Computable General Equilibrium Approaches in Urban and Regional Policy Studies

Computable General Equilibrium Approaches in Urban and Regional Policy Studies

editor **Masayuki Doi**

University of Tsukuba, Japan

World Scientific

NEW JERSEY • LONDON • SINGAPORE • BEIJING • SHANGHAI • HONG KONG • TAIPEI • CHENNAI

Published by

World Scientific Publishing Co. Pte. Ltd.
5 Toh Tuck Link, Singapore 596224
USA office: 27 Warren Street, Suite 401-402, Hackensack, NJ 07601
UK office: 57 Shelton Street, Covent Garden, London WC2H 9HE

Library of Congress Cataloging-in-Publication Data
Computable general equilibrium approaches in urban and regional policy
studies / edited by Masayuki Doi.
p. cm.
Includes bibliographical references and index.
ISBN-13 978-981-256-471-9
ISBN-10 981-256-471-3
1. Urban economics--Mathematical models. 2. Urban policy--Mathematical models.
3. Regional economics--Mathematical models. 4. Regional planning--Mathematical models.
5. Equilibrium (Economics). I. Doi, Masayuki.

HT321.C627 2006
307.7601'5118--dc22

2006044631

British Library Cataloguing-in-Publication Data
A catalogue record for this book is available from the British Library.

Typeset by Stallion Press
Email: enquiries@stallionpress.com

Preface

The computable general equilibrium or, in short, CGE modeling approach has by now a fairly long history of development and policy analysis applications. Although the main application fields were limited to trade and tax policies earlier, the advances in methodology and computation techniques, improved data availability, and increasing needs for many other aspects of policy studies invited a wider range of CGE modeling applications. The emerging application fields include industrial policies, environmental and health policies, transportation and other infrastructure policies for both developed and developing countries. Study areas for CGE analysis by now are not necessarily on a country basis, but also can be multi-countries, regions, multi-regions, or even small regions or cities.

The underlying factor is that complex economies at different levels are requiring policy innovations of structural impacts rather than fragmental or partial problem solving. This is true on the regional level as well as the national level.

In view of such tendencies, we planned to devote a special issue of *Review of Urban and Regional Development Studies* (RURDS), for which the editor of this book acts as Managing Editor, for empirical studies in CGE approaches. It was in early 2002 that we released the call for papers for the special issue, and received an unexpectedly large number of submissions. We then used several issues of RURDS as full or partial collections of them until very recently, even after a considerable number of submissions were unfortunately screened out at the refereeing stage.

This made us perceive the strong need for publishing an extensive but handy collection of urban and regional policy studies in CGE approaches. Most authors of the CGE papers in RURDS were willing to join in the book publication project. We also invited some additional authors for general introductions of CGE modeling as well as for empirical studies published earlier and in other journals. As a result, the chapters cover many different aspects of policies and study areas from all over the world, presumably with rich implications for CGE analysts, policy makers, consultants, students, and many others.

We are grateful for the encouragements and advices consistently given by Dr. Shinichi Ichimura, Professor Emeritus of Kyoto University. We thank all participating coauthors of the book as well as those CGE and related specialists from all over the world who once refereed the papers. The cooperation from both Blackwell Publishing, the publisher of RURDS, and the World Scientific Publishing Co. Pte. Ltd., the publisher of the book, should be acknowledged. This book would never have come into existence without the help from Ms. Juliet Lee, Senior Editor, and Ms. Chean Chian Cheong, Editor, both of the World Scientific Publishing.

MASAYUKI DOI, Professor
Institute of Policy and Planning Sciences
University of Tsukuba
Tsukuba, Ibaraki, Japan

Contents

Part VI: Trade and International Policies

Part I

CGE Model Approach

Chapter 1

Introduction to Computable General Equilibrium Approaches in Urban and Regional Policy Studies

MASAYUKI DOI

Institute of Policy and Planning Sciences, University of Tsukuba, Tsukuba, Ibaraki, Japan

1. CGE Approaches

The computable general equilibrium or CGE model is the generic name to denote numerical models to evaluate economic policies in general equilibrium contexts. In the first step of the CGE modeling approach, it is necessary to construct a social accounting matrix, or in short SAM, which is an arrangement of all transactions in an economic system. It usually starts with an input-output table containing the intermediate input flows between industrial sectors, and extends by capturing income and expenditure flows between households, government, and the rest of the world. Production/supply and consumption in all products and production factors markets including incomplete domestic-overseas substitutional relationships are functionally modeled, with particular details on the segments of policy evaluation concerns. Upon a policy change shock with structural impacts given to the model, it is designed to endogenously compute and solve the prices and quantities of the general equilibrium condition which newly clears each market. Typically, the alternative policy is evaluated comprehensively based on the prices, quantities, welfare and various other criteria of not only the sector of initial shock but also all other sectors at the counterfactual equilibrium as changes from the benchmark equilibrium.

CGE approaches are now widely applied for the evaluation of trade policy including regional economic integration, various taxation policies, income distribution and poverty concerns, industrial policy, environmental problems, transportation and other infrastructure policies both for developed and developing countries. What is common with these policy topics for evaluation is that they cause structural, long-term impacts, including price changes and GDP growth, over various entities (households, enterprises, government and other regions/countries) and industrial sectors of urban, regional, national and international economies. Study areas for CGE analysis are no longer necessarily on a country basis, but also can be multi-countries, regions, multi-regions, or even small regions or cities due to the advances in methodology and computation techniques, improved data availability, and increasing needs for many other aspects of policy studies.

2. From Partial to General Equilibrium Policy Appraisal

Early theories of development economics prior to the mid 1960s emphasized the importance of the expansion of capital through savings and investment and industrialization in the development process because it achieved higher levels of productivity than agriculture. The development of infrastructure to support industrialization was also recognized as a key to economic development. From the mid 1960s infrastructure was still regarded as essential to support an export-oriented industrialization strategy, however, economies of scale and the inducement effects of infrastructure development were no longer exaggerated. It then has become standard practice to evaluate the financial performance and economic effects of infrastructure projects prior to their implementation.

In this context, I. M. D. Little and J. A. Mirrlees (Little and Mirrlees, 1974) were commissioned in 1974 to revise a manual of evaluation methods written by them for the OECD in 1969 and another written by P. Dasgupta, S. A. Marglin and A. K. Sen for UNIDO in 1972. Their revised project evaluation methodology recognized as cost-benefit analysis, which seeks to optimize the allocation of resources taking into account real scarcity and the opportunity costs of goods and labor, has been widely adopted, and is commonly applied to projects by the World Bank and UNIDO. Cost-benefit analysis was thus conceived, and used widely for policy evaluation since then in most developing and also many developed countries. Criteria derived from cost-benefit analysis were used to evaluate and select investment projects, including infrastructure, in order to achieve an optimal allocation of national resources.

Cost-benefit analysis of course is a highly useful tool not only for investment decision but also for soft policymaking, and makes contributions to policy decisions if the impacts are local in the economic system. However, evaluation in use of cost-benefit analysis is a methodology to assess mainly direct costs and benefits of immediate users and suppliers, and is regarded as a kind of partial equilibrium approach, or at most as expanded partial equilibrium approach if some indirect impacts are taken into consideration. One of the reasons that the cost-benefit approach assisted low-income and heavy debtor nations and economic slow-downs due to deferred deregulation or environmental problems only to limited extents was the lack of general equilibrium insights of policy impacts through various channels on various parts of the concerned economies.

Cost-benefit approach as a partial equilibrium approach leads to the same conclusion as the general equilibrium approach if the markets of all sectors besides the analyzed one are perfectly competitive (see, for example, Lesourne, 1975 or Doi, 1986). However, government interventions in the form of import duties and non-tariff restrictions, foreign exchange controls, subsidization and other forms of interventions have been common in every economy, and have been creating the effect of distorting market prices. Cost-benefit approaches try to incorporate shadow prices, shadow exchange rates and some other measures to overcome such evaluation difficulties due to distorted markets. As a result of these distortions, however, criteria of cost-benefit analysis have been critically questioned for decision-making with large impacts. Cost-benefit analysis cannot replace the general equilibrium approach if the impacts of policy changes are structural.

The other side of the coin is that tariff and other trade policies and tax and subsidies are regarded as important policy tools. They can be simulated relatively easily in the CGE modeling, and for these reasons trade policy and tax/subsidization policy has been a main policy to be evaluated in the CGE approach. Distortions in the markets other than that of the immediate policy change can be modeled as discussed in, for example, Chapters 2 and 14. The emerging application fields and study areas for CGE analysis by now are diversified as pointed out above. Besides the advances in CGE data and methodology, another underlying factor is that complex economies at different levels are requiring policy innovations of structural impacts rather than fragmental or partial problem relieves. This is true on regional levels as well as the national level. Methodological difficulties of CGE approach as compared to cost-benefit analysis presumably caused delays in becoming popularly applied, as reviewed in Chapter 2 and some other chapters, and need to be eased. However, now is the time that urban, regional and international policy changes be evaluated empirically and quantitatively in general equilibrium frameworks through CGE approaches, and innovative policy changes be better designed and more persuasively and widely implemented.

3. Purpose and Organization of the Book

This introductive chapter in Part I is followed by Chapter 2, which summarizes the brief history of the CGE model and the two model types, namely, the models of neoclassical type or competitive markets and those of structural rigidities in markets and institutions. This is done by discussing the treatment of market equilibrium or closure of CGE models and the specification of behavioral equations.

Part II has two chapters dealing with the impacts of tax policies on regional economies: Chapter 3 for an island country of Fiji, and Chapter 4 for the Andalusia region of Spain. As discussed above, tax policies are typical and effective application fields of CGE approaches.

Part III collects two papers whose study areas should receive particular attentions, while Chapter 5 deals with employment and tax policies, and Chapter 6 fiscal policy. Although many SAMs and CGE models have been built on a country basis due to data availability and policy identifiabilities, the study area of Chapter 5 is not even at the state level but small cities and towns of the U.S. Their impacts of even minor policy changes are substantially large due to the small size of the areas, and their needs for policy evaluation in a general equilibrium framework are very large. Chapter 6 presents a fairly accomplished version of the multiregional CGE model for Australia which is capable of evaluating spillover effects of regional policies in general equilibrium frameworks.

Part IV includes three studies explicitly evaluating infrastructure and environmental policies. Chapter 7 appraises the impacts of port policy on Japanese economy, Chapter 8 those of carbon tax policy on Thai economy, and Chapter 9 those of land use and housing supply policies on Seoul economy. Resulting welfare and other effects of infrastructure and environmental policies if studied in such CGE approaches are highly profound and indicative.

Two industrial policy studies are found in Part V. Chapter 10 analyzes the importance of the sugar industry for Fiji, and Chapter 11 that of the agriculture sector for Western Australia. Both suggest that the economic contributions by major industrial sectors are broader if studied in CGE approaches.

Chapters 12 and 13 also analyze the agricultural liberalization policies for Europe and China, respectively, but their main concerns are discussed in their international contexts. Therefore, they join into Part VI, which are a collection of trade and international policy studies. Also constituting Part VI are: the economic effects of China's trade and factor market reforms in Chapter 14; the economic, demographic and environmental impacts of globalization simulated as a numerical example in Chapter 15; the economic impacts of Japanese economic cooperation on Asian countries in Chapter 16; and the economic and income distribution impacts of trade liberalization and regional economic integration in different Asia-Pacific member scenarios on the member countries and regions with a focus on Vietnam in Chapter 17. While trade policies have been consistently a most appropriate, important and interesting topic for CGE modelling, the scenarios to be analyzed and policy alternatives to be evaluated are tremendously complicated as the global liberalization tendencies further take place. The data requirements, analytical advances, and resulting findings of the CGE modelling in this topic would continue to get advanced.

It is our hope that this book can be a condensed reference as to how urban, regional and international policies with complex and structural impacts on the concerned economies have been and can be studied in computable general equilibrium or CGE approaches. Also, our wish is that this book can be an important step to having CGE approaches being further developed and more widely applied, satisfying the future need of more innovative problem-solving and policymaking for serious urban and regional issues.

References

Dasgupta P, Sen A, and Marglin S, 1972. *Guidelines for Project Evaluation.* United Nations: New York.

Doi M, 1986. *Multimodal Urban Transportation Pricing Theory.* Ph.D. Dissertation, University of Pennsylvania, University Microfilms International, Inc., Ann Arbor.

Lesourne J, 1975. *Cost-Benefit Analysis and Economic Theory.* North-Holland Publishing Company: Amsterdam.

Little IMD, and Mirrlees JA, 1974. *Project Appraisal and Planning for Developing Countries.* Heinemann Educational Books: London. (A substantially revised version of *Organization for Economic Cooperation and Development*, 1969. Manual of Industrial Project Analysis, OECD, Paris).

Chapter 2

CGE Model and Its Micro and Macro Closures

MITSUO EZAKI

Graduate School of International Development, Nagoya University, Nagoya, Japan

The CGE or "computable general equilibrium" model has by now a fairly long history of development, and is the common name to denote numerical models of general equilibrium type. Differences may become inevitable within the CGE models for developing economies when the models of neoclassical type, which trust markets basically, are contrasted with those of structuralist type, which emphasize structural rigidities in markets and institutions specific to developing countries. Major differences between the two are found in the treatment of market equilibrium (i.e. closures of CGE model) and the specification of behavioral equations (especially for producers). Using a standard prototype CGE model of Lofgren (2003a), we have derived the aggregate identity which leads to Walras' Law for the system with factor markets expressed in efficiency units. We then have clarified two new aspects on the closure of standard CGE model, namely, the supply–demand equalities in factor markets and the macro savings–investment equality.

1. Introduction and Objective

The CGE or "computable general equilibrium" model has by now a fairly long history of development since the Johansen's multisectoral growth model of 1960 for Norway. The Johansen's model was succeeded by the ORANI model of the Australian economy, which became the basis of the GTAP model with global linkage for the world economy. Another line of model development is the Harberger–Scarf–Shoven–Whalley approach with the firm basis on the Herbert Scarf's computer algorithm for numerical solution. It was called AGE or "applied general equilibrium" model and applied mainly to US and other developed economies. The third line of development is the CGE model for developing countries, which originated from the Adelman–Robinson model of income distribution in Korea to be succeeded by the World Bank for the analysis of development planning and policies. The CGE model is now the common name to denote numerical models of general equilibrium type, covering ORANI, AGE and almost all others. It is now widely used for the analysis of trade, taxation, income distribution, structural adjustment, industrial policy, environmental problems and so on, both in developed and developing countries.[a]

There exist no big, essential differences in the framework and structure of CGE models between developed and developing countries, provided that they are the models of neoclassical type which permit basically the working and effectiveness of the markets. Differences, however, may become essential within the CGE models for developing economies when the models of neoclassical type, which trust markets basically, are contrasted with those of structuralist type, which emphasize structural rigidities in markets and institutions specific to developing countries. Major differences between the two are found in the treatment of market equilibrium (i.e. closures of CGE model), the specification of behavioral equations (especially for producers), and so on. As extensions of the neoclassical CGE model, Robinson (1989) discusses clearly in detail three different types: an elastic structuralist CGE model, micro structuralist models, and macro structuralist models. All the three have the problem of closures at the core, i.e. how to treat equilibrium of micro level in each market as well as saving–investment equality of macro level in the national economy, which is relevant and essential also to the CGE models of developed countries.

The objectives of this paper are to (1) discuss the problems of micro and macro closures in the light of Robinson (1989); (2) to focus narrowly on the Walras' Law of the neoclassical CGE model and its extensions, and (3) to show some new aspects of closures in practical use and construction of CGE models for developed and developing countries. Standard CGE models such

---

[a]See Bergman (1990), Dixon and Parmeter (1996), Robinson (1989), Dervis, de Melo and Robinson (1982), etc. There are some other lines of development, of which the econometric approaches to CGE modeling such as the Hudson–Jorgenson model are the least vulnerable to the criticism made from the empirical validation.

as Lofgren, Harris and Robinson (2002) are now available for practical CGE applications, and Lofgren (2003a) provides a model of the simplest version of the prototype economy as exercises using GAMS, the framework of which is used for our discussion of closures without losing any generality in outcome.

2. SAM for a CGE Model: Data, Specification and Walras' Law

Table 1 shows the data of a prototype economy using the framework of SAM (social accounting matrix), which is from Lofgren (2003a, Table 6). The SAM is broken down to the necessary minimum in sectors, factors and institutions to summarize and represent the actual economy. This representative economy consists of two aggregate sectors: agriculture (AGR) and non-agriculture (NAGR), in connection with which activities (*A*), commodities (*C*) and composite goods (*Q*) are defined. The economy has two factors: labor (LAB) and capital (CAP), and three institutional sectors: households (HHD), government (GOV) and the rest of the world (ROW). Households are of two kinds: urban (U) and rural (R). Government levies three kinds of taxes: income tax (YTAX), sales tax (STAX) and tariffs and export duties (TAR). Savings come from households (or the private sector), government, and the rest of the world to be used for investment (S–I). The SAM of Table 1 represents well the actual economy, though corporations as producers are integrated with activities while those as savers with households. It is needless to say that row sums must be equal to the corresponding column sums in the SAM. It is crucial in CGE modeling to give proper economic meanings to these equalities.

Table 2 is the SAM for a CGE model, which corresponds exactly to the data of Table 1. Each of the non-empty cells in Table 1 is expressed in Table 2 by using variables and parameters of an appropriate CGE model.[b] Notations are given in the Appendix (Table 3). The Appendix (Table 3) lists the equations between row sum and column sum for each of the 16 rows and columns (except total) in Table 2. Some of the equations are broken down into two equations of row sum and column sum separated by adding an aggregate total (i.e. Eqs. (5)–(11)), but the two separated equations when combined become identical with the original one. The same is true for Eq. (12) which is broken down into three equations using two aggregate totals. These 16 equations

[b]The model here is basically the same as Lofgren (2003a, pp. 23–32), though notations are partly changed (shortened).

Table 1. The data of a prototype economy using SAM (Social Accounting Matrix): A Numerical Illustration

	AGR-*A*	NAGR-*A*	AGR-*X*	NAGR-*X*	AGR-*Q*	NGAR-*Q*	LAB	CAP	U-HHD	R-HHD	GOV	S–I	YTAX	STAX	TAR	ROW	TOTAL
AGR-*A*			279														279
NAGR-*A*				394													394
AGR-*X*					249											30	279
NAGR-*X*						394										0	394
AGR-*Q*	84	55							30	49	13	28					259
NAGR-*Q*	50	99							165	92	67	85					558
LAB	72	105															177
CAP	73	135															208
U-HHD							95	125			25					40	285
R-HHD							82	83			5					16	186
GOV													25	30	39	15	109
S–I									70	40	−1					4	113
YTAX									20	5							25
STAX					10	20											30
TAR					0	39											39
ROW					0	105											105
TOTAL	279	394	279	394	259	558	177	208	285	186	109	113	25	30	39	105	

Note: Activities (A) are identical with commodities (C), i.e. $A = C$. X means joint products. Q means composite goods

Source: Lofgren (2003a), Table 6, p. 22

Table 2. SAM (Social Accounting Matrix): A CGE Specification

Row \ Column		1 A_1	2 A_2	3 X_1	4 X_2	5 Q_1	6 Q_2	7 L	8 K
1	A_1			PX_1X_1					
2	A_2				PX_2X_2				
3	X_1					PD_1D_1			
4	X_2						PD_2QD_2		
5	Q_1	PQ_1QINT_{11}	PQ_1QINT_{12}						
6	Q_2	PQ_2QINT_{21}	PQ_2QINT_{22}						
7	L	$PL\lambda_1L_1$	$PL\lambda_2L_2$						
8	K	$PK\mu_1K_1$	$PK\mu_2K_2$						
9	HU							$\alpha_u PL\lambda L$	$\beta_u PK\mu K$
10	HR							$\alpha_r PL\lambda L$	$\beta_r PK\mu K$
11	GOV								
12	S–I								
13	YTAX								
14	STAX					$STAX_1$	$STAX_2$		
15	TAR					TM_1	TM_2		
16	ROW					$EXRpwm_1M_1$	$EXRpwm_2M_2$		
	TOTAL	PA_1A_1	PA_2A_2	PX_1X_1	PX_2X_2	PQ_1Q_1	PQ_2Q_2	$PL\lambda L$	$PK\mu K$

Table 2. (*Continued*)

Row	Column	9 HU	10 HR	11 GOV	12 S–I	13 YTAX	14 STAX	15 TAR	16 ROW	TOTAL
1	A_1									PA_1A_1
2	A_2									PA_2A_2
3	X_1							TE_1	$EXRpwe_1E_1$	PX_1X_1
4	X_2							TE_2	$EXRpwe_2E_2$	PX_2X_2
5	Q_1	PQ_1QHU_1	PQ_1QHR_1	PQ_1QG_1	PQ_1QINV_1					PQ_1Q_1
6	Q_2	PQ_2QHU_2	PQ_2QHR_2	PQ_2QG_2	PQ_2QINV_2					PQ_2Q_2
7	L									$PL\lambda L$
8	K									$PK\mu K$
9	HU			TRug					EXR TRuf	YHu
10	HR			TRrg					EXR TRrf	YHr
11	GOV					YTAX	STAX	TAR	EXR TRgf	YG
12	S–I	su (1 − tyu) YHu	sr (1 − tyr) YHr	SAVg					EXR SAVf	SAV
13	YTAX	tyu YHu	tyr YHr							YTAX
14	STAX									STAX
15	TAR									TAR
16	ROW									M
	TOTAL	YHu	YHr	YG	INV	YTAX	STAX	TAR	E + TRf + SAVf	

Note: This table is a CGE specification of Table 1, using variables and parameters of a possible CGE model. See Lofgren (2003a) for a possible CGE model. See Appendix for notation

constitute an essential part of the whole CGE system,[c] representing either identical equations or equilibrium conditions. Let us check the 16 equations one by one.

Equations (1) and (2) are the identities which equate the value of output with the value of input cost. The identities must always be maintained in the model by assuming production functions of constant returns to scale and marginal conditions or by determining profits as residuals. Note that wage rates are different between sectors by constant efficiency coefficients λ_1 and λ_2. The same is true also for rental rates of capital. Equations (3) and (4) are also the identities to equate the value of output with the values of domestic and export sales, which must be maintained in the model by proper functions of commodity transformation.

Equations (5) and (6) are demand–supply equilibrium conditions for composite goods, which determine market-clearing equilibrium prices of those goods (PQ_1 and PQ_2). On the other hand, Eqs. (5′) and (6′) are the identities to define the value of composite goods supply in terms of the value of imports and domestic production, which are maintained usually by assuming the Armington hypothesis based on homogeneous functions for composite goods.

Contrary to the ordinary understanding, Eqs. (7) and (8) are not equilibrium conditions, but the identities to define overall efficiency coefficients for labor (λ) and capital (μ), respectively. λ and μ are assumed to be equal to one at the starting point for the bench mark solution, and to be different from one for other solutions with the levels of (L_1, L_2 and L) or (K_1, K_2 and K) given by factor market equalities, i.e. Eqs. (f1) and (f2) of Appendix (Table 3). When factor prices are flexible, equilibrium conditions [Eqs. (f1) and (f2)] with fixed levels of factor supply (L and K) will determine equilibrium factor prices (PL and PK) so as to clear the factor markets. When wage rate (PL) is rigid and fixed, labor supply (L) will adjust to total demand ($L_1 + L_2$) as in the case of micro structuralist models. When capital stocks are not mobile between sectors and are fixed by sectors (K_1, K_2, and $K = K_1 + K_2$) as in the case of neoclassical CGE models for developing countries, rental rates of capital will be determined at different levels for different sectors, resulting in new efficiency coefficients (μ_1 and μ_2).

Equations (7′) and (8′) are the identities to distribute factor income to urban and rural households by constant allocation shares (α's and β's). Equations (9)

[c]Other essential parts are behavioral equations such as marginal conditions and technological equations such as production function, which do not appear explicitly in SAM.

and (10) are the identities to define income of urban and rural households. Equations (9′) and (10′) are again the identities to allocate household income net of saving and tax payments to the consumption expenditures of composite goods. The identities must always be maintained by adopting proper consumption functions.

Equations (11) and (11′) are the identities which first define government revenue and then allocate it to government expenditures after deducting savings and transfer payments. The latter identity must always be maintained by proper allocation functions. Equations (12) and (12′) are the identities which define total saving in value (SAV) and total investment in value (INV), respectively, while Eq. (12″) is basically an equilibrium condition as discussed below in connection with Walras' Law.

Equations (13)–(15) are the identities which define income tax (YTAX), sales tax (STAX), and tariffs and export duties (TAR), respectively. The final Eq. (16) is basically an equilibrium condition in the market of foreign exchanges which equates the value of imports in US dollars (i.e. demand for US dollars) with the values of exports, transfer receipts and capital inflow in US dollars (i.e. supply of US dollars).

It is noted that, in Table 2, the sum of row sums is identically equal to the sum of column sums since both sums are equal to the sum of all elements:

$$\Sigma_i(\Sigma_j z_{ij}) \equiv \Sigma_j(\Sigma_i z_{ij}) \equiv \Sigma_i \Sigma_j z_{ij} \quad (z_{ij} = \text{ element of } i - j \text{ cell in Table 2})$$

Therefore, by adding up all the equations above [Eqs. (1)–(16) in Appendix (Table 3)], we get the overall aggregate identity leading to Walras' Law, i.e. total excess demand in value must identically be zero [Eq. (17)] in Appendix (Table 3)], so that one equilibrium condition (i.e. excess demand $=0$) becomes redundant when all others hold. In deriving Eq. (17), identities are all dropped except for Eqs. (7) and (8), which are explicitly included in order to show a specific nature of the labor market in terms of efficiency units in standard CGE models, assuming constant relative levels (λ_i or μ_i) between sectors for each factor price.

3. Implications of Walras' Law on Micro and Macro Closures

Let us first consider the case of clearing factor market (say, labor) in terms of efficiency units. In this case, total supply of labor (L) and overall efficiency coefficient (λ) are given exogenously, and the market clearing price (PL) is obtained by the equilibrium condition represented by Eq. (7), giving L_1 and L_2 as employments by sector. However, these sector employments do not satisfy the supply–demand equality in original units shown by Eq. (f1), namely $L_1 + L_2 \neq L$, unless the relative wage levels between sectors (λ_i) are always equal to one. Total employment can be larger or smaller than total available labor, depending on situations. This is not an acceptable specification of the labor market. We must attain the supply–demand equilibrium for labor in original units as in Eq. (f1) to get equilibrium wage (PL), determining overall efficiency (λ) by Eq. (7) which is now the identity but not the equilibrium condition. The same is true for the capital market. The supply–demand equilibrium for capital should be attained by original units as in Eq. (f2), resulting in the determination of overall efficiency (μ) by the identity represented by Eq. (8).

The above is the micro closure of factor markets typically applied in the neoclassical CGE models for developed economies. An alternative micro closure is usually adopted for developing capital markets by fixing capital stock for each sector. Different micro closures of structuralist type are often adopted for developing labor markets by fixing wage rates exogenously, assuming supply adjustments of labor to demand. These alternative cases have already been discussed in the previous section, but it is noted here that Eqs. (f1) and (f2) are no longer equilibrium conditions, but identities. An important fact must be noted in connection with Walras' Law in the standard as well as alternative micro closures of factor markets. That is, the supply–demand equalities in factor markets [Eqs. (f1) and (f2)] are irrelevant to Walras' Law whether they are equilibrium conditions or identities. This is because Eqs. (f1) and (f2) are outside of the aggregate identity [Eq. (17)] which leads to Walras' Law, and do not affect [Eq. (17)] at all. This means that any of the factor prices cannot be taken as numeraire, which must be selected from the prices of composite goods [Eq. (5)], nominal saving or investment [Eq. (12″)], and foreign exchanges [Eq. (16)].

Let us next consider the markets directly relevant to Walras' Law by dropping labor identities in efficiency units from the aggregate one:

$$\begin{aligned}
&\mathrm{PQ}_1(\mathrm{QINT}_{11} + \mathrm{QINT}_{12} + \mathrm{QHu}_1 + \mathrm{QHr}_1 + \mathrm{QG}_1 + \mathrm{QINV}_1 - \mathrm{Q}_1)\\
&\quad + \mathrm{PQ}_2(\mathrm{QINT}_{21} + \mathrm{QINT}_{22} + \mathrm{QHu}_2 + \mathrm{QHr}_2 + \mathrm{QG}_2 + \mathrm{QINV}_2\\
&\quad - \mathrm{Q}_2) + (\mathrm{SAV} - \mathrm{INV})\\
&\quad + \mathrm{EXR}(\mathrm{pwm}_1\mathrm{QM}_1 + \mathrm{pwm}_2\mathrm{QM}_2 - \mathrm{pwe}_1\mathrm{QE}_1 - \mathrm{pwe}_2\mathrm{QE}_2\\
&\quad - \mathrm{TRf} - \mathrm{SAVf})\\
&\equiv 0 \qquad (17')
\end{aligned}$$

This aggregate identity consists of two equilibrium conditions for composite goods (micro closures), one equilibrium condition for nominal saving and investment (macro closure), and one equilibrium condition for foreign exchanges (macro closure). The four equilibrium conditions are not independent due to the aggregate identity pointed out above. We must drop one of the four as redundant and set the corresponding price as numeraire. The savings–investment equilibrium (SAV − INV = 0) is the most natural condition to be dropped as redundant. Then, numeraire is the price of nominal saving or investment, which is unitary or always one, so that the other prices (PQ_1, PQ_2 and EXR) relative to this numeraire are determined in their absolute levels.[d] If one of the other prices (say, PQ_1) is selected as numeraire by dropping as redundant the supply–demand equilibrium condition ($QINT_{11} + QINT_{12} + QHu_1 + QHr_1 + QG_1 + QINV_1 - Q_1 = 0$), then the model needs some appropriate price such as interest rate to be determined by the savings–investment equality (SAV − INV = 0), but standard CGE models often lack such price. Savings- or investment-driven closure is usually adopted in standard CGE models, but this is the case of treating the savings–investment equality as an identity, but not an equilibrium condition, as discussed below, so that the savings–investment equality becomes irrelevant to Walras' Law and numeraire.

If micro closure of structuralist type is adopted for composite goods, say, for the first goods, then its price (PQ_1) is fixed and its supply (or demand) is assumed to adjust to its demand (or supply), changing equilibrium condition into identity which makes the market of the first composite goods irrelevant to Walras' Law and numeraire.

If a macro closure of fixed exchange rate is adopted, then the exchange rate (EXR) is fixed and the foreign saving is usually assumed as adjustment factor to attain supply–demand equality. The market of foreign exchanges is no longer in the framework of Walras' Law and numeraire.

Investment driven by savings or savings driven by investment are usually used as macro closure in standard CGE models. This is the case of treating savings–investment equality as an identity to define either investment in terms of savings or savings (or savings rate) in terms of investment. This macro closure makes the savings–investment equality irrelevant to Walras' Law and

[d]When the model allows explicitly for financial assets, (SAV − INV) becomes equal to the sum of excess demand in the markets of money and other financial assets, reducing itself to the excess demand for money when the markets of other financial assets are cleared in one way or another. Then, the balance between savings and investment coincides with the equilibrium in the money market, resulting in the determination of prices in their absolute levels with the price of money (i.e. unit) as numeraire. See Ezaki (1986) for a CGE model with financial assets.

numeraire. The framework of Walras' Law and numeraire is complete within the markets of composite goods and foreign exchanges to determine relative prices and real quantities. Prices relative to the numeraire price are usually replaced by prices relative to a general price index which is exogenous by using price index equation. Standard CGE models are self-restrained and confined to the real world consisting of relative prices and real quantities. There is, however, a room for expansion to a world of absolute prices and quantities by introducing a new macro closure rule of keeping the macro saving-investment equality as equilibrium condition and dropping it in solving the system with price index equation dropped together.[e]

4. Summary and Conclusion

Using a standard prototype CGE model of Lofgren (2003a), we have derived the aggregate identity which leads to Walras' Law for the system with factor markets expressed in efficiency units. We have clarified two new aspects on the closure of standard CGE model.

First, the supply–demand equalities in factor markets are to be attained in original units before efficiency consideration and irrelevant to Walras' Law whether they are equilibrium conditions or identities. This is because the supply–demand equalities are outside of the aggregate identity which leads to Walras' Law and do not affect it at all. This means that any of the factor prices cannot be taken as numeraire, which must be selected from the prices of composite goods, nominal saving or investment, and foreign exchanges. The supply–demand equalities in efficiency units, on the other hand, give the overall efficiency levels.

Second, the macro savings–investment equality can be regarded as the equilibrium condition to determine the prices of composite goods and the exchange rate in their absolute levels. Either the savings–driven investment or the investment-driven savings is usually adopted for the macro savings–investment closure in the standard CGE model. This macro closure treats savings–investment equality as identity and makes it irrelevant to Walras' Law and numeraire. Therefore, the framework of Walras' Law and numeraire in the standard model is complete within the markets of composite goods and foreign exchanges, resulting in the determination of relative prices and real

---

[e]The price index equation seems to be too restrictive to analyze the case of large inflationary shocks such as oil shock. We are interested in not only changes in relative prices, but also inflation, but the general price level is exogenous in this formulation.

quantities. The standard CGE model may be said to be restrained and confined to the real world consisting of relative prices and real quantities. There is, however, a room for the expansion of standard model to a world of absolute prices and quantities by introducing a new macro closure rule of keeping macro savings–investment equality as equilibrium condition and dropping it along with the price index equation to solve the system. This system may be more effective than the standard model with exogenous general price index in analyzing the case of drastic inflation such as oil shock.

References

Bergman L, 1990. "The development of computable general equilibrium modeling." In: *General Equilibrium Modeling and Economic Policy Analysis.* Bergman L, Jorgenson D, and Zalai E, (eds) Blackwell. 3–30.

Dervis K, de Melo J, and Robinson S, 1982. *General Equilibrium Models for Development Policy.* Oxford University Press.

Dixon PB, and Parmeter BR, 1996. "Computable general equilibrium modeling for policy analysis and forecasting." In: *Handbook of Computational Economics*, Vol. I. Amman HM, Kendrick DA, and Rust J, (eds) Elsevier. 3–85.

Ezaki M, 1986. "A computable general equilibrium model of the Japanese economy." Kobe Economic and Business Review, 32nd Annual Report.

Lofgren H, 2003a. "Exercises in general equilibrium modeling using GAMS." Revised, Microcomputers in Policy Research 4a, International Food Policy Research Institute.

Lofgren H, 2003b. "Key to exercises in CGE modeling using GAMS." Revised, Microcomputers in Policy Research 4b, International Food Policy Research Institute.

Lofgren H, Harris RL, and Robinson S, 2002. "A standard computable general equilibrium (CGE) models in GAMS." Microcomputers in Policy Research 5, International Food Policy Research Institute.

Robinson S, 1989. "Multisectoral Models." In: *Handbook of Development Economics*, Vol. II. Chenery H, and Srinivasan TN, (eds) North Holland. 885–947.

Appendix (Table 3)

Equalities Between Row Sum and Column Sum in SAM (Table 2) and the Walras' Law

$$\mathrm{PX_1X_1 = PQ_1QINT_{11} + PQ_2QINT_{21} + PL\lambda_1}L_1 + \mathrm{PL\lambda_2L_2} \tag{1}$$

$$\mathrm{PX_2X_2 = PQ_1QINT_{12} + PQ_2QINT_{22} + PK}\mu_1 K_1 + \mathrm{PK}\mu_2 K_2 \tag{2}$$

$$\mathrm{PD_1D_1 + EXR\ pwe_1E_1 - TE_1 = PX_1X_1} \tag{3}$$

$$\mathrm{PD_2D_2 + EXR\ pwe_2E_2 - TE_2 = PX_2X_2} \tag{4}$$

$$\begin{aligned}&\mathrm{PQ_1(QINT_{11} + QINT_{12} + QHu_1 + QHr_1 + QG_1 + QINV_1)}\\&\quad\mathrm{= PQ_1Q_1[\rightarrow QINT_{11} + QINT_{12} + QHu_1 + QHr_1 + QG_1}\\&\qquad\mathrm{+ QINV_1 = Q_1]}\end{aligned} \tag{5}$$

$$\begin{aligned}&\mathrm{PQ_2(QINT_{21} + QINT_{22} + QHu_2 + QHr_2 + QG_2 + QINV_2)}\\&\quad\mathrm{= PQ_2Q_2[\rightarrow QINT_{21} + QINT_{22} + QHu_2 + QHr_2 + QG_2}\\&\qquad\mathrm{+ QINV_2 = Q2]}\end{aligned} \tag{6}$$

$$\mathrm{PQ_1Q_1 = PD_1D_1 + EXR\ pwm_1\ QM_1 + TM_1 + STAX_1} \tag{5$'$}$$

$$\mathrm{PQ_2Q_2 = PD_2D_2 + EXR\ pwm_2\ QM_2 + TM_2 + STAX_2} \tag{6$'$}$$

$$\mathrm{PL}\ (\lambda_1 L_1 + \lambda_2 L_2) = \mathrm{PL}\lambda L[\rightarrow \lambda_1 L_1 + \lambda_2 L_2 = \lambda L] \tag{7}$$

$$\mathrm{PK}(\mu_1 K_1 + \mu_2 K_2) = \mathrm{PK}\mu K[\rightarrow \mu_1 K_1 + \mu_2 K_2 = \mu K] \tag{8}$$

$$\mathrm{PL}\lambda L = (\alpha_1 + \alpha_2)\mathrm{PL}\lambda L \quad \text{where } \alpha_1 + \alpha_2 = 1 \tag{7$'$}$$

$$\mathrm{PK}\mu K = (\beta_1 + \beta_2)\mathrm{PK}\mu K \quad \text{where } \beta_1 + \beta_2 = 1 \tag{8$'$}$$

$$\alpha\mathrm{uPL}\lambda L + \beta\mathrm{uPK}\mu K + \mathrm{TRug + EXR\ TRuf = YHu} \tag{9}$$

$$\alpha\mathrm{rPL}\lambda L + \beta\mathrm{rPK}\mu K + \mathrm{TRrg + EXR\ TRrf = YHr} \tag{10}$$

$$\mathrm{YHu = PQ_1\ QHu_1 + PQ_2\ QHr_1 + su(1 - tyu)YHu + tyu\ YHu} \tag{9$'$}$$

$$\mathrm{YHr = PQ_1\ QHr_2 + PQ_2\ QHr_2 + sr(1 - tyr)YHr + tyr\ YHr} \tag{10$'$}$$

$$\mathrm{YTAX + STAX + TAR + EXR\ TRgf = YG} \tag{11}$$

$$\mathrm{YG = P_1QG_1 + P_2QG_2 + TRug + TRrg + SG} \tag{11$'$}$$

$$\mathrm{su(1 - tyu)\ YHu + sr(1 - tyr)YHr + SAVg + EXR\ SAVf = SAV} \tag{12}$$

$$\mathrm{INV = P_1\ QINV_1 + P_2\ QINV_2} \tag{12$'$}$$

$$\mathrm{SAV = INV[\rightarrow SAV = INV]} \tag{12$''$}$$

$$\text{tyu YHu} + \text{tyr YHr} = \text{YTAX} \tag{13}$$

$$\text{STAX}_1 + \text{STAX}_2 = \text{STAX} \tag{14}$$

$$\text{TM}_1 + \text{TM}_2 + \text{TE}_1 + \text{TE}_2 = \text{TAR} \tag{15}$$

$$\begin{aligned}
&\text{EXR pwm}_1\text{M}_1 + \text{EXR pwm}_2\text{M}_2 \\
&\quad = \text{EXR pwe}_1\text{E}_1 + \text{EXR pwe}_2\text{E}_2 + \text{EXR TRuf} + \text{EXR TRrf} \\
&\qquad + \text{EXR TRgf} + \text{EXR SAVf} \\
&\quad [\rightarrow \text{pwm}_1\text{M}_1 + \text{pwm}_2\text{M}_2 = \text{pwe}_1\text{E}_1 + \text{pwe}_2\text{E}_2 \\
&\qquad + \text{TRuf} + \text{TRrf} + \text{TRgf} + \text{SAVf}]
\end{aligned} \tag{16}$$

Walras' Law (i.e. sum of row sums ≡ sum of column sums):

$$\begin{aligned}
&\text{PQ}_1(\text{QINT}_{11} + \text{QINT}_{12} + \text{QHu}_1 + \text{QHr}_1 + \text{QG}_1 \\
&\quad + \text{QINV}_1 - \text{Q}_1) \quad [(5) \rightarrow \text{PQ}_1] \\
&\quad + \text{PQ}_2(\text{QINT}_{21} + \text{QINT}_{22} + \text{QHu}_2 + \text{QHr}_2 + \text{QG}_2 \\
&\quad + \text{QINV}_2 - \text{Q}_2) \quad [(6) \rightarrow \text{PQ}_2] \\
&\quad + \text{PL}(\lambda_1 L_1 + \lambda_2 L_2 - \lambda L) \quad [(7) \rightarrow \lambda] \\
&\quad + \text{PK}(\mu_1 K_1 + \mu_2 K_2 - \mu K) \quad [(8) \rightarrow \mu] \\
&\quad + (\text{SAV} - \text{INV}) \quad [(12'') \rightarrow \text{numeraire}] \\
&\quad + \text{EXR}(\text{pwm}_1\text{QM}_1 + \text{pwm}_2\text{QM}_2 - \text{pwe}_1\text{QE}_1 - \text{pwe}_2\text{QE}_2 \\
&\quad - \text{TRf} - \text{SAVf}) \quad [(16) \rightarrow \text{EXR}] \\
&\equiv 0
\end{aligned} \tag{17}$$

$$L_1 + L_2 = L \quad [(\text{f}1) \rightarrow \text{PL or } L] \tag{f1}$$

$$K_1 + K_2 = K \quad [(\text{f}2) \rightarrow \text{PK or } \mu_i \ (i = 1, 2)] \tag{f2}$$

Note: See rows and columns of Table 2 for the left- and right-hand sides of the 16 equations respectively above.

Notation

X_i = output of activity i $(i = 1, 2)$,
PX_i = price of X_i,

D_i = domestic supply of or demand for commodity i,
PD_i = price of D_i,
E_i = export supply of commodity i,
EXR = exchange rate,
pwe_i = world export price of commodity i,
TE_i = export tax of commodity i,
Q_i = composite goods i,
PQ_i = price of Q_i,
$QINT_{ij}$ = intermediate inputs of composite goods $(i, j = 1, 2)$,
pwm_i = world import price of commodity i,
TM_i = import tariffs on commodity i,
QM_i = import demand for commodity i,
QHu_i = urban household expenditure of composite goods i,
QHr_i = rural household expenditure of composite goods i,
QG_i = government expenditure of composite goods i,
$QINV_i$ = investment demand for composite goods i,
STAX = sales tax,
L_i = labor demand of activity i,
L = total supply of (or demand for) labor,
PL = price of labor,
λ = labor efficiency,
λ_i = labor efficiency of activity i,
K_i = capital stock of activity i,
K = total capital stock,
PK = rental price of capital,
μ = capital efficiency,
μ_i = capital efficiency of activity i,
α_i = distribution of labor income,
β_i = distribution of capital income,
TRug = transfer to urban household from government,
TRuf = transfer to urban household from abroad,
TRrg = transfer to rural household from government,
TRrf = transfer to rural household from abroad,
YHu = urban household income,
YHr = rural household income,
tyu = urban income tax rate,
tyr = rural income tax rate,
su = urban saving rate,
sr = rural saving rate,

YTAX	=	total income tax,
STAX	=	total sales tax,
YG	=	government revenue,
TAR	=	tariffs and export tax,
SAVg	=	government saving,
SAVf	=	foreign saving,
SAV	=	total saving,
INV	=	total investment.

Part II

Tax Policies

Chapter 3

The Macroeconomic Impact of the IMF Recommended VAT Policy for the Fiji Economy: Evidence from a CGE Model*

PARESH KUMAR NARAYAN

Department of Accounting, Finance and Economics, Griffith University, Queensland, Australia

Value Added Tax (VAT) is a general consumption tax levied on goods and services. In September 2002, in the face of mediocre economic performance, deteriorating government finances and stagnant investment levels — all due to the political coups of 2000 — an increase in VAT was recommended to Fijian policy makers by the IMF as a remedy to Fiji's problems. The Fiji government, without an in depth study of the economy wide repercussions of a VAT policy, welcomed it by announcing a 25% increase in VAT in its 2003 budget. Beginning 1 January 2003, all goods and services were levied a VAT rate of 12.5%. In this paper, we use a computable general equilibrium model to examine the economy wide effects of this VAT policy. We find that while the VAT improves government revenue and brings about a small 0.6% increase in real GDP, it fails to address investment levels. VAT actually leads to a decline in investments and a reduction in real consumption and national welfare. We highlight that large amounts of tax revenue are owed to government. This is three times more than what the government will collect from the 25% increase in VAT. In this light, an alternative to VAT is to upgrade

*This chapter was originally published in *Review of Urban and Regional Development Studies*, Vol. 15, No. 3, November 2003, and is reprinted here with minor modifications upon the permission from the publisher.

the government's tax collecting mechanism. From this, we deduce that the IMF policy is misdirected.

1. Introduction

Value Added Tax (VAT) is a general consumption tax levied on goods and services. In general, it covers all commercial activities involving the production and distribution of goods and provision of services. VAT is regarded as a consumption tax for it is borne ultimately by the final consumer. It is charged as a percentage of price, which means that the actual tax burden is traceable at each stage in the production and distribution process. It is usually regarded as a more efficient form of taxation than direct taxation. Efficiency is embedded in the fact that VAT entails little distortionary economic behavior than, say, income taxes. "High marginal rates of tax distort the incentives between work and leisure, between employment and unemployment and underlies the so called poverty trap" (Matthews and Lloyd-Willams, 2000, p. 111). Further, VAT is seen as generating greater revenue than income taxes because it minimizes the scope for evasion.

Fiji's successful bid for the implementation of VAT as a policy for revenue generation was endorsed and came into effect on July 1 in 1992. In the period 1992–2002, goods and services in Fiji attracted a 10% VAT. Exports of locally manufactured commodities such as sugar, gold, ginger, fish, etc. are not charged VAT. In the 2003 budget, the Fiji government announced an increase in VAT by 25%; hence, starting January 1, 2003, all goods and services have a 12.5% VAT levied on them. This policy was recommended to the Fijian policy makers by the International Monetary Fund (IMF). The IMF (2002, p. 2) policy recommendation was as follows:

> . . . directors [IMF] supported the authorities' [Fiji government's] medium-term fiscal strategy of reducing the government debt-to-GDP ratio to 40% . . . . They recommended that the authorities take early action to reduce the fiscal deficit significantly, working towards a sufficient primary surplus to achieve the consolidation target, and using privatization proceeds to reduce debt. This will require expenditure restraint, including on wage costs, as well as improved tax collection, while an increase in the value-added tax should be considered to help finance the desired increase in public investment spending.

The policy of a VAT increase is anchored to Fiji's mediocre economic performance, an upshot of the 2000 coup. The coup, in stunning the government and its people, started an economic collapse which resulted from foreign governments and donor agencies putting a moratorium of their development programs in Fiji coupled with trade bans imposed by the Australian and New Zealand trade unions. Foreign governments also issued negative trade advice to their citizens which substantially weakened Fiji's tourism industry as visitor arrivals plummeted to the extent that hotel occupancy rates floored to 15% as opposed to 70% under normal circumstances (Narayan, 2000). In all, real investment, which was already poor, stalled; real GDP fell by 2.75%; the current account ballooned to 6.5% of GDP; and the external debt reached 43.8% of GDP in 2001 with the prognosis for 2002 at an alarming 47.4% of GDP — any percentage over forty is considered unsustainable. The IMF has used Fiji's poor macroeconomic performance as a rationale to recommend the VAT policy.

The aim of this paper is to delineate the long-run economic impact of the 25% increase in VAT on Fiji's macro-economy. In doing so, we want to gauge the credibility of the IMF policy. In recent times, the IMF has come under heavy criticism for recommending policies that decelerate economic growth and development. (For a detailed critical review of IMF policies, see Stiglitz, 2002.) To accomplish our aim, we use the computable general equilibrium model (CGE). CGE models have been regarded as the most important and superior applied tool in impact studies over its rival — the Input–Output models. Its superiority is embedded in its complete specification of both the supply and demand sides of all relevant markets. Put differently, a CGE model proffers a complete map of an economy. The general equilibrium nature of CGE models means that all sectors are incorporated into a single model. This allows the analysis of shocks or policy changes in one sector that may have effects (direct and indirect) on other sectors.

The balance of the paper is organized as follows. In the next section, we discuss the theoretical structure of the Fiji CGE model. This is followed by the presentation of the simulation results. The final section provides the conclusions and policy recommendations.

2. Theoretical Structure of the Fiji CGE Model

The Fiji CGE model, developed by Levantis (1999) and extended by Narayan (2004), is based on the ORANI model of the Australian Economy. A complete description including the theoretical structure of the ORANI model is provided in Dixon *et al.* (1982). The Fiji model, like ORANI, can be described as an economy-wide, comparative static CGE model of the Johansen class

(Johansen, 1960). The Fiji CGE model consists of $m = 35$ domestic industries, $n = 34$ commodities and $q = 2$ occupational types. In total, there are 13 agricultural sector industries; 10 industrial sector industries; and 12 service sector industries including hotels, cafes and restaurants. Each commodity corresponds to an industry except for gold, which is split into two different industries because of the different cost structures of the industries. Further, the non-farm informal sector is grouped as a separate industry. This is important in Fiji's context given that the informal sector accommodates over 75% of the school dropouts and the unemployed who do not find jobs in the formal sector.

Of the 34 commodities, most have competing imports. In this light, the model adheres to the Armington assumption which takes imports to be imperfect substitutes to domestic goods. A full list of the 35 industries and 34 commodities is in Table 1.

Schematically, the model takes the following form:

$$F[Z_1(t), Z_2(t), Z(0)] = 0.$$

Here, $Z_1(t)$ and $Z_2(t)$ are vectors of values of endogenous and exogenous variables at time t and $Z(0)$ is a vector of initial conditions. At the economy wide level, the equations of a typical Johansen model can be classified into five groups:

1. equations that describe households and other final demands for commodities;
2. equations that describe industry demands for primary factors and intermediate inputs;
3. pricing equations that imply zero pure profit conditions for production;
4. market clearing equations for primary factors and commodities; and
5. other equations, e.g. equations defining GDP, aggregate employment, consumer price index, investment price index, etc.

The equations of the model are derived from neoclassical microeconomic assumptions about the behavior of price taking economic agents. Put differently, consumers maximize utility subject to their budget constraints and producers choose their inputs so as to minimize costs of production. Resources are limited and hence are distributed by market forces, and market imperfections can lead to unemployment. Increasing government expenditure is contingent on raising taxes or borrowing, which has implications on other economic agents such as consumers and firms; this in turn induces other economic effects. The economy is linked to the rest of the world via a foreign exchange market; an

Table 1. List of Industries and Commodities in the Fiji Model

Industry	Commodity
Sugarcane	Raw sugar
Coconuts	Coconuts
Rice	Rice
Ginger	Ginger
Dalo	Dalo
Root crops	Root crops
Kava	Kava
Fruit and vegetables	Fruit and vegetables
Other crops	Other crops
Dairy	Dairy
Livestock	Livestock products
Forestry	Forest products
Fishing	Marine products
Emperor gold mine	Gold
Mt Kasi gold mine	Gold
Quarrying	Quarrying
Sugar manufacturing	Sugar products
Beverages and tobacco	Beverage and tobacco
Food processing	Processed foods
Clothing, footwear and textiles	Clothing, footwear and textiles
Other manufactures	Other manufactures
Electricity and water	Electricity and water
Construction	Construction services
Commerce	Retail/wholesale services
Hotels, cafes, restaurants	Hotels, cafes, restaurants
Transport and communication services	Transport and communication services
Finance	Financial services
Insurance	Insurance services
Property services	Property services
Business services	Business services
Other private services	Other private services
Health	Health services
Education	Education services
Other government services	Other government services
Non-farm informal sector	Informal services

increase in exports in one sector leads to a rise in the exchange rate; hence, discouraging other exports and encouraging imports. The model is solved using the GEMPACK software package, developed by the Centre of Policy Studies and the Impact Project, Monash University. GEMPACK is a flexible model for solving CGE models (Codsi and Pearson, 1988). GEMPACK automates the process of translating the model specification into a model solution program. One needs to only create a text file, the syntax of which resembles ordinary algebraic notation, listing the equations of the model.

The GEMPACK program TABLO then translates this text file into a model specific FORTRAN program, which, when executed, solves the model (Horridge *et al.*, 1993, p. 71).

3. Simulation Results

3.1. *Model Closure*

Figure 1 consists of a stylized representation of the macroeconomic closure encompassing our simulation. The exogenous variables appear in ovals while, to distinguish exogenous variables from endogenous variables, the latter appear in rectangles. The arrows indicate prime casual linkages in the model.

To realize the long-run impact, the conventional wisdom is that capital is mobile between industries in response to changes in rates of return. This assumption is consistent with the fact that Fiji faces an elastic supply of capital from the world market, i.e. the domestic rate of return is assumed to be determined by the world market rate. By holding the after-tax rate of return in each industry fixed, it allows an industry to increase its quantity of capital stock in the event that the cost of capital falls. Notice that if the rate of return is endogenous, in the face of falling cost of capital, there will be an improvement in the rate of return. The exogenous nature of the rate of return on capital implies that a rise in investment levels is needed to build and maintain industry capital — extra capital, here, will add to output. The exogenous nature of the rate of return on capital also implies that if changes in economic conditions induce growth in some industries, they will attract investment expenditure and *de facto* attract capital from other industries. This behavior ensures that when all inter-industry adjustments have taken their course, capital in all industries earns a uniform rate of return.

With regard to the labor market, employment levels are largely fixed in the long-run. It follows that if real wages are endogenous, then either employment or unemployment must be fixed. Employment is held fixed. In the traditional

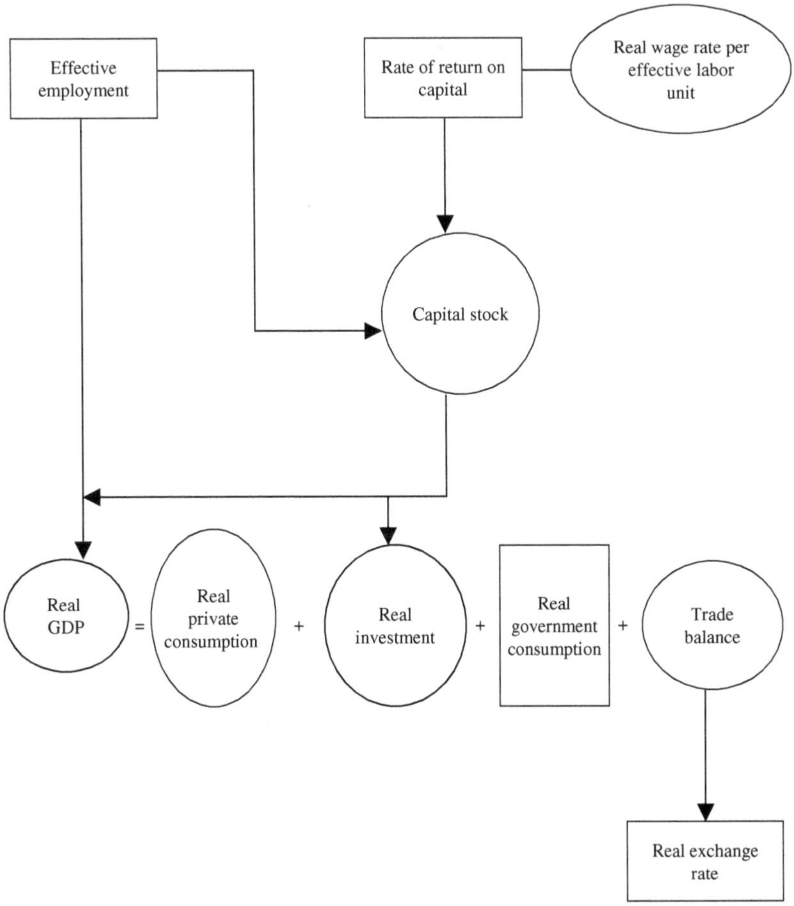

Fig. 1. Macroeconomic Closure

wage-labor setting, the supply curve for labor for each industry and occupation is de facto horizontal. This implies that shifts in the demand for labor will be equilibrated with appropriate adjustments in the wage rate.

With employment growth fixed, the rates of growth of the aggregate capital stock and real GDP are determined. Meanwhile, on the expenditure side, fixing capital growth drives real investment growth via the model's capital-accumulation relationships. The trade balance adjusts to enforce the exogenous setting of the exchange rate. Real public consumption is fixed. Consequently, real private consumption is implied from the GDP identity.

As mentioned earlier, the Fiji model is built in the image of ORANI — a key feature of the model is that it was initially designed for comparative static simulations. The "comparative static" nature of the model implies that it provides projections at only one point in time, which is the solution year. The model refers implicitly to the economy at some future time period to ensure that the economy adjusts after the initial shock(s). This concept is illustrated diagrammatically (Fig. 2), which plots the values of some variable, say exports of Good X, against time. In this setting, A is referred to as the level of exports of Good X in the base period (period 0). Suppose that in period 0 an external shock is applied, say, a 10% fall in the price of Good X. As a result of this shock, C is the level of exports that will be attained in T years time, all other things being equal. In the event of no shock, B will be the level of export of Good X.

The movement from A to B is regarded as the underlying growth path of the export of Good X.

In essence, comparative static analysis is only concerned about the size of the gap between BC, and not the economic path taken to reach either B or C. In a comparative static simulation, then, the model might generate the change

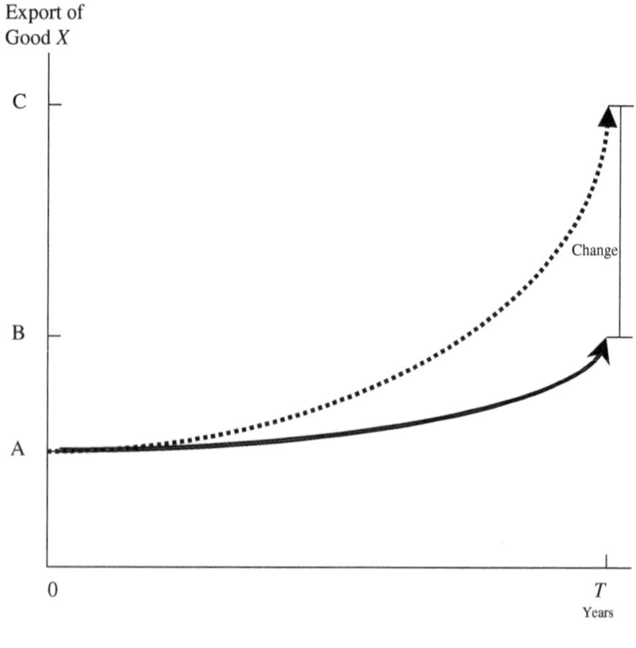

Fig. 2. Comparative Static Interpretation of Results

(C – B), percentage change (100(C – B)/B) or both in the export of Good X, showing how the export of Good X in period T would be affected by the reduction in prices.

It is important to highlight that comparative static models are not dynamic in that they do not describe the adjustment paths, shown as dotted and bold lines in Fig. 1. The other feature of such models is that both short-run and long-run effects of shocks or policy changes can be deduced. The short-run effects are simulated by holding capital stocks at their pre-shock levels. Cooper *et al.* (1985) find econometric evidence in favor of short-run equilibrium established in about two years, i.e. $T = 2$. On the other hand, the long-run effects are derived on the assumption that capital stocks will have adjusted to restore (exogenous) rates of return, which might take 10 or 20 years, i.e. $T = 10$ or 20.

3.2. *Macroeconomic Effects*

The macroeconomic effects of a 25% increase in VAT for Fiji are shown in Table 2.[a] We find that the total imports will fall by 2.1% while total exports will fall by around 3.9%. Notice that the consumer price index has increased by 1.3%, implying the rise in the price of goods and services. This reduces private consumption by 2.1%, which is reflected in the fall in imports. Another reason for the fall in imports can be traced from the rise in the investment price index by around 2.2%. An increase in the investment price index leads to a contraction in real investment by some 1.9%. The fall in investment is reflected in a 3.9% decline in exports. It should be noted that around 64% of Fiji's raw materials used in export production are imported. The fact that exports decline implies that the demand for imported raw materials also decline. Moreover, given that the decline in exports (3.90%) exceeds the decline in imports (2.08%), there is a balance of payment deficit equivalent to 0.12% of real GDP. Further, with additional negative growth in aggregate domestic

---

[a]The enforcement of VAT collections in Fiji are relatively poor and might affect the results, but not our conclusions given our aim in this paper: to test the IMF policy of a 2.5% increase in VAT on Fiji's macroeconomic conditions, we believe that the present analysis is valid. Of course poor tax collections also give further credence to our finding that the IMF policy has failed to improve Fiji's macroeconomic conditions, for the model assumes that Fiji's VAT revenue will increase by 2.5% and hence total government expenditure will increase by an amount equivalent to 2.5% of VAT revenue. This is the same as saying that the model allows 100% VAT collections (for the 2.5% increase). Despite this, we find that in the long run, Fiji's macroeconomic performance is poor. It follows that if we allow only 80% VAT collections, Fiji's macroeconomic performance will further deteriorate.

Table 2. Macroeconomic Effects for Fiji from a 25% Increase in VAT

Variables	Percent Change
Balance of payments surplus as a percent of GDP	−0.1207
Total government savings as a percent of GDP	−0.5584
Imports	−2.0773
Exports	−3.9023
Consumer price index	1.3165
Investment price index	2.1691
Private disposable income	−0.8276
Total government tax revenue	4.3828
VAT revenue	18.8846
Income tax revenue	0.0439
Company tax revenue	−3.4128
Production tax revenue	−2.1776
Excise tax revenue	−2.7558
Tariff revenue	−1.6901
Capital stock	−0.3137
Real GDP	0.6000
GDP deflator	−0.5620
Real private consumption	−2.1260
Real investment	−1.8639
Real national welfare	−1.0780
Labor market	Change
Net after tax rural wage rate for unskilled labor	−1.5024
Net urban wage rate for unskilled labor	1.3229
Wage rate for informal sector labor	14.7545

absorption (consumption plus investment) exceeding additional growth in real GDP, there is an increase in the balance of trade deficit. It follows that despite declining net exports, private investment and private consumption, there is a small rise in real GDP of 0.60%. With employment growth fixed, the positive impact on real GDP reflects the increase in the capital/labor ratio. However, despite an increase in real GDP, there is a deterioration of the real national welfare by around 1.07%. Here, national welfare is defined as consisting of GDP plus net private receipts of investment income from abroad, net private unrequited transfers from abroad and net foreign aid.

3.3. *Impact of Output and Exports on Different Sectors*

Table 3 presents the export effects of a 25% increase in VAT for Fiji. Given that VAT is exempted on exports of domestically produced goods, we find that

Table 3. Export Effects of a 25% Increase in VAT in Fiji

Variables	Percent Change
Coconuts	3.4716
Ginger	0.9504
Dalo	1.4771
Kava	1.2413
Fish	1.7548
Gold	0.1077
Sugar	1.4754
Processed food	11.1048
Textiles, clothing and footwear	0.7326
Other manufactures	4.9320
Hotel	−7.3658
Transport	−4.5887
Other private services	−4.6572
Commerce	−3.0334
Informal	0.1916

the effect of a 25% VAT on all other goods and services will actually increase exports of domestically produced goods. The export sectors that will benefit the most include processed food (11.1%), kava (1.2%), other manufactures (4.9%), fish (1.7%) and dalo (1.5%). On the other hand, given a fall in private disposable income, real investment and consumption, a reduction in real output is imminent (Table 4). Among the agricultural sector, the livestock (−3.5%) and dairy (−1.4%) sectors will experience the largest fall in output. The manufacturing sector, on the other hand, will see a slight increase in output except for beverage and tobacco and textiles, clothing and footwear, which will fall by around 4 and 0.15%, respectively. The commerce and informal sector outputs will fall by 5.5 and 2.7%. Furthermore, the service sector outputs will be among the most affected; the biggest falls in output will be recorded for other private services, business and property services, electricity and water, transport, education and finance.

4. Conclusions and Policy Implications

The aim of this paper is to evaluate the impact of the IMF recommended VAT policy for the Fiji economy, in the process establishing the credibility of such a policy. The idea here is to examine the impact of the policy on the

Table 4. Output Demand Effects from a 25% Increase in VAT in Fiji

Variables	Percent Change
Hotels	−7.5024
Dalo	−0.4482
Root crops	−0.6887
Kava	−0.5870
Fruits and vegetables	−0.5961
Dairy	−1.4494
Livestock	−3.5455
Beverage and tobacco	−3.9607
Electricity and water	−3.1968
Construction	−0.5546
Commerce	−5.4949
Transport	−3.9130
Finance	−3.3235
Insurance	−1.7439
Property services	−3.4059
Business services	−3.1607
Other private services	−11.6238
Health	−1.0783
Education	−1.0948
Other government services	13.6321
Informal	−2.7431
Rice	−0.7381
Quarry	−1.0935
Other crops	−2.3511
Coconuts	2.1284
Ginger	0.9979
Cane	0.7815
Fishing	−0.0335
Forest	0.4127
Sugar products	0.9929
Processed food	0.7926
Textiles clothing and footwear	−0.1515
Other manufactures	1.1698

macroeconomic fundamentals before establishing the verdict. To accomplish this, we use a computable general equilibrium model which is at the forefront of impact studies of policy changes.

The empirical results show that the VAT policy will improve the government's revenue base — VAT revenue is expected to increase by 19% and while revenue from other sources are expected to fall, total government revenue is still expected to rise by over 4%. The Fiji government will collect an additional F$45.1 million from the 25% increase in VAT, assuming that the collection rate is 100%. This is an over optimistic assumption given that the amount of VAT owed, as a percentage of total revenue owed to the government in the period 1997–2001 was 16%. The total amount of revenue owed to the Fiji government has increased rapidly from F$107.9 million in 1997 to F$142.1 million in 2001 (Ministry of National Planning, 2002, p. 68). The average for this period is F$136.4 million, which is three times more than what the Fiji government will collect from the 25% increase in VAT. These large amounts of tax revenue owed to the government and its increasing trajectory reflects a poor tax collection mechanism. In this light, it is obvious that by tightening and revamping its tax collection mechanism, the Fiji government would have generated more revenue than what it will get from the 25% increase in VAT. This together with the fact that both government and real private investments will fall is an outcome contrary to the envisaged objective of the IMF (2002). Though real GDP will grow by 0.6%, private disposable incomes and real consumption will both fall leading to a worsening of the real national welfare by 1.1%. This leads us to the conclusion that the IMF policy of an increase in VAT to boost government revenue and investment will fail to deliver on its objectives.

Finally, a referee highlighted the issue of poor tax collections and their implications on the economy given the assumption of 100% VAT collections (100% of the 2.5% increase in VAT). I concur, and believe that future studies should attempt to incorporate poor tax collections in the Fiji CGE model, for this will give further credence to our finding that the IMF policy has failed to improve Fiji's macroeconomic conditions.

References

Codsi G, and Pearson KR, 1988. "GEMPACK: general purpose software for applied general equilibrium and other economic modellers." *Computer Sci. Econ. Manage.* 1: 189–207.

Dixon PB, Parmenter BR, Sutton J, and Vincent DP, 1982. *ORANI: A Multisectoral Model of the Australian Economy*. North-Holland: Amsterdam.

Horridge JM, Parmenter BR, and Pearson KR, 1993. "ORANI-F: a general equilibrium model of the Australian economy." *Econ. and Finan. Computing* 3(2): 71–133.

International Monetary Fund (IMF), 2002. "IMF concludes 2002 article IV consultation with Fiji." Public Information Notice No. 01/101, September 12, IMF, Washington.

Levatis T, 1999. *The CGE Model of the Fiji Economy: A Working Manual.* National Centre for Development Studies: Australian National University.

Matthews K, and Lloyd-Willams J, 2000. "Have VAT rates reached their limit?: an empirical note." *Appl. Econ. Lett.* 7: 111–115.

Ministry of Finance and National Planning, 2002. *Economic and Fiscal Update: Supplement to the 2003 Budget Address.* Government Printery: Suva.

Narayan PK, 2000. "Fiji's tourism industry: a SWOT analysis." *J. Tourism Stud.* 11(2): 3–15.

Narayan PK, 2004. "An econometric model of tourism demand and a computable general equilibrium analysis of the impact of tourism: the case of Fiji Islands." Unpublished PhD dissertation, Department of Economics, Monash University.

Stiglitz J, 2002. *Globalisation and its Discontents.* WW Norton: New York.

Chapter 4

An Applied General Equilibrium Model to Assess the Impact of National Tax Changes on a Regional Economy*

MANUEL ALEJANDRO CARDENETE

Department of Economics, Universidad Pablo de Olavide de Sevilla, Seville, Spain

FERRAN SANCHO

Department of Economics, Universidad Autónoma de Barcelona, Barcelona, Spain

This paper presents two versions of an applied general equilibrium model for the regional economy of Andalusia, Spain, that differ in the closure rule adopted to describe the behavior of the public sector. We use the model to analyze the impact that the reform of the personal income tax (Act 40/98) implemented in Spain as a whole would have had on the Andalusian region in particular. The model is of the neoclassical variety and includes not only the productive sectors of the economy, but also the foreign sector and the government, which are usually absent from theoretical general equilibrium models. Both versions of the model are calibrated by using a Social Accounting Matrix of Andalusia for 1995. The analysis shows that the reform is not self-financing, not even partially, despite governmental claims. It also indicates that there is a positive, but smaller than anticipated economic stimulus. In welfare

*This chapter was originally published in *Review of Urban and Regional Development Studies*, Vol. 15, No. 1, March 2003, and is reprinted here with minor modifications upon the permission from the publisher.

terms, we find that the category of Urban Salaried consumers is the one that benefits the most in real income terms.

1. Introduction

In 1999, the Spanish government enacted a wide-ranging reform of the personal income tax. This reform aimed at reducing marginal tax rates across the board for all families and was devised by the government as a global stimulus package for the economy. The political justification for the reform was, basically, the fulfillment of the electoral program of the right-of-center governing party. The stimulus, if successful, was thought that it would generate new employment thereby increasing payroll taxes and reducing unemployment benefits, but was not expected to be fully self-financing.

The effects of this tax reform should be studied in a context that allows us to capture the adjustments all consumers undertake under their new budget situation as well as the overall effects on the economy induced by the internal adjustment mechanisms that make an economic equilibrium possible.

Several studies based on micro-simulations have been carried out in Spain to assess and quantify the effects of fiscal reforms at a regional level, for instance Lasheras *et al.* (1994), Castañer *et al.* (1998), and De las Heras *et al.* (2001). These studies, however, mainly deal with welfare indicators and/or income inequality indices, thus ignoring the overall economic impact that this fiscal reform, or any other economy-wide alteration of the tax structure for that matter, will have on resource allocation and the derived major macro magnitudes of the regional economy.

This limitation, however, can be overcome by using one of the most suitable tools for the study of the effects of a wide-range fiscal reform, namely, applied general equilibrium models. In the last 25 years, these models have been profusely used to analyze government economic policies, both in developed and developing countries [Shoven and Whalley (1992), Dervis, de Melo and Robinson (1982)]. An applied general equilibrium analysis permits to capture the changes in the spheres of production and consumption, as well as in income distribution, in response to changes in a given economic policy, since these models explicitly include a representation of the framework of interdependencies among all markets in an economy.

On the empirical side, we should mention that applied general equilibrium models for the whole Spanish economy have been constructed by Kehoe *et al.* (1988, 1989), but ours is one of the first models developed with a regional perspective in mind. Our aim therefore is to evaluate the possible effects of the tax reform in a subset of the Spanish economy, namely, the Andalusian region. This analysis is in principle feasible since Andalusia is one of the few regions in Spain for which a Social Accounting Matrix (SAM) has been constructed. In addition, under the current democratic constitution, regions enjoy a high level of governing and legislative autonomy and recognition and can somehow be considered — for analytical purposes — as "small countries" within the country. In order to achieve this objective, we present a model of the regional economy developed in accordance with the methodology of applied general equilibrium analysis. The model is then numerically implemented by using a SAM database of the region for the year 1995 [*SAMAND95*, Cardenete (2000)].

This paper is organized as follows. In Section 2, we present the main characteristics of our model and its two versions while Section 3 summarizes the database and the calibration procedure. Then we proceed in Section 4 to comment on the basic features of the performed simulations and we present a few tables that describe some of the main results that are obtained. Finally, we draw the main conclusions and at the same time, we discuss the limitations of the analysis, as well as the research lines that we feel should be explored for its improvement.

2. The Model

Any applied general equilibrium model should at least have three basic elements. The first one is the formulation of a theoretical model of the economy; the second one is the numerical specification of the functional parameters that are embedded in the model; and the third one is the use of an algorithm that computes the alternative equilibrium states in different policy scenarios.

2.1. *Model Characteristics*

The nature of the economic situation that is to be studied should suggest the key elements that have to be used in the design of the model. A general requirement is that the model should capture the basics of the economic reality under discussion while at the same time not being so structurally detailed as to make the analysis and the interpretation of results impossible or very difficult. A specific requirement, in our case, is that since we intend to assess the distributional impact of the reform of the direct tax system, desirably the model should include a minimum level of detail as far as consumers' disaggregation is concerned.

Basically, our model includes a disaggregation of 25 production sectors and 4 representative consumers. The government is also an economic agent whose functions are to levy taxes on income and on transactions among the rest of agents, to supply public goods, to transfer income to the private sector, and to demand goods and services from the private sector. The "foreign" or "Rest of the world" sector is a simplified agent that includes three trading partners (the Rest of Spain, the European Union and all the other countries). Finally, although the model is static, it includes a savings and investment sector the behavior of which follows a simple, but commonly used rule in applied general equilibrium. This enables us to account for an activity (savings from the point of view of agents as consumers and other agents, and investment from the point of view of final demand) that cannot be isolated from the flows of income the model attempts to capture.

In the model, relative prices for goods and services, activity levels of the production sectors, the unemployment rate and the foreign deficit are all endogenous variables. The deficit of the public sector is modeled under a double behavior: first, we take the public deficit to be endogenous whereas the public sector activity level (purchases of goods and services and transfers) is kept at the initial level (Scenario I). Alternatively, the second option considers the public deficit as exogenous with activity levels being endogenous (Scenario II). These two versions of the macroeconomic closure rule resume two of the most important ways of representing the public sector behavior. Either we fix the public sector activity level and let the public deficit adjust, or else we keep the public deficit at the given base level and let purchases and transfers adjust to match government tax income. In the first case, we fix the "size" of the government measured simply by its activity level while in the second one, we fix the "size" of the government understood as a dynamic matching to its revenue.

The equilibrium of the economy will determine the values taken up by all these variables. In the next sub-sections, we will describe more fully agents' characteristics and behavior and will explain the concept of equilibrium in further detail.

2.2. *Producers*

The production sphere of the economy is very standard and neoclassical. It is represented by 25 production sectors, whose objective is to maximize after-tax profits, subject to specific technological constraints. Each productive sector produces a homogeneous good using a constant-returns-to-scale technology. This means that there will be no excess profits. Under these conditions, the key elements for the description of the behavior of production sectors are conditional input demand functions.

The inputs to the production function are of two types: domestic production Xd_j, and imports from the three trading partners that we denote by $Xrow_j$. These partially substitutable inputs yield total output using a production technology with Armington input substitution of the Cobb–Douglas variety. Domestic output is obtained as a combination in fixed proportions (Leontief technology) of intermediate inputs and a composite primary factor that we call *value-added* (VA_j). Value-added is in turn produced by combining the primary factors, labor and capital, using a Cobb–Douglas technology.

2.3. *Consumers*

The model includes four different types of households ($h = 1, \dots, 4$) that are classified according to their income source. Households act as consumers demanding goods and services and as workers offering their labor endowment in the market. For each one, income is the result of the sale of the endowments of productive factors, namely, labor L_h and capital K_h, from which they receive a wage w and a capital remuneration r. Every consumer also receives transfers from the public sector TPS_h (these are retirement pensions, social benefits, unemployment benefits, etc.) and transfers from the Rest of the world $TROW_h$. All this gross income is reduced by the social contributions directly paid by workers, in rate WC_h, and by an effective direct taxation rate on income DT_h. Thus, disposable income for each consumer can be written as follows:

$$\begin{aligned} YDISP_h &= \text{Gross Income} - \text{Total Direct Taxes} \\ YDISP_h &= wL_h + rK_h + cpi\,TPS_h + TROW_h \\ &\quad - DT_h(rK_h + cpi\,TPS_h + TROW_h) \\ &\quad - DT_h(wL_h - WC_h wL_h) - WC_h wL_h, \end{aligned} \tag{1}$$

where cpi is a consumer price index that updates transfers in the public sector according to an average change in prices. Notice that in defining disposable income, we need to distinguish between taxable and non-taxable earned income since workers' social contributions are exempted, under the current tax legislation, from the personal income tax.

Consumers' preferences are described by Cobb–Douglas utility functions defined on consumption goods CD_{jh} and a savings good (future consumption) SD_h. Consumers maximize the utility of both goods subject to disposable income $YDISP_h$, which, along with final commodity prices, determines their budget constraint. Thus,

$$\begin{aligned} &\text{maximize} \quad U(CD_{jh}, SD_h) = \left(\prod_{j=1}^{25} CD_{jh}^{\alpha_{jh}} \right) SD_h^{\beta_h} \\ &\text{subject to} \quad \sum_{j=1}^{25} p_j CD_{jh} + invp\ SD_h = YDISP_h \end{aligned} \tag{2}$$

where α_{jh} and β_h represent the share coefficients corresponding to consumption goods and savings, respectively, p_j are present consumption prices and *invp* is the price of the savings/investment good.

2.4. *The Public Sector*

The public sector demands goods and services, collects taxes, and supplies transfers to private agents. The assumptions on the public deficit allow us to obtain two versions of the model. In the first version, the activity level of the government remains constant, although the market value of the public expenditure may vary as a result of changes in prices, and the public deficit, *PD*, is endogenously determined (Scenario I). In the second one, the deficit *PD* remains constant and so the activity level of the government is endogenously determined (Scenario II). Thus,

$$PD = R - \sum_{h=1}^{4} TPS_h cpi - \sum_{j=1}^{25} GD_j p_j \tag{3}$$

where total tax revenues R in turn are determined by all the different taxes — direct and indirect — that are present in the economy and that the model captures. Specifically, the tax revenue function distinguishes the following six tax categories:

$$R = R_P + R_{\mathrm{LF}} + R_{\mathrm{LC}} + R_T + R_{\mathrm{VAT}} + R_I, \tag{4}$$

where R_P is total net indirect production taxes, R_{LF} is the part of the social security contributions paid by employers while R_{LC} is the part levied on working consumers, R_T represents tariffs, R_{VAT} is the consumption value-added tax, and R_I is personal income tax revenues. For each tax category, its collections level depends on equilibrium prices and quantities and effective tax rates.

2.5. *The Foreign Sector*

Since our analysis is based on the Andalusian regional economy, the "foreign" or external sector is modeled in a simple, aggregated way, namely, as a single foreign sector that includes the three trading partners. The level of export activity of the foreign sector is fixed exogenously, whereas the trade deficit is endogenously determined given that imports are also endogenous. Thus, the macroeconomic closure rule for the foreign sector can be written as follows:

$$ROWD = \sum_{j=1}^{25} rowp\ IMP_j - \sum_{h=1}^{4} TROW_h - \sum_{j=1}^{25} rowp\ EXP_j \tag{5}$$

where $ROWD$ is the trade deficit, IMP_j and EXP_j are the demands for imports and exports, $TROW_h$ are the transfers from the rest of the world, and $rowp$ is an aggregate price index for the traded commodities.

2.6. *Savings and Investment*

Following the activity analysis tradition, we model investment as an activity that is produced with a fixed-coefficients technology and whose inputs are the sales of the productive sectors to the investment sector. The output level of the investment activity is driven by total savings in the economy so as to satisfy the macroeconomic rule that total investment equals total savings from all sources (private, public and external to the region). Using previous notation, we have:

$$\sum_{j=1}^{25} INV_j\ invp = \sum_{h=1}^{4} SD_h\ invp + PD + ROWD, \tag{6}$$

where INV_j is the investment level of sector j. Private, public and external savings therefore determine total investment. In static models, the inclusion of an investment sector has to be seen simply as a modeling closure device which guarantees that in the benchmark equilibrium, as well as in any and in counterfactual one, all flows are accounted for and balanced. Without this condition, in fact, we could not recreate a balanced SAM depicting a new simulated equilibrium.

2.7. *Equilibrium*

The two versions of the model (floating deficit + fixed expenditure, and fixed deficit + floating expenditure) follow the standard Walrasian concept of equilibrium. In equilibrium, supply must be equal to demand in all non-labor markets.

About labor and capital demands, we consider that firms minimize the production cost of the value-added composite. In the capital market, we consider that supply is perfectly inelastic. On other hand, in the labor market, we suppose that the supply is perfectly elastic up to the level of total labor endowment where it becomes inelastic. There is also a feedback between the real wage rate and the unemployment rate. This feedback somehow represents rigidities in the labor market that are related to unions' power or other friction inducing factors [see Oswald (1982)]. The simple specification that we adopt picks up in a stylized way some of the labor market rigidities that have been affecting the regional economy. We consider that the real wage satisfies the following feedback condition:

$$\frac{w}{cpi} = \left(\frac{1-u}{1-\bar{u}}\right)^{\frac{1}{\theta}} \tag{7}$$

where u and $\bar{u}$ are the unemployment rates in the simulation and in the benchmark equilibrium, respectively, and θ is an elasticity coefficient that represents the degree of flexibility of the real wage. In our case, it is set equal to 1.

An equilibrium is a price vector, an output vector, an unemployment rate, and a level of tax revenues such that prices follow the unit cost rule, consumers maximize utility, producers maximize after-tax profits, government tax revenues are equal to the amount of taxes paid by all economic agents, and all non-labor markets clear. In addition, in the first version of the model, the public deficit is endogenous (and expenditure is fixed) whereas in the second version, the opposite holds — expenditure is endogenous and the deficit is fixed.

3. Database and Calibration

The numerical specification of the parameters in the model has been made possible using the data assembled in a regional SAM for Andalusia (*SAMAND95*). Calibration consists, as is well known, in determining a set of behavior coefficients and policy parameters that, under the first order conditions derived from the optimization problems of agents, allows the model to replicate the given data in the Social Accounting Matrix as a benchmark equilibrium of the regional economy. We obtain the following set of parameters after calibration:

(a) the technical coefficients of production sectors, both domestic and foreign;

(b) the technical coefficients for primary factors that produce unitary Value-added;
(c) the share coefficients of the utility functions for consumers; and
(d) the tax parameters which allow us to define the effective tax rates for all taxes, both the direct and the indirect ones.

The units we use to express the economic variables in equilibrium have been chosen, for the sake of convenience, in such a way that all prices and levels of activity are unitary in the benchmark equilibrium.

Finally, regarding the database, we have expanded *SAMAND95* to include a finer classification of *Consumers* that comprise our four different types. This disaggregation has been done according to the data in a SAM for Spain in 1990 developed by Uriel *et al.* (1997). A disaggregation based on a more recent SAM would have been more suitable, but Uriel *et al.* is the only official one available at this moment. Thus, the four consumers in *SAMAND95* are: *Rural Consumers* (*RC*), *Urban Salaried Consumers* (*USalC*), *Urban Self-Employed Consumers* (*USelfC*), and *Rest of Urban Consumers* (*RoUC*).

4. Simulations

The tax reform (Act 40/98) took place in 1999, but we use a 1995 SAM for the analysis. This time–distance discrepancy is most of the time an unavoidable, but quite common, restriction in the implementation of applied general equilibrium analysis. The results should therefore be interpreted *as if* the tax reform had taken place in 1995. A comparison between the main macro aggregates in the 1995 SAM and the data in the Regional Income and Products Accounts, whenever this ends up being possible, is called for and would help to indicate to what extent the 1995 simulation results can somehow be safely "adapted", or not, to 1999.

The models compute the effects on relative prices, production and consumption activity levels, unemployment rate, and tax collections, as well as the derived macroeconomic aggregates and welfare distributional effects. Welfare changes are measured using the money-metric Equivalent Variation Index.

The personal income tax rates obtained from the calibration of the models using *SAMAND95* are not statutory, but effective rates. The reform, however, introduces new statutory marginal and average tax rates. Additionally, consumers are not disaggregated by income level or average tax base, but by their income source. Unfortunately, we did not have access to the tax databases to implement a mapping between our effective households' tax rates and their actual tax profile. Therefore, we have followed Castañer *et al.* (1998) and have adopted their estimation of the reduction for the Andalusian region, measured in variation rate on average effective rates. According to their estimates, the tax reform translates to an average reduction of 17.21% in effective tax rates in Andalusia. This is the reduction that has been applied to our four consumers' types. In reality, however, their net tax liabilities are quite different in the benchmark data. Effective tax rates are 3.8% for the *RC* type, 8.6% for *USalC*, 5.9% for *USelfC* and a low 0.2% for the *RoUC* type (this class includes mainly retirees with very low nominal rates). Within each consumer type, we have in fact an aggregation of many different consumers sharing the basic defining trait, and this precludes us from distinguishing in a sensible way consumer-specific tax reductions. We have performed, however, some sensitivity analysis to elucidate the degree of variation in the results.

We perturb the initial equilibrium implementing the reduction of the effective direct tax rate for each type of consumer as shown in the comparative tables below (before and after the reform). As stated above, we present two versions of the applied equilibrium model, one with the public deficit as an endogenous variable and the other with the public deficit as exogenous.

In Table 1, we compare the composition of the GDP, from the point of view of income and expenditure, in both versions of the model. Overall GDP is moderately stable in nominal terms. As expected, due to the newly freed incomes, the share of private consumption increases and does so in fairly equal terms in both scenarios. Its implicit empirical elasticity relative to the tax change is close to −0.06. Each percent point reduction in the effective income tax rate would increase private consumption by approximately 0.06%. Since investment is savings-driven, its behavior is, not surprisingly, directly related to the public sector closure assumption. This assumption does not seem to bear, however, on the income composition of GDP. Labor income falls and business income increases very slightly in both scenarios suggesting a subtle, but small shift of the tax burden towards labor.

Table 2 shows the composition of government tax income. We observe that total tax revenue decreases in net terms (about 1% in nominal terms). This is essentially due to the fall in income tax collections, over a hundred billion pesetas. Indirect taxation remains globally about the same after the direct tax reform showing the lack of self-financing capacity of the tax reform regardless of the closure rule. It is however worth remarking the small, but different behavior of the Value-added tax and Production taxes. This could be traced to the reduction in government production purchases in the fix deficit version.

Table 1. GDP: Expenditure and Income (in Billions of Pesetas)

	Before Reform	After Reform (PD = Endogenous)	After Reform (PD = Exogenous)
Consumption	6276.49	6371.83	6386.45
	69.59%	70.60%	70.65%
Investment	2554.65	2433.78	2632.95
	28.32%	26.97%	29.12%
Government expenditure	2001.00	2003.00	1875.33
	22.18%	22.19%	21.74%
Foreign sector	−1813.12	−1784.60	−1856.04
	−20.09%	−19.77%	−20.53%
GDP-expenditure	9019.02	9024.01	9038.69
Labor income	3190.65	3185.02	3174.70
	35.37%	35.29%	35.12%
Capital income	4534.52	4548.07	4573.11
	50.27%	50.39%	50.59%
Employer's contribution to social security	1119.03	1116.80	1116.87
	12.40%	12.37%	12.35%
Tariffs	97.69	97.50	98.94
	1.08%	1.08%	1.09%
Net production tax	−520.35	−518.18	−529.49
	−5.74%	−5.74%	−5.85%
VAT	597.47	594.80	604.56
	6.62%	6.59%	6.68%
GDP-income	9019.02	9024.01	9038.69

Source: *SAMAND95*

With regard to consumers, we observe in Tables 3 and 4 an increase in disposable income for all four types of consumers, due to the reduction in tax burden. These newly freed incomes do not accrue equally to all households and the *Urban Salaried Consumer* type is the one who benefits most from the tax reform. This is so both in terms of new disposable income and in terms of welfare as measured by the Equivalent variation. All consumers benefit from the reform, but they do not benefit equally and this result is independent of the model version used.

Table 2. Effects on Tax Revenues (in Billions of Pesetas)

	Revenue before Reform	Revenue after Reform (PD = Endogenous)	Revenue after Reform (PD = Exogenous)
Taxes on production	−520.35	−518.19	−529.49
Tariffs	97.69	97.49	98.94
Employer's contributions to social security	1119.03	1116.82	1116.87
VAT	597.48	594.82	604.56
Personal income tax	698.74	579.11	580.29
Workers' contributions to social security	281.90	281.41	280.49
Total taxes	2274.49	2151.46	2151.66

Source: *SAMAND95*

Table 3. Effects on Consumers' Net Income, with PD = Endogenous (in Billions of Pesetas)

	Disposable Income (before Reform)	Disposable Income (after Reform)	Equivalent Variation
Rural Consumer	2017.08	2036.66	16.18
Urban Salaried Consumers	4290.13	4378.90	81.32
Urban Self-Employed Consumers	1277.42	1297.97	18.44
Rest of Urban Consumers	1341.50	1344.47	0.71

Source: *SAMAND95*

Table 4. Effects on Consumers' Net Income, with PD = Exogenous (in Billions of Pesetas)

	Disposable Income (before Reform)	Disposable Income (after Reform)	Equivalent Variation
Rural Consumer	2017.08	2042.61	15.82
Urban Salaried Consumers	4290.13	4384.40	73.03
Urban Self-Employed Consumers	1277.43	1304.58	21.11
Rest of Urban Consumers	1341.50	1349.47	1.51

Source: *SAMAND95*

We have performed some sensitivity exercises to check the dependency of the results to the selected tax policy. We have run simulations where the effective income tax rate has been modified two percent points upwards and downwards. Lack of space precludes showing the alternate simulations here, but we can report that the general direction of the results remains unchanged. In terms of welfare, for instance, the Equivalent variation interval for *Urban Salaried Consumer* goes from 71.88 to 90.77 in Scenario I (endogenous public deficit), an approximate ±12% change relative to the initial estimate. Similar figures apply to the rest of households and the relative ordering of effects is unaltered.

5. Conclusions

We have developed an applied general equilibrium model of the Andalusian economy to analyze the impact of the 1999 enacted income tax reform, with two different public sector closure rules. The main purpose of the analysis has been to use the tax policy induced microeconomic resource allocation shift to obtain the changes in the main macroeconomic aggregates and in real income distribution. A model of these characteristics generates a great amount of information, which can be summarized as follows.

There is a reduction in total government revenue as a result of the reduction of effective rates in the personal income tax. The reform, contrary to government claims, is shown to be not even partially self-financing. The economy does seem to benefit from the stimulus, but at a much smaller pace than expected. This conclusion is robust to the closure rule specification.

Investment behaves differently in both versions. In Scenario I, investment falls because of the increase in the public that follows from the decrease in the tax burden and the corresponding adjustment of savings through the closure rule. This seems to provide some support for the opinion of most macroeconomists who think that an increase in public deficit has a discouraging effect on investment. On the other hand, in Scenario II, there is an increase in investment whose explanation lies on the opposite behavior of the public deficit.

Disposable income, quantified by taking the wage rate as the unit of nominal measurement — *numeraire* — improves, but unequally for all four types of consumers due to the reduction in the tax burden. The improvements are not spectacular, being the *Urban Salaried Consumer* the one who benefits most from the reform in both versions.

As a general conclusion, we must point out that the reform has an overall slight positive effect on the economy, as it is shown by the reported macroeconomic variables. However, the results of this simulation exercise must be interpreted with caution due to the great number of simplifications that have been necessary to develop the model. In addition, the statistical database possesses considerable limitations in regard to its timeliness. All applied economic models are always subject to this kind of constraints. Despite these facts, we feel the model is useful to help us in understanding the economic processes triggered by the tax reform. In the future, it is our aim to improve the model on several respects, such as its technological structure and its supporting database. The latter includes a most important task that should aim at elaborating statistical data more suitable to the requirements of the model, for instance, a finer disaggregation of consumers according to income levels. The updating of the database *SAMAND95* with a new Input–Output table designed by the Regional statistical office, or else with non-survey techniques, such as *RAS* or cross entropy methods can also be undertaken and would clearly yield a better data platform to perform more up to date analysis.

Acknowledgment

The authors wish to thank the support of network grant XT2000-33 and the research project SEC2000-0390. The first author thanks the research project IEA-00 and centrA. The second author is also grateful to research project SGR2001-164. This paper was finished while author Cardenete was visiting the Regional Economics Application Laboratory (REAL), University of Illinois at Urbana-Champaign. This author wishes to thank Prof. G.J.D. Hewings, Director of REAL, and the components of the REAL Seminar by their suggestions.

References

Cardenete MA, 2000. "Modelos de Equilibrio General Aplicado para la Economía Andaluza." Ph.D. Dissertation, University of Huelva, SPAIN, edited by Chadwyck-Healey, 2002.

Castañer JM, Onrubia J, and Paredes R, 1998. "Análisis de los Efectos Recaudatorios y Redistributivos de la Reforma del IRPF por Comunidades Autónomas." Documentos de Trabajo del Instituto de Estudios Fiscales, 19/98.

De las Heras A, Murillo C, and Rodríguez J, 2001. "Información Fiscal y Estimaciones de Diferentes Ganancias en Bienestar Social en las Comunidades Autónomas del Territorio del Régimen Común Derivadas de la Progresividad del IRPF: una Aproximación." VIII Encuentro de Economía Pública, Universidad de Extremadura.

Dervis K, de Melo J, and Robinson S, 1982. *General Equilibrium Models for Development Policy*. Cambridge University Press: New York.

Kehoe T, Noyola P, Manresa A, Polo C, and Sancho F, 1988. "A general equilibrium analysis of the 1986 tax reform in Spain." *European Economic Review* **32**: 334–342.

Kehoe T, Manresa A, Polo C, and Sancho F, 1989. "Un Análisis de Equilibrio General de la Reforma Fiscal de 1986 en España." *Investigaciones Económicas* **XIII(3)**: 337–385.

Lasheras MA, Rabadán I, and Salas R, 1994. "Efectos Redistributivos del IRPF por Comunidades Autónomas." *Hacienda Pública Española* **129**: 105–118.

Oswald AJ, 1982. "The microeconomic theory of the trade union." *Economic Journal* **92**: 576–595.

Shoven JB, and Whalley J, 1992. *Applying General Equilibrium.* Cambridge University Presss: New York.

Uriel E, Beneito P, Ferri J, and Moltó ML, 1997. "Matriz de Contabilidad Social de España 1990." Instituto Nacional de Estadística e Instituto Valenciano de Investigaciones Económicas, Madrid, SPAIN.

Part III

CGE Models for Small Cities and Multi-Regions

Chapter 5

Building Small City and Town: SAMs and CGE Models Revisited*

WALTER SCHWARM

Regional Research Institute, West Virginia University, Morgantown, WV, U.S.A.

HARVEY CUTLER

Department of Economics, Colorado State University, Fort Collins, Colorado, U.S.A.

In this chapter, we attempt to describe both the data sources and organizational methods that allow for effective and easily created SAMs and regional computable general equilibrium (CGE) models. Small cities of around 100,000 people will face very different constraints than a town of 5000 people. Unfortunately, most CGE models typically describe relatively large geographical areas and are therefore not able to capture the uniqueness of individual cities or towns within the region. An illustrative example using these techniques demonstrates the insights and regional characteristics, which such methods allow a researcher to uncover.

*This chapter builds on Schwarm and Cutler (2003, 2005) who used CGE models to highlight how different municipalities have unique responses to the same economic shock. This chapter uses the 2005 extended model including three labor groups, which allowed for a more detailed analysis to be undertaken. The modified model construction results in smaller employment multipliers and the ability to examine changes in the distribution of income and unemployment for the three municipalities. We also include a new simulation describing the economic impact of a one-percent increase in the sales tax rate.

1. Introduction

Most computable general equilibrium (CGE) models typically describe relatively large geographical regions; as such, they are not able to capture the uniqueness of the cities and towns that comprise the region. Examples include Seung and Kraybill (2001) who examine the impact of public investment in the Ohio economy; Hoffmann, Robinson and Subramanian (1996) who investigate the role of Defense cuts in California; and, finally, Jones and Whalley (1989) who construct a CGE model covering most of Canada. In their comprehensive survey of CGE models, Partridge and Rickman (1998) maintain that the "relative slow start of regional CGE models is due to the paucity of regional data." To the contrary, we maintain that regional data of sufficiently high quality exists and therefore social accounting matrices (SAMs) and thus CGE models can be constructed for towns as small as 2000 people. The ability to build city level models is of particular importance since municipalities have specific tax boundaries and therefore such models allow city council members and mayors to develop or assess local economic policies more effectively.

As an illustration, consider the economic consequences of a manufacturing firm of 250 employees locating in a city of 100,000 people versus locating in a town of 5000 people. The impact on the wage structure in the city will be relatively small given the size of the workforce; however, the impact on the wage structure in the town could be comparatively large. While the direct effects will likely be similar across these two municipalities, the indirect effects, such as: differences in household migration, the new demand for city services, and commuting and land use zoning, could be substantial. A decision maker may question the additional benefit gained from the complex exercise of constructing a SAM and CGE model at the town level. There is a tradeoff between the amount of resources employed and the return from conducting such an exercise as opposed to doing a simple I–O analysis or even an ad hoc approach. We present a methodology, which greatly simplifies the construction of a city/town level SAM and CGE model, thereby making the CGE approach more cost-effective.

Prior attempts in the literature to model specific towns or cities have usually resorted to using artificial data due to *perceived* data limitations, or have relied on purely theoretical general equilibrium models as the method of analysis. Using artificial data, Anas and Kim (1996) look at the role of congestion in the performance of a city economy. Kilkenny (1998) examines a two-region model where transportation costs play a significant role in rural development but uses a limited data set. Pasha and Ghaus (1995) and Brueckner and Kim (2000) use a theoretical general equilibrium model to examine optimal taxation (sales and property) policies for a city. We believe that our approach bridges the gap between theoretical models and the use of complex CGE models, and can aid policy makers at the city or town level.

A combination of data sources including ES202 and unemployment insurance (UI) records, county assessor's data, city annual financial records (CAFR), and U.S. Census data are combined with distributional properties derived from IMPLAN and the Consumer Expenditure Survey (CES). These sources when collected and organized are sufficiently rich to allow for consistency checks among the data as well as providing any needed transformations for data reconciliation.

The construction of a CGE model is a lengthy endeavor since data first has to be collected and balanced in a SAM and then calibrated in a CGE model. Our methodology significantly simplifies this process. Utilizing a series of interactive spreadsheets that organize the data into the appropriate household, productive and government sectors, the data is then fed through a final worksheet, which automatically creates a SAM.[a] The resulting SAM is to a great extent self-balancing with the remaining changes requiring some adjustments for flows into and out of the city or town economy. This methodology, given the data, significantly eases the researcher's ability to construct annual SAMs and CGE models. Thus the methodology aids in addressing the criticism that results are difficult to generalize from a given CGE model since only one year's worth of data is analyzed.

The CGE model used in this endeavor is static and loosely based on the California DRAM CGE model of Berck, Smith and Golan (1996) with changes reflecting the level of regional aggregation. This paper's analysis is fundamentally independent of CGE model choice as it is merely a vehicle to demonstrate the value of the data collection and organization methods, and to demonstrate the very different responses to the same economic shock which may result. Our CGE model has been modified to include commuting, a more general method of collecting taxes and the use of land in the production function as well as for household consumption. In addition, labor is now decomposed into 3 groups: L1, comprised of workers earning less than

[a]An excel spreadsheet and users guide are available from the authors on request that presents the coordination of the data into a balanced SAM.

$20,000 annually, L2 workers earning between $20,000 and $50,000 and L3 comprises workers earning over $50,000 annually.

This change allows us to perform a much more detailed examination of the 250 employee expansion in the three municipalities. The use of three labor groups permits modeled firms to make more detailed decisions about hiring and we are able to observe substitution between labor groups and increased competition for workers when the manufacturing sector expands. The increased factors demand specificity in the model results in smaller employment multipliers for all three economic entities when compared to the single labor group model. Given the greater labor supply detail, more realistic migration elasticities were examined using sensitivity analysis which also impacts the employment multipliers as well as influencing gross city product (GCP), tax revenue and commuting. The addition of multiple labor groups also allows an examination of how the distribution of income impacts the three municipalities in ways that were not possible before. The increase in the depth of analysis prompts us to also investigate the variation in results of a one-percent increase in the sales tax rate.

Section 2 presents the structure of the data; Section 3 presents the SAM creation and Section 4 presents the CGE model. Section 5 presents the simulation results and Section 6 is the conclusion.

2. The Structure and Sources of the Data

This section presents the sources and organization of the data for employment, wages, land and capital. Table 1 presents a summary of the data and sectors used in our CGE model. There are 16 productive sectors that demand services from three labor groups, differentiated by level of income. These sectors also demand capital and land. Six household groups in Table 1 are differentiated by income, and they demand goods from the producing sectors as well as housing services. Housing services are divided into four categories: houses less than $100,000 (HS1); houses between $100,000 and $200,000 (HS2); houses valued over $200,000 (HS3); and multiple units such as apartments and condominiums (HS4). The local government provides services such as police, fire, transportation, library, parks and recreation, and city administration. Expenditures for local services are financed by the collection of sales, use, property and other taxes in the local economy. The state and federal governments are also modeled as are school districts and post-secondary education as budget balancers. However, state and federal governments form only a minor part of the model.

Table 1. The Sectors and the Economy

Profit Maximizing Sectors (1–16)	
1) Agriculture Services	9) Computer Manufacturing
2) Agricultural Production	10) Transportation and Utilities
3) Agricultural Processing	11) Communications
4) Low Services: Hair, Cleaners, etc.	12) Wholesale
	13) Retail
5) High Services: Legal, Medical	14) Finance, insurance and real estate (FIRE)
6) Construction	
7) Manufacturing	15) Eating Establishments
8) Mining	16) Lodging
Housing Market	*Public Sectors*
HS1 < \$100,000	1) Local Utilities
\$100,000 < HS2 < \$200,000	2) Local City Government
\$200,000 < HS3	3) State and Federal Governments
	4) Universities and Junior Colleges
	5) School District
Labor	*Household Groups*
	HH1 < \$10,000
Capital Stock	\$10,001 < HH2 < \$19,999
K — Buildings and Factories used by the productive and public sectors	\$20,000 < HH3 < \$39,999
	\$40,000 < HH4 < \$49,999
	\$50,000 < HH5 < \$69,999
	\$70,000 < HH6
Land	
L — Land used by the productive sectors and for residential homes	

2.1. *Employment and Wage Data*

The Colorado Department of Labor collects data on the number of workers in each sector as well as the wages paid to those workers from two different perspectives: ES-202 and unemployment insurance (UI). ES-202 data summarizes quarterly reports by firms concerning the number of workers employed and the total wage bill paid for those workers. Theoretically, every private employer is required to supply this information which is organized by zip code and address. In addition, every worker in the private sector has a UI number, which allows the state to track the individual wages earned by that worker for every quarter. Thus, the state can identify the firm that each worker is employed by and multiple job-holders can be identified and converted to FTEs. Combining ES-202 and UI data, we can create a distribution of employment and wages by sector. There are several employers that are not covered in the ES-202 and UI programs, such as school districts and local, state, and federal governments. These entities must be contacted separately to obtain their wage and employment data. In addition, single proprietors must also be accounted for and added to the data set.[b]

2.2. *Capital and Land*

The standard county assessor's office typically keeps good records on the use of each parcel of land in the county since property taxes differ across commercial and residential properties. The imbedded abstract codes allow one to allocate the commercial parcels into most of the productive sectors presented in Table 1. Included in each parcel are data on market values for acreage and of the structure (capital) on the parcel, thus, reliable data can be obtained for value added in the profit maximizing sectors. Data can also be collected on personal capital (computers, production lines, etc.). However, we are concerned about the accuracy of these value estimates and at the present time, we do not use this data.

Similar data are also available for residential properties. The county collects data on market values for the acreage and the house on each parcel and these values are used to compute the housing expenditures for our six household groups. As Table 1 indicates, homes are divided into three categories determined by prices and there is a sector for multiple unit housing.

At this point, the wage data combined with the land and capital data provides high quality estimates of the value added component in the productive sectors. The relative consistency of the data can be assessed at this point as well, by ensuring that the number of firms correlates between the wage and land data sets. The resultant data aids the estimation of domestic supply across the productive sectors, and is uniquely derived for each town.

2.3. *Household Income and Consumption*

The labor, land and capital income defined from Sections 2.1 and 2.2, can now be mapped into the six different household groups, defined as in Table 1. Outside remittances to the households, such as private retirement or welfare

---

[b]In the case of Colorado, the state demographer had estimates of single proprietors. It may be the case that for other states, different state agencies may have to be contacted to obtain this information.

payments, must also be included in the income stream. The mapping procedure relies on census data as well as some estimates provided by the state demographer on the distribution of household income.[c] The number of multiple income-earning households present in the model is also determined at this point, yielding the "jobcorr" statistic, or the number of wage earners per household.

The calculation of household expenditures across sectors including housing requires both the distribution of expenditures as well as the level of expenditures. Distribution patterns were estimated using a combination of IMPLAN data and the Consumer Expenditure Survey. Both of these sources offer levels of expenditures across household groups, but need to be compared to the level of estimated labor, land and capital income derived in the sections above. Additional wealth that supports expenditures, such as stocks and outside remittances are also used to obtain consistency between expenditures and income.

2.4. *Local Government Data*

The data collected from a local government for a city or town consists of employment and wages, non-labor expenditures for city services and the range of taxes collected by the local government. We have divided the city into five categories; the police department; the fire department; the transportation department; city administration; and library, parks and recreation. Employment and wages for each of these departments are collected as well as the non-labor expenditures made by each department.

The City Auditor's Financial Records (CAFR) were used to identify the array of taxes collected by the city. These taxes are sales taxes, property taxes, use taxes, impact fees and all other taxes. The tax payments are distributed across firms and households. The most challenging category is the school district. Some school districts are responsible for the residents outside of town so it can be difficult to determine the appropriate school district. This is important since many school districts receive tax payments. We contacted the school districts for employment and wage data, as well as non-labor expenditure data.

3. The SAM Framework

The SAM organizes the data in a logical consistent manner (Fig. 1). It ties all the expenditures made by a sector to the receipts of that sector. Column 1

---

[c]Jim Weskott, the state demographer for Colorado was very helpful in supplying data and interpreting a wide range of data issues.

	Commodity (1)	Factors (2)	Households (3)	Govt (4)	World (5)	Totals (6)
Commodity (1)	Intermediate Inputs		Consumption and Housing	Consumption	Exports	
Factors (2)	Value Added				Foreign Value Added	
Households (3)		Distribution of Value Added	Savings	Transfer Payments	Foreign Transfer and Savings	
Govt (4)	Use and Sales Taxes		Income and Property Taxes	Inter-Gov Transfers		
World (5)	Imports					
Totals (6)						

Fig. 1. The SAM

(commodity) represents the private sectors, and summing down the column, we first come to the commodities that the industry demands from other sectors as intermediate demand, this is followed by factor demand, finally use and sales taxes and other costs of doing business are accounted for. These components together represent domestic supply for that sector. In a similar fashion, the household column represents the allocation of household income to consumption, savings and tax payments. Row 1 represents the supply of the commodities as intermediate inputs, household and government consumption, and exports. The household row represents the sources of income (land, labor and capital), government transfers including social security, and outside remittances. All other columns and rows are interpreted in a similar manner.

Our method organizes and links data such that it automatically creates an essentially self-balancing SAM. Worksheets exist for each block in Fig. 1 and are dynamically linked so as to make it self-balancing except for some small sums in the inter-governmental transfer block. Additionally, most of the proportionalization and transformation is done automatically, thus lightening the load on the modeler. This economy of human capital is one of the more attractive features of this data arrangement.

3.1. *The Side Worksheets*

Figure 2 presents the major linkages between the side worksheets and the SAM. These worksheets contain data for household expenditures, wages, I–O relationships, land and capital components, the relationship between wage

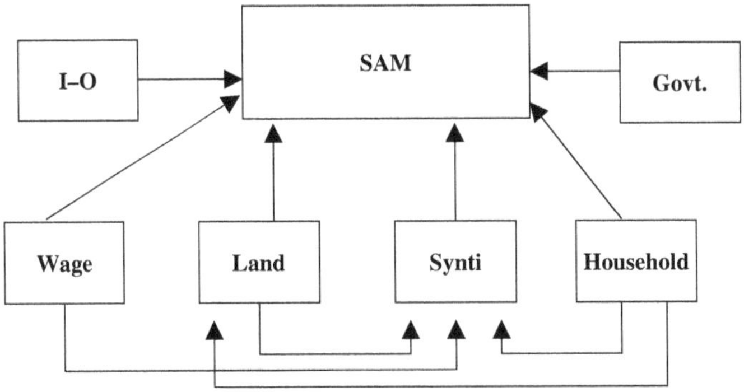

Fig. 2. The Relationship of the Sidesheets to the SAM

earners and the number of households (Synti) and the local government. Each worksheet contains the original input of the data, calculations and proportionalizations to insure that all the worksheets remain consistent with one another. The reconciliation of data acquired from a variety of sources into a coherent SAM representation is a matter of some import in model construction. While there are a number of procedures (RAS, Cross-Entropy, LS) that can achieve final reconciliation, our method uses a variety of pre-SAM manipulations to raise the level of data consistency allowing for easier final balancing. When considering the productive activity component of the SAM, initial balancing starts with estimates of the percentage of domestic supply that is exported. These estimates are obtained from the city government, which collects estimates of these percentages. Given the associated levels of exports, we can derive a good estimate of total demand. With a good approximation of domestic supply, the level of imports can, therefore, reasonably be used to pre-balance this part of the SAM.

Integrating institutions and factor payments follows a similar methodology. From the county assessor's data, we have good estimates of the market value of housing and, therefore, reasonable estimates of annual housing payments. By using the Consumer Expenditure Survey, estimates for the percentage of household expenditures allocated to housing versus other goods were obtained. These estimates allow the expenditures on all other goods to be proportionally-scaled to housing payments. To complete the household expenditure block, state and federal income tax payments are obtained from CES estimates and property tax and other tax payments are obtained from local sources. These tax payments, combined with household consumption estimates, provide a measure of total household expenditures.

These are then compared to labor, land and capital income. Differences between income and expenditures were assumed to be primarily outside remittances such as retirement benefits, stock dividends and contributions made by parents to the some 25,000 Colorado State University students. Thus, imbalances between factors and institutions were essentially removed at this point.

The pre-balancing of the local government sectors; police, fire, transportation, administration, library, and parks and recreation is conducted similarly. The expenditures reported by the city auditor for intermediate inputs and value added components have to balance with the sales, property, use and other taxes collected. Any residual imbalances in the local government sectors were eliminated by adjusting inflows of federal and state monies that help fund education.

Any remaining imbalances in the SAM are ones that data reconciliation methods are unable to address, either because the data is lacking or logical methods do not exist. These imbalances must still be addressed. Cross-Entropy techniques as in Robinson, Cattaneo and El-Said (2001) could be used to adjust the cells in the column as well as balance the new SAM. Additionally, other techniques using Newton scaling algorithms outlined by Schneider and Zenios (1990) could be implemented. We maintain that the choice is largely dictated by the amount of pre-balancing the researcher was able to complete. As we were quite successful in pre-balancing and had few vectors requiring adjustment, therefore, we resorted to a modified RAS procedure. The following sections further describe the major highlights of each worksheet and their connection to the SAM.

3.2. *Households*

This particular sheet has two primary functions: to establish and group local households by income and to provide an accounting of expenditures. The number of households in a town is a crucial value for SAM construction and feeds into may different side worksheets. Census data combined with county business pattern data is reconciled with any other growth or distribution estimates to determine population and household composition. The number of households is also matched up with the number of residential parcels of land in the land worksheet.

The sheet's second task is to determine the level of household expenditures that is consistent with the distribution of households explained above. Data distributions are initially imported from IMPLAN and adjusted with Consumer Expenditure Survey values, resulting in estimates of the level of household expenditures across all private sectors. Adjustments are made so that expenditures on housing are consistent with all other household expenditures. It is also necessary to remove the value of mortgage payments from the finance and real estate sectors as those values are captured in housing service payments entering from the land worksheet.

3.3. *Wages*

Wages can be separated into any number of groups desired (we utilize three, as presented in Table 1) when they are drawn from the UI/ES-202 data sets, and are inserted into this data sheet categorized by sector and group. Once in the sheet, the social security paid by the employers is calculated along with that paid by the employees. This sheet serves as the primary entry point for not only the wages, but also the number of commuters in and out (U.S. Census Data). The income flow from these wages is modified somewhat by calculating and subtracting the wages leaving the city by way of workers commuting in, and adding back income that is earned by workers who commute out. Once adjustments to the incoming wages have been performed, the resulting values are transferred automatically to the Synti worksheet.

3.4. *Land*

The Land worksheet has several tasks to perform. The first is to determine the flow of income derived from land and capital income. To this end, the land and capital stock derived from county assessor's data file is inserted into the model. A depreciation rate of 10% is levied on the capital stock values. The same depreciation rate is also applied to the land stock remaining after maintenance, construction, and finance costs are accounted for. The resulting flow enters the SAM under the productive sectors. This sheet is also responsible for distributing housing stock among the households that come from the household worksheet. In particular, the number of households is reconciled with the number of residential parcels in the city. Parcels within the three housing services groups (HS1, HS2 and HS3) are apportioned across the six households groups according to income level. U.S. Census data is very useful for this stage. Any remaining households are distributed among multiple-unit parcels (HS4). The ensuing matrix is linked to the household sheet, from which it enters the SAM. We have modeled the housing sector as a productive sector similar to Pasha and Ghaus (1995) and Brueckner and Kim (2000).

3.5. *Synti*

This worksheet is primarily responsible for assigning labor, land, and capital income to the resident households in each city. Labor income from the wage worksheet enters this sheet in three income levels with non-resident commuters' (in-commuters) wages already removed. Land and capital income derived in the land worksheet is also used in this worksheet. The core of this sheet is the relative comparison between the income and expenditures of the households. From the total value of expenditures, the capital income, private retirement and social security benefits are subtracted. The remaining expenditure per household group must be derived therefore from labor income.

Logistically, the three labor income categories are correlated to the six household categories by lower triangularizing a 6×3 matrix one column at a time, using the U.S. Census wage earners per household values. In this way, not only is the income distributed, but also the number of workers per household group by income level is determined. The resulting 6×3 "synti" is then linked to the respective block in the SAM (Row 3, Column 2 in Fig. 1), representing the three labor groups payments' to households in the model. A similar procedure is used to distribute the labor income of those workers who commute out-of-town.

3.6. *I/O*

The primary proportions for each productive sector in the model are obtained from IMPLAN. These proportions are then parameterized, by subtracting the intermediate proportions from the total proportional value (unity) leaving the proportion of value added. This amount is multiplied by the sectors' value added components (land, labor and capital) and taxes paid, which is automatically obtained from the SAM, to determine the total value in dollars of the sector. The total amount, minus the dollar amount of value added must represent the dollar value of intermediate demand and is divided among the sectors according to the proportions in the IMPLAN I/O matrix. This final estimate of intermediate demand is then automatically inserted into the correct block in the SAM. Once set up, the only operation, which must be performed manually, is pasting the IMPLAN I/O in the worksheet, all other operations occur automatically.

3.7. *Local Government*

The local government provides services such as a police and fire and also imposes a variety of taxes on firms and households. Local taxes in sales, use, property and other taxes and these taxes are distributed over the private sector as well as the six household groups. In the SAM, these taxes appear in Row 4 and Columns 1 and 3. There are also federal and state taxes such as social security and personal income taxes. Given that we are interested in local issues, these tax payments flow out of the model. The local government's tax revenues are then distributed to pay for the following services: police, fire, transportation, library, administration, and parks and recreation. These expenditures are subdivided into intermediate inputs, labor, land and capital. All of these values are automatically linked to the SAM.

4. CGE Model

All production sectors use the three primary factors of land, labor, and capital, with labor further divided into three subgroups. Each sector produces a composite commodity that goes into domestic supply and exports according to a constant elasticity of transformation (CET) function. Producers are assumed to maximize profits subject to their production technology, represented by a two-stage production function. Intermediate inputs are used in a fixed-proportions, Leontief production function. All primary factors are combined using a Cobb–Douglas function and, following Armington (1969), intermediate demand can be met through a composite of imported and domestic goods.

Consumers are divided into six household groups based on income and they maximize utility subject to a budget constraint, which equals the income from primary factors less taxes, but with private and governmental transfers added. This income is allocated to investment (savings), private consumption, expenditures on housing and net transfers to the outside economy. Utility maximization is achieved using a constant elasticity of substitution (CES) function, and households purchase optimal quantities of the composite private goods, treating local and imported commodities as imperfect substitutes.

The government is modeled in two levels, the state/federal level and the local level. The state and federal component collects income taxes, including social security taxes. The local government generates revenue from property, sales, use and other taxes, in addition to receiving lump-sum transfers from the federal/state level in order to pay for local city services. The local government is required to have balanced budget as they do not go through any maximization process.

Investment is essentially modeled as an unconstrained flow, not limited by domestic savings and exports. Deficits in the balance of payments are met through a balancing inflow from the external economy and external prices are treated as exogenous. Again Armington's approach is followed by assuming that imports are imperfect substitutes for similar domestic commodities. Both the domestic supply and exports of a commodity are a joint product of domestic production. Following Rattsø (1982), neoclassical closure rules for the factor markets are adopted with the overall wage level in the economy and individual sectoral labor supplies flexible. Land and capital levels are proportionally fixed across sectors, but overall flexible throughout the economy taken as a whole.

Four equations merit closer attention as they figure prominently in our simulation results. The first of these is the labor supply equation:

$$\frac{a_h^w}{a_h} = \frac{\bar{a}_h^w}{\bar{a}_h}\left(\left(\frac{\sum_L\left(\frac{r_L^a}{\bar{r}_L^a}\right)}{\left(\frac{p_h}{\bar{p}_h}\right)}\right)\left(\frac{\sum_{Z,L} u_{z,l}^d}{\left(\sum_H a_h^w * \varepsilon_h\right) + \text{CMI}}\right) + \left(\sum_L \frac{Exwage^L}{r_L^a}\right)\left(\frac{\text{CMO}}{\left(\sum_H a_h^w * \varepsilon_h\right) + \text{CMI}}\right)\right)^{\eta_h^{LS}} \times \left(\frac{\sum_{g\in G}\frac{w_{h'g}}{p_h}}{\sum_{g\in G}\frac{\bar{w}_{h'g}}{\bar{p}_h}}\right)^{\eta_h^w} \quad \forall h \in H \tag{1}$$

Labor supply is expressed in terms of the household participation rate, which is the number of working households (a_h^w) divided by the total households in an income class (a_h). This is a function of the initial participation rate ($\bar{a}_h^w/\bar{a}_h$) adjusted by several factors that shift during a simulation. The first factor is a variable economy-wide wage rate (r_L^a), which is deflated by the consumer price level for each household group (p_h) and is calculated relative to the base values of wages and prices ($\bar{r}_L^a$ and $\bar{p}_h$). It is weighted by the proportion of labor demanded within the city ($u_{z,l}^d$) relative to the total supply of labor, which is $((\alpha_\eta^\omega * \varepsilon_\eta) + \text{CMI})$. The first term is the number of laborers from Fort Collins households, based on the working households in each group times, ε_h, the number of workers per household group. CMI is the number of workers who commute into Fort Collins.

Similarly, the external wage, $Exwge_L$, is compared to the local wage rate (r_L^a), and that factor is weighted by the proportion of Fort Collins residents who commute out of town to work, CMO, again relative to the total supply of labor. Thus, households in Fort Collins decide whether to work or not based on a weighted average of the relative wage rates within the city and those available in employment outside the city. The last factor is the household's average transfer payments when not working ($w_{h'g}$), which again is deflated by households specific price indexes and calculated relative to the base levels.

Each household responds to changes in these factors according to elasticities $(\eta_h^{Ld}, \eta_h^{W})$, which vary across households. High-income households have higher elasticities with respect to wages and taxes than low-income households, but high-income households have no responsiveness to transfer payments. Low-income households have lower elasticities with respect to wages and taxes and higher responsiveness to transfer payments. Borjas (1995) contends that the elasticity of factor price is greater for skilled workers than for unskilled and, therefore, immigration surplus is larger, and the native population has more to gain, with the immigration of skilled workers.

The second equation of importance to our results is the determinant of the total number of households in the City, which is in effect a migration function:

$$a_h = \bar{a}_h \cdot \pi + \bar{a}_h^{in} \left(\frac{y_h^d}{a_h} \div \frac{\bar{y}_h^d}{\bar{a}_h} \div \frac{p_h}{\bar{p}_h} \right)^{\eta_h^{yd}} \left(\frac{a_h^n}{a_h} \div \frac{\bar{a}_h^n}{\bar{a}_h} \right)^{\eta_h^u}$$

$$- \bar{a}_h^{out} \left(\frac{\bar{y}_h^d}{\bar{a}_h} \div \frac{y_h^d}{a_h} \div \frac{\bar{p}_h}{p_h} \right)^{\eta_h^{yd}} \left(\frac{\bar{a}_h^n}{\bar{a}_h} \div \frac{a_h^n}{a_h} \right)^{\eta_h^u} \quad \forall h \in H \qquad (2)$$

The number of households of each group that exist in a simulation (a_h) is a function of existing population ($\bar{a}_h$), increased by the natural rate of household growth, π, and by two terms that determine net migration into town. The rate of in-migration is captured in the equation by the term beginning with the parameter $\bar{a}_h^{in}$. Households migrate out of town based on the term starting with $\bar{a}_h^{out}$. Both of these factors depend (inversely) on real per household after-tax incomes ($y_h^d / a_h^w / p_h$) and a household group's fraction of non-working members (a_h^n). Total population is a function of the changing attractiveness of Colorado as measured by real after-tax earnings changes and employment prospects. Higher income households are more prone to being attracted by high after tax wages and lower income homes focus more on employment prospects.

Finally, the commuting equations are specified as follows:

$$\text{CMO} = \text{CMO}_O * \left(\frac{Exwage_L}{r_L^a} \right)^{\eta_{como}^L} \qquad (3)$$

$$\text{CMI} = \text{CMI}_O * \left(\frac{r_L^a}{Exwage_L} \right)^{\eta_{comi}^L} \qquad (4)$$

These equations identify commuting out and in respectively. In Eq. (3), CMO_o is the base number of workers commuting out of Fort Collins, $Exwage_L$ is the external wage rate, which is compared to the internal return on labor (r_L^a). Commuting-in, in Eq. (4), is set up in a similar fashion. Thus, changes in commuting in both directions are a result of the attractiveness working in town versus the rest of the world.

5. Simulations

The first part of this section outlines the primary differences of Windsor, Loveland and Fort Collins. Then we present the simulation results of a 250-employee expansion in the three municipalities as we examine the impacts on gross city product (GCP), household migration, commuting, prices, tax revenue and the distribution of income. The last part of this section analyzes the economic impact of a one-percent increase in the sales tax rate.

For the three municipalities, Table 2 presents the level of employment, the number of workers living and working in each town and the percentage of workers commuting in and out. Fort Collins is the most contained municipality given that of the 64,281 jobs in town, 49,041 of these workers live in Fort Collins. This results in 76% of the jobs in Fort Collins being filled by Fort Collins residents. The picture is different for Loveland as only 13,298 residents fulfill the 25,441 jobs in town or Loveland residents account for 52% of local employment. Windsor has the most dramatic situation given that of the 4,383 local jobs, only 820 workers who live in town, work in town.

The commuting patterns for the three towns differ substantially. Fort Collins has 23.0% of its workforce commuting outside of town, Loveland has 52% and Windsor has 79% of its workers commuting out of town. These differences can be explained by the differences in wages in the three municipalities as well as opportunities for employment. The average wage in Fort Collins is $22,870 and for Loveland, it is $18,780. With wages in Loveland lower, a large portion of its workers seek employment outside of town. With

Table 2. Descriptive Statistics for the Three Towns

City/Town	Total Employment	No. of Workers Living in Town	No. of Workers Live and Work in Town	% Workers Commuting Out (%)	% Workers Commuting In (%)
Fort Collins	64,281	63,688	49,041	23	24
Loveland	25,441	27,553	13,298	52	48
Windsor	4,483	3,920	820	79	87

respect to Windsor, the absence of employment opportunities in town is the primary reason for a significant percentage of the workers commuting out of town. These rather stark differences in employment levels and commuting patterns have important implications when considering the responses to the manufacturing simulations.

The basic simulation performed raised the demand for manufacturing exports in the three municipalities such that manufacturing employment increased by 250 workers for each town. This is a reasonable number of workers employed by a new manufacturing firm entering the area. Table 3 reports the results for the manufacturing expansion for Windsor, Loveland and Fort Collins. The estimated employment multipliers for Windsor, Loveland and Fort Collins are 0.76, 1.01, and 1.2 respectively. The difference in the sizes of the multipliers results from differences in the base number of households and the number of new households migrating into each municipality. Recalling Eq. (2), the base number of households is multiplied by changes in real income and the current unemployment position of the economy. We then raised these values by the elasticities estimated by Schachter and Althaus (1989). Households increase by 25 for Windsor, 64 for Loveland, and 117 for Fort Collins. Even though income increases by more in Windsor, it affects a much smaller base of households, 2955, compared to the 40,119 households in Fort Collins. The net result is that the increase in households is smallest for Windsor even though Windsor's percentage increase in income is the largest.

Schwarm and Cutler (2003) used a single labor group and estimated the multipliers for Windsor, Loveland and Fort Collins to be 1.16, 1.32 and 1.62, respectively. With an expansion in manufacturing, the employment multiplier is influenced by new households entering the economy, changes in commuting patterns and the conversion of non-working households to working households. A fourth factor is the competition for existing workers in other sectors that find it more attractive to switch to the manufacturing sector. It is the difference in commuting patterns and competition for local workers that explains the variation in our estimated multipliers across the three municipalities.

With respect to the competition for workers for Windsor, sectors such as retail and FIRE lost 52 workers to manufacturing which is in contrast to Schwarm and Cutler (2003) where these same sectors only lost 9 workers. In Loveland, 24 workers left existing sectors in the current model while only 8 workers transferred in the one labor group model. For Fort Collins, 57 workers transferred in the new model and 26 transferred in the old model. The three labor groups allow more degrees of freedom and thus more competition for workers who originally resided in the municipality. This is one important reason why our three labor group multiplier estimates are lower than ones for one labor group.

An additional factor influencing the estimate of the multiplier is the level of commuting in the municipality. For Windsor, 86.6% of workers in Windsor commute in from outside the town while 79.1% of people living in town work outside of town. These extremely large values for commuting result from educational/skills mismatch between the existing town and its relatively new high-tech employer.

When there is an expansion in manufacturing in Windsor, see Table 3, the increase in commuting in and the reduction in commuting out accounts for 76% of the new jobs. This effect has a strong negative effect on the Windsor multiplier. Workers who were initially commuting out of town, but now employed in town only have marginal increases in labor income and therefore, the multiplier effect is minimal. The increase in commuting in also has a negligible effect in Windsor as those workers leave town after work and spend their money elsewhere. In summary, the combination of the smaller migration effect and a large commuting effect results in the smallest multiplier effect for Windsor; a relationship further seen in medium size town Loveland, with moderate migration and commuting size, with a multiplier of 1.01, followed by the largest municipality, Fort Collins with a multiplier of 1.2.

The relationship between the multiplier effect and the reduction in unemployment reveals some interesting results. Table 3 decomposes the change in employment into new households, changes in commuting patterns and the conversion of non-working households (unemployed workers) to working households. In Fort Collins, 63.7% percent of the new jobs are taken by new households, for Loveland, it is 46.5% and for Windsor, it is 20.9%. The conversion of non-working households to working households account for 3% of the new jobs, but this is large enough to reduce unemployment from 3.13% to 2.92%. Even though the conversion of non-working households to working households for Fort Collins accounts for 11.4% of the new workers, it only reduces the unemployment rate from 3.94% to 3.90%. Our results indicate that a large multiplier effect does not necessarily lead to the largest change in the unemployment rate. One needs to take into account the impact of migration and commuting to determine the impact on unemployment.

We are also interested in the impact on real income across the six household groups, which consist not just of wage income, but land and capital income as well. As the economy expands, the private sectors require additional land and capital, which causes income from these new assets to rise, and residents benefit to varying degrees. Total real income is calculated by adjusting nominal

Table 3. Economic Impacts of a 250-Employee Expansion in Manufacturing

	Windsor		Loveland		Ft. Collins	
	Amount	% Δ	Amount	% Δ	Amount	% Δ
GCP (mil $)	6.85	5.03	7.70	1.10	11.83	0.50
Households	25	0.85	64	0.40	117	0.30
Employment	191	4.26	253	0.94	292	0.45
Multiplier	0.76		1.01		1.20	
Prop. Tax (mil $)	0.010	1.85	0.0189	0.67	1.25	15.5
Sales Tax (mil $)	0.013	1.80	0.0260	3.0	0.21	0.6
Use Tax (mil $)	0.004	8.45	0.1921	1.3	0.23	3.0
Total Taxes (mil $)	0.060	2.57	0.3030	1.0	1.86	2.1
CPI		0.24		0.13		0.08
	Base	New	Base	New	Base	New
Unemployment Rate	3.13%	2.92	8.00%	7.97	3.94%	3.90
	Composition of New Workers					
Δ in Commuting	145	76.0	129	50.8	73	25.0
New Households	40	20.9	118	46.5	186	63.7
Δ Non-Working HH	−6	−3.0	−7	−2.7	−33	−11.4
	Household Income (mil. of $)					
	Amount	% Δ	Amount	% Δ	Amount	% Δ
HH1	0.01	2.29	0.05	0.9	0.22	1.1
HH2	−0.02	−0.32	0.25	0.6	0.57	0.5
HH3	0.11	0.75	0.38	0.3	2.38	0.9
HH4	0.85	5.85	0.88	1.1	0.65	0.6
HH5	0.59	2.01	2.09	0.9	2.26	0.6
HH6	0.58	0.99	1.92	0.6	5.25	0.7
Total	2.12	1.70	5.58	0.7	11.32	0.7

income by the change in the price level, a value estimated uniquely for each household. For simplicity, Table 3 presents the CPI for each municipality. The CPI for Windsor increases by 0.24%, Loveland increases by 0.13% and Fort Collins increases by 0.08%.

The bottom panel of Table 3 presents the results for changes in real income across the six household groups. Total real income increases the most in percentage terms for Windsor, but it is the change in the distribution of income across the three municipalities that reveals interesting differences. The manufacturing sector primarily employs household groups HH3 and HH4. For Loveland and Windsor, real income increases the most for HH4. HH5 also benefits with a 2.01% increase in Windsor. HH2 in Windsor actually experiences a decline in real income due to the increase in the CPI of 0.24% which offsets the modest gains in nominal income. However, HH1 in Windsor also experiences an impressive real income gain of 2.29%. This results from the fact that most the workers that benefit from the increased competition for workers within town are in labor group L1, and thus in household group HH1.

The situation in Fort Collins is quite different as it is household group HH1 that experiences the largest real income increase is HH1. This is due to the multiplier effect of the new households migrating into the city which increases the demand for retail, low services, restaurants, etc. Since these sectors primarily employ workers from HH1, their wages increase. HH3 gains the second most in Fort Collins, which is due to the indirect multiplier effects. Our results indicate that the change in the distribution of income can vary substantially across the three economies.

We have also examined the economic impact of a one-percent increase in the sales tax rate across the three municipalities. An important distinction between the three economies concerns the size of the component in the economy that charges a sales tax. Loveland has the largest sales tax component, as 42% of GCP is associated with a sales tax. The Fort Collins component is 40% and for Windsor it is 20%. The size of these components plays an important role in determining the economic impact of a sales tax rate increase.

Table 4 presents the results of the sales tax simulations. Since Loveland has a slightly larger dependence on sales tax related sectors, the economic downturn resulting from the increase in the sales tax rate is slightly larger. GCP falls by 0.37% in Loveland and 0.30% in Fort Collins. Since Windsor is much less dependent on sales tax related sectors, GCP falls by only 0.16%. The estimated impact on household income highlights the value of our analysis in the context of a CGE model. On average, household income in all three municipalities falls by a greater percentage for the upper income groups as opposed to the lower income groups. Such declines underscore that the characterization of sales taxes as regressive is largely due to a failure to include not just labor income, but also capital and land income. An increase in the sales tax rate does initially hurt the lower household income groups for two reasons. First, given their low incomes, a one-percent increase in the sales tax rate will reduce real income by a greater amount. The second effect is that the loss of jobs is primarily felt

Table 4. Economic Impacts of a One-Percent Increase in the Sales Tax Rate

	Windsor		Loveland		Ft. Collins	
	Amount	% Δ	Amount	% Δ	Amount	% Δ
GCP (mil $)	−0.22	−0.16	−2.61	−0.37	−6.92	−0.30
Households	−6	−0.20	−47	−0.28	−105	−0.26
Employment	−11	−0.24	−84	−0.31	−199	−0.31
Prop. Tax (mil $)	−0.005	−0.43	−0.005	−0.18	−0.23	−2.78
Sales Tax (mil $)	0.172	24.35	1.161	9.42	3.61	9.46
Use Tax (mil $)	0.001	−0.28	−0.053	−0.37	−0.04	−0.46
Total Taxes (mil $)	0.162	7.01	1.095	3.47	3.30	3.78
CPI		0.13		0.16		0.21
	Base	New	Base	New	Base	New
Unemployment Rate	3.13%	3.06	8.00%	8.06	3.94%	3.98
	Household Income (mil. of $)					
	Amount	% Δ	Amount	% Δ	Amount	% Δ
HH1	−0.002	−0.24	−0.021	−0.35	−0.06	−0.31
HH2	−0.018	−0.24	−0.138	−0.31	−0.48	−0.42
HH3	−0.011	−0.07	−0.660	−0.52	−1.35	−0.51
HH4	−0.048	−0.33	−0.410	−0.51	−0.53	−0.45
HH5	−0.090	−0.31	−1.060	−0.47	−1.62	−0.47
HH6	−0.346	−0.59	−1.418	−0.43	−2.99	−0.39
Total	−0.515	−0.41	−3.706	−0.46	−7.03	−0.43
	Change in Labor, Land and Capital Income (mil. of $)					
Labor	−0.190	−0.18	−0.84	−0.16	−1.87	−0.13
Land	−0.018	−0.54	−0.13	−0.47	−0.45	−0.36
Capital	−0.057	−0.33	−0.55	−0.42	−1.72	−0.25

in the lower wage groups (L1), dominated by the lower household income groups.

However, the indirect multiplier effects further affect household income by reductions in land and capital income. As the bottom panel of Table 4 indicates, land and capital income falls by a greater percentage amount than labor income for all three municipalities. Since the upper household income groups earn a larger percentage of capital and land income, losses in these sectors result in greater declines in household income for these groups. Our results suggest that the indirect multiplier effects cannot be ignored when evaluating the impact of a sales tax increase.

6. Conclusion

Our analysis demonstrates the advantages and feasibility of constructing CGE models for cities and towns of all sizes. Our results reveal significantly different outcomes across cities in important areas such as relative wages, household migration, and commuting. Therefore, disaggregated CGE models have an important potential role in policy consulting and economic impact analysis. There are many issues that towns and cities face that are unique to each municipality and models need to be constructed in a way that captures that fact. We have argued that the data sources and organizational methods outlined above provide basis for sound analysis. Additionally, not only do our methods and sources generate specific models, they do so with an economy of effort and time and therefore, allow the researcher to undertake revisions more often and/or projects that may have once seemed too burdensome.

The results presented as examples of this method, are interesting and provide specific/unique insights about each town or city examined. Models constructed as we have, do react significantly differently to changes, despite nearly identical underlying structure. It is our belief that there is a clear need for this type of analysis in the field. Cities and towns face ever more difficult decisions concerning all matter of problems; models and methods such as those in this paper can provide an important voice to the debate, one that is perhaps all too needed.

Acknowledgments

We would like to thank Dave Kraybill for suggesting the basic idea of the paper and Stephen Davies for ongoing interactions about CGE analysis. We would like to thank the participants of the 14th International Conference Input–Output Techniques, 2002 in Montreal and the participants of the 49th North American Meetings of the RSAI, 2002 in Puerto Rico. This work has been partially supported by the Governor's Smart Growth Initiative, the Office of Energy Conservation, the Department of Local Affairs of Colorado, and thirteen cities in Northern Colorado and the Larimer County government. Special thanks go to Frank Bruno, Alan Krcmarik and Sherry Temple.

References

Anas A, and Kim I, 1996. "General equilibrium models of polycentric urban land use with endogenous congestion and job agglomeration." *J. Urban Econ.* **40**: 232–256.

Armington PS, 1969. "Theory of demand for products distinguished by place of production." *IMF Staff Papers* **16**: 159–178.

Berck P, Golan E, and Smith BR, 1997. "State tax policy, labor, and tax revenue feedback effects." *Ind. Relat.* **36**(4): 339–418.

Borjas GJ, 1995. "The economic benefits from immigration." *J. Econ. Perspect.* **9**(2): 3–22.

Brueckner JK, and Kim H-A, 2000. "Urban sprawl and the property tax." University of Illinois at Urbana-Champaign, Working Paper.

Hoffmann S, Robinson S, and Subramanian S, 1996. "The role of defense cuts in the California recession: computable general equilibrium models and interstate factor mobility." *J. Reg. Sci.* **36**(4): 571–595.

Jones R, and Whalley J, 1989. "A Canadian regional general equilibrium model and some applications." *J. Urban Econ.* **25**(3): 368–405.

Kilkenny M, 1998. "Transport costs and rural development." *J. Reg. Sci.* **38**(2): 293–312.

Kraybill D, and Seung C, 1999. "The effects of infrastructure investment: a two-sector dynamic computable general equilibrium analysis for Ohio." *Int. Reg. Sci. Rev.* **24**(2): 261–281.

Partridge M, and Rickman D, 1998. "Regional computable general equilibrium modeling: a survey and critical appraisal." *Int. Reg. Sci. Rev.* **21**(3): 205–248.

Pasha A, and Ghaus A, 1995. "General equilibrium effects of local taxes." *J. Urban Econ* **38**: 253–265.

Rattsø J, 1982. "Different macroclosures of the original Johansen model and their impact of policy evaluation." *J. Pol. Modeling* 4(1): 85–97.

Robinson S, Cattaneo A, and El-Said M, 2001. "Updating and estimating a social accounting matrix using cross entropy methods." *Econ. Systems Res.* **13**(1).

Schneider MH, and Zenios SA, 1990. "A comparative study of algorithms for matrix balancing." *Operations Res.* **38**: 439–455.

Schachter J, and Althaus P, 1989. "An equilibrium model of gross migration." *J. Reg. Sci.* **29**(2): 143–159.

Schwarm W, and Cutler H, 2003. "Building small city and town SAMs and CGE models." *Rev. Urban Reg. Devel. Stud.* **15**(2): 132–147.

Schwarm W, and Cutler H, 2005. "Multiple labor group effects on small city and town SAMs and CGE models." *Rev. Urban Reg. Devel. Stud.* 17(2): 162–176.

Chapter 6

A Large-Scale Dynamic Multi-Regional CGE Model with an Illustrative Application*

JAMES A. GIESECKE and JOHN R. MADDEN

Centre of Policy Studies, Monash University, Victoria, Australia

This paper describes FEDERAL-F, a large-scale general-purpose multiregional computable general equilibrium model. The model is dynamic and can be used for forecasting, policy analysis and historical analysis. Large-scale CGE models are commonly used in Australia and play a central role in policy analysis. In this paper, we provide an overview of the core of FEDERAL-F's equations via a stylized representation that expresses the model's equations in functional form. An illustrative application demonstrating the power of the model is undertaken. It demonstrates that a feasible state government fiscal policy to halt Tasmania's declining share of national GDP does not exist.

1. Introduction

Australia has been a particularly active nation in the development and use of computable general equilibrium (CGE) models as evidenced by Powell and Snape's (1993) review of the contribution of CGE analysis to policy reform in Australia since the development of Australia's first major CGE model, ORANI, in the mid-1970s.[a] During the nine years since the Powell and Snape article,

*This chapter was originally published in *Review of Urban and Regional Development Studies*, Vol. 15, No. 1, March 2003, and is reprinted here with minor modifications upon the permission from the publisher.

[a]For a full description of ORANI see Dixon *et al.* (1982).

the role of CGE models in Australian policy making has further increased, so much so that government frequently obtains the results of CGE analysis prior to making economic policy decisions.

Initially the only regional dimension of Australian CGE modeling was via a top-down spatial disaggregation of the national model's results across Australia's six states (Dixon, Parmenter and Sutton, 1978).[b] Liew (1984), however, constructed a bottom-up multiregional CGE model of Australia, using ORANI as his starting point. The first bottom-up multiregional CGE model to be used in regular policy analysis in Australia was the FEDERAL model constructed in the late 1980s (Madden, 1996). For well over a decade FEDERAL has been used in a wide range of policy-relevant analysis of Australian regions. Examples of such applications are fiscal federalism (Madden, 1993 and Dixon, *et al.*, 1993), tax policy (Giesecke, 1999), environmental policy (Madden, 1991), resource developments (Wittwer and Bright, 1997), regional development policies (Giesecke and Madden, 1997) and competition policy reforms in transport (Madden and Pant, 1997).

A key attribute of FEDERAL is that it retains all the features of the large-scale national ORANI model, carrying them through into multiregional form.[c] FEDERAL contains very detailed modeling of regional disposable income, including accounting for interregional returns on capital and a wide-range of direct taxes and transfers. There is a detailed treatment of two tiers of government. A primary example of the multi-regional complexity of FEDERAL is its handling of margins, such as wholesale trade, retail trade, transport and insurance. The flow of each commodity from each source of supply can be facilitated by margins supplied from any of the domestic regions. As a general-purpose model FEDERAL contains many features which are generally

[b]The expressions top-down and bottom-up are used in the terminology of Klein and Glickman (1977). A top-down method decomposes results from a national model to regions using base-year shares and local multiplier effects. The bottom-up method explicitly models the behaviour of economic agents at the regional level.

[c]The two main computer software packages used for solving CGE models, GEMPACK and GAMS, provide user-friendly means for economists to build large-scale models. Like most Australian economists we employ GEMPACK (Pearson, 1988, and Harrison and Pearson, 1996) for the simulations reported in this paper. For a description of GAMS, see Brooke *et al.*, 1996. While GAMS is also applicable to other applications, Rutherford (1999) has constructed a version of GAMS specifically for CGE use. GAMS operates in terms of the level of variables. However, while GEMPACK allows users to write their equations in linearised form, the GEMPACK software contains algorithms that allow it to compute the true non-linear solution (see Hertel *et al.*, 1992).

introduced in regional CGE models in other countries only for specific types of applications.[d]

The 1990s saw the introduction of dynamics into Australian regional CGE models. A new multiregional model, entitled MMRF, was constructed with minimal dynamics that enabled average annual forecasting for Australia's six states and two territories (Naqvi and Peter, 1996).[e]

The 1990s also saw the construction of the national CGE model, MONASH, which contained extensive dynamic properties to allow the modeling of structural change over historical periods and year-on-year forecasting (Dixon and Rimmer, 2002a). Subsequently Giesecke (2000) updated FEDERAL to incorporate the key elements of those features of MONASH which relate to its dynamic capabilities and model closure options. The updated model, known as FEDERAL-F, is a recursive-dynamic multi-regional CGE model, linking a sequence of single-period equilibria via stock-flow relationships. The equilibria thus computed change through time as the values for the model's stock variables change. Flows in previous periods (such as investment, inter-regional migration, and government borrowings) influence the values for the endogenous variables computed in each period through their contribution to the values of the model's stock variables (such as capital, population, and government debt) in each period.

MMRF has also recently been upgraded in a similar way, leading to MMRF-GREEN (Adams, Horridge and Parmenter, 2000). While both FEDERAL-F and MMRF-GREEN are each general-purpose models, the former contains features particularly suited to modeling fiscal federalism issues, while the latter contains features facilitating environmental modeling. Both models explicitly treat behavior at the state/territory level.[f] Both models also incorporate a

[d]For a comprehensive survey of regional and multiregional CGE models, see Partridge and Rickman (1998). A notable feature of that survey, however, is a near absence of discussion of Australian models.

[e]The main applications of MMRF (MONASH multi-regional forecasting model) during most of the 1990s, however, were comparative static, with the model's minimal dynamic properties mainly being used for updating the model's database. Examples of MMRF applications are: the economic impact of the Sydney Olympics (Madden, 2002), cumulative-causation in regional development (Dixon and Peter, 1996) and the impact of competition-policy reforms (Whiteman, 1999).

[f]A difference between FEDERAL and MMRF is that the former is usually used as a two-region model with a region-of-focus and a residual region (indeed, early versions of FEDERAL could only be used that way), while MMRF usually separately models all eight Australian states and territories.

top-down facility to decompose results to the sub-state level based on the Dixon *et al.* (1978) regional disaggregation approach.[g]

While many national CGE models are now dynamic rather than comparative static (see, for instance, Harrison, *et al.*, 2000), there are still few instances of large-scale dynamic multiregional CGE models. In the remainder of this paper, we seek to present the essential features of such a model. We begin by outlining the theoretical structure of FEDERAL-F. We then report an application of this model designed to show its properties in: establishing historical trends in unobserved variables; forecasting; and, public policy analysis. Our emphasis in this last section is on the model's capabilities for policy analysis in a dynamic context.

2. A Description of the FEDERAL-F Model

Since FEDERAL-F is large and detailed, it is not possible to provide a full description of its theoretical structure and database in this paper. The interested reader is referred to Giesecke (2000) for a detailed discussion of the full model. However, as Parmenter (1995) has shown, it is possible to provide a good picture of a large-scale CGE model via a stylized representation of its equation structure that presents the model's core equations in general functional form. Such a stylized version of FEDERAL-F is provided in Table 1, and a description of the model's variables is set out in Table 2. Table 3 provides the definitions of the stylized model's sets and set elements. While much of the complexity and detail of the complete model is not captured by this representation,[h] Tables 1–3 do make clear both the core components of the full model, and the relationships between those components. Two preliminary comments about the notation in Tables 1 and 2 are helpful. First, the complete model recognizes many industries and many commodities within each region. For simplicity, the subscripts denoting the commodity and industrial dimensions of the variables of the stylized model have been suppressed. Second, the use of time subscripts in the stylized model has been restricted to those variables relating to the years $t+1$ and $t-1$.

[g]Giesecke (1999), following an idea of Higgs, Parmenter and Rimmer (1988), introduced a limited number of sub-state industries into FEDERAL. This hybrid approach allowed limited bottom-up modelling at the sub-state level while maintaining at this lower regional level the advantages of the top-down method in terms of its relatively small requirements for sub-state data.

[h]The 52 sets of equations and 71 sets of variables of the stylised model summarise the structure and functioning of the 455 sets of equations and 616 sets of variables of the full model.

Table 1. Equations of the Stylized Version of the FEDERAL-F Model

A. Commodity and factor demands

Equation (E1): Intermediate input demands

$$X_s^{(1)r} = F_1\left(Z_r^{(1)}, P_s^{(1)r}, A_s^{(1)r}, A_r^{(1)}\right) \qquad r \in R; \quad s \in S$$

Equation (E2): Primary factor demands

$$H_v^r = F_2\left(Z_r^{(1)}, R_v^r, A_{v,r}^H, A_r^{(1)}\right) \qquad r \in R; \quad v \in V$$

Equation (E3): Inputs to capital formation

$$X_s^{(2)r} = F_3\left(Z_r^{(2)}, P_s^{(2)r}, A_s^{(2)r}, A_r^{(2)}\right) \qquad r \in R; \quad s \in S$$

Equation (E4): Household commodity demands

$$X_s^{(3)r} = F_4\left(Z_r^{(3)}, P_s^{(3)r}, A_s^{(3)r}\right) \qquad r \in R; \quad s \in S$$

Equation (E5): Export demands

$$X_r^{(4)*} = F_5\left(\tilde{P}_r^{(4)}, \Pi_r\right) \qquad r \in R$$

Equation (E6): Regional government commodity demands

$$X_s^{(5)r} = F_6\left(Z_r^{(5)}\right) \qquad r \in R; \quad s \in S$$

Equation (E7): Federal government commodity demands

$$X_s^{(6)*} = F_7\left(Z_*^{(6)}\right) \qquad s \in S$$

B. Technologies and tastes

Equation (E8): Shifts in technology and taste coefficients

$$A_s^{k,r} = F_8\left(F_s^{[E8]k,r}, F_s^{[E8]r}, F^{[E8]}, A_1^{\text{twist}}, A_2^{\text{twist}}\right) \qquad r \in R; \quad s \in S; \quad k = 1-3;$$

Equation (E9): Primary factor technologies

$$A_{v,r}^H = F_9\left(F_{v,r}^{[E9]}, F_v^{[E9]}, F_r^{[E9]}, A_{\text{twist}}^H\right) \qquad r \in R; \quad v \in V$$

Equation (E10): Neutralization of the cost impacts of commodity-specific technical change

$$A_r^k = F_{10}\left(F^{[E8]}, F_s^{[E8]r}, F_{k,r}^{[E10]}\right) \qquad r \in R; \quad k = 1-2;$$

C. Market clearing and zero pure profits

Equation (E11): Market clearing equations for regional outputs

$$Z_r^{(1)} = \sum_{t=1}^{2} \sum_{i=1-3,5} X_r^{i,t} + X_r^{(4)*} + X_r^{(6)*} \qquad r \in R$$

Table 1. (*Continued*)

Equation (E12): National outputs	
$Z^{(1)} = \sum_r Z_r^{(1)}$	
Equation (E13): Zero pure profit in production	
$P_r^{(0)} = F_{13}\left(P_s^{(1)r}, R_v^r, T_{r(1)}^R, T_{(1)}^F, A_s^{(1)r}, A_r^{(1)}, A_{v,r}^H\right)$	$r \in R$
Equation (E14): Zero pure profits in the supply of goods to domestic agents	
$P_s^{i,r} = F_{14}\left(P_s^{(0)}, T_{r(5)}^R, T_{(6)}^F, T_{\text{phant}}^{i,r,s}\right)$	$r \in R; \quad s \in S; \quad i \in D$
Equation (E15): At-port foreign currency export prices	
$\tilde{P}_r^{(4)} = \Phi\left(P_r^{(0)} \cdot T_{\text{phant}}^{(4)r,*} \cdot T_{r(6)}^R \cdot T_{(8)}^F\right)$	$r \in R$
Equation (E16): Domestic currency import prices	
$P_{(3)}^{(0)} = \tilde{P}_{(3)}^{(0)} T_{(7)}^F \big/ \Phi$	
D. Household income, consumption, and savings	
Equation (E17): Income/consumption link	
$Z_r^{(3)} = F_{17}\left(W_r, H_{(1)}^r, R_{\text{net}}^r, Q_r^{(1)}, I_r^{(1)}, \tilde{E}_r^{(1)} \big/ \Phi, T_{(2)}^F, T_{r(2)}^R, T_{(5)}^F, T_{(9)}, U^r, \Psi_r, G^r\right)$	$r \in R$
Equation (E18): Household net capital receipts	
$R_{\text{net}}^r = F_{18}\left(H_{(2)}^h, H_{(3)}^h, R_{(2)}^h, R_{(3)}^h, T_{h(3)}^R, T_{(3)}^F, T_{(4)}^F, M, \Lambda_h^{(1)r}\right)$	$r \in R$
Equation (E19): Aggregate collections of phantom taxes	
$Q_r^i = F_{19}\left(T_{\text{phant}}^{u,k,h}, P_h^{u,k}, \tilde{P}_h^{(4)}, X_h^{u,k}, X_h^{(4)*}, X_h^{(6)*}, \Lambda_h^{i,r}\right)$	$r \in R; \quad i \in O$
Equation (E20): Household savings	
$S_r^{(1)} = F_{20}\left(Z_r^{(3)}, \Psi_r\right)$	$r \in R$
E. Rate of return and investment theory	
Equation (E21): Capital growth rates	
$\left(H_{(2)(+1)}^r \big/ H_{(2)}^r\right) = F_{21}\left(V_r^K, \Xi_r, \Xi\right)$	$r \in R$
Equation (E22): Industry investments by region	
$Z_r^{(2)} = F_{22}\left(H_{(2)(+1)}^r, H_{(2)}^r\right)$	$r \in R$

Table 1. (*Continued*)

Equation (E23): Rates of return on capital	
$V_r^K = F_{23}\left(R_{(2)}^r, T_{r(3)}^R, T_{(3)}^F, P_s^{(2)r}, R, \dot{P}\right)$	$r \in R$
Equation (E24): Rate of inflation	
$\dot{P} = F_{24}\left(P^{(3)}, P_{(-1)}^{(3)}\right)$	
F. Stock-flow relationships	
Equation (E25): Domestic currency value of net interest payments by domestic agents	
$I_r^t = F_{25}\left(\Phi, \tilde{D}_r^t, \Theta\right)$	$r \in R; \quad t = 1-3;$
Equation (E26): Foreign currency value of the net debt of domestic owners	
$\tilde{D}_r^t = F_{26}\left(\tilde{D}_{r(-1)}^t, S_{r(-1)}^t, H_{(2)(-1)}^k, H_{(2)}^k, \Lambda_k^{t,r}\right)$	$r \in R; \quad t = 1-3;$
Equation (E27): Domestic capital ownership shares — Option 2	
$\Lambda_r^{t,k} = F_{27}\left(S_{k(-1)}^t, F_r^{[E27]t,k}\right)$	$t = 1-3; \quad k \in R;$ $r \in R;$
Equation (E28): Foreign capital ownership shares — Option 2	
$\Lambda_r^{(4)*} = F_{28}\left(\Lambda_r^{(1)k}, \Lambda_r^{(2)k}, \Lambda_r^{(3)k}, H_{(2)}^r, H_{(2)(-1)}^r, F_r^{[E28]}\right)$	$r \in R$
Equation (E29): Inter-regional migration	
$M = F_{29}\left(Z_{r(-1)}^{(5)}, G_{(-1)}^r, T_{r(2)(-1)}^R, T_{(5)(-1)}^F, U_{(-1)}^r, W_{r(-1)}, P_{s(-1)}^{(3)r}, F^{[E29]}\right)$	
Equation (E30): Capital accumulation	
$H_{(2)}^r = F_{30}\left(H_{(2)(-1)}^r, Z_{r(-1)}^{(2)}, F_r^{(E30)}\right)$	$r \in R$
Equation (E31): Regional populations	
$G^r = F_{31}\left(G_{(-1)}^r, M, \Delta^r\right)$	$r \in R$
G. Government accounts	
Equation (E32): Regional government net borrowing requirements	
$S_r^{(2)} = F_{32}\left(Z_r^{(5)}, B_{r,t}^R, Q_r^{(2)}, I_r^{(2)}, \tilde{E}_r^{(2)} \big/ \Phi, B^r, P_s^{(5)r}, \Lambda_r^{(2)r}, H_{(2)}^r, R_{(2)}^r\right)$	$r \in R$

Table 1. (*Continued*)

Equation (E33): Regional government production tax revenue

$$B^R_{r(1)} = F_{33}\left(T^R_{r(1)}, Z^{(1)}_r, P^{(0)}_r\right) \qquad r \in R$$

Equation (E34): Regional government revenue from net direct taxes

$$B^R_{r(2)} = F_{34}\left(T^R_{r(2)}, Z^{(3)}_r, S^{(1)}_r\right) \qquad r \in R$$

Equation (E35): Regional government revenue from capital taxes

$$B^R_{r(3)} = F_{35}\left(T^R_{r(3)}, R^r_{(2)}, H^r_{(2)}\right) \qquad r \in R$$

Equation (E36): Regional government revenue from payroll taxes

$$B^R_{r(4)} = F_{36}\left(T^R_{r(4)}, W_r, H^r_{(1)}\right) \qquad r \in R$$

Equation (E37): Regional government commodity tax revenue

$$B^R_{r(5)} = F_{37}\left(T^R_{r(5)}, Z^i_r, P^{i,r}_s\right) \qquad r \in R$$

Equation (E38): Regional government export tax revenue

$$B^R_{r(6)} = F_{38}\left(T^R_{r(6)}, X^{(4)}_r, \tilde{P}^{(4)}_r\right) \qquad r \in R$$

Equation (E39): Federal government net borrowing requirement

$$S^{(3)}_* = F_{39}\left(Z^{(6)}_*, P^{(6)*}_s, B^F_t, T_9, U_r, \Lambda^{(3)*}_r, H^r_{(2)}, R^r_{(2)}, Q^{(3)}_*, I^{(3)}_*, \tilde{E}^{(3)}_* \big/ \Phi, B^r\right)$$

Equation (E40): Federal production tax revenue

$$B^F_{(1)} = F_{40}\left(T^F_{(1)}, Z^{(1)}_r, P^{(0)}_r\right)$$

Equation (E41): Federal income tax revenue

$$B^F_k = F_{41}\left(T^F_k, W_r, R^r_{(2)}, R^r_{(3)}, H^r_v\right) \qquad k = 2 - 4$$

Equation (E42): Federal revenue from net other direct taxes

$$B^F_{(5)} = F_{42}\left(T^F_{(5)}, Z^{(3)}_r, S^{(1)}_r\right)$$

Equation (E43): Federal commodity tax revenue

$$B^F_{(6)} = F_{43}\left(T^F_{(6)}, Z^i_r, P^{i,r}_s\right)$$

Equation (E44): Federal revenue from import duties

$$B^F_{(7)} = F_{44}\left(X^{i,r}_{(3)}, P^{(0)}_{(3)}\right)$$

Equation (E45): Federal revenue from export taxes

$$B^F_{(8)} = F_{45}\left(X^{(4)*}_r, \tilde{P}^{(4)}_r\right)$$

Table 1. (*Continued*)

H. Regional labor markets

Equation (E46): Economy-wide employment

$$L = F_{46}\left(H^{r}_{(1)}\right)$$

Equation (E47): User-price of labor

$$R^{r}_{(1)} = F_{47}\left(W_{r}, T^{R}_{r(4)}\right) \qquad r \in R$$

Equation (E48): Regional real consumer wages

$$W_{r} = F^{W}_{r} \cdot P^{(3)}$$

Equation (E49): Regional labor force

$$L^{S}_{r} = G^{r} \cdot \Gamma^{r} \qquad r \in R$$

Equation (E50): Regional number of unemployed

$$U^{r} = F_{50}\left(L^{S}_{r}, H^{r}_{(1)}\right) \qquad r \in R$$

I. Miscellaneous Equations

Equation (E51): Economy-wide volume of imports

$$X^{M} = F_{51}\left(X^{u,r}_{(3)}\right)$$

Equation (E52): Economy-wide consumer price index

$$P^{(3)} = F_{52}\left(P^{(3)r}_{s}\right)$$

Table 1 contains a system of non-linear equations that are illustrative of the core equations of the complete FEDERAL-F model. The equations of this stylized model, as they relate to the structure of the complete model, are described below.

Equations (E1)–(E7) define factor demands and demands for commodities by six types of agent. Equations (E1) and (E2) define intermediate and factor demands by regional industries. These demand equations are derived from standard cost minimization assumptions relating to firm behavior. Each regional industry produces a single commodity, which is an imperfect substitute for the same commodity produced in other regions or imported from overseas. Firms face a nested production function. At the top of this nest, effective inputs of intermediate inputs, effective inputs of primary factors, and certain other costs, are combined in fixed proportions to produce a given level of output. An effective input of intermediate input commodity i is a CRESH

Table 2. Variable Descriptions and Model Closure

Variable Name and Description		Closure*	
		Standard[(a)]	Historical
$A_s^{i,r}$	Technology coefficients relating to the use of source-specific commodities by domestic agent i ($i = 1 - 3$) in region r.	N	N
A_r^k	All-input using tech change relating to domestic agent k ($k = 1, 2$) in r.	X	N
$F_s^{[E8]k,r}$	User-specific component of shifts in technology/tastes relating to source-specific commodities used by agent k ($k = 1 - 3$) in region r.	X	N ($k = 3$) X ($k = 1, 2$)
$F_s^{[E8]r}$	User-independent component of shifts in technology/tastes relating to source-specific commodities used by agents in region r.	X	N ($r = s = 1$) X (rest)
$F^{[E8]}$	User- and region-independent component in technology/tastes relating to usage of domestically-sourced commodities in general.	X	N
A_1^{twist}	That component of the commodity-use technology coefficients determining the mix between domestic and imported goods.	X	N
A_2^{twist}	That component of the commodity-use technology coefficients determining the mix between region 1 and region 2 sourced goods.	X	N
$A_{v,r}^H$	Technology coefficients relating to the use of primary factor v in r.	N	N
$F_{v,r}^{[E9]}$	Region and primary factor dependent components of technology coefficients relating to primary factor usage by industries.	X	X
$F_v^{[E9]}$	Economy-wide but factor dependent components of technology coefficients relating to primary factor usage by industries.	X	X
$F_r^{[E9]}$	Region-specific technology coefficients relating to the usage of primary factors in general by regional industries.	X	N

Table 2. (*Continued*)

Variable Name and Description		Closure*	
		Standard[(a)]	Historical
A^H_{twist}	That component of primary factor technology coefficients which governs the mix between capital and labor inputs.	X	N
B^r	Federal government grant payment to regional government r.	X	X
B^F_t	Federal government revenue from tax type t.	N	X
$B^R_{r,t}$	Regional government r's revenue from tax type t.	N	X
$\tilde{D}^t_r$	Foreign currency value of net debt of domestic owner t in region r (for $t = 1, 2$).	N	N
$\tilde{D}^t_{r(-1)}$	Foreign currency value of the net debt of domestic owner t in region r (for $t = 1, 2$) at the beginning of the previous simulation period.	X	X
$\tilde{E}^t_r$	The foreign currency value of the non-interest component of foreign receipts/payments by domestic owner t ($t = 1 - 3$) in region r (for $t = 1, 2$).	X	N
$F_r^{[E27]t,k}$	Shift variable on Eq. (E27). Allows switching between alternative treatments of capital accumulation by domestic agents.	X	X
$F_r^{[E28]}$	Shift variable on Eq. (E28). Allows switching between alternative treatments of foreign capital ownership.	X	X
$F^{[E29]}$	Shift variable on Eq. (E29).	X	N
$F_{k,r}^{[E10]}$	Shift variable on Eq. (E10).	N	X
$F_r^{[E30]}$	Shift variable on Eq. (E30).	X	X
F_r^W	Real regional consumer wage	X	X
G^r	Population of region r.	N	N
$G^r_{(-1)}$	Population of region r at $t - 1$.	X	X
$H^r_{(2)(-1)}$	Capital stocks in period $t - 1$.	X	X
$H^r_{(2)(+1)}$	Capital stocks in period $t + 1$	N	N

Table 2. (*Continued*)

Variable Name and Description		Closure*	
		Standard[(a)]	Historical
H_v^r	Demands/supplies for primary factor v in region r.	N ($v = 1, 2$) X ($v = 3$)	N ($v = 2$) X ($v = 1, 3$)
I_r^t	Domestic currency value of net interest payments by domestic owner t ($t = 1 - 3$) in region r (for $t = 1, 2$).	N	N
L	Aggregate employment.	N	X
L_r^S	Labor force of region r.	N	N
M	Number of inter-regional migrants.	N	X
$P_s^{(0)}$	Basic prices of source-specific commodities	N	N
$P_s^{i,r}$	Purchaser's price of source-specific commodities faced by domestic agent i in region r	N	N ($i = 1$) X ($i = 2$–6)
$\tilde{P}_{(3)}^{(0)}$	At-port foreign currency import prices.	X	X
$\tilde{P}_r^{(4)}$	At-port foreign currency export prices.	N	X
$\dot{P}$	Rate of change in the aggregate consumer price level.	N	N
$P_{s(-1)}^{(3)r}$	Consumer prices in period $t - 1$.	X	X
$P^{(3)}$	Economy-wide consumer price index.	X	X
$P_{(-1)}^{(3)}$	Economy-wide consumer price index in period $t - 1$.	X	X
Q_r^t	Phantom tax receipts by owner t in region r (for $t = 1, 2$).	N	N
R_{net}^r	Net capital and land rental receipts by households in region r.	N	N
R_v^r	Per unit cost of primary factor v faced by industries within region r.	N	N
R	Nominal interest rate.	X	X
S_k^t	Net savings of domestic owner t ($t = 1 - 3$) located in region k (for $t = 1, 2$)	N	X
$S_{k(-1)}^t$	Net savings of domestic owner t in region k (for $t = 1, 2$) during ($t - 1$)	X	X

Table 2. (*continued*)

Variable Name and Description		Closure*	
		Standard(a)	Historical
Π_r	Shift variables determining the positions of export demand schedules.	X	N
Ξ_r	Region, and regional industry, shift variables in the functions governing the relationship between expected rates of return and capital growth.	X	N
Ξ	Industry-specific and economy-wide shift variables in the functions governing the relationship between expected rates of return and capital growth rates.	X	X
$T^R_{r,t}$	Power (1 + tax rate) of tax type t levied by regional government r.	X	N
$T^R_{r(2)(-1)}$	Net direct taxes levied by regional government r in $t-1$.	X	X
T^F_t	Power (1 + tax rate) of tax type t levied by the federal government.	X	N
$T^F_{(5)(-1)}$	Net direct taxes levied by Federal government in $t-1$.	X	X
$T^{i,r,s}_{\text{phant}}$	Power (1 + tax rate) of the phantom tax on usage of commodities from domestic source s (for non-export agents) by agent i in region r.	X	X ($i = 1$) N ($i = 2$–6)
T_9	Federal unemployment benefit payments per person.	X	X
U^r	Number of unemployed in region r.	N	N
$U^r_{(-1)}$	Number of unemployed in region r in $t-1$.	X	X
V^K_r	Expected rates of return on capital.	N	N
W_r	Regional gross (pre income tax) nominal wage.	N	N
$W_{r(-1)}$	Regional gross (pre income tax) nominal wage in $t-1$.	X	X
$X^{i,r}_s$	Demand for source-specific commodities by domestic agent i in region r (for $i = 1$–$3, 5$).	N	X ($i = 3$) N ($i = 1, 2, 5$)
$X^{(4)*}_r$	Foreign demands for exports from region r.	N	X
X^M	Aggregate economy-wide import volumes.	N	X

Table 2. (*Continued*)

Variable Name and Description		Closure*	
		Standard(a)	Historical
Z_r^i	Activity level of domestic agent i in region r.	N ($i = 1$–3) X ($i = 5, 6$)	X ($i = 1$ (for $r = 1$ only), 2–6) N ($i = 1$ (for $r = 2$ only)
$Z^{(1)}$	National outputs of commodities.	N	X
$Z_{r(-1)}^{(2)}$	Investment in year $t - 1$.	X	X
$Z_{r(-1)}^{(5)}$	Regional government r consumption spending in year $t - 1$.	X	X
Φ	Nominal exchange rate.	N	N
Ψ_r	Average propensity to consume.	X	N
Θ	Foreign interest rate.	X	X
$\Lambda_r^{t,k}$	Share of physical capital installed in region r which is owned by owner t located in region k (for $t = 1, 2$ only).	N	N
Δ^r	Region r's natural population growth rate (inclusive of foreign immigration)	X	X
Γ^r	Participation rate of region r.	X	X

*"N" denotes endogenous, "X" denotes exogenous

(a)The major features of the standard closure are defined by exogenous real regional consumer wages and (via exogenous participation rates and initial regional populations) exogenous regional labor supply. Regional labor demand and supply are reconciled by endogenous movements in regional unemployment. The start-of-year values for stock variables (industry capital stocks, state and federal government debt, regional populations, household debt, agricultural land) are exogenous. Variables defining structural features of the regional economies — such as rates of technical change, household tastes, capital supply functions, and foreign export demands — are determined exogenously. Government policy variables, such as those defining tax rates and real outlays, are also exogenous. The endogenous variables include regional commodity-specific prices and outputs, export volumes, regional employment, and investment by regional industry. For a similar overview of the historical closure, see Section 3.1

Table 3. Set Names and Elements

T. Federal taxes ($t = 1$–8)	**Q. Regional government taxes** ($q = 1$–6)	**V. Factors** ($v = 1, 2, 3$)
1. Production tax	1. Production tax	1. Labor
2. Labor income tax	2. Net direct taxes	2. Capital
3. Capital income tax	3. Capital taxes	3. Land
4. Land income tax	4. Payroll taxes	
5. Net other direct taxes	5. Commodity taxes	**D. Domestic agents** ($d = 1, 2, 3, 5, 6$)
6. Commodity taxes	6. Export taxes	1. Producers
7. Import tariffs		2. Capital creators
8. Export taxes	**U. Users** ($u = 1$–6)	3. Households
	1. Producers	4. Regional government
R. Regions ($r = 1, 2$)	2. Capital creators	5. Federal government
1. Tasmania	3. Households	
2. Rest of Australia	4. Foreign demands	**O. Owners** ($o = 1$–4)
	5. Regional government	1. Households
S. Sources ($s = 1, 2, 3$)	6. Federal government	2. Regional government
1. Tasmania		3. Federal government
2. Rest of Australia		4. Foreigners
3. Overseas		

combination of i sourced from $r + 1$ regions (r domestic regions, and overseas imports).[i] An effective primary factor unit is a CRESH combination of effective units of labor, regional-industry specific capital, and agricultural land.

In the absence of changes in relative prices and technology, the demand for inputs ($X_s^{(1)r}, H_v^r$) by a regional industry will be proportional to its activity level ($Z_r^{(1)}$). Within any given CRESH nest, changes in relative prices ($P_s^{(1)r}$, R_v^r) invoke substitution towards the relatively cheaper inputs.

Equation (E3) defines demands by regional industries for inputs to the process of capital creation. These equations are derived from an assumption of cost minimization on the part of regional industries in the production of units of their own capital. Capital creation is subject to a two-tiered production function in which effective units of commodities are first formed as a CRESH combination of source-specific commodities, with these effective commodity composites then being input to a fixed-proportions production function.

Regional households maximize a Klein–Rubin utility function by choosing among effective units of commodity i (which are in turn a cost-minimizing CRESH combination of i from the $r + 1$ geographic sources), subject to an

[i] CRESH stands for "Constant ratio of elasticities of substitution, homothetic". See Dixon *et al.*, 1982 for a description of this function.

aggregate expenditure constraint. This gives rise to the household demand equations represented by Eq. (E4). Equation (E5) defines foreign demands for commodities from each region. In the absence of exogenous shocks to the positions of foreign demand schedules, export volumes are inversely related to foreign currency export prices via constant elasticity export demand functions. Equations (E6) and (E7) define current consumption demands by regional and federal governments.

Changes in production technology and household tastes have a direct impact on commodity and factor demands independently of changes in activity levels or relative prices. Equations (E8) and (E9) allow for the technology/taste coefficients appearing in Eqs. (E1)–(E4) to be a function of variables with varying degrees of commodity/factor, source, and regional specificity. One option for technical change within FEDERAL-F's CRESH nests that is frequently employed is that such change be locally cost neutral. This requires a combination of technical changes, operating on more than one input within the given CRESH nest. These movements in the technical coefficients of the CRESH nest are used to simulate secular (i.e. non-price-induced) movements in such things as import/domestic shares, and labor/capital ratios. Following Horridge *et al.* (1998) we call such cost-neutral combinations of technical change variables a "twist".[j] In the stylized model, cost neutral changes in input ratios are represented by shocks to the variables A_1^{twist}, A_2^{twist}, and A_{twist}^{H}.

Equation (E11) imposes market-clearing conditions on domestic production. Equation (E12) calculates national commodity outputs. Equations (E13)–(E16) impose zero pure profit conditions on the activities of: current production Eq. (E13); supplying goods to domestic agents Eq. (E14); exporting Eq. (E15); and importing Eq. (E16). It should be noted that Eqs. (E13)–(E16) suppress much of the detail of the pricing equations of the full model, which include detailed modeling of trade and transport margins, and federal and regional government commodity taxes. One feature of the equations determining the supply-price of goods purchased by domestic agents and foreigners [Eqs. (E14) and (E15)] is the presence of so-called "phantom taxes". These represent an additional mark-up over normal costs, providing an additional[k] cost wedge between basic and purchaser's prices.

---

[j] See Horridge *et al.* (1998) pp. 54–55 for a detailed discussion of such cost-neutral technical change. A detailed discussion of the FEDERAL-F twist terms is provided in Giesecke (2000) pp. 203–210.

[k] That is, additional to standard margins and genuine commodity taxes.

While normally exogenous and zero, these variables can be endogenized in historical simulations to reconcile discrepancies between official statistics relating to output prices and input costs. Any movements in phantom taxes are interpreted as net super-normal profits, and distributed to the owners of capital in the industries producing the goods upon which the phantom taxes accrue.[1]

Equations (E17)–(E20) define household income, consumption and savings. The expenditure constraint of each regional household is defined by Eq. (E17). After-tax income to region r residents from capital and land [Eq. (E18)] is related to the history of inter-regional migration over the simulation period. This explains the presence of M on the RHS of Eq. (E18). Unlike the case in many regional models, inter-regional migrants in FEDERAL-F do not automatically acquire the level and pattern of the capital ownership of the households in the destination region, but rather, carry their initial capital ownership claims with them as they move between regions.

Equation (E19) calculates aggregate collections of phantom taxes by three types of domestic agents. Phantom tax receipts by these agents are related to the rates of phantom tax, the bases upon which these taxes are levied, and the agents' shares in the capital of the industries producing the commodities upon which the phantom taxes accrue.

Equations (E21) and (E22) determine investment in each regional industry. Equation (E21) specifies a positive relationship between year t expectations for the rate of return on each regional industry's capital stock in $t+1$, and the year t rate of growth in the regional industry's capital stock. With the rate of growth in regional industry capital stocks determined by Eq. (E21), Eq. (E22) operates to determine investment in each regional industry. Expected rates of return are determined by Eq. (E23) as a function of net capital rental prices, capital costs, the nominal discount rate, and the inflation rate. The inflation rate appears in Eq. (E23) because expectations of capital rental growth rates are assumed to be adaptive. Equation (E24) defines the inflation rate.

Equations (E25)–(E31) provide the model's dynamic properties, by establishing the links between the year t values for stock variables and the year $t-1$ values for stock and flow variables.

Equation (E25) links the domestic currency value of the net interest payments made by each domestic agent to: the exchange rate, the stock of the agent's net foreign debt, and the foreign interest rate. Equation (E26) relates the stock of the foreign debt of each agent at the beginning of t to their stock

---

[1] See Giesecke (2000) for a detailed discussion of the treatment of phantom taxes in FEDERAL-F.

of foreign debt at the beginning of $t-1$, their saving during $t-1$, and changes in their capital ownership shares ($\Lambda_r^{t,k}$). The presence of $\Lambda_r^{t,k}$ and current and lagged capital stocks ($H_{(2)}^r, H_{(2)(-1)}^r$) in the RHS of this equation arises from the fact that the model provides for two choices in the tracking of changes in capital ownership shares. The first choice links changes in $\Lambda_r^{t,k}$ by domestic agents to changes in the savings of domestic agents Eq. (E27). Foreign capital ownership in each regional industry then adjusts as a residual, reconciling the value of new capital installed with the contributions to the value of that capital by domestic agents [Eq. (E28)]. The second choice assumes that the $\Lambda_r^{t,k}$ are exogenous (requiring that $F_r^{[E27]k}$ and $F_r^{[E28]}$ be endogenous). Under this approach, changes in the aggregate capital ownership of each domestic agent are determined by the underlying growth rates in the capital stocks of the regional industries in which they have a (fixed) ownership interest. The change in each domestic agent's foreign debt is then determined by Eq. (E26) as the difference between the change in their aggregate capital ownership and the value of their savings.

Equation (E29) introduces a two-region adaptation of Jones and Whalley's (1989) migration theory. Changes in inter-regional migration are determined by relative changes in a measure of regional incomes. This income measure excludes those components of income that are invariant to the region in which an individual resides (such as capital returns). It includes only those components that vary with region of residence, such as real per-capita expected wages, real per-capita fiscal variables (such as government consumption and net transfer payments to households) and real per-capita expected unemployment benefits. Expectations of net wage and unemployment benefit receipts are formed using regional unemployment rates as the measure for the probability of employment.

Equation (E30) defines the quantity of capital available to each regional industry at the beginning of each simulation period. This is equal to the depreciated value of the capital available at the beginning of $t-1$, plus any investment undertaken during $t-1$.

Equation (E31) defines the population of each region at the beginning of period t. This is equal to the population at the beginning of period $t-1$, plus natural population growth (inclusive of net foreign immigration), plus net inter-regional migration.

Equations (E32)–(E45) define various elements of the government accounts. Equations (E32) and (E39) define the net borrowing requirements of the regional and federal governments respectively. The RHS's of these equations contain variables relating to the nominal values of government current outlays and current revenues. Equations (E33)–(E38) and (E40)–(E45) define, respectively, regional and federal tax collections from a variety of tax types.

Economy-wide employment is defined by Eq. (E46). Nominal producer wages at the regional industry level differ from the regional nominal wage by the amount of any regional government payroll taxes payable Eq. (E47). Equation (E48) defines the regional real consumer wage. Equations (E49) and (E50) define, respectively, regional labor supply and regional unemployment. The final two equations calculate an economy-wide index of import volumes Eq. (E51) and an economy-wide consumer price index [Eq. (E52)].

3. Analyzing State Government Fiscal Policy with FEDERAL-F

We now describe an application of FEDERAL-F which focuses on the state of Tasmania. Between 1986/87 and 1998/99, Tasmania's share of national output declined from approximately 2.3% to 1.9%. Access Economics (2000) forecast that Tasmania's share of national activity will continue to decline over the period 1999/00 to 2003/04, falling to 1.7% of national activity by the end of this period. The baseline forecast for Tasmania used in the present paper, although generated using a different methodology to that employed by Access Economics, also concludes that Tasmania will account for 1.7% of national activity by 2003/04.

An interesting question is the extent to which it is within the power of the Tasmanian government to influence materially this forecast outcome. Broad policies that state governments might use in this quest are: selective industry assistance; microeconomic reforms to improve industry efficiency, fiscal policy; and population policy. This paper concentrates on fiscal policy, and examines two such policies each involving the budget-neutral manipulation of two tax instruments. These tax instruments are the payroll tax and the direct tax.[m] The two policy packages are investigated in two sets of simulations. In the first simulation, the question asked is whether, over the forecast period, there exists a feasible budget-neutral re-arrangement of the revenue raised by the two tax instruments which maintains Tasmania's share of national GDP at its 1998/99 level. The judgement of feasibility is made on the basis of an

[m]Australian state governments have a number of instruments of the direct tax type. Currently the most important of these is fees and fines, the value of which for Tasmania is approximately one-third of the value of payroll tax collections. The state government also has the power to implement levies, such as fixed charges on household usage of utilities, that would operate effectively as poll taxes. Unlike many other federations, however, Australian state governments do not currently impose income taxes.

informal assessment of plausibility: are the changes in tax instruments required to maintain a constant share of national GDP excessively large, relative to the original tax bases upon which the instruments operate? This is indeed found to be the case, with the state's payroll tax required to become a payroll subsidy in order to achieve the state growth target. Hence, a second policy simulation is undertaken, in which the question now asked is what is the impact on the forecast of the state's share of national output if the state's payroll tax is eliminated over the forecast period and replaced with a direct tax on households. As we shall see, the conclusion that emerges from this simulation is that the impact of such a policy change on the forecast for the state's share of national output is not large.

3.1. *Preliminary Simulation: A FEDERAL-F Baseline Forecast*

Before modeling the state government policy action, it is necessary to generate a baseline forecast that represents the path the Tasmanian and other state/territory economies might be expected to follow over the five year period 1999/00 to 2003/04 in the absence of the policy shock. We present a brief overview of this simulation before proceeding to the policy simulations, since it illustrates one of the major capabilities of FEDERAL-F, namely forecasting. It should be noted that we use a two-region version of FEDERAL-F in this paper. Tasmania is one region, the rest of Australia (or the Australian Mainland) is the other.

Results from historical simulations for the period 1992/93 to 1998/99 formed the starting point for the forecast simulations.[n] The closure of the model in the historical simulations is outlined in the final column of Table 2. The key feature of the historical simulations is that the values for many of the variables for which official statistics provide values (such as national and regional macroeconomic variables, regional industry level variables such as employment and investment, and commodity level variables such as outputs, exports and prices) are determined exogenously. This allows certain unobservable structural variables — such as rates of primary factor and commodity using technical change, household taste changes, positions of export demand curves, rates of government taxation, and such like — to be determined by the model. The results for these structural variables then formed part of the input to the forecasting simulations. It was assumed that over the forecast period, the values for these variables would be equal to the annual average of

[n]A detailed discussion of these simulations is contained in Giesecke (2002).

their values over the historical period. That is, it was assumed that the structural shifts which were calculated to have occurred over the historical period would continue at the same rate over the forecast period. The closure of the model in the forecasting simulation is the same as that of the standard closure (Table 2) with the exception of key national macroeconomic variables, which we determined exogenously equal to values from the independent forecaster Access Economics (2000).[o] Results for Tasmanian macroeconomic variables were determined endogenously, however. Hence the values attained by the Tasmanian macroeconomic variables reflected both the extrapolated values of the technical and taste change variables from the historical simulations, and the impacts on Tasmania of the exogenously specified national macroeconomic environment.

The results of the forecast simulations show the Tasmanian economy continuing to grow at a slower rate than the rest of Australia. The annual average growth rate in Tasmania's real GSP at factor cost is projected to be almost two percentage points below that of the rest of Australia. Hence the forecasts anticipate a continuation of the historical trend of a declining Tasmanian share of national GDP. The factors responsible for the forecast decline in Tasmania's GDP share can be identified by dividing the forecast annual average real regional GDP growth rates into the individual contributions of the many exogenous shocks administered to the model during the forecast simulations.[p] The individual contributions of the many hundreds of exogenous variables

---

[o]The national macroeconomic closure in the forecasting simulation is as follows: real national consumption ($\Sigma_r \Sigma_s X_s^{(3),r}$) is determined exogenously with the economy-wide average propensity to consume ($F(\Psi_r)$) endogenous; real national investment ($\Sigma_r \Sigma_s X_s^{(2),r}$) is determined exogenously with the economy-wide shift variable on regional industry capital supply functions ($F(\Xi)$) endogenous; real national imports (X^M) is determined exogenously with the import/domestic twist (A_1^{twist}) endogenous; real national exports ($\Sigma_r X_r^{(4)}$) are determined exogenously, with the economy-wide shift variable on export demand schedules ($F(\Pi_r)$) endogenous; general state and federal government real outlays ($Z_r^{(5)}$ and $Z_*^{(6)}$) are determined exogenously; with real GDP now effectively determined exogenously from the demand side, economy-wide primary factor productivity ($F(A_{vr}^H)$) is determined endogenously; national employment (L) is exogenous, requiring the labor/capital twist variable (A_{twist}^H) to be endogenous. Note that macroeconomic aggregates like real consumption do not appear in the stylised representation of FEDERAL-F presented in this paper. Hence, in the above representation of the macroeconomic closure, we rely on summations over variables in the stylised model and implicit functions of the shifters in the stylised model, to represent FEDERAL-F macroeconomic variables.

[p]This decomposition is undertaken using the GEMPACK suite of computer programs. The decomposition algorithm is described in Harrison *et al.* (1999).

Table 4. Decomposition of Forecast Annual Average Regional Growth in GDP at Factor Cost

Exogenous Factor	(1) Tasmania	(2) Rest of Australia	(1) – (2) Difference
1. Capital accumulation	−0.08	0.83	−0.92
2. Technical change	1.52	2.26	−0.74
3. Inter-regional migration, natural population growth, and regional unemployment	0.93	1.33	−0.40
4. Other exogenous factors	−0.12	−0.19	0.07
Forecast annual average real GDP growth	2.26	4.24	−1.98

that are shocked during each year of the forecast simulations have been aggregated into four broad sets of factors, and the contribution of each factor to the annual average GDP growth rates of both Tasmania and the rest of Australia have been summarized in Table 4.

The two factors most responsible for Tasmania having a forecast lower rate of growth than the rest of Australia are lower rates of capital accumulation (row 1) and technical change (row 2) relative to the rest of Australia. The rate of capital accumulation in Tasmania is forecast to be just below that required to maintain the size of the Tasmanian capital stock, leading to a small (−0.08% per annum) contraction in real GSP. This result is in part a legacy of the low rates of investment in Tasmania in the period leading up to that covered by the forecast simulations, and in part a result of the extrapolation into the forecast period of the historical shifts in the Tasmanian industry-specific schedules relating capital growth rates to expected rates of return. The overall difference in growth rates attributable to capital accumulation (−0.92% per annum) is driven largely by the positive rates of capital accumulation in the rest of Australia, which contribute approximately 0.83 percentage points per annum to the real GDP growth rate of the rest of Australia. While technical change (row 2) is forecast to increase real output in both regions, the average rate of technical progress in the rest of Australia is higher than that in Tasmania, causing the Tasmanian growth rate to be lower than that of the rest of Australia by 0.74 percentage points per annum. Tasmania is projected to continue experiencing out-migration over the forecast period, although the impact of this on real GSP is somewhat offset by natural population growth and a fall in the number of unemployed in the region, leading to an overall contribution by these labor market factors to the difference in forecast growth rates of 0.4 percentage points per annum (row 3).

3.2. *Labor Market Adjustment under the Policy Simulation*

It will be seen in Section 3.3 that an important factor in determining the results of our two policy simulations is the speed at which the regional real wage rate adjusts to a change in the demand for labor in the region. Modeling this properly required the introduction of a labor market adjustment mechanism into FEDERAL-F. This is done via Eq. (E53), which implements a MONASH-style adjustment mechanism:

$$\left(\frac{W^r}{W^{r*}} - 1\right) = \left(\frac{W^r_{(-1)}}{W^{r*}_{(-1)}} - 1\right) - \Pi\left(\frac{U^r}{U^{r*}} - 1\right) + F^r \qquad \text{(E53)}$$

where W^r is the index of the regional real wage in the policy simulation ($r \in R$), W^{r^*} is the regional real wage index in the forecast simulation, $W^r_{(-1)}$ is the lagged ($t - 1$) value of the index of the real regional wage in the policy simulation, $W^{r^*}_{(-1)}$ is the lagged index in the forecast simulation, U^r and U^{r^*} are the index of the number of unemployed persons in region r in the policy simulation and in the forecast simulation respectively, Π is an adjustment parameter governing the speed with which regional real wages adjust to return regional unemployment in the policy simulation to its baseline value, and F^r is a shift variable allowing Eq. (E53) to be inoperative in all but policy simulations.

Equation (E53) is inoperative during the generation of the baseline forecast (F^r is endogenous). However in the policy simulations, the equation operates to determine the regional real wage. With F^r exogenous, and W^{r^*} and U^{r^*} shocked equal to their values in the baseline forecast simulation, Eq. (E53) allows for short-run rigidity in the regional real wage during the policy simulation, while nevertheless adjusting the regional wage over time to a level that returns regional unemployment to its baseline level after about five years. The intuition behind Eq. (E53) is that, so long as regional unemployment is below (above) its forecast level, the regional real wage will be moving ever further above (below) its forecast level. This means that a shock that is favorable (unfavorable) to regional employment will be expressed in the short-run as a decrease (increase) in unemployment, but expressed in the long-run as an increase (decrease) in the real wage.

3.3. *Simulation Results*

It is particularly important in presenting the results of large-scale CGE models to clearly describe the major model mechanisms that are responsible for the essential character of the results. However, the space limitations on this article means that we will only be able to provide a few major results here, and provide only the broad flavor of the model mechanisms behind the results. Interested readers will find a much lengthier explanation and more detailed results in Giesecke (2003).

It will be recalled that in the first simulation the Tasmanian government targets the maintenance of a constant share of national output. The starting closure for the FEDERAL-F simulation follows the standard closure depicted in Table 2, with each exogenous variable shocked equal to its value in the forecasting simulation.[q] The exceptions to this are detailed in Table 5, which specifies the changes in the standard model closure required to establish the policy closures.[r] In the first simulation, the percentage change in Tasmania's share of national GDP is determined exogenously and set equal to zero, and the Tasmanian payroll tax rate is determined endogenously. Under this closure, the average Tasmanian payroll tax rate adjusts in each period to ensure that Tasmania's share of national GDP remains unchanged. The Tasmanian government's borrowing requirement is not allowed to deviate from its baseline forecast value. This requires that the Tasmanian government's borrowing requirement be determined exogenously and be equal to its baseline value in each period, and also that the average rate of the state government's direct tax be determined endogenously.

Table 5. Closure Swaps Defining the Policy Simulations

Variable Description	Exogenous (X)/Endogenous (N) Status		
	Standard Closure	Policy Simulation 1	Policy Simulation 2
Tasmanian GDP as share of national GDP	N	X	N
Tasmanian payroll tax rate	X	N	X
Tasmanian govt.'s borrowing requirement	N	X	X
Tasmanian govt.'s direct tax rate	X	N	N

[q]Irrespective of whether those variables were determined endogenously or exogenously under the forecasting closure.

[r]It will be noticed that macroeconomic aggregates like gross domestic product do not appear in our stylized representation of FEDERAL-F presented in this paper, and so do not appear in Table 5. Readers interested in the computation of such straightforward accounting relationships should see Giesecke (2000).

Table 6. Selected Tasmanian Results for Simulation 1: Maintenance of Constant Share of National GDP (Percentage Deviations from Forecast Values)

	1999/00	2000/01	2001/02	2002/03	2003/04
Real GSP	1.61	4.26	7.28	4.89	3.19
Employment	2.04	5.33	9.11	5.84	3.66
Unemployment	−20	−62	−100	−72	−51
Payroll tax rate	−147	−575	−967	−967	−967
State direct tax	407	1564	2786	3048	3239
Real investment	1.49	3.05	4.25	1.82	0.71
Capital stocks	0.00	0.08	0.25	0.50	0.59
Population	0.00	0.01	0.04	0.10	0.14

In Table 6, we show just a few of the results from the simulation. Only Tasmanian results are shown as the effects on the Australian Mainland are relatively minor. In the first year of the simulation, 1999/00, the maintenance of a constant Tasmanian share of national output requires the state's real gross state product (GSP) be 1.61 percentage points higher than its baseline value. This requires that Tasmanian employment be 2.04% higher. The contribution of a given percentage increase in employment (l) to real output is summarized by $(S_L/(1 - S_{WC})) \times l$, where S_L and S_{WC} are the shares of wages and working capital rentals respectively in GSP at factor cost. Given the values for S_L and S_{WC}, we can calculate the contribution of the increase in employment to the real GSP result as $2.04 \times (0.68/(1 - 0.11)) \approx 1.57$. The actual increase in real GSP (1.61%) is slightly higher, because the policy causes a slight change in the structure of the economy in a way that favors some sectors experiencing above average rates of productivity growth at the expense of some sectors experiencing below average rates of productivity growth. The increase in employment requires a fall in the producer price of labor, which is generated by a reduction in the payroll tax rate. Via Eq. (E53) the real household wage begins to increase as unemployment falls. However, the household wage does not initially rise by enough to offset the impact of the payroll tax reduction on the producer wage, hence employment rises and regional unemployment falls. The net government revenue foregone from the reduction in the payroll tax rate is recouped through an increase in the direct tax on households.

It can also be seen that the policy causes investment to rise because, with employment rising, so too does the rental price of (and hence the rate of return on) Tasmanian capital. However, investment does not rise as quickly as real output, because the cut in the payroll tax causes the cost of employing labor to fall relative to that of capital. This causes the capital/labor ratio to fall, and with it, the capital/output and investment/output ratios. Real consumption rises in the initial years, but by less than GSP. This is because changes in the disposable income of Tasmanian households are somewhat insulated from changes in GSP at factor cost by receipts of unemployment benefits and other government transfers, interstate capital ownership, and net interest payments and other exogenous household receipts. While interstate trade volumes move roughly in line with gross state product, as do international imports, exports from Tasmania to foreigners rise sharply (by almost 10% in 1999/00). The high elasticities of foreign demand curves, and the relatively higher payroll tax rates paid by export industries, are important in the outcome that the policy change in the tax mix generates increased activity and employment.

It is evident from the Table 6 results that the policy is an infeasible one. Even in the first year, the Tasmanian government must completely cease levying payroll taxes and introduce labor subsidies. The problem becomes progressively harder as a bigger deviation in the percentage change from the baseline forecast is required each year. The required changes in tax rates becomes more and more infeasible. By the third year of the FEDERAL-F simulation, there is insufficient unemployed labor in Tasmania to meet the real GSP growth target. It is assumed that at this stage the Tasmanian government abandons the output target. Once this happens the increase in the regional real wage begins to return unemployment to its baseline level. Despite there being no further changes in the payroll tax rate in these years, the direct tax rate continues to increase (at a decreasing rate), indicating that the policy of the previous three years has caused the structure of the Tasmanian economy to change in a way that has reduced Tasmanian government receipts from other tax bases relative to the value of those receipts in the baseline simulation. The increase in the direct tax in these years causes real consumption spending to fall below its baseline level. In the long run, the policy operates mainly to shift the state government's revenue raising effort from the payroll tax to the direct tax instrument, while leaving real regional activity largely unchanged.

In the second simulation, a more modest proposal, involving the phasing out of the Tasmanian payroll tax over five years, is examined. This requires the Tasmanian payroll tax rate (row 2 of Table 5) to be reduced to zero in five equal installments over the policy period. As in the first simulation, the Tasmanian government's borrowing requirement (row 3) is held on its base-case path via movements in the direct tax rate (row 4). This policy would still be an extreme measure, but it has only a minor impact on gross domestic product and employment, which depart only slightly from the baseline, being higher by 0.63% and 0.78% in 2003/04. In essence, the reduction in payroll tax is offset to a significant degree by rises in the real wage rate to workers. This meant only a small reduction in the real wage paid by producers. In the long run, the producer wage rate, unemployment and real GSP fall to their baseline level. The benefit of the policy is only a small temporary increase in employment which comes at the cost of a long-run major re-alignment in Tasmania's tax structure.

4. Conclusions

The CGE model described in this paper represents the outcome of around two decades of modeling effort in Australia. FEDERAL-F is a large-scale general-purpose model that enables the user to forecast a large number of regional variables in a consistent manner and to examine the effects on those forecasts of changes in policy or other scenarios. FEDERAL-F also allows historical analysis to be undertaken into the reasons underlying regional performance (as undertaken by Giesecke, 2002).

In this paper, we describe an illustrative application that demonstrates the capabilities of the model in forecasting and policy analysis. The simulations examine fiscal options that the Tasmanian government might pursue to prevent a continuation of its declining share in national GDP. The results show that to gain a temporary halt in this decline would involve the introduction of subsidies and taxes which are of an infeasible size. A more modest, but nevertheless extreme measure, of eliminating payroll tax would only slightly alter the rate of decline, and then only for a limited time, at a cost of a major re-alignment of tax measures.

Large-scale regional models have to date been largely confined to Australia. However, such models are readily transferable to other countries, often with only minor changes necessary to cover institutional differences. There is a history of Australian CGE models being adapted for use in other countries.[s] This has involved national models in the main, but there would seem to be scope for the adaptation of FEDERAL-F to other countries, particularly those with a federal structure.

[s]Variants of the ORANI model constructed for other countries include China, Thailand, South Africa, Korea, Ireland, Pakistan, Brazil, the Philippines, Japan, Ireland, Vietnam, Indonesia, Venezuela, Taiwan and Denmark. A large-scale dynamic model of the United States has recently been built for the USA International Trade Commission by Australian researchers (Dixon and Rimmer, 2002b).

References

Access Economics, 2000. *Five Year Business Outlook, September Quarter 2000.* Access Economics: Melbourne.

Adams PD, Horridge MJ, and Parmenter BR, 2000. "Forecasts for Australian regions using the MMRF-green model." *Australasian J. Reg. Stud.* **6**(3): 293–322.

Brooke A, Kendrick D, and Meeraus A, 1996. *GAMS: A User's Guide.* Scientific Press: Danvers.

Dixon PB, Madden JR, and Peter MW, 1993. "The effects of reallocating general revenue assistance among the Australian states." *Econ. Rec.* **69**: 367–381.

Dixon PB, Parmenter BR, and Sutton J, 1978. "Spatial disaggregation of ORANI results: a preliminary analysis of the impacts of protection at the state level." *Econ. Anal. Pol.* **8**: 35–86.

Dixon PB, Parmenter BR, Sutton J, and Vincent DP, 1982. *ORANI: A Multisectoral Model of the Australian Economy.* North–Holland: Amsterdam.

Dixon PB, and Peter MW, 1996. "Export-led growth for a regional economy: a CGE analysis of a south Australian export project." *Australasian J. Reg. Stud.* **2**(1): 11–34.

Dixon PB, and Rimmer MT, 2002a. *Dynamic General Equilibrium Modeling for Forecasting and Policy: A Practical Guide and Documentation of MONASH.* North–Holland: Amsterdam.

Dixon PB, and Rimmer MT, 2002b. "USAGE-ITC: theoretical structure and an illustrative application." Paper presented to 5th Annual conference on Global Economic Analysis. June 5–7, Taipei, Taiwan.

Giesecke JA, 1999. "Modeling the regional consequences of a commonwealth policy — the case of the fringe benefits tax." *Australasian J. Reg. Stud.* **5**(3): 365–376.

Giesecke JA, 2000. "The theoretical structure of the FEDERAL-F model." CREA Paper No. TS-08, Centre for Regional Economic Analysis, University of Tasmania, Australia.

Giesecke JA, 2002. "Explaining regional economic performance: an historical application of a dynamic CGE model." *Pap. Reg. Sci.* **81**: 247–278.

Giesecke JA, 2003. "Targeting regional output with state government fiscal instruments: a dynamic multi-regional CGE analysis." *Australian Econ. Pap.* (forthcoming).

Giesecke JA, and Madden JR, 1997. "Regional government economic policy: assessing the policy instruments." *Australasian J. Reg. Stud.* **3**: 3–18.

Harrison GW, Hougaard Jensen SE, Haagen Pedersen L, and Rutherford TF, (eds), 2000. *Using Dynamic Computable General Equilibrium Models for Policy Analysis.* North–Holland: Amsterdam.

Harrison WJ, and Pearson KR, 1996. "Computing solutions for large general equilibrium models using GEMPACK." *Computational Econ.* **9**(2): 83–127.

Harrison WJ, Horridge M, and Pearson KR, 1999. "Decomposing simulation results with respect to exogenous shocks." Centre of Policy Studies, Monash University, Working Paper No. IP-73.

Hertel TW, Horridge JM, and Pearson KR, 1992. "Mending the family tree: a reconciliation of the linearization and levels schools of AGE modeling." *Econ. Modeling* **9**: 385–407.

Higgs PJ, Parmenter BR, and Rimmer RJ, 1988. "A hybrid top-down, bottom-up regional computable general equilibrium model." *Int. Reg. Sci. Rev.* **11**: 317–328.

Horridge JM, Parmenter BR, and Pearson KR, 1998. "ORANI-G: A general equilibrium model of the Australian economy." Centre of Policy Studies and the Impact Project, Monash University, http://www.monash.edu.au/policy/ftp/oranig/oranidoc.pdf.

Jones R, and Whalley J, 1989. "A Canadian regional general equilibrium model and some applications." *J. Urban Econ.* **25**(3): 368–405.

Klein LR, and Glickman NJ, 1977. "Econometric model-building at regional level." *Reg. Sci. Urban Econ.* 7: 3–23.

Liew LH, 1984. "Tops-down versus "Bottoms-up" approaches to regional modeling." *J. Pol. Modeling* **6**: 351–367.

Madden JR, 1991. "Regional impacts of reducing CO_2 emissions." In: *Regional Modeling and Regional Planning*, edited by Gordon MT, and Gordon BL, Institute of Industrial Economics Conference Series Number 18, University of Newcastle. 119–130.

Madden JR, 1993. "The economics of vertical fiscal imbalance." *Australian Tax Forum* **10**(2): 75–90.

Madden JR, 1996. "FEDERAL: a two-region multisectoral fiscal model of the Australian economy." In: *Modeling and Control of National and Regional Economies: Proceedings*, edited by Vlacic L, et al., Pergamon: Oxford. 347–352.

Madden JR, 2002. "The economic consequences of the Sydney olympics — the CREA/Arthur Andersen study. *Curr. Tourism* 5(1): 7–21.

Madden JR, and Pant HM, 1997. "Modeling the consequences of a microeconomic reform: effects of proposed transport reforms on the Tasmanian economy." Paper presented to Regional CGE Modeling Workshop. Brisbane, 30 June–1 July, 1997.

Naqvi F, and Peter MW, 1996. A multiregional, multisectoral model of the Australian economy with an illustrative application." *Australian Econ. Pap.* **35**(66): 94–113.

Parmenter BR, 1995. "Forecasting and policy analysis with the MONASH model." Paper presented at the International Symposium on Economic Modeling, Bologna, Italy, 19–21 July 1995.

Partridge MD, and Rickman DS, 1998. "Regional computable general equilibrium modeling: a survey and critical appraisal." *Int. Reg. Sci. Rev.* **21**(3): 205–248.

Pearson KR, 1988. "Automating the computation of solutions of large economic models." *Econ. Modeling* 5(4): 385–395.

Powell AA, and Snape RH, 1993. "The contribution of applied general equilibrium analysis to policy reform in Australia." *J. Pol. Modeling*, **15**: 393–414.

Rutherford TF, 1999. "Applied general equilibrium modeling with MPSGE as a GAMS subsystem: an overview of the modeling framework and syntax." *Computational Economics* **14**: 1–46.

Whiteman JL, 1999. "The Inter-regional economic impact of microeconomic reform." *Econ. Pap.* **19**(1): 44–53.

Wittwer G, and Bright M, 1997. "The effects of mining expansion on regional economies in Australia." *Australasian J. Reg. Stud.* 3(1): 71–84.

Part IV

Infrastructure and Environmental Policies

Chapter 7

A Computable General Equilibrium Analysis of Efficiency Improvements at Japanese Ports*

MASAYUKI DOI

Institute of Policy and Planning Sciences, University of Tsukuba, Tsukuba, Ibaraki, Japan

HIDEKAZU ITOH

School of Business Administration, Kwansei Gakuin University, Nishinomia, Hyogo, Japan

PIYUSH TIWARI

University of Aberdeen Business School, Aberdeen, Scotland, United Kingdom

In this paper, we investigate the system-wide impact of increased efficiency of ports in Japan using a computable general equilibrium model developed for 1995. The technological efficiency in the ports reduces the cost of shipping transportation, and the forward and backward linkages of imports and exports introduce some positive gains in the national GDP. Our analysis proves that the spillover effects are substantial on shipping transportation and to a lesser extent on the Japanese economy. Since the port sector brings structural changes to the economies, the impact on the GDP due to productivity gains in the port sector is higher than equivalent gains in other sectors after controlling the size of sectors.

*This chapter was originally published in *Review of Urban and Regional Development Studies*, Vol. 13, No. 3, November 2001, and is reprinted here with minor modifications upon the permission from the publisher.

1. Introduction

In the early 1990s, due partly to adjustment of excessive stocks of production facilities during the "bubble" period, the Japanese economy entered a recessionary phase, starting at the beginning of 1991 just after the "bubble" economy collapsed. In the four years from 1992 to 1995, Japan's growth rate was around 1% or lower. Although the recession touched the bottom in October 1993, the recovery had been very weak. However, since the autumn of 1997, adverse domestic and overseas factors, such as failures of financial institutions in Japan and financial and economic turmoil in Asia, had combined to reduce consumer and corporate confidence in the economy. As a result, the Japanese economy was driven into an extremely severe situation. Consequently, the real GDP had been declining since the fourth quarter of 1997.

Japan's growth record, especially from the 1950s to 1990, was certainly respectable for an economy without major resources. Several institutional factors like lifetime employment, which enhanced productivity due to innovations in manufacturing process and less job mobility, the banking system, which fostered a strong relationship between banks and corporations (where banks held shares of firms and firms borrowed from banks), the education system and a high savings rate, were often cited as the reasons for Japan's booming economic growth. The very feature for which the Japanese economy was praised in the past by academia and policy watchers is being cited as the main cause of economic recession. Table 1 shows the post-war labor productivity growth in Japan during the past three decades for major sectors.

The breakdown by sectors sheds light on the long-run process of Japanese economic growth. First, the primary source of Japan's rapid growth was clearly the high rate of productivity growth in the manufacturing sector and the shift of resources to that sector. The effect is seen across the board, but is especially noticeable in the non-tradable sector. Furthermore, the productivity growth rate of the tradable sector was higher than that of either agriculture or manufacturing. This is because of a substantial relative shift of resources to manufacturing, where the level of productivity has always been higher than in other sectors. The productivity growth rate has been slowing down. Slower productivity growth, particularly after the very high levels reached by Japan from the 1960s to the 1970s, may be inevitable as the economy matures.

However, it may be a signal to review the basic institutional structure. (A detailed analysis of the institutional imperfections is beyond the scope of this paper.) Low factor productivity growth in Japan is often cited as the key economic phenomenon responsible for the slowing of the economy. Other

Table 1. Productivity Growth in Japan (%)

	1960–1971	1971–1981	1981–1992
Tradable			
Total	10.22	5.67	4.59
Agriculture	4.64	3.18	2.79
Manufacturing	10.16	5.31	3.99
Non Tradable			
Total	6.83	2.53	1.90
Energy and transportation	8.08	1.95	2.82
Construction	5.81	0.27	1.99
Distribution and finance	8.75	4.79	2.86
Services	4.00	1.06	0.48
Whole Economy	8.92	3.96	2.88

Source: Ito (1996)

authors have examined the impact of total productivity shocks on the country's economic recovery. Using a dynamic CGE (Computable General Equilibrium) model, Lee and Roland-Holst (2000) conclude that factor productivity growth in the Japanese economy would lead to a growth not only in Japan, but also in other ailing Asian economies through spillover effects. A number of studies have investigated the extent to which rapid output growth in postwar Japan resulted from capital inputs, labor inputs and total factor productivity. Most of these conclude that the postwar economic growth in Japan was attributable to total factor productivity and capital productivity. Most authors have concluded that a structural reform of the economy is necessary to enhance the country's total factor productivity. Each sector is special in its own way and requires very different policy changes. Therefore, it would be more pertinent to analyze the impact of sector specific policy changes on the economic growth.

One sector that we have been keenly following is the port sector in Japan, which has undergone many changes. The sector has limited direct intermediate inputs to various sectors of the economy. It has major inputs to the shipping industry, imports and exports. Through imports and exports, the effects on the port sector affect the economy. Therefore, its efficiency has significant implications on the production structure of various other sectors. The reasons for choosing ports for this study are explained in the next section. Briefly, the motivation to incorporate efficiency gains in the port sector is based on a study by Doi and Ohta (1995). The theoretical study concludes that improved port operations and new port investment leads to enhanced efficiency in this sector and is likely to reduce the cost of port operations followed by economic gains.

Using a static CGE model for Japan, we analyze the impact of the efficiency improvement in the port sector on the Japanese economy. We model the efficiency shock by assuming an improvement in the technology in the production function of this sector.

The rest of the paper is organized as follows: Section 2 briefly presents the developments in the port sector in Japan. Section 3 overviews the Computable General Equilibrium model and the database. Section 4 presents the results, with Section 5 concluding.

2. The Port Sector in Japan

As a component of the overall economy, the port sector is only 0.24% of the GDP. Share of this sector in total employment is 0.09% and capital stock is 0.14%. The structure of port sector is very typical with intermediate inputs of around 35% of the gross output based on the social accounting matrix (SAM) of Japan constructed for this analysis. Most of the intermediate input is from the real estate sector, constituting around half of all intermediate inputs.

Table 2. Cost Structure of the Port Sector

Sector	Share in Total Cost (%)
Labor	53.2
Capital	11.8
Non-durable manufacturing	2.3
Infrastructure manufacturing	0.4
Durable manufacturing	1.3
Construction	0.8
Utilities	0.1
Water	0.1
Trade	0.7
Finance and commerce	5.8
Real estate	17.0
Shipping	0.03
Other transportation	1.8
Communication	1.5
Education and research	0.1
Other services	4.0

Note: Based on the 1995 Japanese SAM constructed for this study

Factor income constitutes 65% of the gross output as a share of GDP; 82% of it accrues to labor and 18% to capital.

Ports comprise the service sector that deals with incoming and outgoing cargo. They require an extensive set of both water and land infrastructure/superstructure to handle various types of cargo. Shippers and shipping lines as well as many other related port users require various administrative and related financial and other services.[a]

The efficiency of port operations is dependent on the design and maintenance of berths, channels, navigation aids, other water-side facilities, stacking areas, cargo handling equipment, warehouses, container freight stations, accessibility and other land-side facilities. Port management, particularly the type of port ownership and administration, stevedoring labor, and the existence of competition determine the operating efficiency of port facilities. Information technology helps improve their operating performance. In turn, port efficiency can be increased by improvements in port design, maintenance, operations, redevelopment, management, labor management, or by inter-port network reform or by a mixture of such approaches.

The types of economic impacts arising from port efficiency improvement differ depending on the flows of cargo handled at the ports. Focusing on containerized cargo which is of higher value than other cargo types, there are three types of flow: local exports and imports, trans-shipments, and re-exports[b] (Doi, 1995). Ports with regional hub functions trans-ship cargoes between large ships of trunk routes and small ships of feeder routes, and tend to have higher trans-shipment ratios.[c] The Port of Singapore is a typical example of the regional hub port covering Southeast Asian countries. Its trans-shipment rate including re-export is as high as 0.8. Another example is the Port of Hong Kong, for which the rate of trans-shipments is about 0.5. The Port of Rotterdam and Port of Hamburg have regional hub functions in Europe, and the Port of Miami, Port of Everglades, and Port of Kingston have similar functions serving Central and South America.

In contrast to countries which host hub ports, Japan is a country of shippers, or cargo origination. The Port of Kobe used to have a trans-shipment rate of more than 0.4 around twenty years ago when Korea was experiencing rapid economic growth and Korean ports were underdeveloped. Major ports in Japan

---

[a]See, for example, Alderton (1999) for the introduction of port systems.

[b]Cargoes are unloaded to ports and then loaded to ships without any or much increase in their value added.

[c]This is the rate of trans-shipment cargo to the total cargo handling at a port.

still carry some trans-shipments of Chinese origin and destination. However, in Japan, local exports, imports, and domestic cargoes would be the main beneficiaries of efficiency improvement to Japanese ports. A study by Tongzon (2001) using data envelopment analysis of sixteen major international ports (including two Japanese ports) indicates that Yokohama and Osaka are among the most inefficient. The major reason cited is huge slack in labor and various infrastructure inputs in the Yokohama and Osaka ports.

We experimentally evaluate the economic impacts of port efficiency improvement using a CGE model, introducing the technological improvements mentioned earlier. We simulate the economic effects of technological improvements that increase the total factor productivity of ports by 20%.

3. The Computable General Equilibrium Model and the Database

Computable general equilibrium (CGE) models have provided an especially useful tool to understand and manage structural change. These models incorporate production at a level of aggregation that permits the analysis of structural change and also captures the essential interdependent nature of production, demand, and trade within a general equilibrium framework that incorporates market mechanisms and works through price incentives. The CGE model that we have used is a static, Dervis, De Melo and Robinson-type model.[d] It has twenty sectors and a detailed disaggregation of non-tradable and services sectors. There are three transportation sectors: shipping, port operations and other transportation. All sectors of the model are assumed to be perfectly competitive and operate under constant returns to scale. Production technology is modeled by a nested CES function. The model has three factors of production: labor, capital and sector-specific, fixed intermediate inputs specified by the sectoral input coefficients in the input-output (I–O) table. The labor supply is determined by a variable linear expenditure system. The labor supply is variable and labor moves freely between the sectors. Thus, there is a single equilibrium wage rate in the economy. Total capital stock is fixed, but capital is free to move among sectors.

All income generated by economic activity is assumed to be distributed to consumers. The income is divided between consumption and savings. The final demand for goods is divided between households, government and investment. Household's demand function is a linear expenditure system. Government and

[d]See Dervis, De Melo and Robinson (1982) for the details.

investment demand for each sector is fixed. This avoids any questions regarding substitution between present and future consumption, which makes the static welfare comparison difficult.

One of the key features of the model is that goods are differentiated as domestic or traded. On the import side, this is reflected by the implementation of the Armington assumption, where a constant elasticity of substitution (CES) specification is used to incorporate imperfect substitution of the imported goods with respect to domestically produced goods. A symmetric specification is used to model export supply, the latter being implemented with constant elasticity of transformation (CET) functions.

The model closure involves fixed real investment demand, fixed real government demands, a fixed price index, and variable government transfers. The exchange rate in the model is the real exchange rate. In this model, macroeconomic balance is achieved via changes in a government transfer variable. The capital stock of the economy does not rise. This model has a fixed numeraire price index (consumer price index), which implies that other prices in the model, including the exchange rate, are real.

Model equations and other relevant details are given in Appendix 1. The model is calibrated to the social accounting matrix of Japan, as well as to various parameters. The SAM is constructed from the I–O table and national accounts data for 1995. The parameters are taken from various sources to the extent available, and the rest are informed guesstimates.[e] Various parameters are listed in Appendix 2.

Let us think about the efficiency improvements of port services again. In the model that we have used, capital stock is fixed, though it is free to move between sectors. Improvement in technology increases the productivity of the sector, while the cost of production of port services declines. Since the cost of production declines as less labor and capital inputs are required to produce the same output, the domestic supply price of port services declines. This shifts the demand away from domestic supply to exports. Export increases, however, are determined by foreign export demand function price elasticities. Domestic prices of composite sales goods of port services decline (a function of domestic supply and domestic export prices). Less labor and capital are required by the port sector per unit of output so the supply factor adjusts to this change and moves out of this sector.

[e]For LES consumption function elasticities: Sasaki (1996). CET and CES function elasticities: Lee and Roland-Holst (1999) and (2000).

At the same time, since the domestic sales price decreases and the domestic import price does not change, the consumer price of port services to other sectors decreases. This increases the value added price in other sectors, as the input cost of port services has reduced. An increased value added price adjusts the wage and capital returns. Through consumption effect, the demand for composite goods in various sectors increases. Besides this, the cost of port services in the trade also declines. This increases the export and import activity. The balance of payment equation ensures that foreign exchange balance is maintained. Foreign savings are fixed, and increased exports of port services require that imports also increase. Imports in various sectors increase. Output that would benefit most from the reduction in the price of port services would shift to those sectors.

4. Modeling Efficiency and Results

In this section, we model the improvement in efficiency of the port sector. As mentioned earlier, only 35% of the gross output is intermediate inputs; the rest is factor payments. Of the total factor payments, the share of labor is around 53%, while that of capital is 12%. The share of labor employed in the port sector is only 0.09% of the total labor, and the port employs only 0.14% of the total capital. The rate of return to the labor and capital is very high.

Improvements of information technology, water-side facilities, land-side facilities, port management, stevedoring labor, and etc. by planning or through keener competition in port networks bring higher operating efficiencies of ports. There can be non-competitive elements that prevent the primary production factors from inter-sectoral movement. A number of policy changes could be discussed which introduce efficiency in this sector. It is not easy to introduce these impediments in the CGE framework.

To show the implications of gains in total factor productivity (TFP) of the port sector, we introduce in the coefficient a_{port} a gain by 20% of the port sector production function

$$X_{\text{port}} = a_{\text{port}}\left(b_{\text{port}}L_{\text{port}}^{(\phi_{\text{port}}-1)/\phi_{\text{port}}} + (1 - b_{\text{port}})K_{\text{port}}^{(\phi_{\text{port}}-1)/\phi_{\text{port}}}\right)^{\phi_{\text{port}}/(\phi_{\text{port}}-1)},$$

where X_{port} denotes gross domestic output for the port sector, L_{port} is labor used, K_{port} is capital used in the port sector, and ϕ_{port} is the elasticity of substitution between labor and capital. a_{port} and b_{port} are the respective intercept (measuring total efficiency) and share parameters.

Total factor productivity's (TFP's) improvement or technological progress corresponds to Hicks neutral technical progress. They increase the total output without changing the marginal rate of substitution between labor and capital.[f] In other words, an increase in total factor efficiency would produce the same output with less labor and capital and reduce the cost of production. This would shift the output towards exports, and various linkages within the economy would determine the impact of this change.

We exogenously increase the total factor efficiency by 20% from its current level (i.e. the benchmark equilibrium or the base case). The consequent changes in macro variables at the counterfactual equilibrium are presented in Table 3, while Table 4 presents changes in price. Table 5 presents sector-wise changes in various components of our model.

With the increase in the productivity of the port sector, the value added price in the port sector decreases. Labor and capital adjust to this change and move out of this sector. The port sector's international competitiveness enhances and the exports of port services increase. Export increases, however, are determined by the price elasticity of the foreign export demand function. At the same time, with the decrease in the domestic sales, the consumer price of port services to other sectors decreases.

The decline in the domestic purchaser price of port services increases the value-added price of other sectors, as input cost of port services has reduced.

Table 3. Percent Changes in Macro Variables (Real Prices)

Gross Domestic Product (real)	0.07
Wage rate (real)	0.05
Rental rate (real)	0.08
Labor supply	−0.01
Private savings	0.08
Consumption demand (real)	0.05
Income tax revenue (real)	0.08
Indirect tax revenue (real)	0.03
Government transfers (real)	0.30
Exchange rate (real)	−0.50

[f]On the other hand, Harrod neutral technical progress (labor-intensive technological progress) can be formulated by increasing the share coefficient of labor in production function of the port sector. Also, Solow neutral technical progress (capital-intensive technological progress) can be formulated by increasing the share coefficient of capital in production function. See, for example, Uzawa (1961) for a detailed discussion of the neutral technical progress, which is practiced in this analysis.

Table 4. Sectoral Changes in Prices (Percentage)

	Domestic Price	Average Output Price	Price of Composite Good	Domestic Price of Export	Domestic Price of Import
Agriculture	0.100	0.100	0.000	−0.498	−0.502
Mining	0.000	0.000	−0.400	−0.100	−0.500
Non durable manufacturing	0.100	−0.100	0.000	−0.499	−0.502
Infrastructure manufacturing	0.000	0.000	−0.100	−0.502	−0.498
Steel	0.000	−0.100	−0.100	−0.500	−0.498
Durable manufacturing	0.199	0.100	0.099	−0.203	−0.598
Construction	0.000	0.000	0.000		
Utilities	0.000	0.000	0.000	−0.500	−0.500
Water	0.000	0.000	0.000	−0.500	−0.500
Trade and commerce	0.000	0.000	0.000	−0.500	−0.500
Finance	0.000	0.000	0.000	−0.500	−0.500
Real estate	0.099	0.099	0.099	−0.500	−0.500
Shipping	−4.409	−2.002	−3.203	−0.500	−0.500
Port	−8.818	−7.114	−7.615	−0.500	−0.500
Other transportation	0.000	0.000	0.000	−0.500	−0.500
Communication	0.100	0.100	0.100	−0.500	−0.500
Public services	0.000	0.000	0.000		
Education and research	0.000	0.000	0.000	−0.500	−0.500
Medical	0.000	0.000	0.000		−0.500
Other services	0.000	0.000	0.000	−0.500	−0.500

Increased value added price adjusts the wage and capital returns. Through consumption effect, the demand for composite good in various sectors increases. The balance of payment equation ensures that foreign exchange balance is maintained. Foreign savings are fixed; increased exports of port services require that imports also increase. Imports in various sectors increase and are determined by the exchange rate, which appreciates slightly, and the elasticity of foreign demand system. Domestic production would shift to those sectors that would benefit most from the reduction in the price of port services. The gainers in the domestic supply in this experiment are the shipping industry, durable manufacturing and construction activity. The largest gain is in the shipping industry, which grows because the intermediate input price of port services has declined and the shipping industry is the largest buyer of the port services. Shipping industry sees significant growth in their domestic and

Table 5. Sectoral Changes in Quantities (Percentage)

	Imports	Exports	Domestic Supply	Domestic Consumption	Labor	Capital
Agriculture	0.706	−2.500	−0.141	0.098	−0.132	−0.145
Mining	0.272	0.000	−0.996	0.000	−1.667	−1.143
Non durable manufacturing	0.699	−0.562	−0.046	0.072	−0.048	−0.095
Infrastructure manufacturing	0.849	−0.590	−0.059	0.083	−0.047	−0.109
Steel	0.828	−0.688	−0.148	0.000	0.000	−0.205
Durable manufacturing	0.084	−0.308	0.016	0.073	−0.040	−0.087
Construction			0.062	0.000	0.067	0.033
Utilities	0.427	0.000	−0.016	0.018	0.000	−0.020
Water	0.000	0.000	0.000	0.000	0.000	0.000
Trade and commerce	1.307	−0.614	0.017	0.026	0.007	−0.019
Finance	1.200	−0.534	0.050	0.027	0.051	0.069
Real estate	0.000	0.000	0.054	0.020	0.140	0.000
Shipping	−1.461	10.554	6.271	1.509	8.000	8.941
Port	−9.623	16.234	6.507	4.545	−10.345	−10.280
Other transportation	1.152	−0.467	0.021	0.079	0.000	−0.035
Communication	1.389	0.000	0.042	0.060	0.000	0.043
Public services			0.000	0.000	0.000	−0.050
Education and research	3.125	0.000	−0.009	0.031	0.000	−0.041
Medical	1.165		0.020	0.084	0.029	−0.046
Other services	1.180	−0.617	−0.005	0.060	0.010	−0.033

international demand. Various service sectors also grow as a result of this experiment. The growth in various services sectors is because there is an additional demand generated for these activities. Appreciation in the exchange rate also leads to increase in the imports of services sectors. Japan imports education and research services as well, and imports in this sector grow with the exchange rate appreciation.

The productivity improvements also reallocate primary factors of production, and there is an increase in the price of value added of all sectors except port services, to which port service is input. Average wage rate and capital rental rate in the economy also grow. This raises household demand and leads to income effect by increasing the demand for agricultural goods and non-durable consumption goods.

Since total investment is fixed in our model, consumption increases. In this experiment, exchange rate depreciates slightly, and to maintain the savings — investment balance, private savings increase a little.

As a result, real GDP grows by 0.07%. It goes without saying that the factor to grow the shipping sector, the main user of port services, is the decrease of port charges. For this reason, the demands in domestic and foreign of the shipping sector increase. And, the various service sectors tend to grow as indirect effects.

Another important issue is: How does the impact of total factor productivity gains in the port sector compare with the similar gains in other supportive sectors of the economy? We simulate the equivalent total factor productivity gains in some other sectors; the results are presented in Table 6. For this simulation, we chose the other transportation sector (mainly road transport) and some of the domestic sectors, namely, utilities supply (electricity and gas supply) and water supply, that have huge investment requirements like ports and thus may be classified as supportive or infrastructure sectors. Some illustrative statistics in Table 6 to emphasize the role that productivity gains have on the port sector in Japan. One important issue to be kept in mind is the relative size of the sector. After controlling the size to make it comparable with the port sector, the impact on the GDP due to productivity gains in the port sector is higher than the other sectors.

The mechanism of transpiring of the TFP shock in the economy for different sectors is very different depending on the nature of the sector. Utilities and water supply are primarily domestic sectors with hardly any exports or imports. The other transportation has a very large domestic road component. The involvement in trade by the port sector is much larger than the other transportation, in terms of percentage share in that sector's output. As the focus of this paper is on ports, we have presented Table 6 for illustration's sake, and refrain from discussing the detailed mechanism of shock transpiration in the economy. Since the port sector brings structural changes to the economies

Table 6. Effect of Sectoral Productivity Gains of 20% in Some Selected Sectors

Sector	Ports	Other Transportation	Utilities	Water
% Change in real GDP due to 20% productivity gains	0.07	0.66	0.38	0.13
Sectoral share in total economy wide GDP	0.24	4.54	2.02	1.01
Sectoral share in total economy wide Output	0.17	4.78	2.01	1.01
Row 2/Row 3	0.29	0.15	0.19	0.13
Row 2/Row 4	0.42	0.14	0.19	0.16

as discussed earlier,[g] however, the impact on the GDP due to productivity gains in the port sector is higher than equivalent gains in other sectors after controlling the size of sectors.

This paper modeled a TFP shock of 20% in the port sector. The level of 20% gains in productivity was chosen for the sake of illustration, i.e. how the productivity shock affects the economy. We tried some alternative TFP shocks in the port sector as a sort of sensitivity analysis; the results indicate that within a small range of shocks, the magnitude of impact can be extrapolated linearly, but that over a large range of TFP shocks, it varies non-linearly. The gains in real GDP due to a 20% TFP shock is around 0.07%, as mentioned earlier. For a shock of 15%, real GDP grows by 0.06%, and for a shock of 10%, by 0.04%. On the upper side, for a TFP growth of 30%, real GDP grows by 0.10%; for 45% TFP growth, it grows by 0.15%. The mechanism of sectoral adjustments for these alternative levels is similar to the TFP growth case of 20%.

5. Conclusion

This is a basic analysis of the impact of port efficiency improvement on the Japanese economy. The port sector currently contributes only 0.24% to GDP. The intermediate inputs to this sector are 35% of the output; the primary factors constitute as much as 65% of the output. We have modeled the impact of total factor productivity in this sector on the economy using a static CGE model.

The results indicate that the impact on the economy is positive: real GDP grows by 0.07%. The typical mechanism increases the exports from port sectors. Increased port service exports require that imports also increase to maintain the trade balance. This increases imports in all sectors. Price of port service declines, which reduces the intermediate input cost of other sectors, thereby increasing the value added price. Factor returns increase, with consumption adjusting to maintain domestic consumption market equilibrium. The major impact is on the shipping industry, which grows all around.

The model requires many simplified assumptions and may at most be considered as rudimentary and indicative. A further model should investigate in a dynamic framework that allows investment decision to be undertaken in a dynamic way. The future possible expansion of our CGE model analysis in

[g]See Doi (2003) for a detailed discussion.

terms of port policy evaluation includes the following:

1. In our CGE model, the port efficiency improvement is evaluated as a 20% increase in the total factor productivity of this sector. A further investigation is required to formally link the productivity gains with improvements in design and technology in the port sector. The efficiency improvement differs from port to port, depending on the port terminal type, due to technological, operational, administrative, and economic management conditions. Further implications can be expected if more detailed port efficiency improvement levels are evaluated in consideration of different cargo types of the industrial sectors.
2. Japan suffers from a shortage of flat land. Therefore, ports and their surrounding areas also act as distribution centers, industrial zones and energy supply bases, trading centers, recreational centers, and other productive and environmental preservation bases. Improved port efficiency brings about changes to the economy through these additional functions of the ports, which are not considered either in the SAM or CGE modeling. Efforts will be made to incorporate at least part of such externalities in a future CGE analysis.

Acknowledgments

The authors express their sincere gratitude to Professor Kim Swales and Professor Mitsuo Ezaki for helping us with the concepts of CGE during our initial stage of this model building. The usual disclaimer applies.

References

Alderton PM, 1999. *Port Management and Operations.* LLP Reference Publishing.

Blonigen BA, Flynn JE, and Reinert KA, 1997. "Sector-focused general equilibrium modeling." in: Francois JF, and Reinert KA (Eds), *Applied Methods for Trade Policy Analysis: A Handbook.* Cambridge University Press, 489–497.

Dervis K, De Melo J, and Robinson S, 1982. *General Equilibrium Models for Development Policy.* Cambridge University Press.

De Melo J, and Robinson S, 1989. "Product differentiation and the treatment of foreign trade in computable general equilibrium models of small economies." *J. Int. Econ.* 27: 489–497.

De Melo J, and Tarr D, 1992. *A General Equilibrium Analysis of US Foreign Trade Policy.* The MIT Press.

Devarajan S, and Rodrik D, 1991. "Pro-competitive effects of trade reform: results from CGE model of Cameroon." *Europ. Econ. Rev.* 35: 1157–1184.

Doi M, 1995. *Transportation Economics for Developing Countries.* Keisoshobo (in Japanese)
Doi M, 2003. *Economics of Ports and Regions.* Taga-Shuppan (in Japanese)
Doi M, and Ohta H, 1995. "Analysis and policy consideration of international production and transport system changes: impacts of port changes." *J. Appl. Reg. Stud.* **1**: 1–11. (in Japanese)
Ito T, 1996. "Japan and the Asian economies: a "miracle" in transition." *Brookings Pap. Econ. Act.* **2**: 205–272.
Lee H, and Roland-Holst D, 1999. "Cooperation or confrontation in U.S.-Japan trade? some general equilibrium estimates." *J. Japanese Int. Economies* **13**: 119–139.
Lee H, and Roland-Holst D, 2000. "Trade and transmission of endogeneous growth effects: Japanese economic reform as an externality for East Asian economies." Mimeo.
Sasaki K, 1996. "Consumer demand in Japan: an analysis using the Deaton-Muellbauer system." *Japan World Economy* **8**: 335–351.
Tongzon J, 2001. "Efficiency measurement of selected Australian and other international ports using data envelopment analysis." *Transp. Res.*: Part A: *Pol. Practice* 35:113–128.
Uzawa H, 1961. "Neutral inventions and the stability of growth equilibrium." *Rev. Econ. Stud.*, February, 117–124.

Appendix 1. Generalized CGE Model Specification

As has been mentioned, the model used in our paper is of Dervis, De Melo and Robinson-type, and relies on the CGE model introduced in Dervis *et al.* (1982) for various structural concepts such as final demand structure, production technology, industrial and factor market structure, and treatment of trade goods. We follow the formulation of Blonigen *et al.* (1997), which is routinely used by the US International Trade Commission, as the core of our modeling works. The model equations and notations are adopted from Blonigen *et al.* (1997).

Final Demand Behavior

The model considers three separate components of domestic final demand: household consumption, government demand, and investment demand. The consumption behavior of households is given in Eq. (1):

$$P_i^Q C_i = P_i^Q \mu_i + s_i\left[(1 - \text{mps})Y - \sum_h P_h^Q \mu_h\right] \quad \forall i, \tag{1}$$

where C_i represents households demand for composite consumption good i, P_i^Q denotes the domestic purchaser price of the composite consumption goods i, s_i is the marginal budget share for composite goods i, mps is the marginal propensity to save, Y is domestic income, and μ_i is the subsistence minimum for composite consumption good i. The functional form is a linear expenditure system (LES). The LES is a generalization of the Cobb–Douglas utility function in which the origin is translated to a point in the positive quadrant. While the income expansion paths are linear, the displaced origin allows preferences to be non-homothetic. That is, income elasticities of demand can differ from unity.

Government and investment spending in each sector (any overall) is held constant in real terms:

$$I_i = is_i I \quad \forall i \tag{2}$$

$$G_i = gs_i G \quad \forall i, \tag{3}$$

where I and G are total investment and government demand, respectively, and is_i and gs_i are the share of the total investment and government demand each sector receives. This specification avoids questions concerning the substitution between present and future consumption which would make static welfare comparisons difficult.

Production Technology

Production technology is modeled by using a constant elasticity of substitution (CES) value added function specified as

$$X_i = a_i\left(b_i L_i^{(\phi_i-1)/\phi_i} + (1-b_i)K_i^{(\phi_i-1)/\phi_i}\right)^{\phi_i/(\phi_i-1)} \quad \forall i, \tag{4}$$

where X_i denotes gross domestic output for sector i, L_i is labor used in sector i, K_i is capital used in sector i, and ϕ_i is the elasticity of substitution between labor and capital for sector i. The parameter ϕ_i is exogenous and is estimated outside the model. a_i and b_i are the respective intercept and share parameters that allow the CES production function to be calibrated for each sector i. A Leontief (fixed coefficients) function is assumed between value added and intermediate products as well as between various intermediates:

$$D_i = \sum_h io_{ih} S_h \quad \forall i, \tag{5}$$

where D_i is the intermediate demand for composite consumption goods i, X_h is the gross domestic output of sector h, and io_{ih} is the input–output coefficient between sectors i and h. The input-output coefficients are determined by calibration to the SAM.

Factor Supplies and Demands

Factor demands are derived from the CES production function:

$$L_i = a_i^{(\phi_i - 1)} X_i \left(\frac{b_i P_i^V}{w} \right)^{\phi_i} \qquad \forall i \tag{6}$$

$$K_i = a_i^{(\phi_i - 1)} X_i \left[\frac{(1 - b_i) P_i^V}{r} \right]^{\phi_i} \qquad \forall i \tag{7}$$

where P_i^V is the value added price in sector i, w is the economy-wide wage rate, and r is the economy-wide rental rate on capital.

While the total capital stock is fixed in the model, we specify a variable labor supply function using a nested linear expenditure system as in De Melo and Tarr (1992) and the Appendix to this chapter:

$$L = L_0 - \left(\frac{\lambda_I}{w} \right) \frac{[(1 - \text{mps})Y - P^{\text{LES}}\Gamma]}{(1 - \lambda_I)} \tag{8}$$

$$P^{\text{LES}} = \frac{\left[(1 - \text{mps})Y - \sum_i P_i^Q \Gamma_i\right]}{\prod_i (C_i - \Gamma_i)^{\lambda_i}}, \tag{9}$$

where L_o is maximum labor supply, λ_i is the marginal budget share for leisure, λ_i is the marginal budget share of composition goods i, P^{LES} is the LES aggregate price index, Γ_i is the LES subsistence minimum for composition good i, and Γ is the aggregate LES subsistence minimum. This represents just one possible labor market closure. One alternative is to fix L and maintain a flexible w. Another alternative is to fix w and allow L to vary.

Treatment of Traded Goods

The treatment of traded goods is the most important component of the model specification. As mentioned, the model views each sector as consisting of three goods, where imports and exports in each industry category are imperfect substitutes for their domestic counterparts. On the import side, the model treats foreign and domestic commodities as imperfect substitutes in domestic use. Therefore, the import composition of domestic demand is influenced by the ratio of domestic and import prices, as well as by any administrative quantity restrictions. The model aggregates imports and their domestic counterparts into an aggregate good for each sector, Q_i, using a CES aggregation:

$$Q_i = \alpha_i\left[\beta_i M_i^{(\sigma_i-1)/\sigma_i} + (1-\beta_i)S_i^{(\sigma_i-1)/\sigma_i}\right]^{\sigma_i/(\sigma_i-1)} \quad \forall i \tag{10}$$

$$\left(\frac{M_i}{S_i}\right) = \left[\left(\frac{\beta}{(1-\beta_i)}\right)\left(\frac{P_i^S}{P_i^M}\right)\right]^{\sigma_i} \quad \forall i \tag{11}$$

$$M_i = M0_i\left(\frac{PW_i^M}{PW_i^{M0}}\right)^{\sigma_{fi}} \quad \forall i. \tag{12}$$

Equation (10) is the aggregation relation in which Q_i denotes the composite good for domestic consumption in sector i, M_i is the imports of sector i, $M0_i$ is the imports of sector i in the base case, S_i is the domestic supply in sector i, α_i and β_i are the respective intercept and share parameters in this CES product aggregation function for each sector i, and σ_i is the elasticity of substitution between imports and domestic competing goods in sector i. Equation (11) is the tangency condition in which P_i^S is the sector i's price of the domestic good and P_i^M is sector i's domestic price of imports.

The use of CES functional form for aggregation implies that preferences with respect to imports and domestic goods within a sector are homothetic, while preferences between sectors are not. For a given level of demand for a product category, determined by the specification of the three components of final demand, the shares of imports and domestic goods are determined in response to relative prices.

On the export side, the model assumes that domestic firms allocate their output between domestic and foreign markets according to a transformation function which depends on the ratio of domestic and foreign prices. Therefore, the export composition of domestic supply is influenced by the ratio of domestic and export prices. The functional form used is a constant elasticity of transformation (CET) as indicated in the following equations:

$$X_i = \gamma_i\left[\delta_i E_i^{(\tau_i+1)/\tau_i} + (1-\delta_i)S_i^{(\tau_i+1)/\tau_i}\right]^{\tau_i/(\tau_i+1)} \quad \forall i \tag{13}$$

$$\left(\frac{E_i}{S_i}\right) = \left[\left(\frac{1-\delta_i}{(\delta_i)}\right)\left(\frac{P_i^E}{P_i^S}\right)\right]^{\tau_i} \quad \forall i \tag{14}$$

$$E_i = E0_i\left(\frac{PW_i^E}{PW_i^{E0}}\right)^{\tau_{fi}} \quad \forall i. \tag{15}$$

Equation (13) is the allocation relation in which S_i is domestic supply in sector i; E_i is the exports of sector i; $E0_i$ is the exports of sector i in the base case, τ is the elasticity of transformation between domestic supply and exports; and γ_i and δ_i are the respective intercept and share parameters used to calibrate the model for each sector i. Equation (14) is the tangency condition in which P_i^E is the domestic price of exports in sector i. The shares of domestic supply and exports are determined in response to relative prices.

Domestic Prices

We next turn to the equations for domestic prices, including those of import and export goods. These are given in the following five equations:

$$P_i^X X_i = P_i^S S_i + P_i^E E_i \quad \forall i \tag{16}$$

$$P_i^Q Q_i = P_i^S S_i + P_i^M M_i \quad \forall i \tag{17}$$

$$P_i^V = P_i^X - \sum_h io_{hi} P_h^Q \quad \forall i \tag{18}$$

$$P_i^M = (1 + t_i)(1 + \rho_i) er PW_i^M \quad \forall i \tag{19}$$

$$P_i^E = er PW_i^E \quad \forall i, \tag{20}$$

where t_i is the tariff rate on imports in sector i, ρ_i is the quota premium rate in sector i, PW_i^M is the world price of import good in sector i, PW_i^E is the world price of the export in sector i, and *er* is the exchange rate (Japanese Yen per unit of foreign currency).

Domestic Market Equilibrium

Three equations are required for domestic market equilibrium, one for the commodity market and two others for the factor markets:

$$Q_i = D_i + C_i + G_i + I_i \quad \forall i \tag{21}$$

$$\sum_i K_i = K \tag{22}$$

$$\sum_i L_i = L. \tag{23}$$

Income and Government Revenue

Income and government revenue are summarized by the following six equations:

$$R_T = \sum_i \frac{t_i}{(1+t_i)} P_i^M M_i \tag{24}$$

$$R_Q = \sum_i \rho_i er PW_i^M M_i \tag{25}$$

$$Y = Y_L + Y_K + GT + R_Q \tag{26}$$

$$\sum_i P_i^Q G_i + GS + GT = R_T \tag{27}$$

$$S = \text{mps}Y + GS + erFS \tag{28}$$

$$I = \sum_i P_i^Q I_i. \tag{29}$$

Equations (24) and (25) represent tariff revenue (R_T) and domestically capital quota rents (R_Q), respectively. Equation (26) defines income, which is the sum of labor income ($Y_L = wL$), capital income ($Y_K = rK$), government transfer payments (GT), and domestically captured quota rents. The government budget constraint is captured in Eq. (27), where *GS* is government savings. Finally, total investments and savings are defined in Eqs. (28) and (29), respectively, where *FS* is foreign savings. As indicated, by Walras's Law, we leave out any savings–investment balance equation.

Foreign Sector Closure

To characterize the foreign sector, we specify the following balance of payments equation:

$$\sum_i PW_i^M M_i + \frac{R_O}{er} = \sum_i PW_i^E E_i + FS. \tag{30}$$

With foreign savings (*FS*) held constant, the balance of payments is maintained in Eq. (30) via changes in the exchange rate, *er*. An alternative foreign sector closure is to fix the exchange rate and allow foreign savings to vary. The closure used here better supports welfare analysis, however. With a numeraire price index held fixed (see the section Macro Closure), the exchange rate behaves as a real exchange rate.

Macro Closure

Because the model is SAM-based, a macroeconomic closure must be specified. A numeraire price index is held fixed, as suggested by De Melo and Robinson (1989). Government and investment demands by sector are fixed in real terms as described. As in Devarajan and Rodrik (1991), real government transfers adjust to maintain the savings–investment balance. The model is homogeneous of degree zero in prices.

Appendix 2. Model Parameters

Demand Elasticities (Sasaki, 1996)

Sasaki estimated household consumer demand income elasticities for the following sectors.

Agriculture	1.10
Construction	0.82
Utilities	0.39
Water	0.25
Durable manufacturing	2.184
Non durable manufacturing	0.98
Medical	1.96
Other transportation	1.42
Education	1.18
Other services	1.30

However, to complete the demand elasticity set in our CGE model, we need additional elasticities. We have imputed the following values for other sectors based on model calibration. The model calibration is done so that we replicate our base case actual values of macroeconomic parameters like GDP, output etc. by adjusting various model parameters. Some of the sectors like mining, infrastructure manufacturing, steel, commerce, finance, port, shipping services are not consumption good and hence we assume that the demand elasticity is 1. The demand elasticity of the real estate sector is assumed to be the same as the construction sector. Communication sector elasticities are assumed to be same as the other transportation sectors.

Mining	1.00
Infrastructure manufacturing	1.00
Steel	1.00
Trade and commerce	1.00
Finance	1.00
Real estate	0.82
Shipping	1.00
Port	1.00
Communication	1.42
Public services	1.00

Trade and Production Elasticities

To the extent possible, we have taken the trade and production elasticities from Lee and Roland-Holst (1999, 2000). Guesstimating procedure for remaining sectors is the same as for demand elasticities. Sectors which are close in nature have been assumed similar parameters and for the left over sectors we derive the parameter value during the calibration of the base case scenario.

	σ	τ	σ_f	τ_f	ϕ
Agriculture	1.65	1.07	55.38	−100	1.19
Mining	2.24	0.88	8.85	−2.0	1.48
Non durable manufacturing	1.65	0.81	5.99	−14.9	1.75
Infrastructure manufacturing	1.93	0.54	9.89	−14.8	1.80
Steel	2.27	0.48	9.64	−4.2	1.80
Durable manufacturing	0.1	0.78	9.95	−0.9	2.15
Construction					1.48
Utilities	1.5	1	100	−90	1.20
Water	1.5	1	100	−90	1.20
Trade	1.5	1	100	−90	1.49
Finance and commerce	1.92	1	100	−90	1.49
Real estate	1.92	1	100	−100	1.49
Shipping	1.92	1	100	−90	1.49
Port	1.92	1	100	−90	1.49
Other transportation	1.92	1	100	−90	1.49

(*To be continued*)

(*Continued*)

	σ	τ	σ_f	τ_f	ϕ
Communication	1.92	1	100	−90	1.49
Public services					1.49
Education and research	1.92	1	100	−90	1.49
Medical	1.92	1	100	−100	1.49
Other services	1.92	1	100	−90	1.49

ϕ: CES parameter in production function
σ: Armington function elasticity
σ_f: import supply elasticity
τ: CET function elasticity
τ_f: export demand price elasticity

Chapter 8

Incorporating Local Health in Assessing GHG Mitigation: An Application to Thailand*

JENNIFER C. LI

Department of Public Policy, University of North Carolina at Chapel Hill, NC, USA

Ancillary benefits of greenhouse gas (GHG) mitigation refer to benefits from GHG mitigation in addition to lowered adverse impacts of global climate change. A major ancillary benefit of GHG mitigation is reduced local air toxins, which improves health. The purpose of the study is not to determine whether ancillary benefits of GHG mitigation can or cannot justify GHG mitigation. Rather, we discuss how an important benefit of addressing GHG emission — the local health effects — should and can be incorporated using the approaches put forth. A Computable General Equilibrium (CGE) model is used for simulating a carbon tax policy. A health effects submodel takes the local air emissions output from the CGE model and assesses the implications for ambient air concentration, health, and labor supply. Labor and medical expenditure changes are fed back into the economy. Applying this approach to Thailand, when health feedback is included, we find that: (1) negative impact on GDP under a carbon tax drops by 45%, and (2) welfare improves for households and cleaner producers.

*This chapter was originally published in *Review of Urban and Regional Development Studies*, Vol. 14, No. 3, November 2002, and is reprinted here with minor modifications upon the permission from the publisher.

1. Introduction

In order to curb greenhouse gas (GHG) emissions, a country needs to reduce fossil fuel use. In this study we examine an economy-wide policy of a carbon tax. The study employs six distinct methodological steps to simulate the feedback of health effects and to assess the influence of this feedback on measures of social welfare used in policy analysis. These methodological steps, shown in Fig. 1 below as the boxes are:

1. Specify the policy measure and how it alters specific parameters in subsequent methodological steps used in the assessment;
2. Alter these parameters in the economic model to determine effects on economic indicators of social welfare and on the emissions from economic activity;
3. From the projected emissions, determine the ambient air concentrations and exposures to the resident population;
4. From these exposures and assumed exposure–response relationships, determine morbidity and mortality rates in the resident population;
5. Assess the impact of these morbidity and mortality rates on labor and on health care expenditures;
6. Simulate the economic model again accounting for the labor and health care impacts;
7. Assess the overall economic impact, through the economic model, considering both primary and secondary (feedback) effects; summarize as economic indicators and GHG emissions; and
8. Assess the welfare distribution implications of the scenario incorporating the feedback effects and the one without.

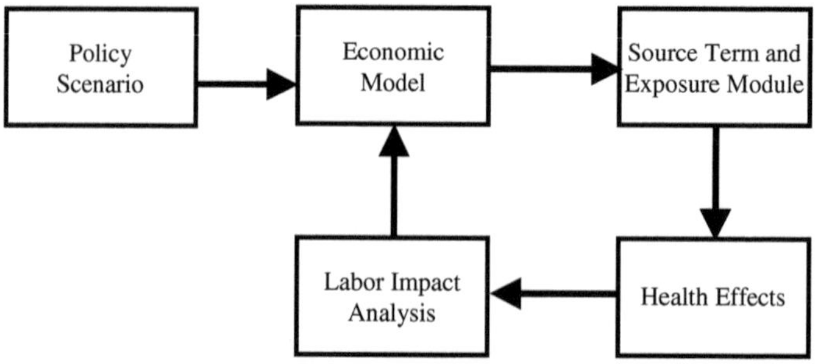

Fig. 1. Conceptual Framework

2. The Model

The model used is a variation of the "standard model" built by the Trade and Macroeconomics Division of the International Food Policy Research Institute (Lofgren *et al.*, 2001). The model is calibrated to a 1998 Social Accounting Matrix (SAM) updated from a 1995 SAM by the Thai Development Research Institute (TDRI). TDRI used the following to update the SAM: Thai National Accounts of 1998;[a] current and capital account information which reported external flows data for 1998; the 1998 Thai household income and expenditure survey;[b] and employment and wages data from the 1998 Thai Labor Force Survey. All data sources were reconciled to resolve inconsistencies among them (TDRI, 2000).

The 1998 SAM obtained for the current study is a more aggregated version of the original 1998 SAM described above. This SAM contains only one type of labor and does not carry detailed employment and wage data. It has 61 production sectors, 3 household categories, and 3 factor types. The following subsections briefly describe the main characteristics of the model.

Structure of the economy: brief background. Traditionally dominated by agricultural production, Thailand today has a much more complex and multi-faceted economy. Several important factors have contributed to Thailand's growth. Its principal comparative advantage has been the abundance and diversity of its natural resources. With its agrarian base as the bedrock, the economy has experienced steady growth. In recent years, manufacturing has surpassed agricultural products in Thailand's GNP, while tourism and the related service sectors have replaced agricultural products as Thailand's largest source of foreign exchange (Mahidol University, 1998).

Production. The production technology for the current model is a nested Constant Elasticity of Substitution (CES) structure taking into account the optimizing behavior in the choice of production factors. Appendix 1 depicts the nested decision process in the choice of production factors. Starting from the top of the structure downwards, outputs from the three composite goods — non-energy intermediates, energy intermediates, and value-added — are aggregated via CES technology. The non-energy intermediate aggregate is obtained by combining all non-energy commodities via a CES structure. The labor–capital bundle is also aggregated via a CES structure, allowing a degree

---

[a]The Thai National Accounts records the aggregate values of final demands and national income.
[b]This survey was used to disaggregate households.

of substitution among the factors. The energy composite is a CES aggregate of eight types of energy that are substitutable: coal and lignite, petroleum natural gas, gasoline, diesel, fuel oil, aviation fuel, LPG, and electricity. The elasticities of substitution reflect the adjustment possibilities in producers' demand for factors when the relative prices of these factors change.

Income distribution and absorption. Labor income is allocated to households according to a fixed coefficient distribution matrix derived from the original SAM. Likewise, capital revenues are distributed among households, private and public enterprises, and the government. The relative incomes of the three households (Agricultural, Non-agricultural, and Government-employed) are 1:3.47:3.88. On average, government-employed household income is the highest, about 3.88 times that of agricultural household income and about 1.14 times higher than the average income of non-agricultural households.

On the consumption side, private consumption demand is obtained through the maximization of household-specific utility function following the Stone–Geary Linear Expenditure System or the Extended Linear Expenditure System (LES) (Lluch, 1973). Household utility is a function of consumption of different goods and saving. The elasticities of household consumption are differentiated by household and product, varying in the range of 0.40 (for basic products consumed) to 2.0 (for services).

The government consumption and investment demands are disaggregated by sector with their shares determined by the SAM data.

International trade. Like most trade-focused CGE models, the model assumes imperfect substitution among goods originating from different geographical areas.[c] Import demand is derived from a CES aggregation of domestic and imported goods. Export supply is symmetrically modeled as a Constant Elasticity of Transformation (CET) function. Producers allocate their output to domestic or foreign markets in response to relative price changes. For Thailand, the Armington elasticities for demand between domestic and imported products are based on Warr (1998) and informed by the base-year shares of imports, exports, and two-way trade.

The transformation elasticities for domestic versus export supply, on the other hand, are obtained from Methakunavut and Jitsuchon (2001).[d] The small-country assumption is applied as Thailand is assumed unable to change world prices. This specification implies that the import and export world prices

[c]Armington (1969).

[d]Contact the author for the Armington and CGE coefficients applied in this study.

are exogenous. Balance-of-payments equilibrium assumes a fixed value for the current account.

Emissions. Two types of polluting substances are considered: CO_2 and PM-10. An abatement policy targeted at CO_2 has the unintended positive effect of reducing a local pollutant, PM-10.[e] We refer to this secondary reduction of PM-10 as an "ancillary effect" or "ancillary benefit" (Burtraw and Toman, 2000). The association between negative health effects and PM-10 exposure is well-established in the epidemiology literature.

Industries that burn fossil fuels emit CO_2 as well as PM-10. PM-10 is also generated during what is called "process emissions" (as opposed to combustion emissions) in the case where dust is generated during a production process that does not involve combustion. Process-emissions are not related to the amount of fuel used, but to the total output produced. One other major source of PM-10 is vehicles, or final consumption-generated PM-10. When a carbon tax is imposed to induce less fossil fuel burning, we do not expect the process-generated PM-10 to drop significantly, but should expect the combustion-generated PM-10, through industrial production and vehicular combustion, to drop more. Emissions coefficients associated with each intermediate and final consumption for CO_2 were derived from the emission coefficients from the U.S. Energy Information Agency. Industry-specific emissions coefficients for PM-10 (for combustion and process-generated emissions) are assumed to follow similar distributions as those applied by Garbaccio *et al.* (2000) in their study on China. The actual process and combustion emission coefficients for PM-10 applied in this study are presented in the tables in Appendix 2.

CO_2 emissions, on the other hand, are emitted through the combustion process only, both from industrial production and vehicle use. The following is a summary of the sources of emissions for PM-10 and CO_2:

CO_2:

- production-generated combustion emission,
- consumption-generated combustion emission.

PM-10:

- production-generated combustion emission,
- production-generated process emission,
- consumption-generated combustion emission.

---

[e]As well as other local pollutants such as SO_2 and NO_x; but here we focus on PM-10 alone.

Formally, the total emission for a given pollutant takes the following form for CO_2:

$$E_{CO_2} = \sum_{A} \sum_{EINP} \alpha_{EINP} QINP_{A,EINP} + \sum_{INST} \tau_{INST} C_{INST},$$

where E = total emissions; A = 61 activity sectors that use energy as an input; EINP = 8 energy inputs; α = sector-specific emission coefficients for combustion-based CO_2 emissions; $QINP_{A,EINP}$ = quantity of each 8 energy input consumed by sector; τ = emission coefficients for consumption-based CO_2 emissions by final consumer groups or institutions; INST = institutions; C_{INST} = amount of good consumed by each institution.

For PM-10, the total emissions take the following form:

$$E_{PM\text{-}10} = \sum_{A} \sum_{EINP} \alpha_{2,EINP} QINP_{A,EINP} + \sum_{A} \beta_A QD_A + \sum_{INST} \tau_{INST} C_{INST},$$

where α_2 = emission coefficients for combustion-based PM-10 emissions by sector; β = emission coefficients for the process-based PM-10 emissions by sector; τ_2 = emission coefficients for consumption-based PM-10 emissions by final consumer groups; QD_A = total domestic output by sector.

Emissions from production can be reduced in three ways: through a lower aggregate output (the scale effect), change in the commodity composition (more or less of dirty goods produced, the composition effect), or the adoption of cleaner technologies (rebalancing the input mix in favor of less polluting inputs, i.e. the technology effect). Note that the abatement of consumption-originated emissions could not be achieved through technology effects, since consumption is only composed of final products.

Household utility functions do not include any term directly related to environmental quality. An emission abatement policy will still have utility effects, however, through its effects on consumption and savings. Similarly, environmental degradation does not affect the productivity of production factors. Productivity gains resulting from a greener environment are not measured in this model. The potential gains from environmental protection policies are therefore most likely underestimated.

Linking expenditures on health to pollution. In Thailand, the government and private institutions (insurance and households) are responsible for covering the medical costs. In the case of "saved" hospital costs due to reduced PM-10, we assume that both the government and the household are able to cut back medical expenditure as a result. The use of this increase in income is assumed to follow the spending pattern (allocation shares) of the existing government and household accounts.

As alluded to earlier, household consumption behavior is assumed to follow a Linear Expenditure System (LES). To link expenditures (household and government) on medical treatments and health (commodity CHLTHMD) to environmental quality, we specify the consumption of CHLTHMD as follows:

- Having a separate definition for the "subsistence" level of demand for the medical and health commodity (CHLTHMD) as a function of total PM-10 emission and an estimated elasticity of demand (ε) for CHLTHMD with respect to the PM-10 emission level.
- Allocating disposable income to the consumption of "all" commodities, including CHLTHMD.
- By these specifications, we allow the subsistence consumption of CHLTHMD to drop when pollution is lessened (price effect), while allowing the income freed up to be spent on all types of goods (income effect).

With respect to government demand for CHLTHMD, it is separated from government demand for all other commodities and tied to the private demand (household demand) for CHLTHMD.[f] With the link between health/medical expenditures and pollution set up in the model, the feedback of health/medical expenditure to a diminished pollution is endogenized.

Policy instruments. The model includes a variety of pre-existing economic instruments, including: direct and indirect taxes on production, consumption; subsidies on production or consumption; and tariffs and other forms of taxes on imports. With respect to a uniform tax based on per unit CO_2 emitted, the tax level can be endogenously determined by having an exogenous emission abatement target. Otherwise, one can set the emission tax exogenously and have the model endogenously determine the corresponding level of emission reduction. For the current paper, the latter approach is adopted. We set the tax rate at a level that would result in a 20% reduction in total CO_2 emissions.

Model closure. The equilibrium condition on the balance of payments is combined with other macro closure conditions to complete the model. The model includes three macroeconomic balances: the (current) government balance,

[f]The government demand for CHLTHMD is tied to the provided demand for CHLTHMD via a pre-selected ratio of government-to-private demand for CHLTHMD.

the external balance (the current account of the balance of payments, which includes the trade balance), and the savings-investment balance.

With regard to government consumption, as the model does not capture its direct and indirect welfare contributions, it is preferable to keep real government consumption fixed. For the government balance, we also set government savings at a fixed level and allow the direct tax rates of domestic institutions to adjust endogenously. The direct tax rates will be adjusted in a manner that would reflect their pre-policy shock rates paid by various institutions. For the external balance, the closure sets the real exchange rate flexible while foreign savings (the current account deficit) fixed. Given that all other items in the external balance (transfer between the rest of the world and domestic institutions) are fixed, the trade balance will also be fixed.

Total investment and total savings are set to equal, with savings originating from households, government, and rest of the world. The closure used is investment-driven, which means that the investment quantities are fixed. Under the chosen savings-investment closure, the investment is fixed and the savings rates of selected institutions are scaled so as to generate enough savings to finance investment. Investment is one component of total absorption. The remaining components are household consumption and government consumption. With the nominal absorption shares of investment and government consumption fixed at base levels, the residual share for household consumption is also fixed.

Reference and carbon tax scenario. The base year of 1998 represents the reference or benchmark economic and environmental scenario in the absence of the environmental policy counterfactual. The impact of the environmental policy is then evaluated against this reference scenario by measuring variations in the economic and environmental aggregates, and the decomposed income distribution effects.

As alluded to before, the environmental scenario considered is a targeted reduction of CO_2 emission. The target is set for a reduction of total CO_2 emissions (production-generated and consumption-generated combined) by 20% with respect to the reference scenario. The instrument used to reach this target is a uniform tax on energy commodities (used as intermediate and final goods) per unit of emission. The carbon tax receipts are then "recycled" to reduce direct income taxes on all three households as well as the public enterprise.[g]

---

[g]See the government closure rule under model closure.

2.1. *From the CGE Model to the Health Module*

Analyzing the carbon tax policy without incorporating health feedback shows that the carbon tax policy has minor costs in terms of output. The GDP is lowered by around 1.2% with respect to the benchmark, and the exports lowered by a higher 2.5%. The reduction in CO_2 emission is primarily due to reductions in production-generated emissions. Production-generated emission was lowered by 20% as a result of the carbon tax whereas consumption-generated emission is lowered by 15%. The greater percentage drop can be attributed to the fact that most of the carbon tax burden is on enterprises, and they are the main polluters through their production activities. With the 20% reduction of CO_2 comes an ancillary (unintended) benefit of reduction in PM-10 by 3.72%. This leads to a lowering of the ambient concentration of PM-10, which is beneficial to the health of urban population.

The following section further explores the links between the total emissions and ambient concentration of PM-10, and assesses the implications of the change in the ambient concentration of PM-10 on public health and labor productivity. (See Appendix 3 for an illustrative flowchart.) The following describes the terms appearing in Appendix 3:

Source term PM-10 from industries before policy $= ST_{\mathrm{N}}^{\mathrm{I}}$
Source term PM-10 from transportation before policy $= ST_{\mathrm{N}}^{\mathrm{T}}$
Source term PM-10 from industries after policy $= ST_{\mathrm{P}}^{\mathrm{I}}$
Source term PM-10 from transportation after policy $= ST_{\mathrm{P}}^{\mathrm{T}}$
Background pollution concentration $= C_{\mathrm{B}}$
Fraction of ambient PM-10 contributed by industries $= F_{\mathrm{I}}$
Fraction of ambient PM-10 contributed by transportation $= F_{\mathrm{T}}$
Fraction of time spent indoor by an average adult $= F_{\mathrm{IN}}^{\mathrm{A}}$
Fraction of time spent outdoors by an average adult $= F_{\mathrm{OU}}^{\mathrm{A}}$
Ratio of ambient air PM-10 concentration over emissions rate contributed by industries $= K_{\mathrm{I}}$
Ratio of ambient air PM-10 concentration over emissions rate contributed by transportation/construction $= K_{\mathrm{T}}$
Ambient air concentration of PM-10 without policy $= C_{\mathrm{N}}$
Ambient air concentration of PM-10 with policy $= C_{\mathrm{P}}$
Indoor air concentration without policy $= C_{\mathrm{IN}}$
Indoor air concentration with policy $= C_{\mathrm{IP}}$

In order to translate the actual emissions at multiple origins into the ambient concentration level of the respective pollutant at a specific locality, we need the dispersion coefficients, which take into account the effects of wind speed and direction, atmospheric turbulence, etc. Usually, these coefficients are obtained using air dispersion modeling. For this paper, since we are evaluating a country-wide average concentration level, we made the important assumption that the contribution by the sources of pollution to the ambient concentration of PM-10 would be similar to their contributions at origin even after accounting for the air dispersion effects.

From the Pollution Control Division (PCD) in Thailand, we obtained the distribution of emission contributions by three sources: point source, line source and area source, corresponding to industrial, transportation, and background emissions. Their respective shares of total emissions emitted at origin (such as at the site of the factories) were reported as 9.78%, 53.94% and 36.28% in 1998.

Assuming the shares of final emissions with air dispersion effects do not depart significantly from the shares of emissions at source, we use 9.78, 53.94, and 36.28 for F_{I}, F_{T}, and C_{B}. The Source Terms, $ST_{\mathrm{N}}^{\mathrm{T}}$ and $ST_{\mathrm{N}}^{\mathrm{I}}$, correspond with total CO_2 emissions emitted by the transportation sectors and the industrial sectors. Note that the only "controllable" share of CO_2 emissions is therefore about 64% of total CO_2 emissions, assuming that background emissions C_{B} is relatively unaffected by the policy. The $ST_{\mathrm{N}}^{\mathrm{T}}$ and $ST_{\mathrm{N}}^{\mathrm{I}}$ information is part of the CGE model outputs under the baseline scenario. With this information, we are able to solve for the dispersion coefficients, Ks (two equations and two unknowns, K_{I} and K_{T}):

$$F_{\mathrm{I}} = \frac{K_{\mathrm{I}}ST_{\mathrm{N}}^{\mathrm{I}}}{\left(K_{\mathrm{I}}ST_{\mathrm{N}}^{\mathrm{I}} + K_{\mathrm{T}}ST_{\mathrm{N}}^{\mathrm{T}} + C_{\mathrm{B}}\right)},$$

$$F_{\mathrm{T}} = \frac{K_{\mathrm{T}}ST_{\mathrm{N}}^{\mathrm{T}}}{\left(K_{\mathrm{I}}ST_{\mathrm{N}}^{\mathrm{I}} + K_{\mathrm{T}}ST_{\mathrm{N}}^{\mathrm{T}} + C_{\mathrm{B}}\right)}.$$

We obtained $K_{\mathrm{I}} = 0.000088$, $K_{\mathrm{T}} = 0.00507$. With these derived dispersion coefficients, we can then assess the ambient air concentration for PM-10 under the baseline scenario through the equation:

$$C_{\mathrm{N}} = K_{\mathrm{I}}ST_{\mathrm{N}}^{\mathrm{T}} + K_{\mathrm{T}}ST_{\mathrm{N}}^{\mathrm{T}} + C_{\mathrm{B}}.$$

The first term on the right expresses the contribution from industry, the second the contribution from transportation, and the third contribution from "background pollution". Under the policy scenario, the economic model will provide us with a new set of source terms. Using the source term information obtained as outputs from the model under the carbon tax scenario and the level of original ambient concentration C_n, we infer the ambient concentration of PM-10 under the carbon tax scenario, C_p, as follows:

$$C_P = C_N \cdot \left[\left(K_I ST_P^I + K_T ST_P^T + C_B \right) \Big/ \left(K_I ST_N^I + K_T ST_N^T + C_B \right) \right].$$

With this expression, we assume that the ambient concentration of PM-10 is proportional to the total source term. The indoor air concentration with a policy then is given by $C_{IP} = C_{PX} R$, where R is the ratio of indoor to outdoor air concentration (R is assumed invariant with policy). R is determined from measurements performed in Thailand. The time-weighted average concentration then equals the weighted sum of the outdoor and indoor concentrations, weighed by the fractions of time spent daily in those two settings.[h]

Based on the observation of Loomis, an epidemiologist and professor of Public Health at the University of North Carolina at Chapel Hill who is familiar with the PM-10 issues in Thailand, the indoor–outdoor concentration of PM-10 in Thailand should not vary by much for two reasons:

1. the fine size of the particulate matter of concern (less than 10 μm in diameter) which is better mixed indoor versus outdoor compared to coarser particulates, and
2. the level of air conditioned housing in Thailand is still relatively low, which makes it more likely for windows to be open and air exchanging between indoor and outdoor air. Given these reasons, we assume that R is equal to 1.

Given the baseline ambient PM-10 concentration of around 68 $\mu g/m^3$ for Thailand in 1998 (ADB, 1999), we were able to derive the post carbon tax PM-10 concentration, C_P, using the procedure laid out above to be around 66.8 $\mu g/m^3$.

3. Exposure–Response Model

Applying the 24–64 age group ERR for PM-10 to our context, with a drop of PM-10 concentration by 1.5 $\mu g/m^3$ or 2.2%, we get the following percentage change/reduction in mortality for the 24–64 age group:

$$\%\Delta H_{MT} = 0.1 \times 2.2(\mu g/m^3) = 0.22.$$

[h]According to Pearce (1996), an average adult in a developing country spends approximately 70% of his or her time indoors and 30% outdoors.

To translate it into the actual number of deaths attributable to exposure to PM-10 (rather than fractional or percentage change in deaths), for the 24–64 population (around 50% of total population in 1998), we go through the following procedure:

$$\Delta H_{\mathrm{MT}} = b \times \Delta \text{PM-10} \times \text{CMR} \times \text{POP}/100$$

(Pearce and Crowards, 1996)

$$\Delta H_{\mathrm{MT}} = 0.1 \times 2.2 \times (6.5/1000) \times 29410375/100$$
$$= 420(261, 547),$$

where ΔH_{MT} stands for the change in the number of mortality cases due to PM-10 exposures in a population (not the percentage change, as in the table above); b is the slope of the dose-response function and equals 0.062, 0.1, 0.13 respectively for lower, central and upper bounds (remember that the slope is in percentage change per μg/m^3). The ΔPM-10 term captures the average change in ambient PM-10 concentration (averaged over some geographic region or population used as the base for the health effects study). CMR is the Crude Mortality Rate for the entire population; applying to all deaths in the respective population exposed in 1998. Here, we assume the CMR for the total population is applicable to that for the 24–64 age population. Sensitivity analysis of using a 25% lower and higher CMR rate showed that the final results are robust to the central, higher, or lower CMR rate assumption.

According to the National Statistical Office of Thailand, the working population in Thailand is defined over a narrower range of 15–59 years of age.[i] In order to extract the incidence of mortality estimated for the 15–59 range from the 24–64 range, we go through two steps: First for the 24–59 range, we estimate its share out of the 24–64 range (67.9%) with respect to mortality (all causes) for Thailand in 1998 with data from the National Statistics Office, Thailand. Then for the 15–23 range, we assumed the mortality induced by exposure to PM-10 in this age range is the same as its relative share over mortality (all causes) vis-à-vis the 24–64 age group (around 10%).

ΔH_{MT} for the working age group 15–59 then becomes:

$$(420 \times 0.679) + 42 = 327. \quad (203, 425)$$

One important feature of the study is that the estimation leaves out long-term chronic effects, e.g. permanent impairment of lung function and the

[i](http://www.nso.go.th/gender/epop.htm).

development of diseases such as asthma and chronic obstructive pulmonary disease. This is appropriate given the short-term focus of our study — we consider only the acute effects resulting from short-term exposure to PM-10. More importantly, we are interested in the changes in these effects with the imposition of a carbon tax policy.

For morbidity calculation, we are informed by the ERRs for acute illnesses applied to short-term exposure to ambient PM-10 concentration. Table 1 lists the ERRs used for estimating the change in the cases of hospital admissions due to a change in PM-10 concentration after the carbon tax imposition.

Given the change in the ambient concentration of PM-10 by 1.5 $\mu g/m^3$ or 2.2% and a total population of 60,763,000, we can proceed to calculate probability weighted respiratory and cardiac hospital admission changes associated with a change in PM-10 concentration using the hospital admission exposure–response relationships for respiratory and cardiac hospital admissions.

Respiratory:

$$\begin{aligned}\Delta H_{\mathrm{RS}} &= [(0.0000028 \times \Delta\text{PM-10}) \times 0.333] + [(0.0000057 \times \Delta\text{PM-10}) \\ &\quad \times 0.334] + [(0.0000085 \times \Delta\text{PM-10}) \times 0.333] \times 60763000 \\ &= 757\end{aligned}$$

Cardiac:

$$\begin{aligned}\Delta H_{\mathrm{RS}} &= [(0.0000028 \times \Delta\text{PM-10}) \times 0.333] + [(0.000005 \times \Delta\text{PM-10}) \\ &\quad \times 0.334] + [(0.0000072 \times \Delta\text{PM-10}) \times 0.333] \times 60763000 \\ &= 668\end{aligned}$$

Table 1. Exposure–Response Functions for Hospital Admissions Associated with PM-10 in Thailand

Health Effect Category	Annual Number of Cases Per Person Per 1 $\mu g/m^3$ Change in Annual Average PM-10 (Probability Weight for Average PM-10 Scenarios in Parentheses)
Respiratory hospital admissions	Low: 2.8×10^{-6} (33.3%) Central: 5.7×10^{-6} (33.4%) High: 8.5×10^{-6} (33.3%)
Cardiac hospital admissions	Low: 2.8×10^{-6} (33.3%) Central: 5.0×10^{-6} (33.4%) High: 7.2×10^{-6} (33.3%)

Source: Chestnut *et al.* (1998)

Again, only a fraction of these applies to the 15–59 working population. Based on NSO data, 44.5% of total reported illnesses in 1998 can be attributed to the 15–59 population. We apply this percentage to derive the respiratory and cardiac hospital admissions changes induced by a change in the ambient concentration of PM-10 to the 15–59 age group: $(0.445 \times 757) = 337$; $(0.445 \times 668) = 297$.

Knowing the mortality and hospital admissions effects of the change in PM-10 concentration, we then want to translate these into labor supply and medical expenditures impacts.

3.1. *Labor Impact and Medical Cost Analysis*

From the former step, we derived the change in the incidences of respiratory and cardiovascular illnesses and premature mortality as a result of a change in ambient air concentrations. Policy analysts would often try to quantify the benefits/costs associated with a change in health status. The major economic benefits/costs are labor productivity gains/losses and medical treatment savings/costs due to a health status change.

With respect to labor change, we adopt an approach similar to that used by Rosendahl (1998) with "reduced activity days" (RADs). With respect to medical costs, we use the hospital admission exposure–response rate (ERRs) results from the morbidity assessment above, coupled with the average costs information for medical and health costs incurred on each type of hospital admission to estimate total costs saved. The estimation of medical costs is for the purpose of cross-checking the resulted reduction in medical expenditure which is captured endogenously by the CGE model.

For the analysis of reduced PM-10 concentration on labor supply, we assume the change does not apply to rural or agricultural household but applies only to two urban household categories: non-agricultural and government-employed.

The change in labor supply includes permanent and temporary change in the availability of workers at the job. In terms of temporary change, there are two components — the days of work lost (due to sick leaves, hospital visits, etc.) and reduced productivity at work both of which cause a temporary effect on labor supply. In terms of permanent effect on labor, the premature mortality avoided due to lowered PM-10 concentration estimated from the last section will add to the "baseline" quantity of labor.

To assess the temporary change in labor supply (both days lost and productivity reduction), we will use a dose-response function that links changes in PM-10 concentration directly to the changes in the RADs.

Using the Dose-Response function for RADs for the working age population from 15–59, developed by Ostro (1994), we will go through the following steps:

- 1 unit rise in PM-10 leads to an increase of 0.058 RAD per person per year or 0.00016 RAD per person per day (Ostro, 1994).
- 62% of all RAD are bed-disability days (100% productivity loss).
- The other 38% are Minor RAD or MRAD (10% productivity loss).
- Multiplying 0.058 by the average wage of the working population, we can get an estimate of the value of work lost per year. The shares of bed-disability days and MRAD can be assessed.

The current policy simulation results in a reduction in PM-10 concentration of 1.5 $\mu g/m^3$ or a drop by 2.2%. This leads to a saved RAD of 0.1276 (0.058×2.2) RAD per person per year. Out of this, 62% are bed-disability days saved, and the rest Minor RAD or MRAD saved.

There are three household types supplying total labor based on the 1998 Social Accounting Matrix for Thailand: Non-agricultural households (HH-NAG), Agricultural households (HH-AGR),[j] and Government-employed households (HH-Gov). The average annual incomes for these households in 1998 were 183275.8, 64454, and 177640.

Total labor saved (sum of labor gained due to avoided mortality and avoided RAD and MRAD) was multiplied by wage to get the labor saving in value term. This is because the dose–response rate or ERR applied for RAD was estimated for the United States (Ostro, 1994). When applied to Thailand, we scale it by the ratio of U.S. Purchasing Power Parity (PPP) to Thai PPP to get the adjusted outcome.[k] The total labor saved in value term for Thailand is estimated to be 1,290,952,484 baht, which is about 8% of the baseline. The U.S. PPP per capita over the Thai PPP per capita in 1998 equals 5.29.[l] Dividing the percentage above by 5.29, we then derive the adjusted total labor saved as around 1.5%.

[j]Again, we do not assume the labor in this household category is affected by the change in the ambient concentration of PM-10. We provide the average income for this household group here as general information.

[k]Pearce and Crowards (1996b), when applying the same ERR for RAD by Ostro (1994) to UK, scaled it by the ratio of U.S. GDP per capita to UK GDP per capita to get the adjusted outcome for UK.

[l]http://www.worldbank.org/data/wdi2000/pdfs/tab1_1.pdf

In terms of relative contributions to total labor supply change, pre-mature mortality change contributes a minimal share (1%) and the change in RAD contributes the bulk of the change in total labor supply (99%). This is observed for the labor from both non-agricultural and government-employed labor categories.

Health impairments due to ambient air exposures demand resources through medical treatment as well. When the health effects incidence caused by air toxic exposures declines, the resources originally spent for health treatment can be used for other purposes. Exposure to PM-10 will result in illnesses for which workers will seek hospital care. Reduction in ambient air pollution concentration of PM-10 will, therefore, lower the case of illnesses and lower the medical expenditures component of the CGE.

One way to quantify this impact is by using the hospital admissions ERR. For Thailand, we have calculated the changes in cardiovascular and respiratory hospital admissions due to a change in ambient PM-10 concentration. The results here recaptured are:

Respiratory hospital admissions are lowered by 337 cases:

$$\Delta H_{\mathrm{RS}} = 337$$

Cardiac hospital admissions are lowered by 297 cases:

$$\Delta H_{\mathrm{CD}} = 297$$

With the ERR information, we will next require hospital data on the mean length of stay[m] and mean total charge[n] for the two disease categories: respiratory and cardiovascular in Thailand. With this information, we can figure out the total medical charges per year for the two respective disease categories. Unfortunately, we were unable to find the MLOS and Mean total charge data for Thailand; instead we acquired such information for the U.S. and scaled it by the purchasing power parity per capita ratio between the U.S. and Thailand to obtain similar information.

---

[m]Mean length of stay (LOS) is calculated by dividing the sum of inpatient days by the number of patients within the DRG category (Diagnosis-related groups (DRGs) are a classification of hospital case types into groups expected to have similar hospital resource use). Inpatient days are calculated by subtracting day of admission from day of discharge, so persons entering and leaving a hospital on the same day have a length of stay of zero (http://www.ahcpr.gov/data/hcup/94drga.htm).

[n]Mean total charge is calculated by dividing the sum of patient charges by the number of patients within the DRG category. Total charges represent the dollar amount charged for the hospitalization rather than the amount paid or the actual costs to provide the care. Physician payments are not included. (http://www.ahcpr.gov/data/hcup/94drga.htm).

With 337 as the total number of annual hospital admissions for respiratory diseases attributable to PM-10 exposure and 297 as the total number of annual hospital admissions for cardiovascular diseases attributable to PM-10 exposure, we next obtained the mean length of stay associated with each of the two types of hospital admissions. After calculation, the numbers are 5.39 for respiratory admissions and 5.37 for cardiac admissions; then we have $337 \times 5.39 = 1816$ total number of bed-days stayed in hospitals for respiratory admissions attributable to PM-10 exposure and $297 \times 5.37 = 1597$ total number of bed-days for cardiac hospital admissions attributable to PM-10 exposure.

We then need the mean total charge for each of the two types of admissions. After calculations, we get the mean 311 baht (US$1646 in 1998 divided by 5.29) per bed day on average for respiratory admissions and 370 baht (US$1846 in 1998 divided by 5.29) per bed day on average for cardiovascular admissions; this gives us 601,407 baht of medical costs for respiratory admissions attributable to PM-10 exposures and 590,973 baht of medical costs for cardiovascular admissions attributable to PM-10 exposures. The total medical costs incurred by particulate induced hospital admissions in 1998 in Thailand therefore add up to 1,192,381 baht.

3.2. *Feeding Back Labor Supply and Medical Expenditure Change into the Model*

Previous studies would normally stop here by reporting the value of the increase/decrease in labor-supply as the health benefits/costs of mitigating GHG. In this paper, however, we feed back the change in labor supply as well as the change in medical spending information into the CGE model to evaluate the secondary general equilibrium effect of these ancillary benefits and costs.

The change in labor supply (output from the previous step) will lead to an adjustment in the amount of labor in the primary factor sector of labor (an input sector in the economic model). Since the health improvement results in a gain of 1.5% of labor in value per year, the labor supply (in value term) will be multiplied by a factor of 1.015.

The change in medical expenditures due to a change in total emissions (CO_2 and therefore PM-10 as an ancillary effect) is automatically taken into account by the model given the model structure which endogenizes the consumption of medical commodity as a function of total pollution emitted.

With a 20% reduction in CO_2, we observe an ancillary reduction in PM-10 emissions by 3.72%, which is translated into a 2.2% reduction in the ambient concentration of PM-10. This leads to a 1.5% increase in total labor supply, applicable only to labor belonging to non-agricultural and government-employed households. A 0.3–2.5% reduction in the consumption of health and medical services is the other effect of reduced ambient PM-10 endogenized in the CGE model.

With the imposition of a GHG mitigation policy such as a carbon tax, the CO_2 emitting production and consumption activities are made to "internalize" the private and social costs of pollution emissions. This has varied cost and benefit implications to different stakeholders, some becoming evident over time and others evident immediately after policy imposition. A CGE model is able to capture the direct costs to economic efficiency which result in a reduction in GDP. It can also capture the indirect benefits of improved labor health and reduced medical expenditures in the form of an increase in GDP.[o] Thus, a CGE model automatically generates estimates of the tradeoffs between these specific economic benefits and costs and yields the net GDP change. In the proposed project, we are interested in comparing the net GDP change under the policy scenario vis-à-vis that under the baseline/no policy scenario. More importantly, we want to compare the net GDP under the "policy scenario with health feedback" vs. the "policy scenario without health feedback". We expect to see that by including the positive health feedback, the net GDP change would be more positive. By including more fully the benefit side of GHG mitigating policy (such as the health improvement feedback and allowing its effect to play out in the economy), we may see a much more positive effect of GHG mitigating policies on GDP and therefore a more accurate policy advice to middle-income countries like Thailand.

Based on the model outputs, we observe 45% less reduction in GDP with the CO_2 tax when the feedback is taken into account. With the feedback, we also observe a slightly greater trade composition change: with relatively less reduction in exports/imports of clean goods than that of dirty goods. Aside from the composition effects, with the feedback the carbon tax induces greater input substitution away from polluting energy intermediates to both non-energy intermediates and other factors (technology effect). Table 2 captures

[o]The health effects considered in the current paper do not include the quality of life benefits associated with environmental risk reduction. Should such valuation data be available, they could be incorporated at the social welfare analysis stage. Not taking into account the quality of life, benefits in the policy analysis means we will underestimate the local health benefits of GHG mitigation.

Table 2. Economic Impact Comparison

	Tax Vs. No Policy (%)	(Tax + Feedback) Vs. No Policy (%)
GDP	−1.2	−0.66
Exports (total)	−2.5	−2.1
Exports of pollution intensive goods	−2.6	−2.2
Exports of goods from non-pollution intensive industries	−0.8	−0.3
Exports of agricultural goods	−0.5	−0.3
Exports of service	+0.2	+0.7
Imports (total)	−3.4	−2.8
Imports of pollution intensive goods	−3.7	−3.2
Imports of goods from non-pollution intensive industries	−2.5	−1.6
Imports of agricultural goods	−2.1	−1.5
Imports of service	−2.6	−2.0

these differences under the "no feedback" and "with feedback" scenarios. All effects are nominal. Production changes are captured by total production in nominal terms.

4. Social Welfare Analysis

In addition to examining the aggregate criterion of GDP, it is important to compare the income distribution effects of the policy with and without the health feedback. In terms of health, non-agricultural households and government-hired households are likely to gain more from a carbon emission reduction policy (as opposed to agricultural households) since the secondary effects of reduced local air pollution will mostly benefit the urban population. However, due to the lack of air dispersion modeling data, we cannot trace location specific pollution change and location specific welfare change in terms of health. We can, however, evaluate income distribution changes as a result of the carbon tax.

Here the welfare effects were measured using Equivalent Variation (EV). Household EV are measured by total nominal consumption, and industrial EV by total nominal production. Table 3 reports the welfare effects.

Table 3. Welfare Change Comparison

	Tax Vs. No Policy (%)	Tax + Feedback Vs. No Policy (%)
Households		
Agricultural	−2.6	−1.8
Non-agricultural	−2.2	−1.0
Government-hired	+1.7	+2.4
Energy intensive industries	−0.04	−0.03
Non-energy intensive industries	−0.21	−0.17
Energy producers	−0.26	−0.25
Transportation industries	−0.03	−0.02
Agricultural sectors	−0.023	−0.02
Service sectors	−0.01	−0.005

With respect to effects of the carbon tax on household welfare measured with EV (in nominal value), we see around 50% less effect of the tax when the health feedback is included across household categories. This has already factored in the effect of recycling the carbon tax revenue for reducing income taxes. The higher EV observed for government-hired households is the artifact of the revenue recycling scheme which compensates government-hired households by a relatively greater share than the other two households.

Some sectoral welfare distribution information is also provided. Not surprisingly, lower levels of production are observed for most pollution-intensive manufacturing sectors when the tax is imposed.[p] However, the welfare effects of the carbon tax on these and all other sectors are lessened when the health feedback is incorporated.

5. Conclusion

The previous literature on ancillary benefits of GHG mitigation policies tends to understate the social welfare benefits by not including the ancillary ones. This in part has led to insufficient GHG mitigation in certain countries. These include middle-income countries (e.g. Thailand, Malaysia, Brazil and China) that have highly polluted mega-cities where labor forces are concentrated. The purpose of the study is not to claim that local health benefits from saved acute health effects can or cannot justify GHG mitigation. Rather, we discuss how an

[p]On the extreme side, we observe up to 28% reduction for the production of basic metal and a 19% reduction for the production of plastic and rubber.

important benefit of addressing GHG emission — the local health effects — should and can be incorporated using the approaches laid out. The study can be seen as an effort to better inform decision-makers in developing countries on the "real" costs of addressing GHG emissions are (which, when the benefits are better included, are naturally lower).

This paper considers the question: By capturing the local health effects of reduced air toxins as a secondary effect of reducing GHG emissions, and allowing this benefit to feed-back into the economy, do we observe any change in the desirability of policies aimed at GHG emissions reduction from the standpoint of social welfare benefits? The study explored the specific policy of a carbon tax. The results of the study show that when these important ancillary benefits of reducing GHG emissions are captured, we observe the following impacts:

1. 45% less impact on GDP;
2. emissions reductions through a "cleaner" trade composition and more pronounced substitution of energy inputs with non-energy and factor inputs; and
3. on average, 28% less welfare effect across households and producer sectors excluding government-employed households which experience a net gain in welfare under both scenarios, but a 40% higher one under the "with feedback" scenario.

These results are robust under lower and higher bound values for the input substitution elasticity values, CMR used for the 15–59 population, and the slope for the mortality and morbidity dose-response functions. Some caveats are necessary. This paper does not attempt to include all possible secondary effects of GHG mitigation. Secondary effects not included are those on chronic health, ecosystems, visibility and traffic accidents, and related quality of life improvements. This will be left for future work.

With respect to data quality, the health evaluations of acute morbidity effects rely on exposure–response rates established for the US and Canada and are adjusted by income level for Thailand. This has the potential of over-estimating the effects.

Regarding methodology, for the ambient and indoor PM-10 concentration estimations, the study employed an empirical model rather than an air dispersion model. Information on the shares of PM-10 contributions from transportation/construction, industrial, and background sources were acquired from the pollution control division of Thailand, and these shares were assumed fixed. Such an approach does not take into account the meteorological factors affecting pollution emitted from the industrial and transportation sources. This could lead to over- or under-estimation of the ambient average concentration of PM-10.

Acknowledgments

The author would like to thank Sherman Robinson, Xinshen Diao, and Hans Lofgren at TMD, IFPRI, and Professors Douglas Crawford-Brown and Mort Webster at the University of North Carolina at Chapel Hill for their comments on an earlier version.

References

Anderson K, and Blackhurst R, 1992. *The Greening of World Trade Issues.* University of Michigan Press: Ann Arbor.

Armington P, 1969. "A theory of demand for products distinguished by place of production." *IMF Staff Papers* **16**: 159–178.

Birdsall N, and Wheeler D, 1992. "Trade policy and industrial pollution in latin America: where are the pollution havens?" In: *International Trade and the Environment* (Low P, ed.) World Bank Discussion Paper No. 159. The World Bank Washington.

Braga CAP, 1992. "Tropical forests and trade policy: the case of Indonesia and Brazil." In: *International Trade and the Environment* (Low P, ed.) World Bank Discussion Paper No. 159. The World Bank Washington.

Chestnut LG, Ostro BD, Nuntavarn V-V, Adit L, Wichai A, Smith KR, and Tsai FC, 1998. "Executive summary: Health effects of particulate matter air pollution in Bangkok." Prepared for Air Quality and Noise Management Division, Pollution Control Department. Bangkok, Thailand.

Copeland BR, and Taylor SM, 1993. "Trade and transboundary pollution." University of British Columbia Discussion Paper, No. 93-42.

Copeland BR, and Taylor SM, 1994. "North-south trade and the environment." *Quart. J. Econ.* **109**: 755–787.

Copeland BR, and Taylor SM, 1995. "Trade and the environment: a partial synthesis." *Am. J. Agri. Econ.* 77: 765–771.

Cropper ML, and Frances GS, 1990. "Valuing future risks to life." *J. Environ. Econ. Management*, **19(2)**: 160–175.

Dallas B, and Toman M, 2000. "Ancillary benefits of greenhouse gas mitigation policies." Climate Change Issues Brief No. 7. Resources for the Future, Washington, D.C.

Dervis K, de Melo J, and Robinson S, 1982. *General Equilibrium Models for Development Policy.* Cambridge University Press, 1982. Reprinted by the World Bank, 1989.

Dessus S, and Maurizio B, 1998. "Is there a trade-off between trade liberalization and pollution abatement?" *J. Policy Modeling* **20(1)**: 11–31.

EIAa. "Emissions of greenhouse gases in the United States." http://www.eia.doe.gov/oiaf/1605/1605aold.html.

EIAb. "Assumptions to the annual energy outlook 201 — table 2. carbon dioxide emission factors." http://www.eia.doe.gov/oiaf/aeo/assumption/tb12.html.

Food Market Exchange, 2001. "Thailand's proposal for the fourth WTO ministerial conference." http://www.foodmarketexchange.com/datacenter/laws/detail/dc_1r_reference_Doha.html.

Garbaccio RF, Ho MS, and Jorgenson DW, 2000. "Modeling the health benefits of carbon emissions reductions in China." Preliminary Draft, Kennedy School of Government, Harvard University, Cambridge, MA.

Hettige H, Lucas REB, and Wheeler D, 1992. "The toxic intensity of industrial production: global patterns, trends and trade policy." *Am. Econ. Rev.* **82**.

Lee H, and Roland-Holst D, 1997. "International trade and the transfer of environmental cost and benefits." In: *Applied Trade Policy Modeling* (Francois J, and Reinert K, eds.) Cambridge University Press: Cambridge.

Lluch C, 1973. "The extended linear expenditure system." *Europ. Econ. Rev.* 4.

Lofgren H, Harris RL, and Robinson S, with the assistance ofThomas M, and El-Said M, 2001. "A standard computable general equilibrium (CGE) model in GAMS." Discussion Paper No. 75, Trade and Macroeconomics Division, International Food Policy Research Institute.

Low P, and Yeats A, 1992. "Do dirty industries migrate?" In: *International Trade and the Environment* (Low P, ed.) World Bank Discussion Paper No. 159. The World Bank: Washington.

Mahidol University, 1998. http://www.mahidol.ac.th/Thailand/economy/charac-econ.html.

Methakunavut N, and Jitsuchon S, 2001. "Productivity growth and external accounts in a computable general equilibrium model." Mimeo, Thailand Development Research Institute, Bangkok, Thailand.

OECD, 1993. *Environmental Policies and Industrial Competitiveness.* OECD Documents: Paris.

Pearce D, 1996. "Economic valuation and health damage from air pollution in the developing world." *Energy Policy* **24**(7): 627–630.

Perroni C, and Wigle RM, 1994. "International trade and environmental quality: how important are the linkages?" *Can. J. Econ.* **27**: 551–567.

Rosendahl KE, 1998. "Health effects of air pollution and impacts on economic activity." In: *Social Costs of Air Pollution and Fossil Fuel Use — A Macroeconomic Approach* (Rosendahl KE, ed.).

TDRI, 2000. "The construction of computable general equilibrium." A paper submitted to National Economic and Social Development Board (NESDB). (in Thai).

Thanh BD, and Lefevre T, 2000. "Assessing health impacts of air pollution from electricity generation: the case of thailand." *Environ. Impact Assessment Rev.* **20**: 137–158.

Tobey JA, 1990. "The effects of domestic environmental policies on patterns of world trade: an empirical test." *Kyklos* **43**: 191–210.

Warr PG, 1998. "Estimation of elasticity of substitution/transformation between domestic and imported/exported commodities." Australian National University (ANU).

Appendix 1.

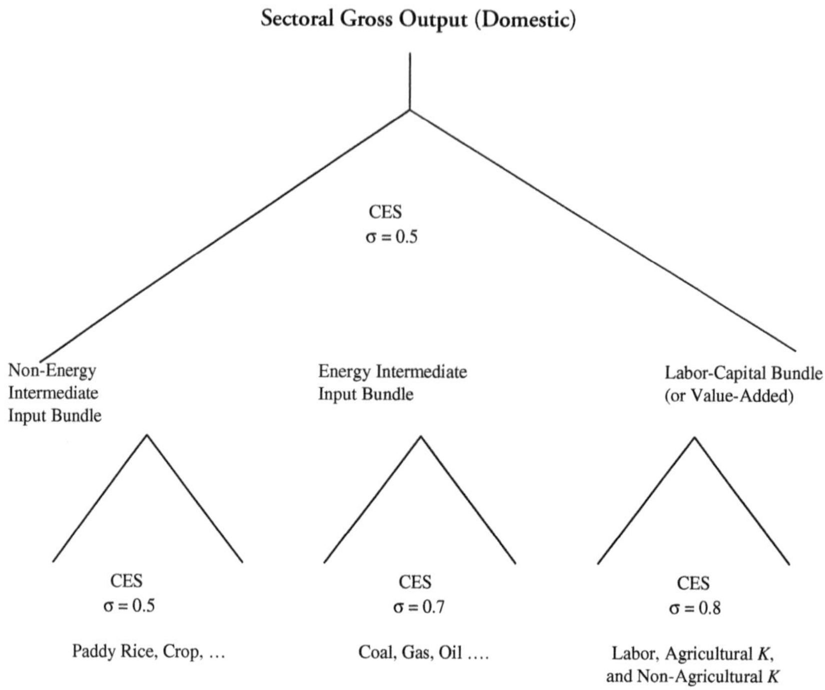
Sectoral Gross Output (Domestic)
CES
σ = 0.5
Non-Energy Intermediate Input Bundle
Energy Intermediate Input Bundle
Labor-Capital Bundle (or Value-Added)
CES
σ = 0.5
CES
σ = 0.7
CES
σ = 0.8
Paddy Rice, Crop, …
Coal, Gas, Oil ….
Labor, Agricultural K, and Non-Agricultural K

Appendix 2.

Table A1. Particulate Matter Combustion Emission Coefficients (Tons of PM Per kg of Coal and Lignite, Per scf of Petroleum Natural Gas, and Per Liter of Gasoline)

Sectors	COALIG	PTRONG	GASLNE	Sectors	COALIG	PTRONG	GASLNE
PADDY	1.50×10^{-5}	3.67×10^{-16}	9.48×10^{-11}	BASMTL	9.1×10^{-7}	8.92×10^{-17}	2.30×10^{-10}
OCROP	1.50×10^{-5}	3.67×10^{-16}	9.48×10^{-11}	FABMTL	8.88×10^{-7}	1.98×10^{-17}	5.48×10^{-12}
VGFRU	1.50×10^{-5}	3.67×10^{-16}	9.48×10^{-11}	MACHIN	3.21×10^{-6}	7.93×10^{-17}	2.02×10^{-11}
OAGR	1.50×10^{-5}	3.67×10^{-16}	9.48×10^{-11}	ELCMNU	3.21×10^{-6}	7.93×10^{-17}	2.02×10^{-11}
LIVSTK	1.50×10^{-5}	3.67×10^{-16}	9.48×10^{-11}	TRANEQ	3.21×10^{-6}	7.93×10^{-17}	2.02×10^{-11}
FISHIN	1.50×10^{-5}	3.67×10^{-16}	9.48×10^{-11}	OINDST	9.90×10^{-6}	2.48×10^{-16}	6.24×10^{-11}
COALIG	3.55×10^{-6}	8.92×10^{-17}	2.23×10^{-11}	ELCITY	5.22×10^{-6}		2.20×10^{-10}
PTRONG	3.55×10^{-6}	8.92×10^{-17}	2.23×10^{-11}	CONSTR	1.50×10^{-5}	3.67×10^{-16}	9.48×10^{-11}
OMINE	3.55×10^{-6}	8.92×10^{-17}	2.23×10^{-11}	TRADE	1.50×10^{-5}	3.67×10^{-16}	9.48×10^{-11}
MEAT	7.99×10^{-6}	1.98×10^{-16}	5.06×10^{-11}	RESTAU	1.50×10^{-5}	3.67×10^{-16}	9.48×10^{-11}
CANFDS	7.99×10^{-6}	1.98×10^{-16}	5.06×10^{-11}	HOTEL	1.50×10^{-5}	3.67×10^{-16}	9.48×10^{-11}
OFOOD	7.99×10^{-6}	1.98×10^{-16}	5.06×10^{-11}	TRANLD	1.50×10^{-5}	3.67×10^{-16}	9.48×10^{-11}
OAGRPD	1.50×10^{-5}	3.67×10^{-16}	9.48×10^{-11}	TRANOC	1.50×10^{-5}	3.67×10^{-16}	9.48×10^{-11}

Table A1. *(Continued)*

Sectors	COALIG	PTRONG	GASLNE	Sectors	COALIG	PTRONG	GASLNE
BEVER	7.99×10^{-6}	1.98×10^{-16}	5.06×10^{-11}	TRANWR	1.50×10^{-5}	3.67×10^{-16}	9.48×10^{-11}
TEXTLE	4.74×10^{-6}	1.19×10^{-16}	2.99×10^{-11}	TRANAR	1.50×10^{-5}	3.67×10^{-16}	9.48×10^{-11}
APPARL	1.12×10^{-6}	2.97×10^{-17}	7.16×10^{-12}	TRANOT	1.50×10^{-5}	3.67×10^{-16}	9.48×10^{-11}
LEAFOT	1.12×10^{-6}	2.97×10^{-17}	7.16×10^{-12}	COMMUN	1.50×10^{-5}	3.67×10^{-16}	9.48×10^{-11}
WOODPR	5.06×10^{-6}	2.48×10^{-16}	4.02×10^{-10}	BANKIG	1.50×10^{-5}	3.67×10^{-16}	9.48×10^{-11}
FURNIT	5.06×10^{-6}	2.48×10^{-16}	4.02×10^{-10}	INSURE	1.50×10^{-5}	3.67×10^{-16}	9.48×10^{-11}
PAPER	5.06×10^{-6}	2.48×10^{-16}	4.02×10^{-10}	RESTAT	1.50×10^{-5}	3.67×10^{-16}	9.48×10^{-11}
PRNTPB	5.06×10^{-6}	2.48×10^{-16}	4.02×10^{-10}	BUSISR	1.50×10^{-5}	3.67×10^{-16}	9.48×10^{-11}
BASCHM	2.52×10^{-6}	2.48×10^{-16}	6.38×10^{-10}	PUBADM	1.50×10^{-5}	3.67×10^{-16}	9.48×10^{-11}
GASLNE	1.44×10^{-6}	1.39×10^{-16}	3.63×10^{-10}	EDUCAT	1.50×10^{-5}	3.67×10^{-16}	9.48×10^{-11}
DEISEL	1.44×10^{-6}	1.39×10^{-16}	3.63×10^{-10}	HLTHMD	1.50×10^{-5}	3.67×10^{-16}	9.48×10^{-11}
AVIFUL	1.44×10^{-6}	1.39×10^{-16}	3.63×10^{-10}	NONPRF	1.50×10^{-5}	3.67×10^{-16}	9.48×10^{-11}
FULOIL	1.44×10^{-6}	1.39×10^{-16}	3.63×10^{-10}	RPAIRS	1.50×10^{-5}	3.67×10^{-16}	9.48×10^{-11}
NONMTL	1.77×10^{-6}	1.78×10^{-16}	4.48×10^{-10}	PERSSR	1.50×10^{-5}	3.67×10^{-16}	9.48×10^{-11}

Table A2. Particulate Matter Process Emission Coefficients (Tons Per Million Baht)

COALIG	0.12
PTRONG	0.12
MEAT	0.09
CANFDS	0.09
OFOOD	0.09
BEVER	0.09
TEXTLE	0.03
WOODPR	0.03
FURNIT	0.03
PAPER	0.03
PRNTPB	0.03
BASCHM	0.51
GASLNE	1.09
DEISEL	1.09
AVIFUL	1.09
FULOIL	1.09
NONMTL	2.23
BASMTL	0.88
FABMTL	0.03
MACHIN	0.09
TRANEQ	0.09
OINDST	1.3
ELCITY	0.39

Appendix 3.

From Source Term to PM-10 Concentration Calculation Flowchart

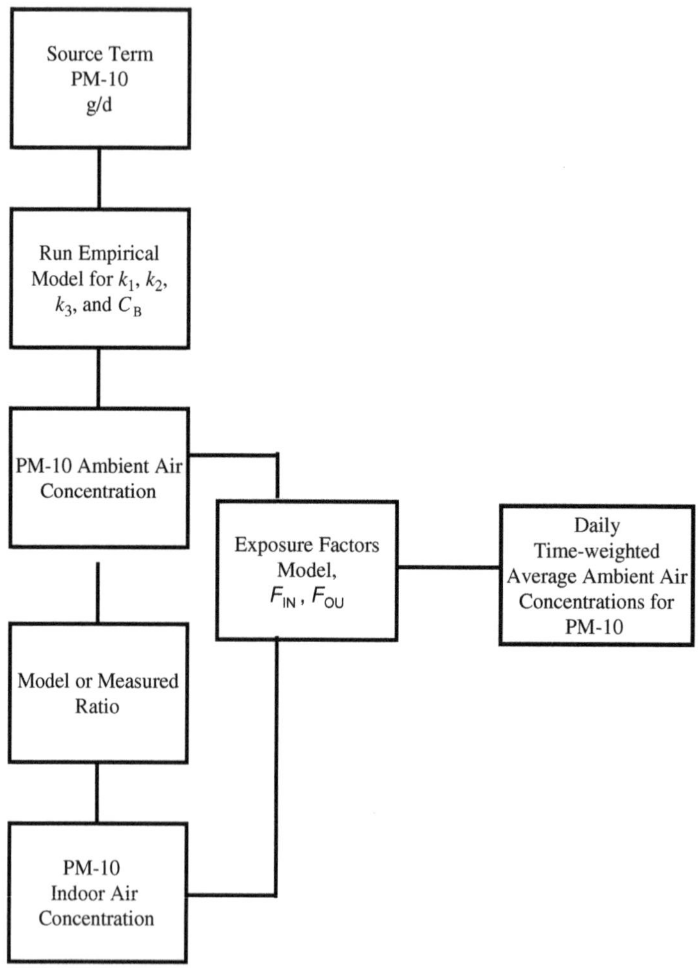

Chapter 9

Economic Analysis of Urban Land Use and Housing Supply: An Application of Urban Land Use and a CGE Model for Seoul*

EUIJUNE KIM

Department of Agricultural Economics and Rural Development, Seoul National University, Seoul, Korea

Regional Economics Applications Laboratory, University of Illinois, Urbana, IL, USA

JAEUK JU

Department of City and Regional Planning, Cornell University, Ithaca NY, USA

This paper assesses economic effects of housing supplies on the urban growth and income distribution of Seoul, using an urban land use and Computable General Equilibrium (CGE) model of Seoul economy. The simulation shows that the housing development with the transformation of the green or the industrial land uses into the residential land use leads to an increase of the Gross Regional Product (GRP) by approximately 1% at the worse income inequality. The aggregate welfare effects in terms of Hicksian Compensating Variation range from 1.746 trillion Korean Won to 1.768 trillion Korean Won on a ten-period average, depending on the type of the land use re-designation.

*This chapter was originally published as "Growth and distributional impacts of urban housing supply: an application of urban land use and computable general equilibrium model of Seoul." In: *Review of Urban and Regional Development Studies*, Vol. 15, No. 1, March 2003, and is reprinted here with minor modifications upon the permission from the publisher.

1. Introduction

Local and national governments of Korea have innovated a number of growth management instruments for controls of urban land uses and economic activities to discourage an excessive concentration of population on a few large cities including Seoul (Kim and Gallent, 1998; Cho, 2002). In the early 1970s, the Restricted Development Zone (RDZ) was designated around 14 large cities in order to preserve their open space and farmlands from urban sprawl and leapfrog development, covering 5.4% of the national land areas.[a] In the 1990s, congestion charges were imposed in Seoul on the development of either new offices with floor space in excess of 25,000 m^2 or commercial buildings with floor space in excess of 15,000 m^2. The government has set an upper limit on the floor space sizes of the new construction and the expansion of existing facilities to promote the redevelopment of industrial estates (Levin, 1999; Cho, 2002). One of adverse consequences of spatial restrictions on urban development is a substantial increase in housing price because of a lack of housing supply. The ratio of housing supply to demand has remained at about 80%, much lower than the national average in the 1990s. The Seoul government announced plans to construct 100 thousand units of housing in 2002 in order to meet the housing needs. Recently, urban housing policy has been more concerned with housing quality and demand side of residential redevelopment rather than increase of housing stock (Jang, 2001). For example, more than 100,000 squatters and substandard housing units replaced with 217,000 new units in 228 renewal districts of Public Substandard Housing Renewal Program of Seoul (Kim, 2001).

This paper attempts to analyze economic effects of housing supply on the growth and income distribution of Seoul, developing an urban land use and Computable General Equilibrium (CGE) model for Seoul's economy. In the sense that a housing unit consists of both land and building structure, the residential development can lead to changes in not only construction activities, but also land productivity. That is, the economic impacts of the housing supply depend on investment expenditures as well as land development approaches, such as urban regeneration and urban sprawl. We perform three types of counter-factual analysis based on type of land transformation for the residential land uses. The model integrates an urban land supply module with an applied version of an elasticity structuralist CGE model to focus on the institutional

[a]It is composed of forestry (61.6% of total RDZs), agricultural land (24.0% of total RDZs), and housing and miscellaneous development land (14.4% of total RDZs) (Gallent and Kim, 2001).

structure of Seoul urban economy. The model can capture a cause-and-effect relationship between urban economic development and land use by specifying the behavior of economic agents such as eight producers, five income groups, and the Seoul and national government. The simulation can identify which type of land use transformation for housing supply should deserve high priority in terms of income growth, welfare and the income distribution in the long run. In this paper, we begin with a brief review of CGE models related to the housing and land policies. We then present a structure of our CGE model to examine the land use policy impacts on Seoul's economy. In the next sections, we measure the effects of housing investments and land use re-designation on the economic growth and income inequality of Seoul, discussing policy implications and further research directions in terms of model structure.

2. CGE Model for Urban Economy and Land Use of Seoul

2.1. *Literature Review*

CGE models have been applied to various economic issues such as international trade, public finance, agriculture, structural adjustment policies, and income distribution, growing in popularity as an analytic framework of the regional economies (Partridge and Rickman, 1998; Devarajan and Robinson, 2002). However, only a few CGE models have been developed to address impacts of land and housing development policies. Luk (1991) was one of the pioneer works to demonstrate how the housing market could be incorporated into the CGE model. The urban housing market module was modeled with indivisibility and a fixed-point algorithm in a framework of general equilibrium theory. Housing was interpreted as a discrete unit, with a household having a preference for housing characteristics. The Logit model was applied to solve the problem of rigid household response and of the discontinuity in the discrete choice model. The numerical simulation showed that the CGE model could trace changes in land rent, housing price and population density gradient. Hofe (2002) assessed the policy impact of supply- and demand-side housing policies on New York's economy. The housing policies included mortgage rate reductions, property tax reductions, public housing investment, and allowance and voucher programs. The CGE model was static and neoclassical, following a trade-focused structuralist approach. The housing market was linked with the residential construction sector, the owner-occupied housing sector and the real estate market. Bye and Avitsland (2003) analyzed the welfare effect of imposing a neutral system of housing taxation between the housing capital and the financial capital (an increase in the marginal effective tax rate on housing capital), using an inter-temporal CGE model for the Norwegian economy. The housing investment was financed by loans, and the user cost of capital for housing was mainly determined by that of owner-occupied housing. They revealed that the neutral housing tax reform gave an intra-temporal efficiency gain, but that this gain with lump sum rebating of the additional tax revenue could be less than the efficiency loss in the labor market and the inter-temporal efficiency loss.

With respect to the relationship between economic growth and land development via a natural resource policy, Wong and Alavalapati (2003) examined the potential economy-wide impact of forest carbon policy with US participation on the national economic welfare and the land use distribution for the US, employing a dynamic version of a Future Agricultural Resources Model composed of a CGE model and Geographic Information System (GIS). The land was differentiated into six classes in terms of climate characteristics, water supply, and length of growing season. They found that the establishment of carbon plantations in the US would have a small, but favorable impact on the overall economy, and particularly on the farm and forest sectors. US inaction with regard to ratifying the Kyoto Protocol might have a negative effect on the economy, particularly when taking into consideration the loss of benefits foregone. Olatubi and Hughes (2002) examined the impact of the Wetland Reserve Program on the regional economy of Louisiana, using a CGE model. They showed that the policy effects on output, the income, and prices were insignificant, recognizing the probable distributional impact of policy choices on factor owners.

2.2. *Structure of a CGE Model for Land Use Policy of Seoul's Economy*

The CGE model for Seoul is developed to assess the effect of housing investment and urban land use on urban economic growth and income distribution. The framework of the model draws on the structure of an elasticity structuralist model. That is, the model assumes an endogenous determination of price and quantity from market equilibrium under no excess profit, but limiting the degree of substitution in sectoral supplies and demands. In the Seoul CGE model, there are three economic regions: (1) Seoul; (2) the rest of the nation; and (3) the rest of the world. The regional agents are composed of producers, households, and Seoul and national governments. The production sector is divided into eight sub-sectors: (1) agriculture; (2) mining and manufacturing; (3) public utility; (4) construction; (5) wholesales; (6) transportation; (7) finance; and (8) other services. Urban land use is classified into (1) industrial land use, (2) commercial land use, (3) residential land use, and

(4) green land use including agricultural land use. Among them, the industrial and commercial land uses are factor inputs for mining and manufacturing production and the five service-relevant sectors, respectively. The residential land indirectly affects household utility levels through a change in the demand for housing consumption. However, there is no linkage between green land use and urban economic activity due to a data problem. The household is disaggregated into five groups based on income level: (1) low; (2) low-middle; (3) middle; (4) high-middle; and (5) high-income. Every agent is assumed to be a price-taker, and the equilibrium price is obtained by clearing any excess demand in labor, capital, and commodity markets. Each producer and household chooses an optimal set of factor inputs and commodity demand bundles under the maximization principles of constrained profit and private utility, respectively. We do not, however, impose an optimizing behavior on the government sector.

In the commodity market, each production sector produces a single representative commodity, assuming a constant return to scale and perfect competition. It implies that the supply price is equal to the marginal cost. We take into account the cross-hauling of commodities, reflecting their imperfect substitution and heterogeneity. Thus, the commodities to be consumed in Seoul market are (1) intra-regional supplies from Seoul, (2) interregional supplies from the rest of the nation, and (3) foreign imports in terms of the origin of the product. The commodities produced in Seoul are also classified into (1) intra-regional supplies to Seoul, (2) interregional supplies to the rest of the nation, and (3) foreign exports in terms of the destination of the product.

There are two broad categories of production inputs, primary factors and intermediate inputs, and the production structure consists of four-stages. At the top of the structure, the producer chooses quantities of intermediate demands and value-added using a fixed proportion to the gross output following Leontief production technology. In the next stage, the producer chooses an optimal set of labor and capital in order to produce a given level of the value-added using the production technology of Constant Elasticity of Substitution (CES). Each labor input is assumed to be homogeneous and intersectorally mobile, while the capital stock and land in each sector are fixed within the same period. Labor demand is derived from the producers' profit maximization activities subject to the total production cost in Eq. (5), with the average wage rate of each period depending on the consumer price level and the lagged wage rate. This wage indexation scheme can identify how total employment changes in response to wage level, while in general, the labor market can clear via either wage adjustment under the neoclassical closure rule (full employment condition) or quantity adjustment under Keynesian closure rule (fixed wage condition) (Thissen, 1999). These two stages allow for the substitution between labor, capital, and land, but no substitution among the intermediate inputs and production factors.

The third stage is concerned with the substitution between the demand for the domestic product and foreign imports. Namely, demand is satisfied with foreign imports and domestic products supplied by both Seoul and the rest of the nation. We employ the Armington function, which can distinguish the commodity by industry and place of origin under an assumption of a *small open economy*, specifying the imperfect substitutability between the commodities. The cost minimization with the Armington function leads to an optimal level of the import-domestic commodity ratio. The demand for foreign imports relies on the domestic product, the price of domestic product relative to the domestic price of foreign imports, the share parameter and the elasticity of substitution. At the final stage, the same specification as the case of international trade is applied to regional trade. Namely, the demand for the regional imports from the rest of the nation is determined by the relative price of two competing commodities of Seoul and the rest of the nation and the degree of the substitution.

The optimal allocation of the gross output into three types of commodities (intra-regional supply to Seoul, interregional supply to the rest of the nation, and foreign exports) is derived from profit maximization with a two-level Constant Elasticity of Transformation (CET) function. At the top stage, the ratio of foreign exports to gross output depends on the relative difference between the price of domestic product and the domestic price of foreign exports, the share parameter, and the elasticity of transformation under the revenue maximization. In the same manner, the regional export to the rest of the nation is determined by the relative ratio of two competing commodity prices, the quantity of the intra-regional supply of Seoul and the interregional trade elasticity. From this, we see the following:

$$\mathrm{SX}_i = \sum_j \mathrm{io}_{ji} \cdot \mathrm{SX}_i + \mathrm{VA}_i \tag{1}$$

$$\mathrm{VA}_i = A_i \cdot \left(\alpha_i \cdot \mathrm{L}_i^{-\rho_i} + \beta_i^K \cdot \mathrm{K}_i^{-\rho_i} + \beta_i^L \cdot \mathrm{KLI}_i^{-\rho_i}\right)^{-1/\rho_i} \tag{2}$$

$$\mathrm{XS}_i = \mathrm{AC}_i \cdot \left(\delta_i \cdot \mathrm{M}_i^{-\rho c_i} + (1-\delta_i) \cdot \mathrm{XDS}_i^{-\rho c}\right)^{-\frac{1}{\rho c_i}} \tag{3}$$

$$\mathrm{XDS}_i = \mathrm{ADC}_i \cdot \left(\delta d_i \cdot \mathrm{XLS}_i^{-\rho dc_i} + (1-\delta d_i) \cdot \mathrm{XSS}_i^{-\rho dc_i}\right)^{-\frac{1}{\rho dc_i}} \tag{4}$$

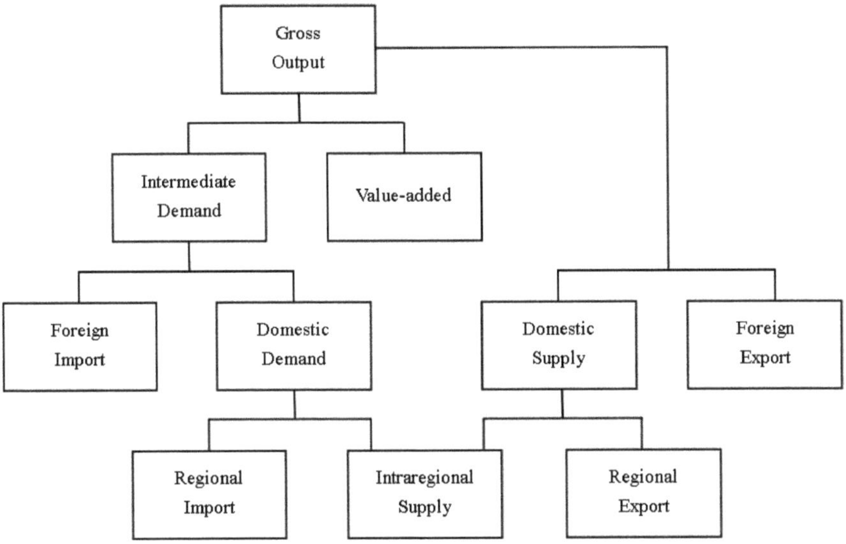

Fig. 1. Production Structure of the Seoul CGE Model

$$\mathrm{WA} \cdot \mathrm{wdist}_i \cdot \left(\alpha_i \cdot \mathrm{L}_i^{-\rho_i} + \beta_i^K \cdot \mathrm{K}_i^{-\rho_i} + \beta_i^L \cdot \mathrm{KLI}_i^{-\rho_i}\right)$$
$$= \mathrm{PX}_i \cdot \mathrm{VA}_i \cdot \alpha_i \cdot \mathrm{L}_i^{-(\rho_i+1)} \quad (5)$$

$$\mathrm{SX}_i = \mathrm{AT}_i \cdot \left(\gamma_i \cdot \mathrm{E}_i^{\rho t_i} + (1-\gamma_i) \cdot \mathrm{XSD}_i^{\rho t_i}\right)^{\frac{1}{\rho t_i}} \quad (6)$$

$$\mathrm{XSD}_i = \mathrm{ADT}_i \cdot \left(\gamma d_i \cdot \mathrm{XSL}_i^{\rho dt_i} + (1-\gamma d_i) \cdot \mathrm{XSS}_i^{\rho dt_i}\right)^{\frac{1}{\rho dt_i}} \quad (7)$$

where E_i = foreign export by sector; K_i = capital stock by sector; KLI_i = land input by sector; L_i = labor input by sector; M_i = demand for foreign import by sector; VA_i = value-added by sector; SX_i = gross output by sector; WA = average wage rate of Seoul; XS_i = demand for composite commodity for Seoul by sector; XDS_i = demand for domestic product by sector; XLS_i = demand for regional import by sector; XSD_i = domestic supply by sector; XSL_i = regional export to the rest of the nation by sector; XSS_i = intraregional supply to Seoul by sector; io_{ji} = input–output coefficients; wdist_i = wage proportionality by sector.

Total household income of each household group consists of wage, capital income and exogenous subsidy from the government. The total consumption amount is a linear function of the total household income, income tax rates of the national and Seoul governments and the marginal propensity to save. There are five consumption goods: (1) clothes; (2) food; (3) housing; (4) leisure; and (5) others. Consumption disposable income, price, and lagged consumption level are determinant factors of demand for consumption goods, with the residential land use variable additionally affecting the demand for housing service. The consumption expenditure by consumption commodity is transformed into private consumption by the industrial sector through a consumption matrix, which can keep the material balance in the demand side. Household savings is linearly dependent on the household disposable income with the marginal propensity to save.

For the consumption goods of clothes, food, leisure, and others:

$$\frac{\mathrm{YHCONN}^c_{h_t}}{P^c_{t-1}} = \mathrm{cles0}^c_h + \mathrm{cles1}^c_h \cdot \mathrm{YH}_h \cdot (1 - \mathrm{shtax}_h - \mathrm{nhtax}_h) + \mathrm{cles2}^c_w \cdot \frac{\mathrm{YHCONN}^c_{h_{t-1}}}{P^c_{t-1}} \tag{8}$$

For the consumption goods of housing:

$$\frac{\mathrm{YHCONN}^c_{h_t}}{P^c_{t-1}} = \mathrm{cles0}^c_h + \mathrm{cles1}^c_h \cdot \mathrm{YH}_h \cdot (1 - \mathrm{shtax}_h - \mathrm{nhtax}_h) + \mathrm{cles2}^c_w \cdot \mathrm{YHCONN}^c_{h_{t-1}} + \mathrm{cles3}^c_h \cdot \mathrm{LRESI} \tag{9}$$

where LRESI = area of residential land use; P^c_t = consumer price by commodity c in period t; YH_h = total incomes of household group h; $\mathrm{YHCONN}^c_{h_t}$ = consumption of commodity c by household group h in period t; shtax_h = income tax rate of Seoul government by household group h; nhtax_h = income tax rate of national government by household group h; $\mathrm{cles0}^c_h$, $\mathrm{cles1}^c_h$, $\mathrm{cles2}^c_h$, $\mathrm{cles3}^c_h$ = parameters in consumption equations.

A two-tier government structure is specified in the model: Seoul and national governments. The common revenue sources of both governments are household incomes and value-added of producer sectors, and their expenditure sources are composed of consumption expenditures, subsidies to producers and households, and savings. In addition, the government of Seoul receives a transfer from the national government to make up a government deficit, while the national government levies a tax on foreign imports. With respect to the macroeconomic closure rule for the capital market, aggregate savings determine total investments. Total savings consist of the household and government savings, the capital depreciation, and the foreign borrowings. The sectoral allocation of total investment by destination at the real term is determined by the capital price by sector and the allocation coefficient of investment, and is transformed into the sectoral investment by origin through a capital coefficient matrix.

$$\mathrm{GR} = \mathrm{TITAX} + \mathrm{HHTAX} + \mathrm{EGR} \tag{10}$$

$$\mathrm{GR} = \mathrm{GDTOT} + \mathrm{GOVSAV} + \mathrm{GOVSUB} \tag{11}$$

$$\begin{aligned}\mathrm{SAVINGS} = {} & \mathrm{HHSAV} + \mathrm{DEPRECIA} + \mathrm{GOVSAV} \\ & + \mathrm{FSAV} \cdot \mathrm{ER} + \mathrm{ECAP}\end{aligned} \tag{12}$$

where DEPRECIA = capital depreciation; ECAP = exogenous saving from the rest of the nation; ER = foreign exchange rate; EGR = transfer from national government; FSAV = net foreign borrowings; GR = total revenues of Seoul government; GDTOT = government consumption expenditure of Seoul government; GOVSAV = government savings of Seoul government; GOVSUB = government subsidy expenditure of Seoul government; HHSAV = household savings; HHTAX = direct tax revenue of Seoul government; SAVINGS = total savings; TITAX = value-added tax revenue of Seoul government.

The equilibrium between demand and supply for each commodity, labor, and capital flow is achieved by the fully flexible adjustment of the price in response to the excess demand. This price adjustment process is called an average cost pricing rule or marginal cost pricing rule under the assumption of constant returns to scale and profit maximization (Gottinger, 1998). For example, the composite commodity price is a weighted average of the price of domestic product and the domestic price of foreign imports, while the gross output price is that of the primary factor payment, the value-added tax rate, and the intermediate input prices.

$$\mathrm{P}_i \cdot \mathrm{XS}_i = \mathrm{PDS}_i \cdot \mathrm{XDS}_i + \mathrm{PM}_i \cdot \mathrm{M}_i \tag{13}$$

$$\mathrm{PDS}_i \cdot \mathrm{XDS}_i = \mathrm{PLS}_i \cdot \mathrm{XLS}_i + \mathrm{PSS}_i \cdot \mathrm{XSS}_i \tag{14}$$

$$\mathrm{PX}_i \cdot \mathrm{SX}_i = \mathrm{PSD}_i \cdot \mathrm{XSD}_i + \mathrm{PE}_i \cdot \mathrm{E}_i \tag{15}$$

$$\mathrm{PSD}_i \cdot \mathrm{XSD}_i = \mathrm{PSS}_i \cdot \mathrm{XSS}_i + \mathrm{PSL}_i \cdot \mathrm{XSL}_i \tag{16}$$

$$\mathrm{PX}_i \cdot (1 - \mathrm{sitax}_i - \mathrm{nitax}_i) = \mathrm{PVA}_i + \textstyle\sum_j \mathrm{io}_{ji} \cdot P_j \tag{17}$$

where P_i = composite commodity price by sector; PDS_i = price of domestic demand by sector; PE_i = domestic price of foreign export by sector; PLS_i = price of regional import by sector; PM_i = domestic price of foreign import by sector; PSD_i = price of domestic supply by sector; PSL_i = price of regional export by sector; PSS_i = price of intraregional supply by sector; PX_i = gross output price by sector; PVA_i = value-added price by sector; $sitax_i$ = indirect tax rate of Seoul government by sector; $nitax_i$ = indirect tax rate of national government by sector.

2.3. *Model Calibration*

The Seoul CGE model specifies the economic activities of production, consumption, savings and investment, government revenue and expenditure, international and interregional trades, and capital mobility in the real side economy. The development of the CGE model requires a benchmark data set that should be internally consistent with the overall economic activity. A SAM is satisfied with this condition, tracking the purchases and expenditures of services and commodities. In this paper, the starting point for the SAM was Han and Kim's (1999) Seoul SAM, whose sectoral classification has been modified based on compatibility of industry structure and availability of historical data. This modified SAM is treated as an initial equilibrium for the Seoul CGE model, providing useful information in calibrating parameters in the CGE model. The modified Seoul SAM consists of 13 accounts including production factor, household, production, Seoul and national governments, the rest of the nation, the rest of the world, investment and capital accumulation and so on.

In the Seoul CGE model, there are two kinds of parameters: structural coefficients and behavior parameters. The former is a set of point estimates based on the short-term observation and SAM, such as intermediate input coefficients, government expenditure shares, and saving and tax rates. The latter is the parameter derived from the historical data or long-term structural behavior of economic agents (Devarajan and Robinson, 2002). The behavior parameters include the elasticities of substitution and transformation in import demand functions and export supply functions, and the parameters of utility functions, sectoral household consumption functions and wage functions. All parameters should be adjusted so that the model can reproduce the benchmark data of 1995, given the values for policy variables.[b]

The CGE model is a recursive dynamic regional model composed of a within-period model and a between-period model. The within-period model

[b]The sensitivity analysis to test the robustness of the model shows that the Seoul CGE model is less responsive to the changes in the values of parameter of substitution and trade elasticities.

Table 1. Social Accounting Matrix of Seoul 1995 (Unit: Trillion Korean Won)

		1	2	3	4	5	6	7	8	9	10	11	12	13
1.	Labor input					42.76								
2.	Capital input					30.96								
3.	Household	42.76	30.96				0.06							
4.	Commodity			49.87										
5.	Production				49.87	69.01	5.54	25.64			129.52	20.43		
6.	Seoul Gov't			1.70		2.64	5.60			0.45				4.54
7.	Investment								25.64					
8.	Capital account			11.20		9.74						28.80		20.68
9.	National Gov't			11.02		5.14							5.78	
10.	Rest of Korea					84.74			44.78					
11.	Rest of world					49.23								
12.	Tariff					5.78								
13.	Others						3.73			21.48				

Source: Han and Kim (1999)

determines equilibrium quantities and prices under an objective and constraints of each economic agent, where the balance between supply and demand is achieved in a perfectly competitive market. The between-period model finds a sequent path of equilibrium of within-period model over the multiple periods using a stock-flow interaction. The within-period model is a square system of equation with 392 equations and 471 variables, including the exogenous variables such as foreign exchange rate, world market prices, and government expenditures. A unique solution can be found with the same number of endogenous variables as the equations, and the numeraire of the model is foreign exchange rate at nominal terms.

3. Economic Effects of Urban Land Use on Seoul's Economy

3.1. *Simulation*

Seoul contains about 605 km^2 of urban area: 302 km^2 of residential land use, 253 km^2 of green land use, 29 km^2 of industrial land use, and 21 km^2 of commercial land use. Over the last decade, there has been a substantial increase (8.3%) in the share of the residential land use in Seoul reducing the sizes of industrial and green land. This trend results from housing supply through land use re-designation.

This section measures the effects of housing investments and the allocation of urban land use on the economic growth and income distribution. For simplicity, we make four assumptions on the housing development based on Seoul government plan.

1. The total number of new housing units is 100,000, and the construction period is set at four years.
2. The type of dwelling is an apartment with 81 m^2 of the floor space size.
3. The ratio of total floor space size to lot size is 150%, and the total lot size of the new housing development is 5.4 km^2.
4. The total investment expenditure of the housing development is 1.27 trillion Korean won, and is financed by the private saving.

We set three alternatives based on the type of the land input for supplying 100,000 units of new housing as shown in Table 2.[c] The *green zone scenario* is to use 5.4 km^2 of the current green development zone as construction sites for housing development through land use transformation. In general, the

[c]The housing configurations are characterized by building structure and land input (Luk, 1991).

Table 2. Changes in Area Sizes of Development Zone by Scenario (Unit: km^2)

Scenario	Residential Zone	Industrial Zone	Commercial Zone	Green Zone
Green Zone	+5.4	0	0	−5.4
Industrial Zone	+5.4	−5.4	0	0
Commercial Zone	+5.4	0	−5.4	0

Note: + and − mean the increase and the decrease, respectively

green land is located around the edge of Seoul, so this scenario is understood as urban sprawl. The *industrial zone scenario* and the *commercial zone scenario* involve designating 5.4 km^2 of the industrial and commercial development zones as a residential development zone. Because the industrial development zone has concentrated on two of five sub-centers in Seoul, the construction of new housing in the industrial land zone (*industrial zone scenario*) implies urban regeneration. According to the model structure, the decrease in the non-residential development zone and the increase in the residential development zone have major impacts on the levels of production and price through the supply and the demand sides, respectively.

The effects of three housing development alternatives are measured as a deviation from the base case in terms of the growth rate of Gross Regional Product (GRP), the price inflation, the income disparity, and the sectoral changes in the value-added, the employment, and the product price. The base case is defined as a subsequent path of the economic behavior following an inter-temporal consistency for ten periods, keeping the area size of each land development zone constant at the benchmark year of 1995. The price effect is measured by a percentage change in the consumer price index from the base case, and the relative degree of income inequality among the five income classes is measured by a coefficient of variation.[d]

Table 3 shows that the housing supply with the transformation of the green land use into residential land use (*green zone scenario*) has the largest effect on the GRP of Seoul over ten periods on one hand, but the least impact on price inflation on the other. It increases the GRP by 1.010% and the consumer price level by 0.2025% over the ten period time horizon on average. For the *industrial zone scenario*, the GRP and the consumer price index are 1.0005% and 0.2048%, respectively. For all scenarios, there is a substantial rise in the price level during the construction phase (first–fourth periods) due to an exogenous

[d]The percentage change should be carefully interpreted because it is relative to the size of the quantity in Seoul economy.

Table 3. Dynamic Impacts of Housing Supply on Income, Price, and Income Inequality (Unit: %)

Period	1	2	3	4	5	6	7	8	9	10	Average
GRP											
Green zone	1.4981	1.2189	1.1441	1.0362	1.1166	1.0240	0.9192	0.8202	0.7323	0.6564	1.0100
Industrial zone	1.4900	1.2103	1.1347	1.0267	1.1076	1.0146	0.9096	0.8102	0.7220	0.6457	1.0005
Commercial zone	1.4615	1.1787	1.0996	0.9892	1.0690	0.9740	0.8672	0.7663	0.6766	0.5991	0.9613
Price											
Green zone	1.0880	0.7674	0.9848	0.8355	−0.2219	−0.2050	−0.1891	−0.1741	−0.1534	−0.1469	0.2025
Industrial zone	1.0880	0.7674	0.9934	0.8438	−0.2219	−0.2050	−0.1891	−0.1672	−0.1534	−0.1469	0.2048
Commercial zone	1.0880	0.7674	0.9934	0.8438	−0.2219	−0.1974	−0.1818	−0.1602	−0.1467	−0.1405	0.2087
Income inequality											
Green zone	0.0175	0.0159	0.0228	0.0192	−0.0066	−0.0055	−0.0045	−0.0037	−0.0030	−0.0025	0.0011
Industrial zone	0.0177	0.0161	0.0230	0.0193	−0.0065	−0.0054	−0.0044	−0.0036	−0.0030	−0.0025	0.0012
Commercial zone	0.0177	0.0161	0.0230	0.0194	−0.0064	−0.0053	−0.0044	−0.0035	−0.0029	−0.0024	0.0013

increase in aggregate demand. As for income distribution, the housing development can lead to narrowing the income gaps regardless of the type of land to be transformed into the residential land use. During the construction phase, the provision of housing in the commercial development zone (*commercial zone scenario*) has the largest impact on the reduction in income inequality, inducing a decrease of the coefficient of variation by 0.0177% during the first period to 0.0194% during the fourth. Interestingly, the coefficient of variation keeps rising at a decreasing growth rate after the completion of the housing. It implies that the generation of employment opportunities through housing construction has a higher impact on the horizontal income distribution than the increase in housing stock.

The aggregate impacts on the price and the income between the scenarios are relatively similar in Table 3, but the sectoral impacts on the value-added, the employment, and the price level are very differentiated depending on the industrial sector and the type of land to be transformed into the residential land use (Table 4). The largest impacts are observed in the construction sector with increases in value-added by 2.7741 to 2.8510%, employment by 3.0388 to 3.1282%, and production price by 2.7510 to 2.8647%. For the agricultural and transportation sectors, the value-added and the employment increase with the decrease in product price. On the contrary, the growth rates of the finance and other service sectors fall down with the product price inflation (0.1969% for finance and 0.3058% for the other service sector). Each scenario has substantial impacts on the industrial sector to directly be linked with land use transformation: the agricultural sector for the *green zone scenario*; the manufacturing sector for the *industrial zone scenario*; and the service sectors (public utility, construction, wholesales, transportation, finance, and others) for the *commercial zone scenario*. For example, when the commercial development zone is designated into residential use for the construction of housing, the growth rate of the value-added and employment for the service sectors would be lower, but their price level would be higher than any other scenario.

The Hicksian Compensating Variation (HCV) measures the change in household utility by the housing development. It refers to the amount of income to be taken away or added in order to recover the old utility of the household (Kim and Kim, 1998). The aggregate welfare benefits from residential development are estimated at 1.1808 to 1.9829% of the GRP for the *green zone scenario*, 1.1814 to 2.0070% for the *industrial zone scenario* and 1.1415 to 1.9910% for the *commercial zone scenario*. These are equivalent to 1.7455 trillion Korean Won per year (*commercial zone scenario*) to 1.7680 trillion Korean won per year (*industrial zone scenario*) at a 1995 constant price.

Table 4. Sectoral Changes in Value-Added, Employment, and Price by Scenario (Unit: %)

	Green Zone	Industrial Zone	Commercial Zone
Value-added			
Agriculture	1.5010	1.5314	1.5192
Manufacturing	1.5525	1.4322	1.5391
Public utility	−0.0430	−0.0602	−0.1118
Construction	2.8245	2.8510	2.7741
Wholesales	0.6811	0.6885	0.6602
Transportation	1.9820	2.0000	1.9762
Finance	−0.1939	−0.2064	−0.2593
Others	0.4663	0.4692	0.3345
Employment			
Agriculture	0.7389	0.7389	0.7389
Manufacturing	0.9494	0.8266	0.9258
Public utility	−1.1547	−1.1547	−1.1547
Construction	3.0957	3.1282	3.0388
Wholesales	0.0340	0.0359	0.0009
Transportation	1.3469	1.3514	1.3379
Finance	−1.4302	−1.4484	−1.5030
Others	−0.3798	−0.3816	−0.5236
Price			
Agriculture	−0.0149	−0.0157	−0.0157
Manufacturing	0.0229	0.0298	0.0229
Public utility	0.1023	0.1031	0.1075
Construction	2.7510	2.8083	2.8647
Wholesales	1.0058	1.0142	0.9989
Transportation	−0.3767	−0.3833	−0.3862
Finance	0.1969	0.1937	0.1993
Others	0.3058	0.3080	0.3762

The construction of the housing in the industrial development zone has the highest welfare effect on all household groups. In addition, the *green zone scenario* could result in the largest reduction in the welfare inequality between the household groups, dropping the coefficient of variations by 0.37 to 1.07%.

4. Conclusion

This paper attempts to quantify the economic effects of the housing supplies on the urban growth and income distribution in Seoul, using the urban land use

Table 5. Annual Average of Hicksian Compensating Variation Alternative

	Green Zone		Industrial Zone		Commercial Zone	
	HCV[1]	HCV/GRP[2]	HCV[1]	HCV/GRP[2]	HCV[1]	HCV/GRP[2]
Low-income	0.0630	1.1808	0.0630	1.1814	0.0611	1.1451
Low-middle-income	0.1713	1.5299	0.1723	1.5385	0.1688	1.5076
Middle-income	0.2062	1.5140	0.2073	1.5223	0.2031	1.4914
Middle-high-income	0.3508	1.7073	0.3539	1.7222	0.3488	1.6973
High-income	0.9598	1.9829	0.9715	2.0070	0.9637	1.9910
Coefficient of variation[3]	1.0164 (98.92)		1.0202 (99.30)		1.0274 (100.0)	

[1] unit: trillion Korean won
[2] unit: percentage
[3] The value in parenthesis is the percentage ratio of coefficient of variation of each scenario to the commercial zone scenario

and CGE model. The quantitative simulation confirms that the housing construction with the transformation of either green land development zone (*green zone scenario*) or industrial land development zone (*industrial zone scenario*) into the residential land use leads to an increase of the GRP by approximately 1% at the worse income inequality. Their aggregate welfare effects range from 1.7511 trillion Korean won to 1.7680 trillion Korean won on a ten-period average in terms of Hicksian Compensating Variation. These findings imply that opportunity costs of the commercial and industrial development zones in Seoul are relatively high. It provides an economic rationale for the promotion and the national-wide networking of knowledge-based service industries that Seoul government has implemented recently. The urban regeneration projects in sub-centers are expected to improve the overall land productivities of Seoul, partially decreasing commuting costs by a spatial mismatch between working places and residential locations. For the case of *green zone scenario*, considerable caution should be taken in interpreting with its highest income, because there is no trade-off mechanism between the preservation of the green land use and the urban economic growth in the model. That is, the model fails to estimate negative impacts of the reduction in the green development zone on Seoul economies. If the CGE model accounts for the values of fragile forests, health benefits, and environmental qualities, the income effect of the *green zone scenario* in the long-term could be much lower than the estimate of this paper.

The paper provides an insight into an interaction between urban land uses and economic activities with respect to the housing development, but the policy implication should be understood within the context of the model structure and the background of Seoul economy. One of major drawbacks in the model for analyzing the economic effects of the housing policies is to neglect connections among the financial market, the property market, and the real side market (Thissen, 1999). In general, the financial rates of return on assets and wealth affect the consumption of the housing space in the property market as well as the housing investment in the asset market (DiPasquale and Wheaton, 1992). Because the housing asset tends to be imperfectly substitutable with the financial assets such as money and bonds, the demand can be estimated with the relative rates of return on the competing financial assets in a framework of portfolio model (Thissen, 1999). The demand for the housing space in the property market can be also specified with the rental price of the space and the level of household income according to DiPasquale and Wheaton (1992). Therefore, the attempt should be made to incorporate financial and housing markets into the CGE model, while the rental and asset prices of the housing are modeled with the rental housing sector of the property market and the owner occupied housing sector of the asset market, respectively. Another limit is that the model has no explicit land market under an assumption that the land supply determines the demand. The integration of the land market with the CGE model captures the bid rent under the competition among production sectors and the spatial pattern of the urban land use to maximize the land productivities. In addition, if GIS and the housing hedonic price model are incorporated in the CGE model, we could explore the relationship between the spatial distribution of economic and human resources and the spatial land and housing markets.[e]

References

Abdelgalil EA, and Cohen SI, 2001. "Policy modelling of the trade-off between agricultural development and land degradation — the Sudan case." *J. Policy Modeling* **23**: 847–874.

Atkinson AB, 1983. *The Economics of Inequality*. Clarendon Press: Oxford.

Bye B, and Avitsland T, 2003. "The welfare effects of housing taxation in a distorted economy: a general equilibrium analysis." *Econ. Modelling,* forthcoming.

Cho, C-J, 2002. "The Korean growth-management programs: issues, problems and possible reforms." *Land Use Policy,* **19**: 13–27.

Decaluwe B, and Martens A, 1988. "CGE modelling and developing economics: a concise empirical survey of 73 applications to 26 countries." *J. Policy Modeling* **10**: 529–568.

Devarajan S, and Robinson S, 2002. "The influence of computable general equilibrium models on policy." TMD Discussion Paper No. 98, International Food Policy Research Institute, Washington, D.C.

DiPasquale D, and Wheaton WC, 1992. "The market for real estate and space: a conceptual framework." *J. Amer. Real Est. Urban Econ. Assoc.* **20**(1): 181–197.

Gallent N, and Kim KS, 2001. "Land zoning and local discretion in the korean planning system." *Land Use Policy* **18**: 233–243.

Giesecke J, 2002. "Explaining regional economic performance: an historical application of a dynamic multi-regional CGE Model." *Pap. Reg. Sci.* **81**: 247–278.

Gottinger HW, 1998. "Greenhouse gas economics and computable general equilibrium." *J. Policy Modeling* **20**: 537–580.

Han YJ, and Kim E, 1999. *Development of Seoul Economic Model (I)–A Social Accounting Matrix Approach.* Seoul Development Institute: Seoul (in Korean).

[e]Because the housing is a joint consumption commodity of the residential land use, the location, and the building structure, the housing commodity needs to be disaggregated by the floor space size and the lot size, the locational factor such as distance and neighborhood, and the dwelling type as discussed in Luk (1991).

Hofe RV, 2002. "A regional computable general equilibrium model for housing policy: the case of New York state." Paper presented at the 49th Annual North American Meetings of the Regional Science Association International, San Juan, Puerto Rico, November 14–16.

Jang Y-H, 2001. "Directions of housing policy in Seoul: from quantity to quality." In: *Urban Management in Seoul: Policy Issues and Responses.* Kwon W-Y, and Kim K, (eds) Seoul Development Institute. 147–1661.

Kim E, 1998. "Economic gain and loss from public infrastructure investment." *Growth and Change* **29**: 445–469.

Kim E, and Kim W, 1998. "Economic effects of ITS development strategies in Korea." *IATSS Research* **22**(2): 43–53.

Kim E, and Kim K, 2002a. "Impacts of regional development strategies on growth and equity of Korea: a multiregional CGE model." *Ann. Reg. Sci.* **36**: 165–180.

Kim K-J, 2001. "Residential redevelopment in Seoul: public substandard housing renewal program." In: *Urban Management in Seoul: Policy Issues and Responses.* Kwon W-Y, and Kim K, (eds) Seoul Development Institute. 189–211.

Kim KS, and Gallent N, 1998. "Regulating industrial growth in the south Korea capital region." *Cities* **15**: 1–11.

Levin N, 1999. "The effects of local growth controls on regional housing production and population redistribution in California." *Urban Stud.* **36**: 2047–2068.

Luk FK, 1991. "A general equilibrium simulation model of housing markets with indivisibility." *Reg. Sci. Urban Econ.* **23**: 153–169.

Olatubi WO, and Hughes DW, 2002. "Natural resource and environmental policy trade-offs: a CGE analysis of the regional impact of the wetland reserve program." *Land Use Policy*, **19**: 231–241.

Partridge MD, and Rickman DS, 1998. "Regional computable general equilibrium modeling: a survey and critical appraisal." *Int. Reg. Sci. Rev.* **21**: 205–248.

Thissen M, 1999. *Financial CGE Models; Two Decades of Research.* SOM Research Memorandum. University of Groningen: Groningen.

Wong GY, and Alavalapati JR, 2003. "The land-use effects of a forest carbon policy in the US." *Forest Policy Econ.* **5**(3): 249–264.

Part V

Industrial Policies

Chapter 10

The Economic Importance of the Sugar Industry for Fiji*

PARESH KUMAR NARAYAN

Department of Accounting, Finance and Economics, Griffith University, Queensland, Australia

BIMAN CHAND PRASAD

Department of Economics, The University of the South Pacific, Fiji

For over a century, the sugar industry has been perceived as the backbone of the Fijian economy, given its contributions to gross domestic product (GDP) and employment generation. However, due to the non-renewal of land leases and the gradual withdrawal of the preferential prices by the European Union, the industry is on the verge of collapse. We use the Fiji computable general equilibrium model to simulate the economy-wide impact of a 30% reduction in sugar production. Amongst our key results, we find that in the long-run a 30% reduction in sugar production leads to a 2.1% fall in exports, and government expenditure and real consumption fall by 1.9 and 1.6%, respectively. These declines in the aggregate demand components are reflected in a fall of around 1.8% in Fiji's GDP. The negative repercussion of declining economic growth is reflected in a 1.5% decline in real national welfare.

*This chapter was originally published in *Review of Urban and Regional Development Studies*, Vol. 17, No. 2, July 2005, and is reprinted here with minor modifications upon the permission from the publisher.

1. Introduction

After independence in 1970, Fiji pursued an inward-looking import-substitution strategy for growth in agriculture and manufacturing, with sugar production being Fiji's main export. While Fiji has adopted tourism and export-led manufacturing strategy over the last 15–20 years as the basis for economic growth, sugar exports still drive the rural economy where the bulk of the population resides. Currently, sugar export constitutes approximately 7% of gross domestic product (GDP) and generates approximately 22% of total exports. It accounts for 8.5% of total foreign earnings and generates direct and indirect employment for about 51,000 people (Government of Fiji, 2002). The government in its 2003–2005 strategic development plan has put forward a number of policy objectives. These include:

- the restructure of the sugar industry into a commercially viable and efficient industry;
- improving the milling efficiency and introducing a cane quality payment system; and
- improving the efficiency of sugarcane production, diversifying production into a range of sugar by-products and initiating long-term reforms to make the sugar sector internationally competitive

(Government of Fiji, 2002).

However, over the last decade, the sugar industry has been on the decline due to: (i) non-renewal of sugarcane land leases, and (ii) expiring benefits under the trade agreement.[a] In light of the poor performance of Fiji's sugar industry, the goal of this paper is to examine the long-run impact of a 30% reduction in sugar production on Fiji's economy. To achieve this goal, we use the computable general equilibrium model, which is at the forefront of research on "impact studies". Given the economic and social importance of the sugar industry, its performance has implications on the land, capital, labor, and trade markets, all of which are fully represented within a CGE framework. For instance, the industry structure is well detailed and the links between industries are well specified in CGE models. The equations of the model are derived from neoclassical microeconomic assumptions about the behavior of price taking economic agents. For example, consumers maximize utility subject to their

[a]Levantis *et al.* (2003) provides an analysis of the potential consequences for Fiji from eroding EU price incentives. See also Narayan (2004b) and Prasad and Narayan (2004) for recent analysis of Fiji's sugar industry.

budget constraints and producers choose their inputs so as to minimize costs of production. Market forces play an important part in distributing limited resources, and market imperfections can lead to unemployment. Government expenditure is contingent on raising taxes or borrowing, which has implications on other economic agents such as consumers and firms; this, in turn, induces other economic effects. The economy is linked to the rest of the world via a foreign exchange market; an increase in exports in one sector leads to a rise in the exchange rate; hence, discouraging other exports and encouraging imports.

The balance of the paper is organized as follows. In the next section, we provide an overview of Fiji's sugar industry and draw the main motivation for this study. The methodology is presented in Section 3, and the simulation results are presented in Section 4. In the final section, we conclude with some policy implications.

2. An Overview of Sugarcane Production in Fiji

2.1. *Trends in Sugarcane and Sugar Production*

During the first twenty years after independence, one of the key policy objectives of successive governments in Fiji was to stimulate sugarcane production: from its inception, it was believed that this was needed to provide Fiji the economic stimulus required for development. Between 1975 and 1980, the number of sugarcane growers (farmers) increased from 16,995 to 19,567, leading to an increase in sugarcane production from 2.1 to 3.3 million tons. The land area under sugarcane production in this period increased from 44,000 to 64,000 hectares, and sugar production increased from 272,000 to 396,000 tons. From 1980 to 1990, the number of farmers increased to 22,000 tons and the land area under production increased by 6,000 hectares. Over this period, sugarcane production increased to 4 million tons and sugar production increased to 408,000 tons. Between 1990 and 1995, sugarcane production increased from 4 to 4.1 million tons while sugar production increased from 408,000 to 454,000 tons. However, since 1996 when sugarcane production reached 4.3 million tons, sugarcane production has continued to decline, reaching a low of 2.6 million tons in 2003. During the same time, not surprisingly, sugar production also declined, reaching a low of 294,000 tons in 2003.

The decline in sugarcane production and sugar production can be attributed to the existing problems in the industry. These include: (i) the non-renewal of land leases for the sugarcane farmers, (ii) the impending expiry of preferential prices from the European Union, and (iii) the rising level of inefficiency in sugar production, milling and transportation.

2.2. *The Reform of the Sugar Industry*

The process of reform in the sugar industry is part of the bigger agenda of economic reforms that Fiji has pursued since the mid 1980s. The military coups of 1987 caused serious economic decline and the whole viability of the import-substitution policies pursued by Fiji since 1970 could not be sustained (Akram-Lodhi, 2000). Market-led reforms driven by the world economic environment provided Fiji with the impetus to change its economic policies. The main thrust of the policies since the mid 1980s has been to promote exports as a strategy for economic growth.

The restructuring of the sugar industry is premised on two fundamental problems in the industry. First, the bulk of Fiji's sugar is sold to the European Union (EU) under a preferential price agreement, where the sugar price received by farmers in Fiji is about three times the world market price. The sugar protocol of the Lome Convention allows seventeen countries in Africa, the Caribbean and the Pacific preferential access to the EU market. The sugar protocol has been extended under the new Cotonou agreement. This agreement is expected to conclude in 2008 as per the World Trade Organization (WTO) requirements. The increase in the quantity of sugar produced over the years is a direct result of the preferential price under the guaranteed market. While Fiji has a fixed quota under the agreement, there has been some variation over the years with respect to the amount of sugar sold under preferential prices. Special access to the European Union market has determined Fiji's sugar industry policies over the last 30 years. This is also the case in many other sugar producing countries such as Cuba, the Philippines, and Zimbabwe (Borell and Larsen, 2001).

Second, the mills are owned by the government and like many public enterprises in developing countries, the sugar mills in Fiji have been poorly managed and have become very inefficient (Prasad, 2002). As pointed out by Larson and Borrell (2001), most sugar producing countries are undertaking reform of the industry and they each have their unique problems with respect to production of sugarcane, manufacturing and marketing of raw sugar.

Since 2000, both sugarcane and sugar production have been falling. For example, there was a decline in sugarcane production of 9% and 16% in 2000 and 2003, respectively. This trend is likely to continue in the coming years given the problems with respect to property rights in land and the impending expiry of preferential prices in 2008. To address this issue, the industry stakeholders, including government, which owns the four sugar mills, have put in place a plan for restructuring the industry. The main thrust of the restructuring plan is to increase the efficiency of the sugarcane farms, transportation system and milling so as to advance Fiji's competitiveness in the international market when the preferential prices end in 2008. The need for restructuring is summarized by the ADB (ADB, 2003b: 1) as follows:

The combination of deteriorating world sugar market prices, declining efficiencies in all sections of Fiji's sugar sector, and the adverse effects of the Master Award[b] which result in an inequitable distribution of Fiji's sugar proceeds that does not permit reinvestment in the sugar sector's infrastructure, has resulted in a situation that dictates an immediate restructure of the Fiji sugar sector. Without immediate restructuring, either the Fiji Sugar Corporation (FSC) will have to cease production due to its technical insolvency and declining credit rating or the government of the Fiji Islands will have to provide an immediate cash injection to FSC of up to F$ 33 million to ensure continuing operation of the four mills for 2003–2004. Future annual cash injections can be expected to rise as the deteriorating sugar sector infrastructure maintenance and replacement costs escalate.

The restructuring plan put forward by the stakeholders in the sugar industry, including the government, millers, and growers, envisage a smaller industry in terms of the number of farmers (Government of Fiji, 2003). The plan also envisages that production will be maintained at a level that would still contribute significantly to the economy. However, the problem with the land leases and the lack of agreement on the proposed restructuring will continue to cause production to decline. For example, between 2003 and 2005 more than 7,492 native land leases are expected to expire. Non-indigenous farmers hold all these leases. If we accept the current trend of non-renewal of leases, then it is reasonable to assume that about 27% of the land under sugarcane will be removed from the tenants. This is consistent with the Fiji Sugarcane Growers Council's prediction for a 30% production decline over the next 3 years. The 30% decline in production is based on the number of factors. The first is based on the number of sugarcane land leases that have been taken away from sitting tenants. New and inexperienced farmers have already proven to

[b] Fiji's current Master Award, which came into existence in 1989, sets the guidelines for sharing proceeds between the millers and the growers. Under the Master Award growers receive 70% of the proceeds while the millers get 30%. While there have been conflicts between the millers and growers in the past, the situation has never been as serious as it is at present.

be less productive and hence the actual cane production in 2004 declined. It is estimated that sugarcane production in 2005 will decline by about 28%–30% (Reserve Bank of Fiji, 2005). The 30% decline in sugar production used in this paper may be conservative as the trend overall is a declining sugar industry not only due to internal factors such as land lease problems, but the decline is also in anticipation of the erosion of preferential prices from the European Union.

3. Methodology: Theoretical Structure of the Fiji CGE Model

The Fiji CGE model developed by Levantis (1999) and extended by Narayan (2004a) consists of 35 domestic industries, 34 commodities and 2 occupational types. The model consists of 13 agricultural sector industries, 10 industrial sector industries and 12 service sector industries (see also Narayan, 2003). A feature of the model is that gold production is categorized into two different industries given different cost structures, leading to a 35 industry model. A list of the 35 industries and 34 commodities is given in Appendix 1. The Fiji model is a "comparative static" model, implying that it provides projections at only one point in time, which is the solution year. The model refers implicitly to the economy at some future time period to ensure that the economy adjusts after the initial shock(s). Schematically, the model takes the following form:

$$F\left[Z_1(t),\ Z_2(t),\ Z(0)\right] = 0$$

Here, F denotes function, $Z_1(t)$ and $Z_2(t)$ are vectors of values of endogenous and exogenous variables at time t and $Z(0)$ is a vector of initial conditions. At the economy wide level, the equations of a typical Johansen model can be classified into five groups:

1. equations that describe household and other final demand for commodities;
2. equations that describe industry demand for primary factors and intermediate inputs;
3. equations that describe prices;
4. market clearing equations for primary factors and commodities; and
5. other equations, e.g. equations defining GDP, aggregate employment, the consumer price index and investment price index.

The equations of the model are derived from neoclassical microeconomic assumptions about the behavior of price taking economic agents, and is solved using the GEMPACK software package, developed by the Centre of Policy Studies and the Impact Project, Monash University.

3.1. *Model Closure and Solution*

To simulate the long-run impact, we allow capital to move between industries in response to changes in rates of return. This assumption is consistent with the fact that Fiji faces an elastic supply of capital from the world market, i.e. the domestic rate of return is assumed to be determined by the world market rate. Notice that if the rate of return is endogenous, in the face of falling cost of capital, there will be an improvement in the rate of return. The exogenous nature of the rate of return on capital implies two things; (i) that a rise in investment levels is needed to build and maintain industry capital, and (ii) that if changes in economic conditions exert growth in some industries, they will attract investment expenditure and *defacto* attract capital from other industries. This behavior ensures that when all inter-industry adjustments have taken their course, capital in all industries earns a uniform rate of return.

With regards to the labor market, employment levels are largely fixed in the long-run. It follows that if real wages are endogenous, then either employment or unemployment must be fixed. We hold employment fixed. This implies that shifts in the demand for labor will be equilibrated with appropriate adjustments in the wage rate.

4. Simulation Results

Table 1 presents the key macroeconomic impacts of a 30% reduction in sugar production in Fiji. The impact on real GDP and exports is profound. Real GDP, for instance, will fall by 1.85% and this is significant given that Fiji's growth rate over the last decade has averaged only 2.8%.

Exports, on the other hand, will decline by 2.1% and imports will decline by 1.7%. This will contribute to a deterioration of the balance of payment for Fiji. Another very important result is the impact on tax revenue for the government from declining sugar production. The income tax revenue will decline by about 3% followed by a decline in value added tax (VAT) revenue by about 1%. The biggest decline will be in the company tax and production tax revenues, representing 3% and 6%, respectively.

The sugar industry has a bigger multiplier effect than most other industries in Fiji (Narayan, 1999). Given the economic and social importance of the sugar industry, its performance has implications on the land, capital, labor, and trade markets, all of which are fully represented within a CGE framework. It is, therefore, expected that a negative shock to the sugar industry will have a

Table 1. Macroeconomic Effects for Fiji from a 30% Reduction in Sugar Production

Variables	Change (%)
Private savings	−2.6796
Balance of payments	−F$ 703,043
Total government consumption	−1.8761
Total government investment expenditure	−0.8924
Total government savings	−26.5760
Imports	−1.6652
Exports	−2.1434
Consumer price index	−1.0763
Investment price index	−0.8237
Private disposable income	−2.6796
VAT revenue	−1.0436
Income tax revenue	−2.9898
Company tax revenue	−3.0141
Production tax revenue	−6.2675
Excise tax revenue	−2.5254
Tariff revenue	−1.5425
Real GDP	−1.8467
GDP deflator	−0.7160
Real consumption	−1.6466
Real national welfare	−1.4690
Labor Market Effects for Fiji from a 30% Reduction in Sugar Output	
Variables	Change (%)
Net after tax rural wage rate for unskilled labor	−1.8776
Net urban wage rate for unskilled labor	−1.0763
Wage rate for informal sector labor	−7.1587
Aggregate demand for informal unskilled labor	3.7379

direct impact on other sectors of the economy. Table 2 reports the real output effects of a 30% decline in sugar production. While the hotel and transport sectors will benefit most, other sectors will experience a decline in output. The decline in the outputs of dalo, root crops, kava, fruit and vegetables, dairy and livestock will be more than 1%.

This decline could be explained in two ways. First, the demand for these crops from the sugarcane farming community will decline. This is because while many farmers do not grow these crops, they are part of their daily household consumption. Furthermore, during the sugarcane-harvesting season, the demand for these crops is even higher, as they form the bulk of the

Table 2. Real Output Effects for Fiji from a 30% Reduction in Sugar Production

Variables	Change (%)
Hotels	2.0169
Transport	1.2054
Commerce	−1.4891
Dalo	−1.0374
Root crops	−1.7961
Kava	−1.5571
Fruits and vegetables	−1.2209
Dairy	−1.1992
Livestock	−1.4343
Beverage and tobacco	−2.3741
Electricity and water	−2.4094
Construction	−1.3899
Finance	−2.6732
Insurance	−1.2192
Property services	−2.8516
Business services	−0.8516
Other private services	3.1779
Health	−2.0105
Education	−2.6769
Informal	−3.3907
Rice	−0.8314
Quarry	−1.5548
Other crops	−1.1552
Coconuts	0.4919
Ginger	0.5300
Cane	−15.0111
Fishing	0.0839
Processed food	0.6855
Textiles clothing and footwear	0.7683
Other manufactures	0.6535

food for laborers harvesting cane. Third, the commercial and business activities in at least four major urban centres in Fiji are largely driven by sugarcane farming activity. Hence, it follows that any decline in production is likely to affect economic activity in the urban areas. Consequently, there would be a reduction in demand for agricultural products. There is also a significant decline in the beverage and tobacco sector. Of more concern is the decline in electricity and water, construction, finance and insurance where output decline will be between 1% and 2%. These sectors together contribute 15% to GDP, implying that reduction in their output will be reflected in a fall in GDP. The most important social sectors — education and health — will suffer a decline of 2.7% and 2%, respectively. The impact on the informal sector will be the largest, amounting to 3.4%. This is because the bulk of the labor force in sugar cane farming comes from the informal sector.

The impact on the textile and footwear sector, which gained prominence in Fiji in the post-1988 period for employing a large proportion of female workers, will be positive but less than 1%. Other manufactures will experience an increase, but again these will be relatively small in magnitude.

The export effect of a 30% reduction in sugar production on other export crops such as dalo, kava, fish, gold, coconuts and ginger will be positive (see Table 3). However, ginger and gold exports will increase by less than 1%. Dalo and kava show potential in that the increase will be more than 2%. Textiles, clothing and footwear exports will increase modestly and remain less than 2%.

The average prices of all the commodities will experience a decline and in some cases (beverages and tobacco) it will be between 4% and 5%. This is expected: as sugar export earnings decline, the exchange rate is likely to depreciate and therefore domestic prices of goods and services are expected

Table 3. Export Effects for Fiji from a 30% Reduction in Sugar Production

Variables	Change (%)
Coconuts	1.0133
Ginger	0.4958
Dalo	2.4202
Kava	2.7073
Fish	1.2346
Gold	0.6754
Sugar	−37.8016
Processed food	7.8114
Textiles, clothing and footwear	1.7480
Other manufactures	2.2591
Hotel	3.1811
Transport	1.9139
Other private services	19.4257
Commerce	12.6526

to decline. The price effect is consistent with the results in Table 1, where wages in both rural and urban areas will decline by more than 1%. The brunt of the wage decline will be felt in the informal sector. Again this is consistent with the decline in income resulting from declining wages, and increasing exports of some of the traditional crops such as kava, dalo and other manufactures.

The widely held view amongst policy makers in Fiji is that the tourism industry has the potential to compensate for the collapse of Fiji's sugar industry, and lead economic growth in Fiji (Budget Address, 2003). This may be one reason why the problems in the sugar industry have not been given much prominence until it became very obvious that the industry will collapse. Here, we provide a glimpse of the reaction of Fiji's tourism industry in the event of a contraction in Fiji's sugar industry. The results on Fiji's tourism industry from a 30% reduction in sugar production are presented in Table 4. We find that tourism prices will decline which will boost tourism exports. However, an important result here is that the growth in tourism exports will not be big enough to compensate for the contraction in sugar exports and exports of other sectors. Notice that, overall, a 30% reduction in sugar production results in a balance of payments deficit (see Table 1).

Table 4. Impact on Fiji's Tourism Industry from a 30% Reduction in Sugar Production

	Change (%)
Tourism Prices in Fiji for Visitors from:	
Country	
Australia	−0.2105
New Zealand	−0.2199
United States	−0.1969
Tourism Exports by Country:	
Country	
Australia	0.6275
New Zealand	0.4742
United States	0.2822
Tourism Exports as a Percent of:	
Variables	
Total tourism exports	1.9784
Total exports	1.0355
GDP	0.3375

5. Conclusions and Policy Implications

The sugar industry in Fiji is at the crossroads. There are a number of problems that beset the industry, such as the impending expiry of preferential European Union sugar prices, the non-renewal of land leases, and the milling and transportation inefficiencies. In this paper, using a CGE model, we show that a decline in sugar production will have a deleterious impact on Fiji's economy. For instance, real GDP will decline by about 1.8%, negatively affecting government's tax revenues. The decline in sugar production will also have a negative impact on the nation's welfare. This is reflected in the declining levels of wages in other sectors of the economy as well. The decline in wages in the informal sector by more than 7% is of particular concern. The result can be explained by the fact that the contribution of the agricultural sector in Fiji declined from 22% in 1990 to 16% in 2000 concomitant with a 10% increase in urbanisation (ADB, 2002). However, the urban manufacturing sector's contribution to GDP increased only marginally. Therefore, the informal sector has been the natural absorber of the labor released from the agricultural sector. Within the sugar industry, it is expected that by the year 2008, some 5,000 families will abandon sugarcane farming if leases are not renewed. The resulting increase in unemployment in the informal sector signals a major social problem, which will be a burden on both government resources and resources of the community.

This study has made a significant contribution to the understanding of the importance of the sugar industry to Fiji's economy. In this light, it is dangerous to play down the importance of the industry, as we believe has been done by the government. Our study clearly shows that the sugar industry is still vital to the national well being of Fiji. It provides evidence that a decline in sugar production is likely to have significant negative consequences on most sectors of the economy. This study should dispel the view that there are real alternatives to the sugar industry in the short to medium term. Sugar industry reform must, therefore, be carefully implemented so that there are alternatives to farmers who, on current evidence, are likely to be forced out of the industry as a result of the reforms. A longer time frame will be required to allow the transition to a more urban-based manufacturing sector in a less painful manner.

References

Akram-Lodhi AH, 2000. *Confronting Fiji Futures*. Asia Pacific Press: Canberra.

Asian Development Bank (ADB), 2002. *Key Indicators 2002: Population and Human Resource Trends and Challenges*. ADB: Manila.

Asian Development Bank (ADB), 2003a. *Intermediation of Sugar Sector Restructuring, Draft Report.* ADB and Government of Fiji: Suva.

Asian Development Bank (ADB), 2003b. *Alternative Livelihoods Project: Mid-Term Report.* TA No. 3887-FIJ, Lincoln International Ltd: Suva.

Borrell B, and Larson DF, 2001. *Sugar Policy and Reform.* World Bank Country Economics Department, World Bank, Washington D.C.

Codsi G, and Pearson KR, 1988. "GEMPACK: general purpose software for applied general equilibrium and other economic modellers." *Comput. Sci. Econ. Manag.* **1**: 189–207.

Cooper R, McLaren K, and Powell A, 1985. "Macroeconomic closure in applied general equilibrium modelling: experiences from ORANI and agenda for further research." In: Piggot J, and Whalley J (eds) *New Developments in Applied General Equilibrium Analysis*, Cambridge University Press: New York.

Dixon PB, Parmenter BR, Sutton J, and Vincent DP, 1982. *ORANI: A Multisectoral Model of the Australian Economy.* North Holland: Amsterdam.

Fiji Bureau of Statistics, 2005. *Household Income and Expenditure Survey — Rural.* FBS: Suva.

Horridge JM, Parmenter BR, and Pearson KR, 1993. "ORANI-F: a general equilibrium model of the Australian economy." *Econ. Fin. Comput.* **3**(2): 71–133.

Levantis T, 1999. *The CGE Model of the Fiji Economy: A Working Manual.* National Centre for Development Studies, Australian National University, Canberra.

Levantis T, Jotzo F, and Tulpule VC, 2003. "Ending of EU sugar trade preferences: potential consequences for Fiji, Australian Bureau of Agricultural and Resource Economics (ABARE)." ABARE Current Issues 03.2, Canberra. (This report can be downloaded from http://abareonlineshop.com/prodsearchresults.asp?x=597259515).

Johansen L, 1960. *A Multi-Sectoral Study of Economic Growth.* North Holland: Amsterdam.

France P, 1969. *The Charter of the Land: Custom and Colonization in Fiji.* Oxford University Press: Melbourne.

Government of Fiji, 2003. *Fiji Sugar Industry Restructure Plans.* Prime Minister's Office: Suva.

Government of Fiji, 2002. *Rebuilding Confidence for Stability and Growth for a Peaceful, Prosperous Fiji.* Strategic Development Plan 2003–2005, August 2002, Government Printer: Suva.

Government of Fiji, 1985. *Laws of Fiji.* Chapter 134, Government Printer: Suva.

Government of Fiji, 1978. *Laws of Fiji.* Government Printer: Suva.

Government of Fiji, 1976. *Laws of Fiji.* Chapter 270, Government Printer: Suva.

Kumar S, and Prasad B, 2002. "Fiji's economic woes: a nation in search of development progress." *Pacific Econ. Bull.* 17: No. 1.

Lal P, Lim-Applegate H, and Reddy M, 2001. "ALTA or NLTA, what's in the name — land tenure dilemma and the Fiji sugar industry." Paper presented at the Australian Agricultural and Resource Economics Society Conference, AARES 2001, 22–25 January 2001, Adelaide, South Australia.

Moynagh M, 1981. *Brown or White: A History of the Fiji Sugar Industry, 1873–1973.* Australian National University: Canberra.

Ministry of Finance and National Planning, 2002. "2003 budget address: securing sustained growth." Suva.

Narayan PK, 2003. "The macroeconomic impact of the IMF recommended VAT policy for the Fiji economy: evidence from a CGE model." *Rev. Urban Reg. Dev. Stud.* **15**: 227–236.

Narayan PK, 2004a. "An econometric model of tourism demand and a computable general equilibrium analysis of the impact of tourism: the case of Fiji islands." Unpublished PhD Dissertation, Department of Economics, Monash University.

Narayan PK, 2004b. "An empirical analysis of sugarcane production in Fiji, 1970–2000." *Econ. Policy Analysis*, **34**: 53–62.

Nayacakalou R, 1971. "Fiji: manipulating the system." In: Crocombe R (ed.) *Land Tenure in the Pacific*, Oxford University Press: Melbourne.

NLTB, 1995. "Vanua." Native Land Trust Board Annual Report: Suva.

Overton J, 1994. "Land tenure and cash cropping in Fiji." In: Crocombe R, and Meleisea M (eds) *Land Issues in the Pacific*, Institute of Pacific Studies and Macmillan Brown Centre for Pacific Studies: Canterbury.

Prasad B, 2003. "Sugar restructuring." Friday, 21 February, Fiji Times.

Prasad B, and Kumar S, 2000. "Institutional rigidities and economic performance in Fiji." In: Akram-Lodhi AH (ed.) *Confronting Fiji Futures*, Asia Pacific Press: Canberra.

Prasad BC, and Tisdell C, 1996. "Institutional constraints to economic development: the case of native land rights in Fiji." *Asia Pacific Dev. J.* **12**: 112–122.

Prasad BC, and Narayan PK, 2004. "The relationship between Fiji sugar corporation's profitability and sugarcane production." *Pacific Econ. Bull.* **19**: 19–32.

Reddy M, 1998. "Production economic analysis of Fiji sugar industry." PhD dissertation, University of Hawaii, Honolulu (unpublished).

Reserve Bank of Fiji, 2005. *Quart. Rev.*, March, RBF, Suva.

Verebalavu J, 1998. "Indigenous Fijians in business — a study of cane farmers." Unpublished Masters Thesis, The University of the South Pacific.

Ward M, 1965. *Land Use and Population in Fiji. A Geographical Study*. Her Majesty's Stationery Office: London.

Ward M, 1965. "Land, law and custom: diverging realities in Fiji." In: Ward RG, and Kingdon E (eds) *Land, Custom and Practice in the South Pacific*, Cambridge University Press: Cambridge.

Appendix 1

Table A1. List of Industries and Commodities in the Fiji Model

Industry	Commodity
Sugarcane	Raw sugar
Coconuts	Coconuts
Rice	Rice
Ginger	Ginger

Table A1. (*Continued*)

Industry	Commodity
Dalo	Dalo
Root crops	Root crops
Kava	Kava
Fruit and vegetables	Fruit and vegetables
Other crops	Other crops
Dairy	Dairy
Livestock	Livestock products
Forestry	Forest products
Fishing	Marine products
Emperor gold mine	Gold
Mt Kasi gold mine	Gold
Quarrying	Quarrying
Sugar manufacturing	Sugar products
Beverages and tobacco	Beverage and tobacco
Food processing	Processed foods
Clothing, footwear and textiles	Clothing, footwear and textiles
Other manufactures	Other manufactures
Electricity and water	Electricity and water
Construction	Construction services
Commerce	Retail/wholesale services
Hotels, cafes, restaurants	Hotels, cafes, restaurants
Transport and communication services	Transport and communication services
Finance	Financial services
Insurance	Insurance services
Property services	Property services
Business services	Business services
Other private services	Other private services
Health	Health services
Education	Education services
Other government services	Other government services
Non-farm informal sector	Informal services

Source: Levantis (1999)

Chapter 11

A CGE Approach to Measuring the Sectoral Contribution to an Economy: An Application to Western Australian Agriculture*

HELAL AHAMMAD

Australian Bureau of Agricultural and Resource Economics, Canberra, Australia

Typically, sectoral contribution to an economy is estimated by measures such as shares in gross domestic/regional product, employment and exports. According to these measures, agriculture's contribution declines as the economy grows. However, in the process of economic growth, the indirect contribution of the sector is likely to rise due to the expansion of agriculture-based processing activities. Input–output multiplier analysis is often used to capture such flow-on contributions of the sector. This chapter proposes to use a computable general equilibrium framework to estimate the direct as well as indirect contributions of agricultural growth in an economy. It also develops a methodology to distinguish the broader effects of agricultural output growth by source — input growth and productivity growth. The proposed methodologies are illustrated by applying these to analyze the contribution of agriculture to the economy of Western Australia, an agriculture and resources based State of Australia. The results for Western Australia suggest that the indirect benefits of agriculture exceed its direct contributions and that the contributions made by enhancing productivity in agriculture are indeed substantial. Importantly, the broader

*This chapter was originally published in *Review of Urban and Regional Development Studies*, Vol. 14, No. 3, November 2002, and is reprinted here with minor modifications upon the permission from the publisher.

contribution of the agriculture sector depends critically on the specific source of the sectoral growth — input or productivity growth.

1. Introduction

This chapter proposes to employ a computable general equilibrium (CGE) framework for quantifying the broader (direct plus indirect) contributions of agriculture to an economy. Traditionally, the contribution of the agricultural sector in an economy is measured by its shares in gross domestic (or regional) product, employment and exports. This conventional approach shows that as an economy grows, agriculture's shares decline relative to other sectors (e.g. Martin and Warr, 1994). Nevertheless, this decline of agriculture's relative share during economic growth does not necessarily imply that the overall economic significance of the sector diminishes as well. As the sector itself grows, so do its absolute contributions to the economy. Beyond the direct contributions of the sector, one also has to take into account its contributions to the growth of the light manufacturing devoted to processing agricultural produce and further value-adding as well as its contribution to the growth of the transport and marketing sectors. Similarly, one also has to consider agriculture's backward linkages through which it contributes to the growth of those sectors that service farm activities. For example, the fertilizer, chemical, machinery industries and various services to the agricultural sector also benefit from expansion in agriculture. Often the indirect contributions flowing through the linkages in production, trade and consumption are complex and may not be obvious, so that the broader contributions of the sector could easily be underestimated. Accordingly, for a comprehensive account of the sector's contributions to the economy, a proper account of the wide-ranging linkages of the agricultural sector with the rest of the economy should be taken. Often input–output multiplier analysis is undertaken to capture these linkages, which is based on some restrictive assumptions on both the demand side and the supply side. For example, on the supply side, this approach does not recognize any constraints on the supplies of primary factors nor does it assume any balance of payments constraints. Furthermore, a major inadequacy of the input–output approach is its inability to explicitly take into account public policies such as direct and indirect taxes, and trade and exchange rate policies. The chapter thus proposes to employ a computable general equilibrium model, which does not suffer from these weaknesses, to quantify the overall contribution of agriculture. Given its theoretical superiority, a CGE approach to measuring sectoral contribution would represent an improvement over the input–output methodology.

The chapter also develops a methodology to decompose the total contribution of agriculture into those attributable to agricultural productivity growth and input growth. Agriculture is facing declining terms of trade as well as intensified competition stemming from trade liberalization. Accordingly, productivity growth in agriculture is quintessential for the sector to grow. The proposed decomposition analysis will contribute to a better understanding of the economics of agricultural productivity growth.

The proposed methodologies are applied to analyze the contributions of agriculture to the economy of Western Australia (WA), one of the six States of Australia. WA presents a classic case of the relative decline of the agricultural sector in the process of economic development. The chapter proceeds to present in Section 2 an overview of the key characteristics of WA agriculture, followed by a review of the growth performance of WA agriculture in the past two decades. It then analyses the broader effects of the sector's average growth p.a. over the period, and decomposes the effects by sources of agricultural growth in Section 4. To be self-contained, Section 3 presents an overview of the CGE model of the WA economy that is used to simulate the broader effects of agricultural growth. Section 5 concludes the chapter.

2. Key Characteristics of WA Agriculture

Agriculture remains an essential component of the economy of WA. For more than a century and a half, the sector, in addition to providing the bulk of the basic domestic needs for food and fibre, was the mainstay of WA's and Australian exports. However, as the national and State economies have grown over the years, their structure has undergone changes characterizing a decline in the relative importance of the agricultural sector (in terms of "direct" contributions). The changes in factor endowments, technology, relative commodity prices and consumer demands *inter alia* contributed to this process. Until the Second World War, agriculture, with wool as a major export, remained the outstanding sector of both the WA and national economies. In WA, until the early 1930s, agriculture was at least as big as manufacturing and a lot bigger than mining (predominantly gold and coal) (ABS, 1998). Subsequently, the contributions of agriculture relative to other sectors have diminished both nationally and in WA (see, e.g. ABS, 1998, Johnston and Girdlestone, 1983, and Productivity Commission, 1999). The growth of manufacturing and mining during and following the Second World War and more recently the marked growth in the services sector have accompanied the relative decline of agriculture's share in WA's gross state product (GSP).

Table 1. WA Agriculture in the State and National Economies[1]

(Percent)

Item (1)	Share in the WA Economy (2)	WA's Share in Australian Agriculture[2] (3)
Value-added	5	15
Exports	17	16
Employment	6	12

Notes: [1]The data are averages over five years to 1995/96
[2] The column represents WA agriculture's share in the national agriculture sector; e.g. for the "value-added" row, it shows WA agriculture's share in value-added of the national agriculture sector
Source: Ahammad (2000a)

Agriculture's direct contributions to the WA economy in recent years can be readily understood from its shares in the State's GSP, employment and exports as presented in Table 1.[a] In the first half of the 1990s, the sector accounted for about 5% of WA's GSP, 17% of the State's overseas exports and 6% of the total employment (column 2). It grew at a rate of about 6% p.a. in this period (Islam, 2000), contributing about 6% directly to the growth of WA's GSP. By comparison, during the same period, mining and manufacturing (the latter includes mineral processing) sectors respectively accounted for about 16% and 10% of WA's GSP, grew at the average rate of 11% and 2% per annum, and directly contributed about 35% and 3% to GSP growth (ABS, various issues). Nevertheless, agriculture is one of the few sectors in WA whose contributions to the national counterparts far exceed the State's average. More specifically, WA comprises about 10% of the national GDP, but its agriculture accounts for about 15% of the national agricultural output (column 3 of Table 1). WA's agricultural exports account for over 16% of the national agricultural exports.

Despite the respectable average annual growth of the sector in the 1990s, agriculture's relative decline in WA is evident in recent years. The sector

[a]In its State Accounts (Catalogue No. 5220.0), the ABS includes forestry, logging and fishing with agriculture. While in the remaining sections of this chapter agriculture is treated separately from forestry, logging and fishing, throughout this section, the ABS' broad definition of agriculture is used because of the lack of data. Since forestry, logging and fishing constitute only a small part of the ABS broader sector, the discussion on the role of agriculture based on the ABS statistics for broader sectors remains largely valid.

accounted for over 9% of WA's GSP in 1984 and by 2000, its share had reduced to below 4% (ABS, various issues). Nonetheless, agriculture still directly accounts for a sizeable share of the WA economy. Given the size of the sector, its indirect contributions to the State economy are likely to be substantial.

As regards the "multifunctionality" of the sector, agriculture continues to underpin regional WA. In Australia, the interests in regional development, and for that matter agriculture's role in regional development, are likely to prevail in the presence of policy distortions and immobile factors. This study is undertaken at a time when there is a surge of public interests in rural and regional development in Australia (e.g. Chaney, 1999, and Productivity Commission, 1999). As such, analysis of the performance of agriculture and its broader impacts on the economy is therefore important, as it will shed light into aspects of WA's regional economic development.

WA agriculture faces very challenging economic circumstances. Agriculture is highly export orientated in WA and is therefore exposed to intense international competition (Ahammad, 2000a). An alarming aspect of the WA farm activities is that agricultural producers are confronting an intensified "cost-price squeeze" as output prices (in absolute terms) tend to rise more slowly than prices paid for inputs. This is evident from the trends in farmers' terms of trade for WA over the last two decades, which have been declining, *albeit* with some notable fluctuations, at an alarming rate of 3.7% per annum (Ahammad, 2000a).[b] One way to stimulate and sustain agricultural growth in the face of intensified competition and declining terms of trade is through technical progress and productivity growth. In the past, to cope with the above challenges producers used to receive government assistance in the forms of price supports, input subsidies, tax concessions, export promotion subsidies and concessional interest rates, etc. In recent years, due to the National Competition Policy and other related reforms, farmers in Australia are confronted with changing economic circumstances. While there may be net beneficial impacts of such reforms on the economy (see, e.g. Productivity Commission, 1999), under a more competitive environment, the importance of productivity growth in agriculture for its survival and growth has become ever more obvious.

The rest of the chapter is devoted to analyzing the growth trends of WA agriculture over the last two decades and then to quantifying the economy-wide

[b]It should be noted that this rate relates to the WA agricultural sector as a whole and may not necessarily apply to individual agricultural outputs or industries.

impacts of the historical growth. In this regard, the contributions of agricultural productivity growth are also quantified and analyzed.

Figure 1 presents production indices for WA broadacre agriculture together with those of five broad agricultural commodities namely, Sheep meat, Wool, Grains, Beef & other meat and Agriculture n.e.c. These indices are constructed by applying Divisia methods to the "farm productivity data" for Western

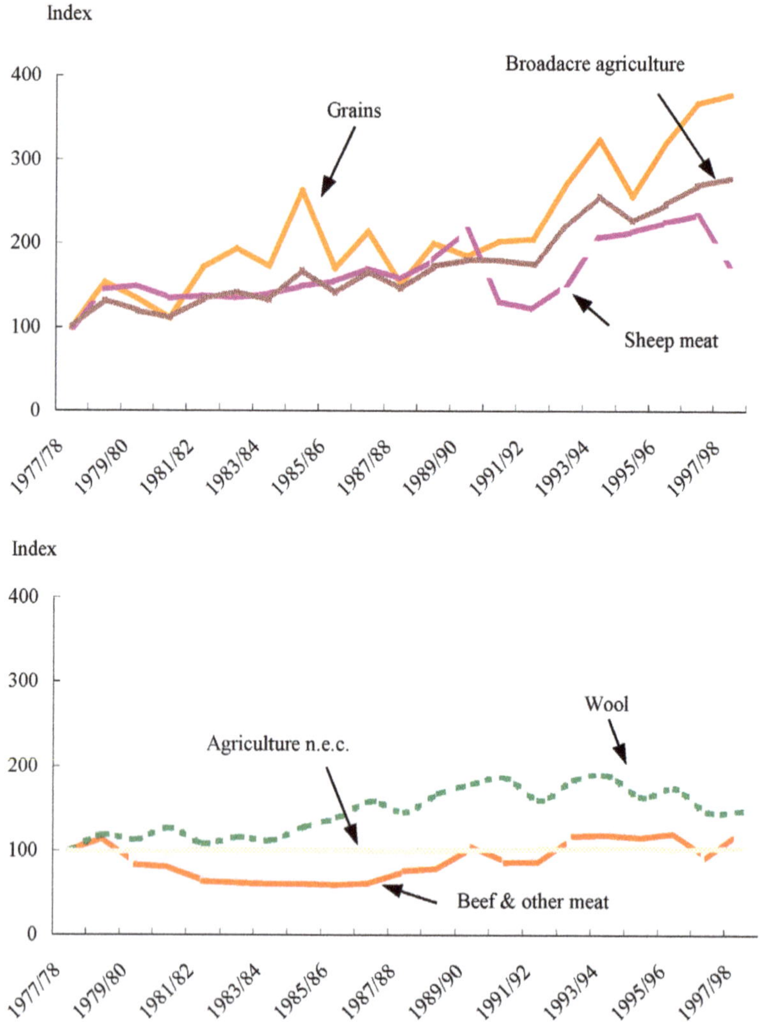

Fig. 1. Production trends of broadacre agricultural commodities in WA, 1977/78–1997/98 (Indexes with 1977/78 = 100). *Source*: Ahammad (2000b)

Australia made available by the Australian Bureau of Agricultural and Resource Economics (ABARE, 1999), and represent real growth net of the inflationary effects. Column 3 of Table 2 presents the underlying average rates of production growth for the period extending from 1977/78 to 1997/98. As can be seen, the overall production of agriculture grew at an average rate of over 6% p.a. between 1977/78 and 1997/98. However, this growth was uneven both across the commodities and over time. Grains production recorded the fastest growth with an average rate of over 10% p.a., reflecting primarily the surge in wheat production, attributable to strong productivity growth during the period (Islam, 2000).[c] Throughout the period, there has been very high variability in growth for all five broad commodities, with Grains being the most volatile.

To evaluate the more recent growth performance of WA agriculture, column 2 of Table 2 presents the average growth rates for the period 1992/93

Table 2. Estimates of Typical-Year Growth Rates for WA Broadacre Agriculture[1]

(Percent p.a.)

Commodity[2] (1)	Growth Rate	
	1992/93–1997/98 (2)	1977/78–1997/98 (3)
Sheep meat	4.75	4.58
Wool	−3.93	2.56
Grains	9.18	10.52
Beef & other meat	3.05	2.67
Agriculture n.e.c	0.42	0.20
Broadacre agriculture[3]	5.35	6.21

Notes: [1]The growth rates are estimated using ABARE's survey data on an average farm, popularly known as "farm productivity data" (ABARE, 1999)
[2]The commodity classification is based on that of WAG, the economy-wide model of the WA economy used in this chapter (see Section 3)
[3]The growth rates for broadacre agriculture estimated as the weighted average of the growth rates for the above commodities, using the WAG shares in gross output as weights, are 4.75% and 6.40% p.a.
Source: Ahammad (2000a)

[c]Factors contributing to the strong growth in grain productivity include the successful adoption of technology, improved farm management, advances in plant breeding, crop rotations, pest and weed control, efficient usage of fertiliser, advances in tractor and machinery design, and large scale farming.

to 1997/98. On average, as can be seen from the table, the growth performance of the individual commodity groups in recent years is not significantly different from the trends over the whole period under review. The only exception is Wool. Wool production has actually declined in the 1990s, due to the slump in the world markets over the past decade, as against a 2.6% growth p.a. for the period since 1977.[d] Nevertheless, WA broadacre agriculture has recorded a growth of over 5% p.a. in the 1990s. While the direct contribution to the whole economy of such growth in agriculture is readily understood, its indirect contribution, which operates through inter-industry linkages, input markets, government revenue and expenditure, etc., is not visible to the naked eye. The next section presents an overview of a new economy-wide model for WA that incorporates the above linkages in some detail. In Section 4, the model is used to estimate the broader contributions of agriculture to the economy.

3. WAG: A CGE Model for WA Agriculture

The CGE model used for simulating the broader effects of growth in WA agriculture is called WAG. Unlike other economy-wide models for the WA economy (e.g. WAM developed by Clements *et al.*, 1996), WAG gives a more detailed coverage of the State's agricultural sector, drawing on the production systems of WA agriculture estimated by Ahammad and Islam (2004). The details on WAG are available in Ahammad (2000b). For expositional convenience, however, a brief description of the main features and assumptions of the model follows.

WAG is a single-region, multi-sectoral CGE model of the WA economy. As a CGE model, WAG captures the linkages among WA industries in some detail. It incorporates explicitly the decisions made by producers and consumers, embodies relevant government policies and recognizes the constraints the economy confronts, such as limited supplies of the primary factors of production. At the core of WAG are (i) input demands by industries and their commodity supplies; (ii) demands for commodities by households and government; and (iii) the external sector comprising imports into and exports from WA.

WAG has 105 industries, of which all but two are non-agricultural. The two agricultural industries are broadacre agriculture (henceforth Agriculture for short) and Dairy. Agriculture produces nine commodities (Table 3)

---

[d]In recent years, prices of wool have gone up. This, combined with the depleted wool stockpile in recent years, may lead to a slow recovery of wool production in WA.

Table 3. Commodities and Industries in WAG

Commodity	Industry
Sheep meat	
Wool	
Cereals	
Pulses & oilseeds	
Beef cattle	1. Agriculture
Pigs	
Poultry	
Horticulture	
New industries & other agriculture	
+ 104 other commodities[1]	+ 104 other industries[1]

Note: [1]Includes Dairy. The sector is treated as a single-product industry in WAG. For the complete lists of WAG commodities and industries, see Table A1 in Ahammad (2000b)

based on a technology described in Appendix 1. Accordingly, with a multi-product Agriculture industry, WAG has more commodities (113) than industries (105).

As regards the non-Agriculture industries, each of them produces a single commodity using materials, labor and capital as inputs so as to minimize costs subject to a nested production technology. All producers face competitive markets. The production structure is based on the assumption of constant returns to scale and that each of the material inputs is separable from the others, as well as from primary inputs. Substitution takes place between the primary factors. WAG considers consumers who own primary factors, and a consolidated government which collects revenue and spends on current consumption. Household consumption demand is based on the assumption of preference independence and utility maximization. All goods are distinguished according to their source of supply, WA and non-WA. Locally sourced good is treated as an imperfect substitute for imports. WAG can be viewed to comprise four main building blocks:

- Equations describing the final demands for consumption, investment and government expenditure; and equations describing industrial demands for intermediate inputs and primary factors.
- Zero profit equations which ensure that revenue equals costs, as implied by competitive markets.

- Market clearing-conditions for domestically produced goods and primary factors.
- Miscellaneous definitional equations for prices, revenue from taxation, gross state product, total consumption and total trade.

The equations constituting WAG are in log-changes of variables and involve numerous shares and elasticities. The model uses the 1992/93 input–output table for Western Australia[e] to calculate the shares, including the revenue and cost shares. The values for the elasticity parameters are adapted from Ahammad and Islam (2004), Dixon *et al.* (1982) and Johnson (2003). Ahammad (2000b) presents further details on the WAG database.

Table 2 presented the average rates of growth of production of five broad agricultural commodities for two (overlapping) periods. The average annual growth rates for the longer period from 1977/78 to 1997/98 (column 3 of Table 2) are taken to characterize the performance of WA broadacre agriculture in a typical year, which are then used as inputs into WAG for simulating the typical-year effects of agricultural growth.[f] The economy-wide effects of WA agriculture based on its recent performance in the 1990s (for example, the one that was represented by column 2 of Table 2) might seem more appropriate for policy purposes. However, in view of the volatility that exists in agricultural markets, for simulations in this study, the average growth rates for the longer period are used, as this will tend to smooth out fluctuations in production.

Under the assumption of constant returns to scale, output growth is the sum of input growth and productivity growth. Accordingly, the effects of (broadacre) agricultural output growth can be disaggregated by source — agricultural

---

[e]The original input–output table by Islam and Johnson (1997) has been updated in 1999 at the Economic Research Centre of the University of Western Australia.

[f]As already noted in Section 2, these growth rates are estimated using ABARE's survey data for an average farm known as "farm productivity data". As a result, they differ from the growth rates estimated using the Australian Bureau of Statistics' (ABS') data on gross value of agricultural production. For example, in the 1990s, the ABS growth rates for the outputs in question are 13.6, 2.2, 8.0, 8.9 and 6.7 while the corresponding ABARE rates are 4.8, −3.9, 9.2, 3.1 and 0.42 (column 2 of Table 2). However, ABARE's survey data are popularly used to estimate farm productivity in Australia and as this chapter also aims to evaluate the economy-wide effects of productivity growth, the growth rates based on the ABARE data-set are used for WAG simulations.

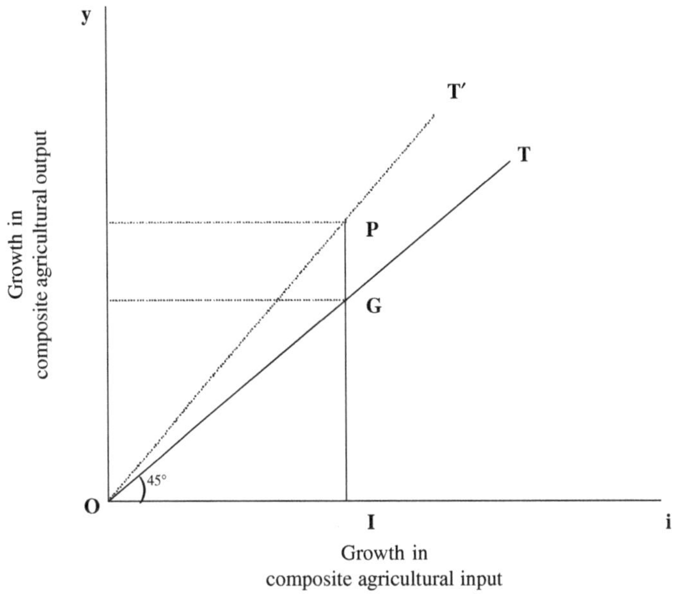

Fig. 2. Sources of Output Growth: Input and Productivity Growth

input and productivity growth.[g] The rationale for the decomposition can be laid out using Fig. 2 as follows. The vertical axis of the diagram measures the growth in composite agricultural output while the horizontal axis measures the growth in composite agricultural input. The 45° line, OT, measures the relationship between input growth and the corresponding output growth under the assumptions of constant-returns-to-scale and no productivity growth. It may be noted that, by construction, the assumption of the constant-returns-to-scale production technology is maintained in WAG. If, however, productivity growth does occur due to the improved quality of human and physical capital, it will shift the ray OT to OT′. Any point on the ray OT′, say P, will then measure the output growth resulting from the input growth (IG) and the productivity growth (PG).

[g]This is based on the supply-side decomposition of output growth and does incorporate the effects of any factor accumulation due to new investment. One may wish to decompose the effects of output growth from the demand side into the effects due to export and domestic absorption growth. Unless based on compatible assumptions about the factor markets, results may differ between the two approaches.

Based on the above technical relationship among output, inputs and productivity, it is possible to simulate WAG for the economy-wide effects of agriculture growth in two alternative ways:

- Directly by exogenously increasing agricultural output, with agricultural inputs and productivity adjusted endogenously and sufficiently to support the increased output, as described earlier. This is labeled the "output-augmenting" approach.
- Indirectly by exogenously increasing agricultural inputs and productivity so as to simulate the observed growth in agricultural outputs. This is labeled the "decomposing" approach.

Except for the different exogenous changes (called "model shocks") discussed above, the two approaches do not entail any changes in the other exogenous variables of the model. Accordingly, the two approaches are symmetrical in terms of the simulation results. However, one distinct advantage of the latter approach is that it allows for the decomposition of the agricultural-growth effects into those due to agricultural productivity growth and those due to agricultural input growth. The "decomposing" approach involves two separate simulations — one for agricultural productivity growth and the other for agricultural input growth. To ensure that the results of these two simulations are comparable and additive, they should be carried out under identical economic environments whereby the agricultural outputs (as well as all other endogenous variables) were determined by the model. Added together, the two sets of effects represent the effects of growth in agricultural production and equate the results from the "output-augmenting" simulation.[h]

The economic environment under which the above simulations are carried out is characterized by an unchanged (nominal) exchange rate and sticky nominal wages. This broadly agrees with the workings of Australia's federal system whereby the exchange rate and wages for WA are largely determined by the rest of Australia (Ye, 1999). Furthermore, it is assumed that no autonomous changes occur in consumers' demands (due to, for example, changes in tastes and attitudes), or in government and investment expenditure. Government policies with regard to tax rates and the production technologies of the non-agricultural industries are also assumed to remain unchanged.

[h]Further details on the technical aspects of the WAG simulations are available on request from the author.

4. Broader Benefits of Growth in WA Agriculture

Table 4 presents the simulated results for the Agriculture growth discussed above. As can be seen, a 6.4% growth in Agriculture (see note 3 to Table 2) generates about 0.47% growth in real gross state product (GSP). We can decompose this growth in GSP into direct and indirect contributions of the agricultural sector. Agriculture in WAG comprises about 3% of the WA economy. Accordingly, the direct contribution of 6.4% agricultural growth to the GSP growth would be about $0.03 \times 6.4 \approx 0.19\%$. The remaining $0.47 - 0.19 = 0.28\%$ can be regarded as the indirect contribution of Agriculture to GSP growth, so that $0.47 \div 0.19 \approx 2.5$ is a type of multiplier. To put it in perspective, this multiplier is much greater than the similar general equilibrium multiplier of 1.7 estimated for the minerals sector, the key driver of the WA economy, by Ahammad and Clements (1999). It may also be noted that the above multiplier for agriculture is broadly in line with the most recent estimates by Johnson (2003) of the Type-2A-value-added multipliers, which range from 1.5 to 3.5 for various agricultural outputs with an average of 2.3 for agriculture as a whole.[i] The indirect contribution can be viewed to reflect the economy-wide linkages of Agriculture. The initial impact of agricultural growth (with productivity enhancement accounting for only

Table 4. Typical-year Macroeconomic Effects of Growth in Broadacre Agriculture

Variable (1)	Effects of Growth in Agriculture (%) (2)
GSP (real)	0.47
Employment	0.57
Consumption (real)	0.42
CPI	0.30
Imports	0.57
Exports	0.53

Note: The percentage changes are relative to 1992/93 (the base year) levels
Source: WAG simulations

[i]Strictly speaking, the WAG "multiplier" and Johnson's input–output multipliers cannot be compared because of the differences in the assumptions underlying the two methodologies and the WA inter-industry flow tables used.

a part of the growth) is to boost demands for inputs by the industry which, in turn, stimulates other industries to scale up their output and employment. The results suggest that the agricultural growth stimulates substantial growth in non-agricultural sectors.

Increased GSP means higher incomes and higher overall consumption. Increased demand for consumer goods and intermediate inputs leads to higher imports. However, agricultural growth also boosts aggregate exports.

As pointed out earlier, the effects of agricultural output growth can be disaggregated according to its sources — agricultural input growth and agricultural productivity growth. The decomposition analysis conforms to the observed (historical) contributions of productivity and input to agricultural growth. In other words, of the 6.4% average annual growth in broadacre agriculture, three-quarters are due to productivity growth and the remaining quarter is due to input growth.

It is of interest to know how the two sources of agricultural growth account for the macroeconomic effects reported in Table 4. Figure 3 presents the decomposition of the effects by sources of agricultural output growth. The figure shows that about 40% of the contribution of Agriculture to GSP growth is due to the industry's productivity growth. However, productivity growth in Agriculture seems to boost the economy's consumption, exports and employment significantly more than the input growth under consideration. Interestingly,

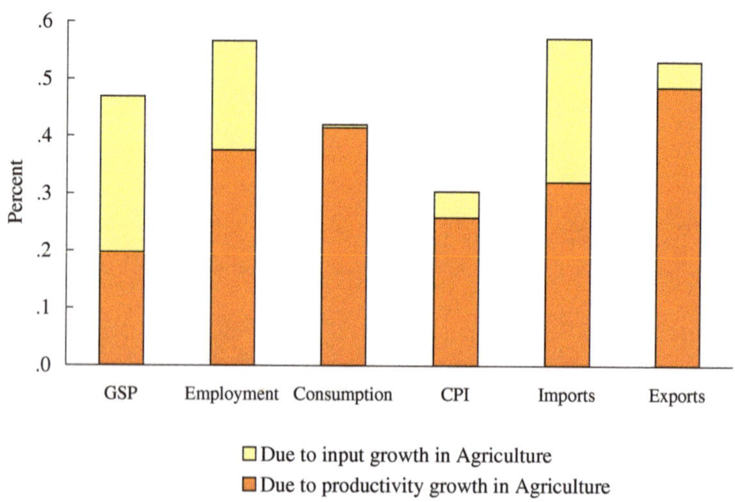

Fig. 3. Decomposition of the Typical-year Macroeconomic Effects of Growth in Broadacre Agriculture (Percent change). *Source*: WAG Simulations

the growth in the overall consumption and the consumer price index (CPI) are both higher under the agricultural productivity growth than under the agricultural input growth. The underlying economics are explored and explained below.

Productivity growth in Agriculture leads to a substantial fall in production costs and, hence, the supply price of agricultural output (column 3 of Table 5). This induces an increase in the demand for final consumption, as well as for further processing, of agricultural commodities. On the other hand, the productivity-led substantial growth in agricultural output means that farmers' income rises considerably despite the fall in their output price. The increased income in turn leads to increased demands for non-agricultural goods and services, pushing their prices up (column 3 of Table 5). The prices of non-agricultural goods and services (in particular, Services to agriculture, Trade & transport, Financial & business services and Other services) rise enough to more than offset the fall in prices of the primary and processed agricultural commodities, with the overall effects of a higher CPI and consumption than otherwise. In contrast, under the input-growth simulation, the additional demands for material inputs by Agriculture push their prices up, which in turn results in a rise in the cost of production in Agriculture and hence a rise in the prices of agricultural commodities. However, except for Services to agriculture, the rise in prices is not all that significant (column 4 of Table 5). Thus, with the given world prices of imports, the CPI has remained virtually unchanged. With reduced consumption of agricultural goods as well as financial and business services and only a slight increase in others, overall consumption has not recorded much growth following the growth in agricultural inputs.

4.1. *Effects on Economic Structure*

Table 6 presents the effects of agricultural growth on the production of nine broad non-Agriculture sectors.[j] As would be expected, sectors with strong linkages with Agriculture benefit the most. Among these beneficiaries, foremost is the sector Services to agriculture which includes *inter alia* aerial seeding, crop and pasture dusting or spraying services, wool shearing services, packaging services, farm irrigation services, and veterinary services. Overall, this sector grows by over 2% most of which is driven by the growth in agricultural inputs (Fig. 4), followed by the sector Trade & transport services. Various other services as well as industries engaged in processing primary agricultural

[j]More detailed results and the composition of the broad sectors are available on request.

Table 5. Typical-year Effects of Growth in Broadacre Agriculture on Prices[1]

Sector (1)	Effects of Decomposing the Effects by Source (%)		
	Growth in Agriculture (2)	Productivity Growth in Agriculture (3)	Input Growth in Agriculture (4)
Producers' Price			
Agriculture	−0.42	−0.49	0.07
Dairy	0.21	0.04	0.17
Services to agriculture	4.63	0.46	4.17
Forestry, logging & fishing	0.03	0.01	0.01
Mining	0.01	—	—
Agriculture processing	0.03	−0.05	0.08
Other manufacturing	0.08	0.05	0.04
Trade & transport	0.23	0.17	0.06
Financial & business services	0.25	0.18	0.07
Other services	0.28	0.23	0.06
Total	**0.18**	**0.12**	**0.05**
Consumers' Price[2]			
Agriculture	0.03	−0.38	0.41
Dairy	0.11	0.02	0.09
Services to agriculture	4.41	0.44	3.97
Forestry, logging & fishing	0.01	0.01	—
Mining	0.01	—	—
Agriculture processing	0.04	—	0.04
Other manufacturing	0.04	0.02	0.02
Trade & transport	0.20	0.16	0.04
Financial & business services	0.20	0.15	0.06
Other services	0.50	0.46	0.04
Total	**0.30**	**0.26**	**0.05**

Notes: [1]The percentage changes are relative to 1992/93 (the base year) levels. More detailed results and the composition of the broad sectors are available on request

[2]Refers to the composite price of a good from both local and imported sources. The consumers' price for locally produced commodities includes sales taxes on the top of the corresponding producers' price

"—" implies a number less than 0.005

Source: WAG simulations

Table 6. Typical-year Effects of Growth in Broadacre Agriculture on Sectoral Production

Sector (1)	Effects of Growth in Agriculture (%) (2)
Dairy	0.04
Services to agriculture	2.33
Forestry, logging & fishing	−0.03
Mining	−0.04
Agriculture processing	0.30
Other manufacturing	0.13
Trade & transport	0.46
Financial & business services	0.25
Other services	0.30
Total	**0.45**

Note: The percentage changes are relative to 1992/93 (the base year) levels. More detailed results and the composition of the broad sectors are available on request
Source: WAG simulations

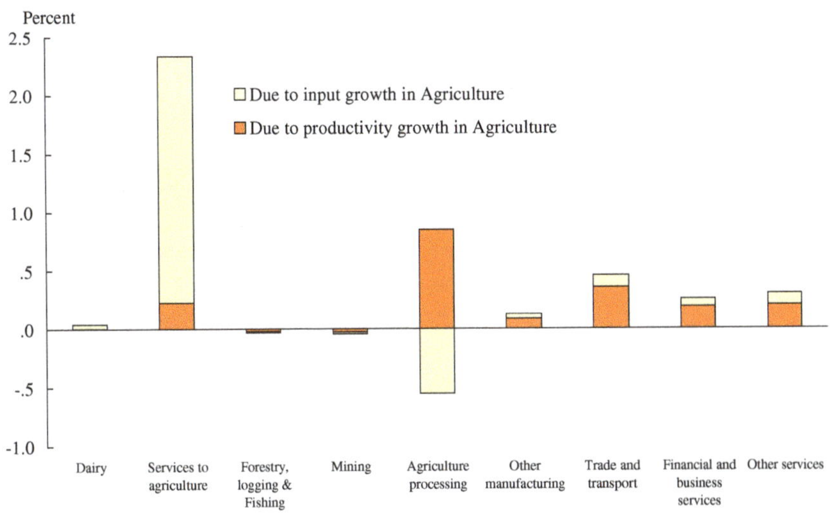

Fig. 4. Decomposition of the Typical-year Effects of Growth in Broadacre Agriculture on Sectoral Production. *Source*: WAG Simulations

commodities also benefit from the agricultural growth. However, the sector Agriculture processing grows only by a meager 0.3%. This is not a surprising result once the effect is decomposed according to the sources of agricultural growth (Fig. 4). The positive growth in Agriculture processing associated with the Agriculture productivity growth is largely offset by the contractionary effect of the agricultural input growth on agricultural processing.

It needs to be noted that the highly export-oriented, non-Agriculture sectors such as Mining and Forestry, logging & fishing (in particular, fishing) suffer a contraction, though not significant contraction. This is a reflection of the "booming sector" phenomenon (see, e.g. Cordon and Neary, 1982) — an expansion of highly export-oriented Agriculture leads to a real appreciation of the exchange rate which hurts non-agricultural exports.

Overall, a 6.4% growth in Agriculture leads to approximately a 0.5% growth in WA's total production (column 2 of Table 6), of which over three-quarters can be attributed to the productivity growth in Agriculture. In the short-run, employment effects are highly and positively correlated with the output effects. The differential output effects largely explain the relatively larger employment effect associated with the agricultural productivity growth demonstrated in Fig. 3.

Table 7 presents the effects on sectoral exports of agricultural growth. As expected, agricultural exports record a substantial growth in volumes (column 2). Interestingly, all non-agricultural sectors suffer a reduction in export volumes. This can be due to the cost-price squeeze associated with the real exchange rate appreciation discussed before, and/or rises in domestic demand whereby the goods and services which otherwise would be exported are absorbed locally. The real exchange rate appreciation largely explains the reduction in exports of the sectors Mining and Forestry, logging & fishing. As for the other non-Agriculture sectors, exports of their outputs decline despite the expansion in production (column 2 of Table 6). Clearly, domestic absorption for these commodities increases more than the increase in their production. Nonetheless, the overall impact of agricultural growth on State's exports is positive — the substantial export growth for Agriculture, combined with an increase in exports of processed agricultural commodities, leads to a growth in WA's total exports (in real terms) of about 0.6%.

The decomposition analysis shows that about three-quarters of the 9% export growth in agriculture is due to agricultural productivity growth. Almost the entire 0.6% growth in WA's total exports can be attributed to agricultural productivity growth (columns 2 and 3).

Table 7. Typical-year Effects of Growth in Broadacre Agriculture on the Volume of Sectoral Exports[1,2]

Commodity (1)	Effects of Decomposing the Effects by Source (%)		
	Agriculture Growth (2)	Productivity (3)	Input (4)
Agriculture	9.43	6.91	2.51
Dairy	—	—	—
Services to agriculture	—	—	—
Forestry, logging & fishing	−0.17	−0.13	−0.03
Mining	−0.06	−0.04	−0.02
Agriculture processing	0.25	2.13	−1.88
Other manufacturing	−0.41	−0.24	−0.17
Trade & transport	−0.25	−0.19	−0.06
Financial & business services	−0.39	−0.26	−0.12
Other services	−0.38	−0.23	−0.15
Total[3]	**0.56**	**0.51**	**0.05**

Notes: [1]The percentage changes are relative to 1992/93 (the base year) levels
[2]"—" implies no or negligible exports in the base year 1992/93
[3]The figures differ from the corresponding figures in Table 4 and Fig. 3 as the latter represent the effects on export value rather than the volume
Source: WAG simulations

5. Summary and Conclusion

This chapter has illustrated the methodologies of using a CGE model to quantify and decompose the overall contribution of agriculture. It has introduced and applied a CGE model of the WA economy (known as WAG) to quantitatively analyze the direct and indirect effects of the output growth of WA broadacre agriculture on the State economy of WA. It then has decomposed the economy-wide effects of agricultural output growth by its sources on the supply side — agricultural input growth and productivity growth.

Between 1977/78 and 1997/98, broadacre agricultural production grew at an average annual rate of over 6% in WA. This has been considered to be the typical-year output growth of the sector. According to WAG simulation results, this agricultural growth, in the absence of any policy changes or other external shocks, causes WA's real GSP to grow by 0.5%. The direct effect of this growth on GSP is about 0.2%. The remaining 0.3% is the indirect contribution of the sector. In other words, the indirect effect of agricultural growth is $0.3 \div 0.2 = 1.5$ times the direct effect. As expected, sectors with strong linkages to agriculture benefit most from the expansion of the sector. Foremost among these is the sector "services to agriculture" which grows by over 2%, followed by "trade & transport services".

Growth in agricultural production brings about a 0.6% growth in aggregate exports (both agricultural and non-agricultural) from WA. Although broadacre agricultural exports grow by over 9%, the low growth in total exports is due to the contraction of mining and fishing exports. This is a "booming sector" phenomenon — an expansion of agriculture, other things being unchanged, leads to a real appreciation of the exchange rate which hurts non-agricultural exports.

Above we stated that the 6% agricultural growth leads to an expansion of GSP of approximately 0.5%. According to our estimates, about 40% of this 0.5% GSP growth is derived from agricultural productivity growth. Input growth accounts for the remaining 60%. On the other hand, about three-quarters of the 9% of export growth in agriculture can be attributed to agricultural productivity growth.

Thus, the results suggest that the indirect benefits of agriculture exceed its direct contributions and that the contributions made by productivity enhancement in agriculture are indeed substantial. More importantly, the broad contribution of agriculture depends critically on whether the agriculture growth itself is due to input growth or productivity growth. In particular, productivity growth in agriculture leads to a substantial increase in farmers' income. It results in a reduction in production costs and a reduction in the supply price of agricultural output. This in turn induces an increase in the demand for agricultural commodities and produces a resultant increase in farmers' income.

In conclusion, it needs to be pointed out that the CGE approach, though a useful tool for analyzing sectoral contributions, also has its limitations. In particular, CGE models are based on a number of assumptions, including about production technologies, and product and factor markets. Some of these assumptions may not represent the real world as it is; but these assumptions are made nevertheless to keep the model manageable and tractable while retaining a strong resemblance to the real world. Often the model results are sensitive to various parameters. As for the current exercise, while the CGE model WAG is based on some simplifying assumptions, the specification of its agricultural sector and hence the critical parameters are based on the econometric estimates by Ahammad and Islam (2004).

Acknowledgments

This chapter is part of the project "Living Standards and WA Agriculture", jointly funded by the Australian Research Council and Agriculture Western Australia. The author would like to acknowledge the helpful comments by Kenneth Clements of the University of Western Australia. The views expressed in this chapter are author's own and should not be implicated in any way to the positions of his current organization.

References

ABARE, 1999. "Farm productivity data: 1977/78–1997/98." Australian Bureau of Agricultural and Resource Economics, Canberra (through personal communication via Agriculture Western Australia).

ABS, 1998. *1998 Western Australian Year Book.* Catalogue No. 1300.5, Australian Bureau of Statistics: Perth.

ABS, 1998. (various issues). *Australian National Accounts: State Accounts.* Catalogue No. 5220.0, Australian Bureau of Statistics: Canberra.

Ahammad H, 2000a. "The effects of growth in agriculture on the Western Australian economy: a CGE investigation." Discussion Paper No. 2000.08. Department of Economics, The University of Western Australia: Nedlands.

Ahammad H, 2000b. "WAG: A computable general equilibrium model of the Western Australian economy." Discussion Paper No. 2000.11. Department of Economics, The University of Western Australia: Nedlands.

Ahammad H, and Islam N, 2004. "Regional agricultural production systems: estimates for Western Australia." *Rev. Urban Reg. Develop. Stud.* **16**: 189–209.

Ahammad H, and Clements KW, 1999. "What does minerals growth mean to Western Australia?" *Resources Policy* **25**: 1–14.

Chaney M, 1999. "Towards a blueprint for revitalising rural and regional Australia." Keynote Presentation, Regional Australia Summit, Canberra.

Clements KW, Ahammad H, and Ye Q, 1996. "New mining and mineral-processing projects in Western Australia: effects on employment and the macroeconomy." *Resources Policy* **22**: 293–346.

Corden WM, and Neary JP, 1982. "Booming sector and de-industrialisation in a small open economy." *Econ. J.* **92**: 825–848.

Dixon PB, Parmenter BR, Sutton J, and Vincent DP, 1982. *ORANI: A Multisectoral Model of the Australian Economy.* North-Holland: Amsterdam/New York/Oxford.

Islam N, 2000. "An analysis of productivity growth in Western Australian agriculture." Discussion Paper No. 00.15. Department of Economics, The University of Western Australia: Nedlands.

Islam N, and Johnson P, 1997. *Agriculture and the Western Australian Economy: An input-output analysis.* Agriculture Western Australia: South Perth.

Johnson P, 2003. "Aspects of regional economic analysis." PhD thesis. Economic Research Centre, Department of Economics, The University of Western Australia.

Johnston B, and Girdlestone J, eds., 1983. "Implications for future research of recent developments and trends in agriculture." Bureau of Agricultural Economics and Commonwealth Scientific and Industrial Research Organization, Canberra.

Martin WJ, and Warr PG, 1994. "Determinants of agriculture's relative decline: Thailand." *Agric. Econ.* **11**: 219–235.

Productivity Commission, 1999. "Impact of competition policy reforms on rural and regional Australia." Commonwealth of Australia, Canberra.

Ye Q, 1999. "How different is mining from mineral processing? A general equilibrium analysis of new resources projects in Western Australia." *Australian J. Agric. Res. Econ.* **43**: 279–304.

Appendix 1. WA Agriculture in WAG

The joint-production[k] nature of Agriculture distinguishes it from the non-Agriculture industries. The specification of the joint-production technology for WAG Agriculture is based on the optimising assumption that a representative farm chooses a combination of output and input quantities so as to maximise its profit given a set of prices for outputs and inputs (characterising competitive markets for outputs and inputs), and fixed factors (i.e. the area of land holdings and the capital stock, characterising a short run) and the level of technology. The distinguishing feature in this optimisation problem is that the agricultural firm chooses the output mix simultaneously with the input mix. By comparison, a non-Agriculture firm does not have to choose the output mix as it produces only one good.

WAG considers a three-level nested production technology for Agriculture as presented in Fig. A1. In other words, the choice problem of the farm in WAG is modelled to entail a three-level production decision making process as follows:

- At the top, the farm chooses the quantities of five outputs, the amount of labour and the level of composite materials and services so as to maximise its profit, given a production technology, the prices of inputs and outputs and the supply of an input which is a composite of land and capital. The five top-level outputs are Sheep meat, Wool, Grains, Beef & other meat, and Agriculture n.e.c. (column 1 in Table A1).

[k]In this study, jointness is used to mean jointness in input quantities and to imply that decisions about production of one commodity are dependent on those about the production of other commodities. Note that one farm producing many outputs does not necessarily mean jointness in input quantities.

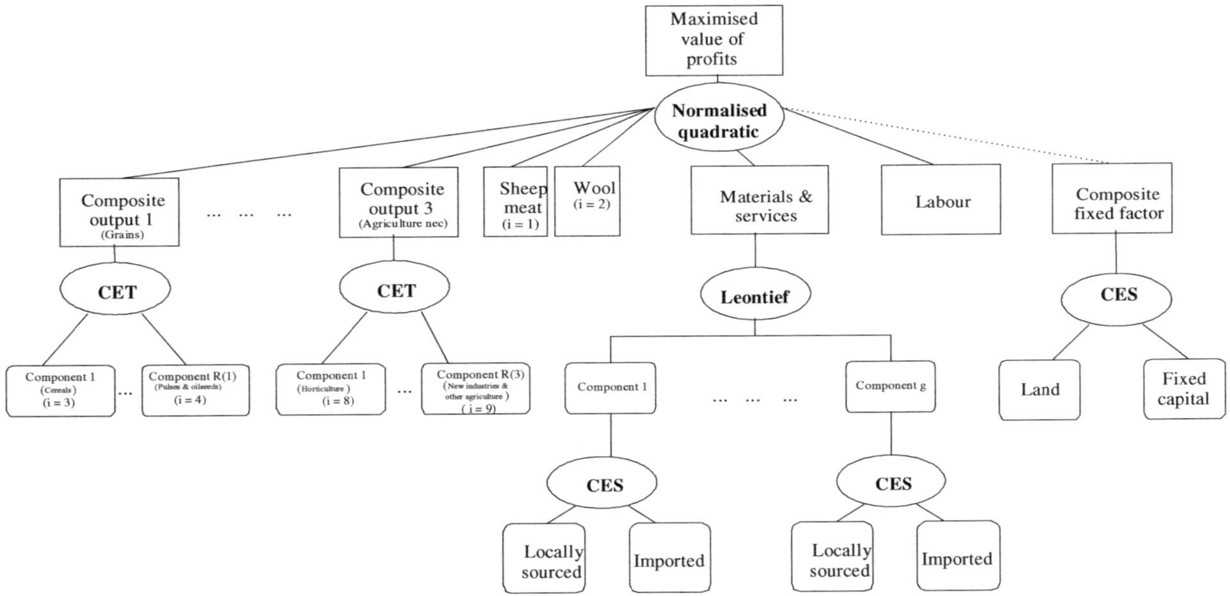

Fig. A.1. Production Technology for WAG Agriculture. *Notes*: (1) The nine WAG commodities listed in Table 3 are denoted by $i = 1, \ldots, 9$. (2) At the top panel, the dotted line for the composite fixed factor denotes that the factor, unlike other netputs at the top level, is fixed in supply in the short run and not determined in the farm's profit maximization process

Table A1. WAG Commodity Mapping

Top-level WAG Commodity	Commodity Component
1. Sheep meat	1. Sheep meat
2. Wool	2. Wool
3. Grains	3. Cereals 4. Pulses & oilseeds
4. Beef & other meat	5. Beef cattle 6. Pigs 7. Poultry
5. Agriculture n.e.c.	8. Horticulture 9. New industries & other agriculture

Note: The prefix numbers (1 to 9) in the second column are according to Table 3

- At the second level, given the quantities of the composite outputs and inputs from above, the farm chooses the quantities of their components such that:
  1. A composite crop is a CET (constant elasticity of transformation) aggregate of its components. Table A1 presented the list of three composite crops (numbered 3, 4 and 5) and their components. Accordingly, the output Grains is a CET composite of two commodities namely Cereals and pulses & oilseeds; Beef & other meat is a CET composite of three commodities namely Beef cattle, Pigs and poultry; and Agriculture n.e.c. is a CET composite of Horticulture and New industries & other agriculture.
  2. The composite materials & services input is a Leontief aggregate of the individual intermediate inputs i.e. the individual inputs are combined into the composite in fixed proportions.
  3. The only fixed primary input is a CES (constant elasticity of substitution) aggregate of its components — land and capital.

At the bottom, the individual intermediate inputs are chosen from local and imported sources so that each individual material input is a CES aggregate of the same commodity from both local and imported sources.

Part VI

Trade and International Policies

Chapter 12

The Impacts of Redesigning European Agricultural Support*

SØREN E. FRANDSEN, BIRGITTE GERSFELT and HANS G. JENSEN

Institute of Food and Resource Economics, The Royal Veterinary and Agricultural University, Frederiksberg, Denmark

The objective of this paper is to assess the impact at the individual member state level in the European Union and in non-member regions of liberalizing domestic support in the EU. Three scenarios are analyzed in order to illustrate the impacts of eliminating or decoupling the European agricultural support. We found that the existing domestic support payments in the EU are indeed coupled to production and hence affect production decisions and distort international trade with adverse effects on the export potential of developing countries as a consequence. Further, the value of this support is capitalised in significant higher land prices in Europe than would otherwise prevail. The scenarios illustrate the economic implications of transforming all domestic support payments (as well as other distorting policies) into a nationally homogenous and fully decoupled payment to all agricultural land, irrespective of a farmer's decision to crop or not. The analysis suggests that it is possible to convert the existing agricultural support into a fully decoupled payment which would not distort international trade and it indicates a way forward to offset the negative impact on land prices. Such a policy would also comply with the WTO rules (i.e. fall within the green box as decoupled income support). The

*This chapter was originally published in *Review of Urban and Regional Development Studies*, Vol. 15, No. 2, July 2003, and is reprinted here with minor modifications upon the permission from the publisher.

analysis also suggests that such a policy reform could be achieved at somewhat lower budgetary costs as compared with the existing costs of the Common Agricultural Policy.

1. Introduction

The Uruguay Round Agreement on Agriculture (URAA) marked the integration of agriculture into the multilateral trading system governed by WTO rules. The agreement covers the traditional WTO areas of market access and export competition, requiring member countries to reduce tariffs and export subsidies. However, it also contains an innovative feature as it seeks to discipline the use of domestic support by restricting member countries' use of trade-distorting domestic support policies.

The primary policy instruments in the European Common Agricultural Policy (CAP) are market price support and area and headage payments supplemented by a number of quantitative restrictions. The URAA stipulations on market access, export competition, and domestic support policies commit the EU to reduce its use of market price support. Furthermore, although area and headage payments are not currently subjected to reduction requirements, international pressures for reform of these payments are expected to increase during the upcoming WTO negotiations. It is therefore pertinent to investigate the options for reforming European agricultural support in accordance with the WTO rules.

In this paper, three decoupling or liberalization scenarios are presented with particular attention given to the importance of domestic support. We stress that the results presented are illustrative as our research has identified needs for further adjustments and improvements of the data underlying the analysis.[a]

2. Background

The inclusion of domestic support into the URAA is a formal recognition of the long-known fact that any domestic policy, which affects production (or consumption) of agricultural commodities, will generally have an effect on the country's international trade in agricultural commodities. Therefore, in order

[a]As the analysis underlying this paper was undertaken in the spring of 2002, this paper does not pretend to analyze the European Commission Midterm Review proposal of July 10, 2002. Our paper simply addresses the economic impacts of decoupling the direct support and possible avenues for reforming the Common Agricultural Policy.

to establish a "fair and market-oriented agricultural trading system" (URAA), it is not enough to deal with the issues of market access and export competition. The issue of coupled domestic support policies (i.e. policies which affect the producer's production decision or the consumer's consumption decision) must also be addressed.

In the URAA, domestic support policies are assigned to one of three boxes depending on their impact on international trade. Policies considered to have "no, or at most minimal trade-distorting effects or effects on production" (URAA) are placed in the green box and are not subjected to the requirement that support be reduced. All domestic support policies considered to distort trade are placed in the amber box and subjected to reduction requirements, except for certain distorting policies, which are implemented under production limiting programs. These latter policies are placed in the blue box, which exempts them from reduction requirements. One of the major issues in the upcoming negotiations is what will happen to these boxes — should the reduction requirements for amber box policies be tightened, should the blue box policy measures be subjected to some sort of reduction requirements, or should the blue box be scrapped all together by moving these policies into the amber box etc. (WTO, 2002).

The issue of what will happen to the three boxes has profound implications for the CAP. Market price support has long been considered the epitome of coupled support, and the provisions of the amber box along with the stipulations on market access and export subsidies seek to limit the use of this policy instrument significantly. The EU reforms of the CAP, which started with the MacSharry reform in 1992 and continued in Agenda 2000, have replaced some of the market price support with area and headage payments, which are less coupled and hence cause less distortions of international trade. However, the area and headage payments are not decoupled and do not qualify for the green box. Instead they are declared as blue box payments at present (Beard and Swinbank, 2001).

The blue box is currently a permanent provision of the agreement, and it can only be removed through negotiation. However, blue box policies are protected from challenge by the so-called "Peace Clause" (cf. article 13 of URAA), and it expires at the end of 2003. If the Peace Clause is not extended, other countries will have greater opportunity to take action against the EU area payments and headage payments, even if the box remains in place. And the blue box may not remain in place, as a number of developed and developing countries are proposing to get rid of the box and move the current blue box policies into the amber box. At the same time, there are also proposals to tighten the reduction requirements for amber box policies, and some countries even want amber box subsidies to eventually be eliminated (WTO, 2002). The EU is thus under pressure not only to reduce or eliminate its use of market price support, but also to reduce or reform its use of area and headage payments. This paper will explore the consequences of reforming the CAP by replacing these policies with fully decoupled area payments, which would be permitted under the green box.

Green box policies are often referred to as "decoupled" policies, but although the notion of "no, or at most minimal, trade-distorting effects or effects on production" is clearly related to the concept of decoupling, it should be noted that the green box also encompass some policies which typically will not be fully decoupled and probably should not be evaluated in reference to the decoupling criteria.[b] In fact, in the URAA the term decoupled is only used in connection with one policy — the type of green box direct payments to producers dubbed "decoupled income support". The URAA defines "decoupled income support" in the following way (URAA Annex 2).[c]

- Eligibility for such payments shall be determined by clearly-defined criteria such as income, status as a producer or landowner, factor use or production level in a defined and fixed base period.
- The amount of such payments in any given year shall not be related to, or based on, the type or volume of production (including livestock units) undertaken by the producer in any year after the base period.
- The amount of such payments in any given year shall not be related to, or based on, the prices, domestic or international, applying to any production undertaken in any year after the base period.

---

[b]The issue is whether the rationale for the policy is market failure correction or income redistribution. Certain market failure correcting policies neither can nor should be decoupled, since they aim to influence the farmer's production decision. However, if the rationale for the policy is purely income redistribution, the policy should be designed in accordance with the criteria for decoupling.

[c]In order to qualify for inclusion in the green box under the heading of "decoupled income support" the policy must also comply with the fundamental green box requirement of having "no, or at most minimal, trade-distorting effects or effects on production" and (URAA Annex 2):

1. The support in question shall be provided through a publicly-funded government programme (including government revenue foregone) not involving transfers from consumers; and
2. The support in question shall not have the effect of providing price support to producers.

- The amount of such payments in any given year shall not be related to, or based on, the factors of production employed in any year after the base period.
- No production shall be required in order to receive such payments.

This URAA definition of decoupling is clearly very application-oriented in that it is basically a checklist of requirements that a policy must fulfil in order to be considered decoupled. However, although these requirements capture the core implications of the concept of decoupling, they do not fully reflect the economic meaning of the concept. Some additional theoretical analysis is therefore given below.

3. Decoupling: Concept and Theory

In a recent paper, OECD explores the concept of decoupling and offers two possible definitions of the term: "effective full decoupling" and "full decoupling (in the restrictive sense)". A policy is effectively fully decoupled if "it results in a level of production and trade equal to what would have occurred if the policy were not in place . . . The shape of the supply or demand curves could be changed by an effectively decoupled policy, even if the equilibrium production and consumption are not changed" (OECD, 2001a).

On the other hand, a policy is fully decoupled in the restrictive sense if "it does not influence production decisions of farmers receiving payments, and if it permits free market determination of prices" (OECD, 2001a). That is, full decoupling is a very restrictive concept that requires no change in the way farmers and consumers take decisions: "After the introduction of a fully decoupled policy, both the shape and the position of the supply and demand curves should not be changed".

The important difference between these two concepts is that while effective decoupling is a concept that focuses on equilibrium quantities, decoupling in the restrictive sense also considers the adjustment process. Thus for a policy to be fully decoupled in the restrictive sense not only do equilibrium quantities have to remain unchanged, but the market must also respond to exogenous shocks as it would if the policy were not in place (OECD, 2001a). However, although the concept of decoupling in the restrictive sense may be the most theoretically appropriate concept, it is also very difficult to operationalize this concept. Therefore, empirical studies typically rely on the less restrictive concept of effective decoupling, and this is also the concept that the present paper will employ.

Comparing the two definitions of decoupling offered by OECD to the definition in URAA, one difference that immediately stands out is that the URAA defines decoupling in terms of policy design, whereas the two OECD definitions define decoupling in terms of policy effects. Policy design and policy effects are obviously intimately connected, but there is not always a one-to-one correspondence, as the same policy may result in different effects when implemented in different locations (cf. Gohin *et al.*, 1999). As it is the policy's effect on production and trade that matters rather than the policy design per se, this raises questions as to whether the URAA requirements will always be appropriate for determining whether a policy is decoupled in the true economic sense of the word.

When exploring the concept of decoupling theoretically, it is convenient to distinguish between decoupling from production and decoupling from trade. Decoupling from production refers to the notion of breaking the link between agricultural policies and the farmer's production decision. To move from "decoupling from production" to "decoupling from trade", it is necessary to also include the policy's effect on consumption and stockholding (OECD, 2001a). Market price support is of course the classic example of a policy that affects both production and consumption by increasing both the price received by the producer and the price paid by the consumer. Designing policies to be decoupled from trade thus requires attention to the policy's effect on the farmer's production decision as well as its effect on the consumer's consumption decision.

In order to design agricultural policies that are decoupled from production, it is necessary to understand the mechanisms through which agricultural policies may affect the farmer's production decision. The primary mechanism for a policy to affect the farmer's production decision is for the policy to affect the relative prices the farmer faces, be they market prices or shadow prices. Policies may change relative prices directly by subsidizing or taxing certain factors or commodities (e.g. area and headage payments), or they may change relative prices indirectly by altering regulations or market conditions, which in turn induces changes in market or shadow prices (e.g. market price support).

As changing the price pertaining to the production of a particular commodity changes the relative profitability of producing this commodity, policies targeting a subset of commodities will generally produce cross-commodity effects affecting the production of the other commodities the farmer could produce. The magnitude of these effects will depend in part on the design and coverage of the policy package. A policy package that covers a wide array of commodities in a homogenous fashion may well have smaller cross-commodity effects than a policy, which only targets one commodity.[d]

While a large number of agricultural policies work through the price mechanism to affect the quantity of outputs and/or inputs, other policies target these quantities directly. Typical examples of such policies would be quantity constraints on output or input use. Such policies may be introduced to offset the production effects of non-decoupled policies. By introducing a quantity constraint, the policy package may become effectively decoupled, although it is highly unlikely that it will also be decoupled in the restrictive sense. This issue of combining policy instruments as well as the issue of policies targeting one commodity affecting the production of other commodities highlights an important point for policy evaluation. As it is the aggregate effects that matter, policy evaluation should also focus on the aggregate effects of the policy package rather than only focusing on the effects of the individual instruments. Furthermore, the evaluation should not be limited to the commodities targeted in the policy package, but should be extended to also include non-targeted commodities that may be effected through cross-commodity effects. Relating the former point to the URAA definition of decoupling, it becomes clear that one of the problems with the URAA definition is that it does not allow for several policy instruments to be evaluated as one policy package. Instead, each policy instrument must be evaluated individually (cf. Gohin *et al.*, 1999).[e]

The effects discussed so far can all be modelled and evaluated in a static and deterministic framework. However, agricultural policies may affect the farmer's production decision through other channels relating specifically to the dynamic dimension or the presence of uncertainty. Starting with the former, farmers do not merely make decisions pertaining to current production, they also need to make decisions about future production and what investments to undertake. Statically coupled support will always affect the farmer's investment

[d]Of course, the aggregate supply response will also depend on, e.g. the elasticity of input supply. If all inputs are in fixed supply, this will temper the overall supply response to a change in policy, as the farmers will only be able to use existing resources. However, if input supply is very flexible, then the aggregate supply response to the policy package, which covers all commodities in a homogenous fashion, may be a large increase in output quantities, even if the relative resource allocation *within* the sector is largely unchanged (i.e. even if the cross-commodity effects are very small).

[e]A combination of a coupled payment and a quantity constraint that achieves an effectively decoupled outcome will thus not qualify for the green box under the heading "decoupled income support". However, this policy may qualify for the blue box, which would at present exempt it from the requirements to reduce domestic support.

decision, since it affects his production decision. Statically decoupled support, on the other hand, will not affect the farmer's investment decision if markets are perfect. However, if capital markets are imperfect, even decoupled income support will affect the farmer's investment decision as the market imperfection results in a breakdown of separability between the farmer's production and consumption decision (cf. OECD, 2001a).

Through the investment mechanism, current policies can affect future production. However, through the expectation mechanism, future policies can affect current production. This will be the case, if the farmer's current production affects the policy payments he will receive in the future, either because the policy is explicitly designed this way, or because the farmer expects the government to change the policy so that current production will become the determining factor for future payments (OECD, 2001a).[f] In either of these cases, farmers will generally have an incentive to retain more resources in agricultural use and possibly produce more than justified by current market conditions.

Moving on to the issue of uncertainty, agricultural production is generally characterized by a high degree of uncertainty, and this suggests some additional channels through which agricultural policies may affect the farmer's production decision. If farmers are risk averse, and market failure results in a breakdown of separability between the farmers production and consumption decision, then risk aversion will affect the farmer's production decision. Agricultural policies may either mitigate the farmer's response to risk or reduce the amount of risk the farmer faces. The former will be the case, if policy payments increase the farmer's wealth, provided the farmer's preferences exhibit decreasing absolute risk aversion (DARA). Even lump-sum income support payments, which would be fully decoupled in a static deterministic world, may thus induce the farmer to produce more, if he is risk averse and has DARA preferences. On the other hand, policies can reduce the amount of risk faced by the farmer, if policy payments partially (or fully) offset the fluctuations in prices (OECD, 2001a). However, this kind of policy may be market failure correcting rather than income redistributing, and as such it may not be appropriate to evaluate it based on the decoupling criteria.

---

[f]This would for instance be the case, if farmers expect the government to update the base year used for determining the amount of support each farmer receives. This problem is explicitly dealt with in the URAA, as green box decoupled income support payments may not be based on "output, prices or factors used in any year after a fixed base year" (OECD, 2001).

Empirical studies on decoupling of agricultural policies often focus on the relative price effects, which can be analyzed in a static deterministic framework. As the preceding discussion has shown, taking dynamic aspects and uncertainty into consideration suggests additional channels through which agricultural policies may affect the farmer's production decision. These effects should be kept in mind when designing policies to be decoupled from production, and it should also be considered how the presence of these effects might skew the results of empirical studies using a static, deterministic framework. It is therefore important to obtain estimates of the relative magnitudes of these effects. However, OECD suggests "it seems reasonable to postulate that the static relative price effects are more significant for assessing the effective degree of decoupling and that the effects associated with risk and dynamics are more likely to be significant for assessing the degree of responsiveness with respect to external shocks and market signals (full decoupling in the restrictive sense)" (OECD, 2001a). As this paper will focus on the issue of effective decoupling, the analysis will be restricted to considering relative price effects in a static, deterministic world.

4. European Agricultural Support

Up until 1992, market price support was the primary policy instrument of the European Common Agricultural Policy. However, in response to the Uruguay Round negotiations, the EU implemented the so-called McSharry reform in 1993. The reform entailed a reduction of the guaranteed prices for a number of commodities while compensating farmers for the price cuts by introducing direct payments to producers in the form of area payments and headage payments (Walter-Jørgensen and Jensen, 2001). The latest CAP reform, Agenda 2000, extends and deepens the McSharry reform for several commodities by further reducing the intervention prices and partially compensating farmers for these price cuts by increasing area and headage payments for the affected commodities (OECD, 2001b). A new direct subsidy to milk production was also introduced.

EU area payments. Under the EU area payment scheme, farmers can request area payments for land used for cereals, oilseed, and protein crops (COP). The farmer, who wishes to receive area payments, has to choose between two schemes: the simplified scheme and the general scheme. Under the simplified scheme, the farmers may not request payments for an area exceeding what corresponds to 92t cereals in his yield region. He is not obliged to set aside land, and he receives a non crop-specific payment corresponding to the cereal payment for all the eligible COP areas. Under the general scheme, the farmer is obliged to set aside a certain percentage of his declared area, and he receives crop-specific payments for the land he is farming, plus compensatory payments for the land he is setting aside. The total area, on which COP area payments are payable, is fixed on a Member State basis. In case of the planted area being expanded beyond the defined base area, there will be a proportionate reduction in the payment per hectare. However, overshooting of the national base areas has been rare (Walter-Jørgensen and Jensen, 2001).

From this description it is clear, why the current EU area payments are not likely to be decoupled from production. These payments are directly linked to the current use of land inducing the farmer to farm more land than he otherwise would. In theory, a set aside requirement could limit production just enough to ensure effective decoupling, but this would probably be quite difficult to implement in reality. Furthermore, since the area payments differ across commodities, they will distort the output mix. Under Agenda 2000, the area payment for oilseed is scheduled to be reduced to align it with the area payment for cereals and the set aside compensatory payment (OECD, 2001b). However, as long as area payments are not identical for all uses of agricultural land, the area payment scheme will continue to distort the farmer's production decision.

Comparing these issues to the green box criteria for decoupled income support, it becomes clear that the current EU area payments violate most of these criteria, as they depend on current factor use and type of production, and the farmer is required to engage in production to receive the payments. Furthermore, the payments also violate the eligibility criterion, as these payments are presently available to all current and future farmers.

EU headage payments. Under the headage payment schemes, farmers can request payments for bovine animals. The production of beef and veal is subject to several direct support programs, which are linked to production (special premium, suckler cow premium, slaughter premium, and additional payments), as well as some direct support programs, which are aimed at leveling seasonal variation in slaughtering or extensification of production (Walter-Jørgensen and Jensen, 2001). Most of these premiums and payments are subject to national or regional ceilings (European Commission, 2001). Producers of sheep may request a premium per head of ewe, and producers of goat meat in less-favored areas are also granted support under a similar system (Walter-Jørgensen and Jensen, 2001).

From this description, it is clear that the various payments are directly linked to production, which would generally induce the farmers to increase production. However, the national or regional ceilings in the premium schemes serve to limit the supply response.

5. Adjusting the Standard Model and Database

The base GTAP model is a standard multi-regional, static computable general equilibrium (CGE) model.[g] Regional production is produced according to a constant return to scale technology in a perfectly competitive environment, and the private demand system is represented by a non-homothetic demand system (a Constant Difference Elasticity function).[h] The foreign trade structure is characterised by the Armington assumption implying imperfect substitutability between domestic and foreign goods, cf. Hertel (1998).

In order to analyze the impacts of reforming the Common Agricultural Policy, i.e. decoupling the agricultural support, it is important to capture the key institutional features of CAP (the policy instruments) and the recent reform of the CAP (Agenda 2000). We have therefore explicitly modelled the following features of the CAP, cf. Bach, Frandsen and Jensen (2000):

- Direct payments to arable land and livestock, together with set-aside requirements and base area restrictions.
- Budgetary limits on the total amount allocated to land and livestock according to the institutional rules of the Common Agricultural Policy.
- Milk and sugar quotas.[i]
- The European Union agricultural budget and the important effects of interregional transfers between member states.

In this paper, the point of departure is version 5 of the GTAP database, cf. Dimaranan and McDougall (2002). This implies that all 15 members of the EU are explicitly represented in the database, including the important transformation of the OECD Producer Subsidy Estimates to the GTAP level of aggregation plus a full disaggregation of the EU-15 aggregate of domestic support to the individual EU member country level, cf. the discussion in Frandsen, Jensen and Yu (2001).

[g]GTAP is the abbreviation for Global Trade Analysis Project.

[h]Hence, the present analysis abstracts from features such as imperfect competition and increasing return to scale, which may however be important in certain sectors.

[i]In this study, the representation of the EU sugar policy is rudimentary and not as detailed as in Frandsen *et al.* (2003). The results for the production of sugar should therefore be considered with great care. Similar considerations relate to the dairy sector.

A number of important adjustments have been made to the standard database to allow a more precise representation of the CAP instruments and the level of domestic support. First, the GTAP database is updated to allow for the recent adjustments as reported by the OECD secretariat, i.e. the level of domestic support reflects the 1998-PSE numbers as reported in the OECD PSE edition 2001. Second, the database is adjusted to include all domestic support reported by the OECD's PSE tables (the standard GTAP database does not include domestic support for vegetables, fruits and nuts, plant based fibers and other crops). Third, hectare premiums given to silage crops in the EU, being included as an intermediate input subsidy, are moved to input subsidies to land and male animal premiums are moved from capital input subsidies to output subsidies. Fourth, the database has been adjusted to reflect the quota rents associated with the EU milk and sugar quota regimes. The data incorporated are based on two recent studies undertaken by Frandsen *et al.* (2001) and Jansson (2002). Finally, the common agricultural budget has been explicitly represented in the database (the 1998/99 budget) at the member state level, including the contribution of the individual member states to the financing of the agricultural expenditures.

6. Experimental Design

Before analyzing the impacts of reforming the Common Agricultural Policy, a baseline for the period 1997–2013 is constructed.[j] The baseline provides a benchmark against which alternative scenarios can be compared. It features projections of the world economy, plus incorporation of policy changes and the effects of changes in the CAP as outlined in the Agenda 2000 reform. In terms of results from the baseline, only a few important characteristics will be presented, including the resulting level of market price support and domestic support, i.e. the support measures being eliminated in the following three scenarios.

Scenario 1: Elimination of domestic agricultural support in the EU. This entails a complete elimination of all domestic support given to European agriculture, i.e. all output subsidies, intermediate input subsidies, land-based payment and capital-based payment are phased out. The requirement to set-aside is also eliminated. The budgetary savings are reflected in a lower common contribution rate to the financing of the EU CAP budget.

[j]The model is solved using GEMPACK (Harrison and Pearson, 1996).

Scenario 2a: Decoupling domestic agricultural support in the EU. All existing domestic support measures in each of the 15 EU member countries are converted into a region specific homogenous payment to land. This implies that all distorting payments are converted into a land subsidy which is given irrespective of the use of the pre-defined and fixed agricultural area. The requirement to set-aside is again eliminated. The budgetary costs of the domestic support correspond to the costs prior to the change in the policy.

Scenario 2b: Elimination of the homogenous and decoupled payment to land in the EU. The land subsidy defined in scenario 2a is now removed. The budgetary savings are reflected in a lower common contribution rate financing the EU CAP budget.

Scenario 3: WTO reform scenario. All export subsidies and all domestic support measures are eliminated. Market access is improved by reducing tariff barriers by 30%. Quantitative restrictions are eliminated. To compensate the owners of agricultural land for the significant capital loss in terms of lower land prices, a region specific homogenous payment to land is introduced. The payment exactly offset the negative impact on land prices in each of the member states. Again the payment is given irrespectively of the farmer's decision to crop or not. The design of the scenarios is illustrated in Fig. 1.

7. Quantitative Description of the Scenarios

For all the scenarios described above, the analysis is undertaken in the year 2013 in a world shaped by the baseline scenario.[k]

The border protection and domestic support levels in the EU are shown in Table 1 for the beginning (1997) and the end of the baseline period (2013). Import protection in the European Union for rice, wheat, other grains, bovine meat products, and sugar and dairy products is relatively high in both 1997 and 2013. In 2013, only rice, other grains, and in particular sugar receive noteworthy export subsidies. According to the post Agenda 2000 simulation,

[k]The macroeconomic closure used is a neo-classical closure where investments are endogenous and adjust to accommodate any changes in savings. This approach is adopted at the global level and investments are then allocated across regions to equalize the marginal rate of return in all regions. Although global investments and savings must be equal, this does not apply at the regional level, where the trade balance is endogenously determined as the difference between regional savings and regional investments. This is valid as regional savings enter the regional utility function. The numéraire used in the model is a price index as suggested by de Melo and Robinson (1989) and de Melo and Tarr (1992), namely the global primary factor price index.

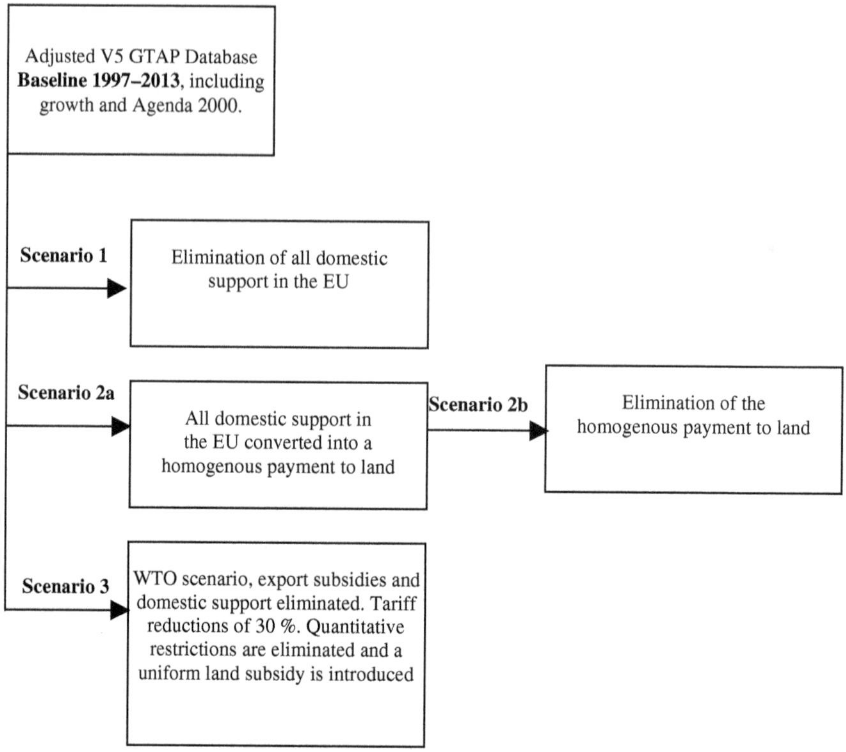

Fig. 1. Experimental Design

the export subsidies to bovine meats and dairy products amounts to 1.7% and 5.6%.

In a number of cases, the database reflects significant domestic support measures in primary agriculture. In the case of wheat, the domestic support measures amount to 66% and 69% of the value of the domestic wheat production in 1997 and 2013, respectively. The changes from 1997 to 2013 reflects both the implementation of the Agenda 2000 reform and the deflation of the nominally fixed direct payments by 2% per annum.

In Table 2 below, the aggregate power of domestic support for EU-15 is shown. The power of support equals 1 plus the ratio of total value of the payment (the sum of the value of output subsidies, intermediate input subsidies, land-based payments and capital-based payments) over the value of production. The total value of direct payments in the European Union amount to 38.3 billion EURO in 1998 or approximately 18% of the total value of agricultural

Table 1. Protection and Domestic Support, EU-15, 1997 and 2013 (Percent)

	Import Tariff Equivalent		Export Subsidies		Domestic Support	
	1997	2013	1997	2013	1997	2013
Paddy rice	64.9	64.9	13.8	13.8	12.4	8.0
Wheat	61.4	61.4	9.1	0.0	65.7	68.6
Other grains	38.6	38.6	34.2	14.1	60.3	66.2
Vegetables, fruit, nuts	14.5	14.5	0.8	0.8	3.6	3.3
Oilseeds	0.0	0.0	0	0.0	52.6	28.7
Sugar cane and beet	251.4	251.4	0	0.0	6.6	5.8
Plant based fibers	0.0	0.0	0	0.0	65.7	45.8
Other crops	3.1	3.1	0.4	0.4	7.8	6.8
Bovine animals	36.6	36.6	0	0.0	54.2	85.6
Other animal products	6.7	6.7	0	0.0	4.2	4.3
Raw milk	0.0	0.0	0	0.0	5.2	15.5
Wool	0.0	0.0	0	0.0	0.0	0.0
Fish	3.6	3.6	0	0.0	0	0
Resource extraction	0.0	0.0	0	0.0	0	0
Bovine meat products	88.9	88.9	27.1	1.7	0	0
Other meat products	30.9	30.9	4.2	4.2	0	0
Vegetable oils and fats	11.4	11.4	0.1	0.1	0	0
Dairy products	87.7	87.7	24.2	5.6	0	0
Processed rice	87.4	87.4	13.8	13.8	0	0
Sugar	76.4	76.4	54.4	54.4	0	0
Other processed foods	28.8	28.8	4.5	4.5	0	0
Beverages and tobacco	8.3	8.3	0	0.0	0	0
Textiles/wearing apparel	10.2	10.2	0	0.0	0	0
Wood/paper products	2.4	2.4	0	0.0	0	0
Petro/chemicals/minerals	3.2	3.2	0	0.0	0	0
Manufactures	3.7	3.7	0	0.0	0	0
Utilities	0.0	0.0	0	0.0	0	0
Transport	0.0	0.0	0	0.0	0	0
Services	0.0	0.0	0	0.0	0	0

Source: GTAP version 5 database, OECD PSE tables and own calculations

Table 2. The Aggregate Power of Domestic Support, EU-15, 1998 (Million Euros)

GTAP Item	Total	Wheat	Rice	Course Grains	Oil-seeds	Sugar (Refined)	Milk	Beef & Sheep	Other Meat	Wool	Misc.
Value of production (1)	213534	12347	754	10684	3801	4917	33904	22072	32370	0	92685
Value of payments (2) of which (in percent)	38349	7651	111	6187	2564	304	1834	10954	1367	0	7377
Output subsidy	14.49	−0.23	−0.33	−0.19	−0.20	−3.15	−3.13	13.04	−7.80	0.00	58.77
Intermediate input subsidy	5.54	2.75	11.66	2.87	2.62	21.78	6.39	0.65	39.82	0.00	11.60
Land-based payment	51.72	95.26	80.00	94.96	95.68	63.25	58.23	14.66	16.15	0.00	14.10
Capital-based payment	28.26	2.22	8.67	2.35	1.90	18.12	38.50	71.65	51.83	0.00	15.52
Power of domestic support ((1 + 2)/1)	1.180	1.620	1.147	1.579	1.674	1.062	1.054	1.496	1.042	1.000	1.080

Source: OECD PSE Tables and own calculations

production of which for example 7.7 billion EURO relates to the support of wheat production.

Table 3 shows the distribution of domestic support on member states. The value of domestic support to wheat producers in France amounts to 2.2 billion EURO or 48.7% of the French total value of wheat production, which is somewhat lower than the average EU level of domestic support for wheat. About 96% of these payments are area-based payments. In total, France receives almost 30% of the total amount spent on domestic support for the production of wheat in the EU. Germany receives another 20% of the total support given to wheat producers in the European Union.

Finally, it is evident from Table 4 that the importance of the domestic agricultural support varies significantly across the agricultural commodities as well as across the individual EU member countries. The variations across the commodities reflects the different policy regimes for the different agricultural commodities — some commodities being highly dependent on border protection, e.g. sugar and dairy products, while others are more dependent on the direct support payments, e.g. grains, oilseeds and plant-based fibers.

The variations across the member countries for a given commodity reflects a number of national characteristics, including differences in the historical reference yields and eligible hectares for the major crops, the actual harvested area and yields in 1997, as well as different crops and animals being produced in different regions (compositional effects). For a detailed description of the methods used in disaggregating the EU-15 power of support across the agricultural commodities at the EU member country level, see Frandsen, Jensen and Yu (2001).

This structure of domestic support is replicated in the data after undertaking the baseline simulation, including the introduction of the full Agenda 2000 reform and an implicit deflation of 2% per annum of the nominal fixed area and headage payments, cf. Table 5. Note that in particular, the domestic support for the production of milk and bovine animals increases significantly from 1997 to 2013 (the Agenda 2000 reform), and that the domestic support declines slightly for a number of the other commodities.

In the scenarios analyzed, a number of different and significant changes will therefore take place simultaneously. Not only will the farmers in the individual member countries be affected differently in terms of different reductions in the domestic support received (relative to the value of production), but the relative competitiveness between the different agricultural commodities within a given region as well as between different member countries will change and impact significantly on the final outcome. Also, the initial trading pattern will

Table 3. Domestic Support for Wheat, EU-15 and at Member State Level, 1998 (Million Euros)

	EU15	Bel	Dk	Ger	Gre	Spa	Fra	Ire	Italy	Lux	Neth	Aus	Por	Fin	Swe	UK
Value of production (1)	12347	202	561	2303	294	688	4627	77	1221	7	122	157	18	45	261	1763
Value of payments (2) of which (in percent)	7651	82	277	1642	373	574	2252	42	923	3	133	129	71	53	167	930
Output subsidy	−0.23	−0.13	−0.22	−0.47	0.00	−0.13	−0.19	−0.17	−0.00	−0.19	−0.68	−0.38	−0.48	−0.57	−0.36	−0.15
Intermediate input subsidy	2.75	1.53	2.62	5.61	−0.00	1.59	2.27	1.97	0.05	2.26	8.06	4.53	5.65	6.76	4.28	1.81
Land-based payment	95.26	97.36	95.48	90.33	100.00	97.26	96.08	96.66	99.92	96.11	86.12	92.19	90.26	88.35	92.63	96.88
Capital-based payment	2.22	1.23	2.12	4.52	−0.00	1.28	1.83	1.59	0.04	1.82	6.50	3.65	4.56	5.46	3.45	1.46
Power of domestic support (1 + 2)/1)	1.62	1.41	1.49	1.71	2.27	1.83	1.49	1.55	1.76	1.40	2.09	1.82	4.92	2.17	1.64	1.53

Source: OECD PSE Tables and own calculations

Table 4. Domestic Support, EU Member Countries, 1998 (Percent of the Value of Domestic Production)

	EU15	Bel	Dk	Deu	Gre	Spa	Fra	Irel	Italy	Lux	Nld	Aut	Por	Fin	Swe	UK
Paddy rice	14.7	0.0	0.0	0.0	14.7	14.7	14.7	0.0	14.7	0.0	0.0	0.0	14.7	0.0	0.0	0.0
Wheat	62.0	40.8	49.4	71.3	126.8	83.4	48.7	54.5	75.6	40.3	109.3	82.4	392.4	116.8	64.3	52.7
Other grains	57.9	40.0	69.4	76.5	26.2	45.3	50.1	64.8	39.6	48.0	157.6	57.3	58.8	82.7	95.7	83.4
Vegetables, fruit, nuts	3.8	1.2	4.6	0.8	7.6	6.7	5.2	0.2	2.8	0.0	1.6	2.0	3.9	1.9	2.2	0.7
Oilseeds	49.1	65.0	59.2	59.1	40.4	50.8	65.3	71.9	36.1	39.5	61.0	104.5	45.3	125.8	94.5	58.3
Sugar cane and beet	6.2	6.9	9.8	5.2	2.7	7.8	6.1	5.9	4.5	0.0	6.0	7.0	2.1	4.9	4.7	11.6
Plant based fibers	60.4	81.3	0.0	0.0	51.9	78.8	118.6	0.0	0.0	0.0	110.5	0.0	0.0	0.0	0.0	340.6
Other crops	6.6	1.2	8.2	3.6	35.1	11.5	5.5	5.4	7.0	3.1	0.2	11.0	9.0	9.1	14.3	11.8
Bovine animals	49.6	24.5	35.2	48.3	77.7	60.8	37.5	66.6	30.5	36.9	8.1	77.0	127.9	102.6	60.4	82.2
Other animal products	4.2	0.7	0.4	3.8	16.7	6.8	2.5	18.9	3.4	9.6	5.2	8.5	14.9	9.5	4.3	1.1
Raw milk	5.4	12.5	2.0	3.4	6.7	5.9	7.6	11.9	4.1	0.1	7.9	4.8	11.7	4.5	2.7	2.2
Wool	0.0	0.0	0.0	0.0	0.0	0.0	0.0	0.0	0.0	0.0	0.0	0.0	0.0	0.0	0.0	0.0

Source: OECD PSE Tables and own calculations

Table 5. Domestic Support, EU Member Countries, 2013 (Percent of the Value of Domestic Production)

	EU15	Bel	Dk	Deu	Gre	Spa	Fra	Irel	Italy	Lux	Nld	Aut	Por	Fin	Swe	UK
Paddy rice	8.0	0.0	0.0	0.0	10.2	9.2	9.2	0.0	12.4	0.0	0.0	0.0	12.4	0.0	0.0	0.0
Wheat	68.6	37.2	45.8	75.0	110.7	77.0	46.6	63.8	86.5	35.7	101.9	92.2	620.6	137.3	64.5	53.1
Other grains	66.2	38.1	65.9	87.0	26.5	43.8	52.5	72.9	50.1	47.4	144.7	67.8	51.6	122.5	100.2	83.5
Vegetables, fruit, nuts	3.3	1.2	4.2	0.8	6.3	6.0	5.1	0.1	2.6	0.0	1.5	0.8	4.7	2.7	3.5	0.7
Oilseeds	28.7	32.3	26.8	26.6	19.3	29.0	33.7	324.8	19.2	13.5	46.3	58.7	29.0	75.6	47.1	30.8
Sugar cane and beet	5.8	6.4	9.0	4.4	2.1	7.3	5.6	5.2	3.7	0.3	5.3	5.9	4.3	4.4	4.1	10.6
Plant based fibers	45.8	63.4	0.0	0.0	36.7	66.4	92.3	0.0	0.0	0.0	67.3	0.0	0.0	0.0	0.0	237.0
Other crops	6.8	1.1	5.8	2.2	34.6	10.7	4.6	2.3	6.7	3.4	0.2	9.1	8.2	7.3	10.7	6.1
Bovine animals	85.6	46.6	62.7	87.1	77.6	71.9	57.5	85.1	52.7	52.9	20.5	125.8	142.4	183.8	131.8	185.0
Other animal products	4.3	0.8	0.4	4.0	15.0	6.9	2.6	17.1	3.3	9.2	5.6	7.6	16.0	9.2	3.9	1.1
Raw milk	15.5	27.7	11.2	18.4	7.7	14.5	20.9	23.0	10.3	13.1	26.1	17.0	23.7	10.7	9.8	13.5
Wool	0.0	0.0	0.0	0.0	0.0	0.0	0.0	0.0	0.0	0.0	0.0	0.0	0.0	0.0	0.0	0.0

Source: OECD PSE Tables and own calculations

influence the impact on the agricultural production in each of the 15 member countries depending on, for example, whether the major export markets for a given commodity are other European markets or markets outside the European Union.

8. Results

8.1. *Scenario 1: Eliminating Domestic Support Measures*

Supply response in the EU. Eliminating domestic support in the European Union impacts significantly on the European production of a number of primary agricultural products, cf. Table 6. At the aggregate level, the production of wheat, other grains and oilseeds declines by 6.9%, 5.6% and 8.9%, respectively, as a result of the elimination of the land-based payments given to these crops. The production of plant based fibers, receiving domestic support that correspond to almost 60% of the value of production, declines by 63% — a decline that also reflects the relative week competitiveness of these crops in Europe (cotton etc.). The production of vegetables and fruits and other crops, however, increase marginally — a result of increased competitiveness of these sectors relative to the other land using sectors in the European Union.

The production of bovine animals decrease by approximately 11% following the elimination of the relatively significant payments to cattle. The average EU production of other animals — pork and poultry — is unaffected by the elimination of the domestic support measures, which only constitute some 4% of the total value of production of pork and poultry. At the individual EU member state level, most of the production changes mirror the changes at the aggregate EU level reflecting the relative reductions in domestic support in the individual EU member countries. It is also evident, that the production of a few agricultural commodities changes significantly, examples being the production of plant-based fibers and rice. This is explained by either a significant reduction in the subsidies received in the countries producing these commodities (for plant-based fibers, this is Belgium, Greece, Spain, France, Netherlands and the UK; in the case of rice, it is France, Italy, Spain, Greece and Portugal) or simply changes to an almost absent production of these commodities in the other countries.

The analysis also shows some interesting results. First, the raw milk quota is no longer binding in Germany, Italy and Austria. This is a result of a significant lower value of the milk quota in year 2013 compared to 1997 (cost increases due to higher prices of a number of important factors of production

Table 6. Scenario 1: Change in Production, EU Member Countries (Percent)

	Bel	Dk	Deu	Gre	Spa	Fra	Irel	Italy	Lux	Nld	Aut	Por	Fin	Swe	UK	EU15
Paddy rice	12.1	22.1	38.5	23.6	−1.7	−0.5	26.4	−2.2	11.9	9.4	22.6	11.7	25	22.1	43.1	5.5
Wheat	−9	2	−13	−19.1	−5	−2.2	−7.2	−4.7	−7.2	−30.9	−16.6	−53.3	−7.2	−0.5	−9	−6.9
Other grains	−16.9	−0.2	−10.3	−6.1	−3.3	−0.7	−8.3	−1.3	−13.1	−70.3	−1.4	−3.8	−5.1	−8	−12.3	−5.6
Vegetables, fruit, nuts	1.1	7.2	18.5	5.1	−5.1	−4.6	28.2	3.3	16	−5.3	39.4	10.2	22.7	45.8	5.5	2.2
Oilseeds	−42.8	8.4	−2	−14.7	−18.7	7.2	−18.5	−7.7	16.1	−76.3	−6.6	−19.6	−8.8	−2.4	−2.2	−8.9
Sugar cane and beet	−0.2	0	0.3	−5.2	0	0.5	0.2	0	0.2	0.3	0.1	41.9	0.6	0	−0.7	0.0
Plant based fibers	−95.9	26.9	87.9	−80.5	−96.9	−95.7	6.5	12.9	40.1	−96.2	33.7	94.8	4.3	122.1	−99.8	−63.1
Other crops	−1.3	0	33.4	−36.3	−12.9	4.2	26.6	−2.8	5	9.7	−0.4	2.7	13.6	18.4	14.2	3.1
Bovine animals	−12.4	−26.6	−12.4	−13.7	−13.6	−7.7	−52.8	−6.7	−22.2	21.1	−7.5	−11.6	−6.9	−11.9	−12.7	−10.7
Other animal products	6	17.9	0	−5.8	−1.8	1.6	−5.7	0.2	−8.4	1.2	−0.3	−2.9	−4.1	0.9	−9.3	0.0
Raw milk	0	0	−1.2	0	0	0	0	−3.3	0	0	−4.7	0	0	0	0	−0.5
Wool	19.7	11.2	70.5	12.6	18.9	3	66.2	9.3	31	9.3	33.1	36.1	29.3	7.3	−22.6	−5.1
Fish	−1	−0.8	0	1	0.1	−0.2	0.2	−0.1	−0.5	−0.6	−0.8	−0.1	−0.4	−0.6	−0.3	0.4
Resource extraction	0	0	0	0.3	0.1	0	0	0	0	0	0	0.1	0.1	0	0	0.0

Table 6. (*Continued*)

	Bel	Dk	Deu	Gre	Spa	Fra	Irel	Italy	Lux	Nld	Aut	Por	Fin	Swe	UK	EU15
Bovine meat products	−14.9	−27.9	−14.1	−13.5	−13.6	−8.5	−57.7	−7.2	−25.2	24.6	−7.6	−11.1	−7	−12.2	−10.8	−10.9
Other meat products	7	21.4	−0.1	−5.5	−1.8	2.1	−7.3	0.7	−9.2	0.7	−0.4	−3.1	−5.9	1	−20.7	−1.6
Vegetable oils and fats	1.4	4.7	0.1	−14.8	−5.7	2	4.2	−4.1	−0.1	−1.4	0.7	−3.5	−0.8	−1.3	−5.2	−1.5
Dairy products	0.6	0.7	−0.9	3.1	2.5	1.7	5.4	−2.8	3.9	−0.8	−7.6	3	0.2	0.1	0.6	0.1
Processed rice	6.8	−0.7	32	19	−1.1	−0.8	3.6	−1.4	4.4	−4.3	26.3	2.1	17.6	16.3	37.5	2.2
Sugar	0.1	0	0	0	0	0	−0.2	0	0.1	0.1	0	−1.4	−0.3	0	0	0.0
Other processed foods	−2.3	−0.5	−1.1	−23.2	−1.6	0.9	0.6	−0.8	−5	0.4	0.5	−0.5	−3.8	−0.9	−1.2	−0.8
Beverages and tobacco	0.9	−0.4	0	1.9	0	1.5	4.1	−1.5	1.2	−0.3	0.5	0.7	−2.7	−0.8	−0.6	0.0
Textiles/wearing apparel	−0.1	−0.5	0	8.7	0.6	−0.6	−3.4	−0.9	−0.1	−0.7	−1.7	2.6	0.9	−1.2	−2.7	−0.3
Wood/paper products	0	−0.5	−0.1	1.7	0.9	0.2	1.6	0.1	0.2	−0.1	0.2	0.9	0.3	−0.1	0.3	0.2
Petro/chemicals/minerals	−0.2	−0.9	−0.3	3.1	0.7	0.1	2.8	0	0	−0.3	0	0.8	0.2	−0.2	0.4	0.1
Manufactures	−0.3	−1.3	−0.6	9	3.2	0.2	3.3	0.3	0	−0.5	−0.1	2	0.4	−0.3	0.7	0.3
Utilities	0	−0.1	0	0.9	0.3	0.2	−0.1	0	0.3	0	0	1.1	0.3	0	0.3	0.2
Transport	0.1	−0.1	0	2.3	0.2	0.1	0.6	0.1	0.3	0	0.1	0.7	−0.1	0.1	0.3	0.2
Services	0.2	0	0.1	0.8	0.1	0	0	0.2	0.3	0.1	0.1	0.1	0.2	0.1	0.4	0.2

in these countries) and the removal of the domestic support measures, which amount to 18.4%, 10.3% and 17.0% of the value of production in 2013 in the three countries, respectively (recalling the milk payments being introduced according to the Agenda 2000 reform).

Second, the production of pork and poultry increases significantly in Denmark — a result of an increased market share in most export markets in Europe. The price of producing pigs in Denmark decline marginally — approximately 1% due to lower costs of production (whereas it increases in all other European countries). Furthermore, the initial domestic support constitute only 0.4% of the total value of production in Denmark — somewhat lower than in the other European Countries — which also impacts positively on the Danish competitiveness in the European markets for pork and poultry meat. This also implies that the demand for grains in Denmark increases correspondingly, wherefore the negative impact of lower domestic support for wheat and other grains is more or less offset by the increased demand from the Danish producers of pigs (as opposed to the impact in most other European countries).

The impacts on industries outside agriculture and the processing industry are generally minor and slightly positive — the industrial production increases in the range of 0.1% to 1.0%.

Supply response outside Europe. For countries outside Europe, the impacts of eliminating EU domestic agricultural support is typically positive, cf. Table 7. In particular, there is a positive impact on the production of grains, oilseeds, plant-based fibers (the latter not shown) and both the production of bovine meats and other meats (pork and poultry meat) increase in the range of 0.5% to 3.0% — the variation being mainly explained by the initial trading structure between the region/country in question and the European Countries.

The production of vegetables, fruit and nuts and other crops, however, fall marginally in a number of countries outside Europe (e.g. Eastern and Central European Countries and the Former Soviet Union) — in the range of 2% to 5%. This is caused by slightly declining European export prices due to in particular lower land and capital prices.

In Fig. 2, the impacts on the world market prices of liberalizing the domestic support in the European Union are shown. In particular, the price of grains and bovine meats increase and only in the case of rice, vegetables and fruits and other crops do the average world market prices fall (marginally). The positive terms of trade effect and increased exports from a number of countries outside Europe also leads to a positive macroeconomic effect in terms of a higher value of GDP in these countries — typically around 0.1% to 0.2% (not shown).

Table 7. Scenario 1: Change in Production in Third Countries, Selected Commodities and Regions (Percent)

	Hungary	Poland	RCE	FSU	China	XSS	Australia	NAFTA
Wheat	3.5	1.4	2.8	2.7	0.6	3.6	1.2	1.6
Other grains	3.3	0.9	2.5	1.3	0.3	0.3	0.3	0.7
Vegetables, fruit, nuts	−2.2	−0.7	−0.7	−0.7	0	−0.1	−1.4	−0.7
Oilseeds	2.2	1.7	2.3	1.9	0.3	0.9	0.1	1.5
Bovine meat products	14.8	2.4	3.1	3.4	0.5	3.1	13	1
Other meat products	3.7	1.7	0.9	0.3	0.8	1.5	0.5	0.5
Vegetable oils and fats	−0.5	1.1	1.1	−0.3	0.1	0.9	0.7	0.5
Dairy products	−0.6	0	−0.4	−0.3	−0.1	−1	−1.2	−0.1

RCE = Rest of Central European Associates; FSU = Former Soviet Union; XSS = Rest of Sub-Saharan Africa

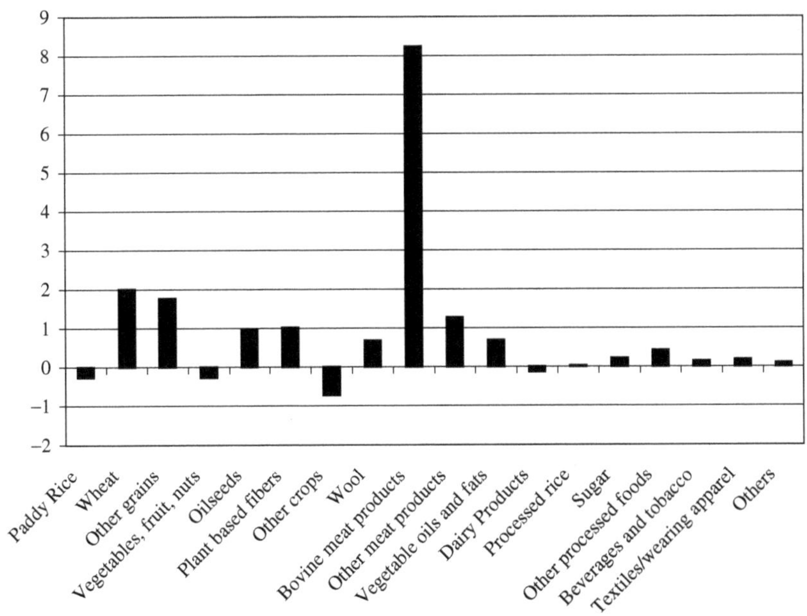

Fig. 2. Scenario 1: Changes in World Market Prices, Selected Commodities (Percent)

Table 8. Scenario 1: Macroeconomic Results

	Real GDP (% Change)	Total EV Bill. 1997 (EURO)	of which CAP Transfers Bill. 1997 (EURO)	of which Allocative Efficiency Bill. 1997 (EURO)	Land Prices (% Change)
EU15	0.1	10.7	0.0	10.5	−78.4
Belgium	0.1	0.6	0.4	0.2	−54.9
Denmark	0.1	0.2	0.0	0.1	−71.7
Germany	0.1	5.0	3.2	1.2	−82.6
Greece	0.7	−1.4	−1.8	0.8	−76.3
Spain	0.2	−1.8	−2.5	1.1	−74.1
France	0.1	−0.5	−1.8	1.0	−78.4
Ireland	0.5	−0.7	−1.1	0.4	−85.7
Italy	0.1	1.6	1.3	0.8	−80.1
Luxembourg	0.2	0.0	0.0	0.0	−62.6
Netherlands	0.1	1.1	0.5	0.3	−41.1
Austria	0.1	0.3	0.1	0.2	−84.5
Portugal	0.4	−0.3	−0.6	0.4	−95.2
Finland	0.2	0.3	0.0	0.3	−91.7
Sweden	0.1	0.6	0.3	0.2	−91.5
United Kingdom	0.3	5.7	2.1	3.4	−77.8

Macroeconomic results. Liberalizing the domestic support in the European Union results in a slightly higher gross domestic product for EU-15 of 0.1%, cf. Table 8. Measured in terms of equivalent variations, this corresponds to a welfare gain of 11 billion 1997 EURO — a significant result given the relative limited overall importance of the agricultural sectors in the European Economy.[1]

At the EU member state level, real GDP increases by 0.1% to 0.7%, of which a major part is explained by the significant changes in the interregional transfers between the individual EU member countries (the common financing of the Common Agricultural Policy). In particular, Germany gains in terms of significant lower contribution to the common financing of the CAP, and the UK gain of 0.3% of GDP is explained by significant budgetary savings as well as a noteworthy efficiency gain. Among the losers, measured in terms of the

[1]The differences between total equivalent variation and the sum of CAP transfers and allocative efficiency are primarily due to terms of trade effects.

equivalent variation, are the major recipients of domestic support, including Greece, Spain, France, Ireland and Portugal. Also, and as expected, the average land prices fall significantly across all EU member states in particular as a result of the removal of the area payment. The regional differences reflect the relative importance of the different agricultural commodities and the policy regimes related to those commodities.

8.2. *Scenario 2: Converting Domestic Support Measures into a Uniform Hectare Payment*

Supply response in the European Union. Scenario 2a analyzes the impacts of converting all domestic support in each member state into a uniform hectare payment given to all agricultural land (i.e. no budgetary savings). Scenario 2b analyze the removal of this subsidy (i.e. budgetary savings). As land is only used in agricultural production in the GTAP model and as the supply of land is pre-determined and fixed, a uniform subsidy given to all agricultural land irrespective of its use (cf. Scenario 2a) should result in the same supply response as would occur if the subsidy were eliminated (cf. Scenario 1), save for minor budgetary effects of eliminating CAP domestic support transfers between member countries. These minor budgetary effects arise as eliminating CAP transfers result in positive/negative income (and demand) effects in the net-contributing/-receiving countries and they are captured in scenario 2b. As Table 9 shows, the supply response in Scenario 2a is very close to being identical to the supply response in Scenario 1, and when the minor budgetary effects are taken into account (cf. Scenario 2a+b), the supply response is indeed identical to that of Scenario 1. It is therefore concluded that a uniform hectare payment to all agricultural land (where the eligible number of hectares are pre-determined and fixed) can be termed effectively fully decoupled.

Macroeconomic results. Comparing the macroeconomic results of Scenario 2a with those of Scenario 1 (cf. Table 8 and 10) shows that decoupling all domestic support results in a similar increase in real GDP as eliminating this domestic support would. In terms of welfare, Scenario 2a yields an increase for EU-15 of almost 11 bill. EURO, which is also comparable to the EU-15 welfare gain in Scenario 1. However, at the individual member state level, the welfare gains differ from those of Scenario 1, as Scenario 2a maintains the previous level of CAP transfers.[m] Thus, while elimination of CAP domestic support entails a

[m]The reason why the United Kingdom "looses" 0,1 bill. EURO in CAP transfers is primarily due to an increase in UK imports from third countries resulting in higher tariff revenues, which are transferred from the UK to the EU.

Table 9. Supply Response, EU-15, Scenario 1 and 2 (Index)

	2013	Scenario 1	Scenario 2a	Scenario2a + b
Wheat	100.0	93.1	93.1	93.1
Other grains	100.0	94.4	94.5	94.4
Vegetables, fruit, nuts	100.0	102.2	102.2	102.2
Oilseeds	100.0	91.1	91.0	91.1
Bovine meat products	100.0	89.1	89.2	89.1
Other meat products	100.0	98.4	98.5	98.4
Vegetable oils and fats	100.0	98.5	98.5	98.5
Dairy products	100.0	100.1	100.2	100.1

Table 10. Scenario 2a: Macroeconomic Results

			of which		
	Real GDP (% Change)	Total EV Bill. 1997 (EURO)	CAP Transfers Bill. 1997 (EURO)	Allocative Efficiency Bill. 1997 (EURO)	Land Prices (% Change)
EU15	0.1	10.9	0.0	10.7	75.1
Belgium	0.1	0.2	0.0	0.2	66.1
Denmark	0.1	0.3	0.0	0.1	15.2
Germany	0.0	1.2	0.0	0.9	38.6
Greece	0.8	0.8	0.0	1.0	101.6
Spain	0.2	1.0	0.0	1.2	110.1
France	0.1	1.8	0.0	1.3	56.1
Ireland	0.6	0.6	0.0	0.5	234.1
Italy	0.1	0.2	0.0	0.7	59.1
Luxembourg	0.2	0.0	0.0	0.0	82.1
Netherlands	0.1	0.5	0.0	0.3	62.0
Austria	0.1	0.2	0.0	0.2	71.1
Portugal	0.4	0.4	0.0	0.5	73.6
Finland	0.2	0.3	0.0	0.3	44.4
Sweden	0.1	0.2	0.0	0.2	44.3
United Kingdom	0.3	3.2	−0.1	3.3	142.9

reduction in total welfare for the major recipient-countries in spite of allocative efficiency gains, decoupling of domestic support results in total welfare increases in all countries as allocative efficiency gains are realized without the impacts of redistributing funds between the member countries. Furthermore, by decoupling domestic support rather than eliminating it, the negative impact on land prices is also avoided. As shown in the table, converting domestic support into a land subsidy actually entails substantial increases in land prices throughout the EU as the support, which prior to the decoupling was given not only to land, but also to other input factors, is now allocated exclusively to land.

8.3. *Scenario 3: WTO Liberalization Scenario*

Supply response in the European Union. In addition to eliminating all direct support as illustrated in Scenario 1, this scenario eliminates all export subsidies (which mainly affects the export of other grains, dairy products, processed rice and sugar) supplemented by a 30% reduction in the import tariff equivalents across all the agricultural commodities. Note also, that the set-aside requirement and the production quotas on milk and sugar are removed in this scenario. By definition, the average price of land is unaffected, as the decoupled payment to land is exactly determined to neutralize the negative impact on land prices of the reduction of the distorting support.

The production response in the EU and the member countries are shown in Table 11. The production of grains and oilseeds decline by 11% and 8%, respectively, and the production of beef and veal as well as pork and poultry fall by 17% and 4%. Again, these supply effects reflect the importance of both the domestic support measures as well as the assumed reductions in the border protection rates.

The overall EU production of dairy products increase by 7% — the net result of both the reductions of the domestic support and the border protection as well as the impact of lifting the restrictive milk quota system. Although the market prices for dairy products decline somewhat, the net impact in this scenario implies that milk production in the European Union increases (a result of the assumed initial quota rent and the estimated price reduction). It is also evident from the table, that the impact on the dairy production in each of the EU member states varies significantly — a reflection of the underlying and assumed relative quota rents prior to the subsidy cuts and the lifting of the national milk quotas. As the competitiveness of milk production in particularly Germany, Italy and Austria decreases in the constructed baseline and that the quota rent is relatively small in Finland, Sweden and the UK prior to the policy changes, the result of the lower level of support in this scenario leads to a somewhat smaller milk production in these countries. The Netherlands, Denmark and Ireland gain in terms of a higher export of dairy products to these countries.

Table 11. Scenario 3: Change in Production, EU Member Countries (Percent)

	Bel	Dk	Deu	Gre	Spa	Fra	Irel	Italy	Lux	Nld	Aut	Por	Fin	Swe	UK	EU15
Paddy rice	−15.9	−15.2	3.1	−4.5	−29.6	−21.5	−15.0	−20.1	−24.1	−32.9	−10.6	−10.4	−0.7	−4.0	0.2	−20.6
Wheat	−16.4	−1.1	−18.0	−22.5	−8.6	−6.1	−14.5	−11.0	−20.2	−37.7	−22.2	−54.5	−13.6	−5.9	−11.3	−11.1
Other grains	−28.3	−7.9	−15.5	−7.3	−7.4	−8.9	−13.5	−4.9	−22.9	−74.6	−6.2	−3.0	−12.4	−23.5	−16.2	−11.4
Vegetables, fruit, nuts	0.2	7.3	18.1	4.3	−7.1	−5.9	21.1	2.4	4.0	−16.1	38.9	8.6	22.4	46.7	5.5	0.1
Oilseeds	−39.0	8.9	1.1	−17.4	−18.5	9.8	−17.8	−8.1	−0.6	−76.9	−4.9	−20.1	−7.3	−2.6	−2.0	−8.3
Sugar cane and beet	−17.0	0.9	−4.3	11.4	−0.9	−2.1	0.9	−4.2	−16.6	−1.1	−2.9	−53.8	10.7	6.5	14.5	−0.5
Plant based fibers	−95.9	30.8	101.5	−78.7	−96.6	−95.6	10.5	13.7	25.8	−95.9	39.9	137.1	5.6	141.4	−99.8	−60.9
Other crops	0.0	1.8	37.9	−37.6	−15.1	4.1	23.9	−3.8	−4.9	−6.3	−0.2	1.2	11.8	20.6	16.1	1.5
Bovine animals	−24.3	−38.1	−20.8	−16.4	−15.7	−9.5	−55.8	−8.8	−31.9	−5.8	−11.0	−10.5	−8.4	−17.5	−15.8	−15.0
Other animal products	3.2	11.4	−2.0	−6.2	−2.1	1.4	−5.5	−0.4	−10.7	−6.1	−1.3	−2.4	−4.7	−0.8	−11.5	−1.8
Raw milk	11.1	21.3	−20.4	10.8	−0.9	2.7	20.3	−11.4	128.8	168.7	−12.0	21.6	−1.2	−7.8	−3.9	11.4
Wool	41.7	11.8	86.1	27.5	31.3	4.1	65.2	10.0	50.6	0.9	37.3	103.5	29.7	9.2	−19.1	−0.4
Fish	−4.2	−2.3	−0.1	0.9	−0.8	−0.7	−0.8	−0.4	−1.9	−1.8	−1.1	−1.3	−0.7	−2.1	−0.8	0.0
Resource extraction	0.0	0.0	0.0	0.3	0.1	0.0	0.0	0.0	0.0	0.0	−0.1	0.1	0.0	0.0	0.0	0.0

Table 11. (*Continued*)

	Bel	Dk	Deu	Gre	Spa	Fra	Irel	Italy	Lux	Nld	Aut	Por	Fin	Swe	UK	EU15
Bovine meat products	−27.6	−39.5	−22.4	−16.2	−15.8	−10.9	−61.0	−10.2	−35.2	−6.5	−11.2	−10.5	−8.6	−17.9	−21.7	−17.2
Other meat products	3.9	13.6	−2.2	−5.9	−2.1	1.7	−6.7	−0.8	−11.6	−9.0	−2.5	−3.0	−6.8	−1.0	−21.5	−3.7
Vegetable oils and fats	−3.5	3.5	−0.7	−18.5	−8.2	−0.9	−0.4	−5.4	−5.7	0.3	−0.1	−4.9	0.6	−1.9	−6.6	−2.6
Dairy products	15.9	24.1	−24.7	18.1	1.6	2.9	31.0	−12.1	185.8	180.6	−19.8	28.1	−1.1	−8.0	−5.0	7.1
Processed rice	−18.7	−42.5	−4.1	−7.8	−26.1	−9.7	−35.8	−28.6	−27.1	−42.4	−20.3	−11.5	−15.2	−13.1	−4.6	−22.2
Sugar	−18.0	0.8	−3.5	18.7	−5.1	−2.2	−2.7	−15.5	−17.6	−2.0	−2.7	−72.0	1.6	5.2	38.1	2.1
Other processed foods	−10.6	−9.4	−5.7	−27.0	−6.7	−3.0	−8.0	−4.1	−12.6	−4.3	−2.8	−3.2	−10.1	−4.9	−3.1	−4.9
Beverages and tobacco	−2.2	0.2	1.3	1.6	−0.6	1.1	6.3	−2.1	−3.0	−0.6	1.8	−0.4	−1.3	1.4	2.2	0.6
Textiles/wearing apparel	1.8	−0.1	0.9	7.4	1.3	0.0	−3.3	0.2	−0.6	−1.4	−0.4	2.1	0.9	−0.7	−2.2	0.4
Wood/paper products	0.4	−0.5	0.1	2.1	1.0	0.2	1.7	0.3	0.1	−0.2	0.4	1.0	0.3	0.0	0.4	0.3
Petro/chemicals/minerals	0.2	−0.5	0.1	2.9	0.6	0.2	2.7	0.2	−0.7	−0.8	0.0	0.6	0.2	−0.3	0.5	0.3
Manufactures	0.6	−1.1	0.2	7.7	3.3	0.4	3.2	0.8	−1.0	−2.4	0.2	1.2	0.2	0.0	1.1	0.6
Utilities	0.1	−0.3	0.2	1.1	0.1	0.2	0.1	0.0	0.3	0.1	0.0	1.0	0.2	0.1	0.2	0.2
Transport	0.1	−0.1	0.2	2.4	0.5	0.1	0.7	0.2	0.2	−0.3	0.1	0.7	0.2	0.1	0.4	0.2
Services	0.2	0.0	0.2	0.5	0.2	0.0	0.1	0.2	0.4	0.1	0.1	0.2	0.2	0.2	0.4	0.2

Table 12. Scenario 3: Change in Production in Third Countries, Selected Commodities and Regions (Percent)

	Hungary	Poland	RCE	FSU	China	XSS	Australia	NAFTA
Wheat	4.5	2.9	3.8	3.5	1.1	4.8	2.3	2.6
Other grains	6.4	3.0	5.5	3.3	0.6	0.7	1.2	1.6
Vegetables, fruit, nuts	−1.8	0.1	−0.1	0.0	0.0	0.1	−0.9	−0.6
Oilseeds	−3.2	1.6	1.8	1.0	0.4	0.9	−0.2	1.2
Bovine meat products	29.2	5.1	7.3	3.8	0.6	3.2	27.3	2.0
Other meat products	17.2	6.5	3.1	1.6	1.6	3.6	2.3	1.3
Vegetable oils and fats	−5.0	1.3	1.4	−0.5	−0.1	1.0	0.7	0.8
Dairy products	−5.6	−5.2	−4.8	−3.4	−4.1	−23.6	−10.9	−0.9

RCE = Rest of Central European Associates; FSU = Former Soviet Union; XSS = Rest of Sub-Saharan Africa

Supply response in third countries. The impact on countries outside Europe is generally positive in terms of a slightly higher level of agricultural production and somewhat higher world market prices, cf. Table 12 and Fig. 3. The supply responses correlate with the relative cuts in the European agricultural protection and with the trading structure — those countries trading initially most with the European Countries gain the most in terms of export increases to the European markets or a lower level of imports of European commodities. In particular, the world market price of grains and beef and veal increase by 2% and 7%, respectively whereas the world market price of dairy products decline by 9% — a result of both slightly higher exports of dairy products from the European Union and lower intra-European union prices.

Macroeconomic results. Real GDP in the European Community increases by 0.2% and the aggregated equivalent variation increases by 14.6 billion EURO of which the community gains 15.2 billion EURO in efficiency due to the (partial) liberalisation of the Common Agricultural Policy.[n] The efficiency gain is therefore 50% higher in this scenario as compared with Scenarios 1 and 2.

At the member state level, real GDP increases by 0.1% to 0.8%, as shown in Table 13. Real GDP increases the most in Greece (0.8%), Portugal (0.5%) and Ireland (0.5%), whereas the German gain is more limited (0.1%) — Germany being relative large in the European Economy as well as the agricultural sector is only of minor economic importance in Germany. Nevertheless, Germany

[n]This difference between total equivalent variation and the sum of the CAP transfers and allocative efficiency is primarily due to a negative impact from changes in terms of trade.

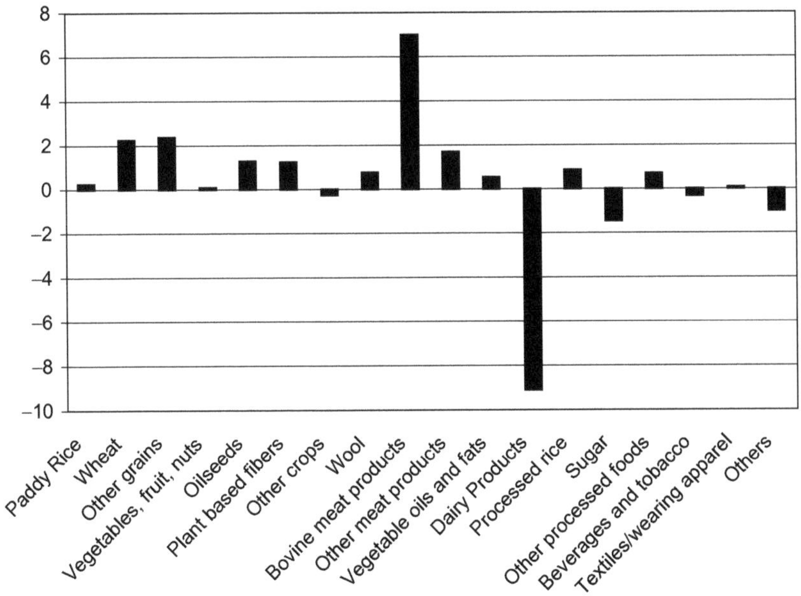

Fig. 3. Scenario 3: Changes in World Market Prices, Selected Commodities (Percent)

saves some 2.8 billion EURO in lower net-transfers to the common agricultural budget. In Germany and the UK, the efficiency gain amounts to 1.9 and 4 billion EURO, respectively.

Comparing this scenario with Scenario 2a demonstrates an interesting feature in our scenario design. In Scenario 2a, there are no savings on the common agricultural budget as all domestic support is converted into a homogenous and decoupled land payment. This in turn implies that the land prices in all the European countries increase tremendously. In Scenario 3, on the other hand, the landowners are only just compensated as the negative impact on land prices is just offset by the introduction of uniform payments to land in each member state. However, this does not imply that there will not be adjustments in the agricultural sector. The level of agricultural employment and capital stock will typically decline as a result of this reform, and, as shown in Fig. 4, agricultural gross factor income will decline in most countries. The reason why agricultural gross factor income increases in the Netherlands, Luxembourg, and Denmark is that raw milk production increases significantly in these countries (cf. the milk quotas are eliminated in this scenario) and in the case of Denmark, the production of pork and poultry also increases significantly.

Table 13. Scenario 3: Macroeconomic Results

	Real GDP (% Change)	Total EV Bill. 1997 (EURO)	of which CAP Transfers Bill. 1997 (EURO)	of which Allocative Efficiency Bill. 1997 (EURO)	Land Prices (% Change)
EU15	0.2	14.6	0.0	15.2	0.0
Belgium	0.2	0.3	−0.1	0.4	0.0
Denmark	0.2	0.4	0.1	0.3	0.0
Germany	0.1	5.2	2.8	1.9	0.0
Greece	0.8	−0.3	−1.1	1.0	0.0
Spain	0.2	−0.5	−1.7	1.4	0.0
France	0.1	1.6	−0.4	1.7	0.0
Ireland	0.5	−0.7	−1.1	0.5	0.0
Italy	0.1	2.0	1.0	1.2	0.0
Luxembourg	0.4	0.1	0.0	0.0	0.0
Netherlands	0.3	0.2	−0.6	1.3	0.0
Austria	0.1	0.5	0.1	0.3	0.0
Portugal	0.5	0.2	−0.2	0.6	0.0
Finland	0.2	0.5	0.1	0.3	0.0
Sweden	0.1	0.7	0.3	0.3	0.0
United Kingdom	0.3	4.6	0.6	4.0	0.0

The size of the homogenous area payment has been determined to exactly offset the negative impacts on the average land price in each of the EU member states and consequently the payment differs somewhat across the individual member states. However, the overall budgetary cost is still being financed through a common contribution rate across all member states. The impact on the EU budget is a decrease from a total cost of 53 billion EURO in 2013 (measured in current prices) to roughly 26 billion EURO, and the common contribution rate decrease from 0.45% of GDP to 0.21% in this scenario, cf. Table 14.

9. Conclusions

The analysis demonstrates that the existing domestic support payments in the European Union are indeed coupled to production and hence they affect production decisions and distort international trade with adverse effects on the

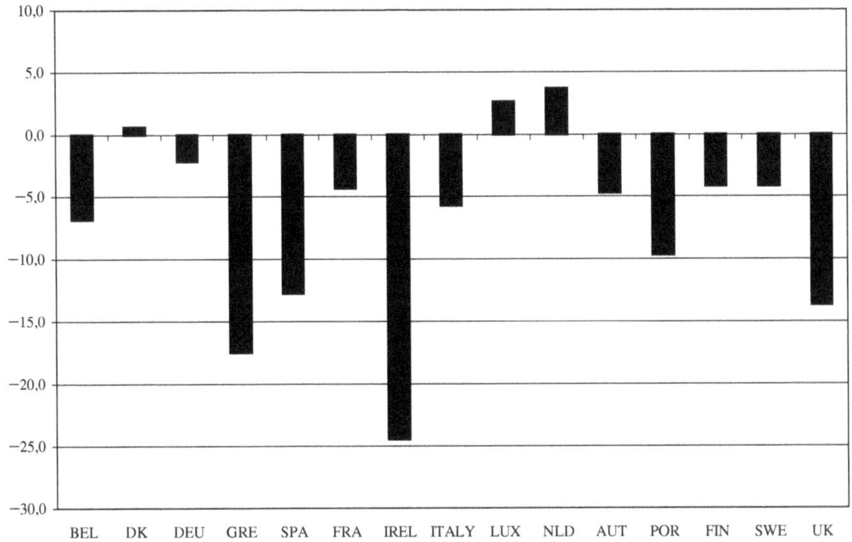

Fig. 4. Scenario 3: Changes in Agricultural Gross Factor Income (Percent)

Table 14. Implication for the Common Agricultural Budget, Billion Euros (Current Prices)

	1997	2013	Scenario 1	Scenario 2a	Scenario 2b	Scenario 3
Total CAP budget	43.2	52.9	4.1	52.8	4.1	25.5
Homogenous land subsidy	0.0	0.0	0.0	48.7	0.0	25.5
Area premium	15.5	16.0	0.0	0.0	0.0	0.0
Animal premium	5.3	13.0	0.0	0.0	0.0	0.0
Other subsidies	17.6	19.6	0.0	0.0	0.0	0.0
Export restitutions	4.8	4.2	4.1	4.1	4.1	0.0
Levies on imports	−1.1	−0.9	−1.1	−1.1	−1.1	−1.0
Net Cost	42.1	52.0	3.1	51.8	3.1	24.5
% of GDP	0.598	0.453	0.027	0.451	0.027	0.213

export potential of e.g. developing countries as a consequence. Furthermore, the value of this support is capitalised in significant higher European land prices than would otherwise prevail. The discussion of the Enlargement of the European Union and the international trade talks under the auspices of the WTO also underlines the need for reforming these policies.

In this paper, we analyzed the economic implications of transforming all domestic support payments (as well as other distorting policies) into a nationally homogenous and fully decoupled payment to all agricultural land, i.e. irrespective of the farmers decision to crop or not. Specifically, the analysis suggest that it is possible to convert the existing agricultural support into a fully decoupled payment which would not distort international trade and it indicates a way forward to offset the negative impact on land prices. Such a policy would also comply with the WTO rules (i.e. fall within the green box as decoupled income support). The analysis also suggests, that such a policy reform could be achieved at somewhat lower budgetary costs as compared to the existing costs of the Common Agricultural Policy.

The results estimated in this analysis are of course no better than the data and parameters used, and the results are therefore illustrative. Our research has identified several important characteristics in the database that need to be addressed in the future as well as a need for further improving aspects of the modelling of the Common Agricultural Policy, where the milk quota regime and the explicit representation of the tariff quota regimes are important examples. Also we recognise, that we have not addressed all relevant issues related to the discussion of decoupling the existing agricultural support. For example, we have not addressed a number of politically relevant distribution issues — both among different types of farms and landowners in European agriculture — and we have not addressed the design of the financing scheme of the European common policies.

References

Bach CF, Frandsen SE, and Jensen HG, 2000. "Agricultural and economy-wide effects of European enlargement: modelling the common agricultural policy." *J. Agri. Econ.* **51**(2): 162–180.

Beard N, and Swinbank A, 2001. "Decoupled payments to facilitate CAP reform." *Food Policy* **26**(2): 121–145.

Dimaranan BV, and McDougall RA, 2002. "Global trade, assistance, and production: the GTAP 5 data base." Center for Global Trade Analysis, Purdue University.

The European Commission, 2001. "Common organisation of the agricultural markets — beef and veal." europa.eu.int/scadplus/leg/en/lvb/l60009.htm.

Frandsen SE, Jensen HG, Yu W, and Walter-Jørgensen AA, 2001. "Domestic support in agriculture." Version 5 of the GTAP database: The case of the European Union. Paper presented at the Fourth Annual Conference on Global Economic Analysis, June 27–59, 2001, Purdue University, Indiana, USA.

Frandsen SE, Jensen HG, Yu W, and Walter-Jørgensen AA, 2003. "Reform of EU sugar policy: price cuts versus quota reductions." *European Review of Agricultural Economics* **30**(1): 1–26.

Frandsen SE, Jensen HG, and Vanzetti D, 2000. "Expanding 'Fortress Europe': agricultural trade and welfare implications of European enlargement for non-member regions." *The World Economy* **23**(3): 309–329.

Gohin A, Guyomard H, and Le Mouël C, 1999. "Measuring the degree of decoupling of alternative internal support policy instruments: The green box issue." European Agriculture Facing the 21-st Century in a Global Context. EAAE IX Congress, Warsaw, 78–95.

Hertel TW, (ed.) 1998. *Global Trade Analysis, Modeling and Applications*. Cambridge University Press: Cambridge.

Jansson J, 2002. "Abolishing milk quotas — economic consequences for agriculture in Sweden and the EU." Swedish Institute for Food and Agricultural Economics. Paper presented at the Conference on Future of Milk Regime, CEPS Brussels, April 2, 2002.

OECD, 2001. *OECD Agricultural Databases*, 2001 Edition. Paris.

OECD, 2001a. "Decoupling: a conceptual overview." www.oecd.org/pdf/M00002000/M00002887.pdf.

OECD, 2001b. "Agricultural policies in OECD countries — monitoring and evaluation." www1.oecd.org/publications/e-book/5101101E.PDF.

Rude J, 2000. "Green box criteria: A theoretical assessment." Economic & Policy Analysis Directorate, Policy Branch, Agriculture and Agri-Food Canada. www.agr.gc.ca/policy/epad/english/pubs/wp-tp/tms/99036wp/all.pdf.

Uruguay Round Agreement on Agriculture (referred to as URAA). www.wto.org/english/docs_e/legal_e/14-ag.pdf.

Walter-Jørgensen A, and Jensen TV, 2001. "The CAP and the international trade negotiations." Report No. 123, Statens Jordbrugs- og Fiskeriøkonomiske Institut.

WTO. 2002. "WTO agriculture negotiations — The issues, and where we are now." www.wto.org/english/tratop_e/agric_e/agnegs_bkgrnd_e.pdf (updated version).

Chapter 13

Regional and National Perspectives of China's Integration into the WTO: A CGE Inquiry with Emphasis on the Agricultural Sector*

XINSHEN DIAO

International Food Policy Research Institute, Washington, DC, USA

AGAPI SOMWARU and FRANCIS TUAN

Economic Research Service, U.S. Agricultural Department, Washington, DC, USA

China's integration in the World Trade Organization (WTO) is already on its fast track. Understanding the complexity of China's dynamic adjustment resulting from its membership in the WTO and the differential regional impacts within China is very important and poses a crucial challenge in evaluating its impacts. In this study, we make an attempt to incorporate seven regional commodity-detailed models into a dis-aggregated multi-sector and multi-region China Computable General Equilibrium (CGE) framework. This framework has allowed us to evaluate the impacts of China's integration into the WTO at both national and regional levels and analyze the interlinkages between China's provincial agricultural markets. Using the framework and assumptions about factor mobility, we assess the impacts on China's agricultural and non-agricultural sectors (regionally and nationally) by reduction

*This chapter was originally published in *Review of Urban and Regional Development Studies*, Vol. 15, No. 2, July 2003, and is reprinted here with minor modifications upon the permission from the publisher.

of its trade policy distortions, such as tariffs rate changes and quantitative restrictions. We also evaluate the structural changes on China's national and regional production and trade as China implements its commitments and moves into the WTO.

1. Introduction

After fifteen years of continuous efforts, China was finally admitted to the World Trade Organization (WTO) in December 2001. During this period, China has witnessed considerable progress in economic liberalization and reforms even without being a WTO member. This process is in harmony with the general trend of globalization elsewhere, which, through the flows of trade, financial capital movement, technology and information transfer across national boundaries, has led to and continues to lead to restructuring of the world economy.

As a result of the economic reform and opening-up since 1979, China has achieved a remarkable rate of economic growth. The nation's GDP has grown at 9% to 10% per annum, outperforming most of developing countries in the world. The reform was initiated in the agriculture sector, and has led to a rapid transformation in rural China. Grain output increased from 508 million tons in 1999 to 469 million tons in 2004, with an annual growth rate of 1.7% per annum. Such growth is much faster than China's population growth rate of 1% per annum. The value added of agriculture rose at an even higher annual rate of 4.8%, due to increased diversification of agricultural production. Rapid growth in agriculture has led to an even more impressive reduction in rural poverty (Zhang and Fan, 2001).

Many studies based on data in the past several decades have shown a strong positive relationship between openness in trade and economic growth and this relationship is particularly strong for low-income countries (Easterly and Levine, 2000; Wazing, 2001). Thus, we can expect that China's accession to the WTO will accelerate its economic growth as the country becomes more integrated into the world economy and has more opportunity to take advantage of globalization.

However, the gains from past reforms are not equally distributed among China's regions. Less-developed areas, such as the Northwest and the Southwest, have seen less progress and regional inequality has become increasingly large over the last two decades (Kanbur and Zhang, 1999). With China's entry into the WTO, the economic prospects of these less developed regions are questionable, especially in the short-run, as the regions' economies are still predominantly agricultural with poor access to capital and markets. With inadequate infrastructure and shortage in human capital, it will be hard for farmers in these regions to switch and adopt new production activities of high value-added crops or to engage into non-farm activities. This, in turn, could hold back China's economic progress and perhaps increase the concentration of rural poor in these regions.

The objective of this study is to quantify the effect of WTO entry on China's economy at both national and regional levels. The analytical framework to be used in the study is a multi-sector, multi-region CGE model. Previous CGE studies on China's WTO accession have mainly focused on the possible impacts at the national level (DRC, 1998; USITC, 1999; Wang, 1999; Martin *et al.*, 1999; Walmsley *et al.*, 2000; Lejour, 2000; Fan and Zheng, 2000[a]). Almost all these studies were conducted before China's entry into the WTO, when information on China's WTO commitments was not available to the public. Thus, most of these studies were not able to accurately assess the impacts of China's WTO accession using China's commitment schedule. Most of these studies only considered the reductions in tariffs (or tariff equivalents), while quantitative trade barriers such as tariff-rate-quotas were ignored. It is well known that quantitative barriers, instead of tariffs, mainly restrict China's imports of grain, vegetable oils, and cotton. One of the most important commitments that China made to the WTO is the implementation of a tariff-rate-quota (TRQ) system for these commodities. Accounting for TRQ barriers is crucial for estimating the impact of WTO accession on China's grain imports.

Most previous studies only evaluate China's agricultural trade protection policy effects at the national level and may overestimate the impact of China's WTO entry. This might be the case, as under WTO accession, these studies show that China's production would shift away from protected grain crops to more profitable high-value crops such as vegetables and fruits. Although China is a large country, the switch from low into more profitable crops might be limited by land quality, climate conditions, and capital availability in the various regions. Moreover, under existing gaps among the regions in economic development and openness, a positive impact at the national level does not imply that all regions in China would benefit equally; in fact some regions may be hurt.

This paper tries to fill in gaps in analysis on China's WTO accession. Specifically, we conduct our CGE model simulation based on China's announced

[a]For a comprehensive survey of CGE assessments of trade liberalization in China, see Gilbert and Wahl (2000).

WTO commitments, and we incorporate into the model the quantitative constraints of TRQs for major agricultural commodity imports in a manner consistent with the theory. Furthermore, the national data are disaggregated to the regional level. This allows greater realism in evaluating the impact on China's crop production. The paper is organized as follows. We first describe differences in economic development and openness across regions within China. Then we employ a CGE model with disaggregated regional production to simulate the effects of the WTO accession on the agricultural and rural economy at the national and regional levels. Policy implications from the study conclude the paper.

2. Regional Disparities in the Rural Economy

We divide China into seven regions based on geographic location, agricultural production structure, and the level of economic development at the provincial level. The classification of the regions is listed in Table 1. Differences in economic development among the seven regions can be gauged by the per capita GDP and the agricultural share in regional GDP, as well as per capita income in the rural areas (Table 2). Measured by both per capita GDP and rural income, the Northwest and the Southwest are the two least-developed regions in China with poor factor endowments. In 2000, per capita GDP in the Southwest and Northwest was around 5,000 yuan, about half the income level in the East and the South (Table 2).

The rural income gap between the two poor regions, the Northwest and the Southwest, and the other five is particularly large. Per capita rural income in these two regions was 1,518 and 1,662 yuan, respectively, only 40% of the income level in the East. Shares of agricultural GDP in total GDP for these two regions (20% and 23%) are much higher than those in the other regions (11–15%) indicating that farming is still the major source of rural income in these two areas (Table 2).

The difference in the share of the rural labor force employed by the rural non-farm sector contributes significantly to the regional gap in rural income (Rozelle, 1994). Many factors, including economic, social, institutional, and other factors have restricted labor mobility in the less-developed regions. Such restrictions have been shown to contribute to widening regional disparities and differential rates of economic development (Kanbur and Zhang, 1999). In 1997, for the nation as a whole, about 29% of the rural labor force was engaged in non-agricultural activities, such as rural industry, construction and services, and the non-farm sector provided rural residents more than one-third

Table 1. Regions in the Study

Region (Number of Provinces)	Province
Northeast (3)	1. Liaoning
	2. Jilin
	3. Heilongjiang
North (7)	4. Beijing
	5. Tianjin
	6. Hebei
	7. Shanxi
	8. Shandong
	9. Shaanxi
	10. Henan
Northwest (6)	11. Inner Mongolia
	12. Gansu
	13. Qinghai
	14. Ningxia
	15. Xinjiang
	16. Tibet
Central (4)	17. Anhui
	18. Jiangxi
	19. Hubei
	20. Hunan
East (3)	21. Shanghai
	22. Jiangsu
	23. Zhejiang
Southwest (4)	24. Sichuan
	25. Chongqing
	26. Guizhou
	27. Yunnan
South (4)	28. Guangdong
	29. Guangxi
	30. Hainan
	31. Fujian

of income. However, in the Northwest and Southwest, the two least-developed regions, the percentage of the rural labor force employed in non-farm activities is below 20%, compared to 40% in the more developed areas such as the East.

With an overwhelmingly large share of the rural labor force employed in agricultural activity, labor productivity is low in these less developed regions.

Table 2. Major Economic Indicators in the Seven Regions, 2000

Region	Population (1,000)	Per Capita GDP (Yuan)	AgGDP/GDP (%)	Rural Per Capita Income (Yuan)
Northeast	104,540	9,328	13	2,175
North	355,600	7,747	15	2,592
Northwest	54,090	5,317	20	1,518
Central	163,580	6,092	19	2,200
East	189,420	11,716	11	3,845
Southwest	190,270	4,496	23	1,662
South	155,450	10,280	15	2,733

Source: Fan *et al.* (2001b)

In 1997, for example, labor productivity in the Southwest was half of the national average. Poor natural resource endowments and infrastructure limit the potential yield of agricultural land, while the high illiteracy rate and lack of investment and personnel in science and research restrain the adoption of new technology and the improvement of agricultural productivity. Moreover, difficulties in accessing both national and international markets constrain the choice of cropping mix and the development of high value agricultural products in these regions. A study by Fan *et al.* (2001a) shows that the growth rates of agricultural land and labor productivity in the Northwest and the Southwest have been far below the national average in the last two decades. With the rise in the gap of agricultural productivity and rural income between the less developed regions and the rest of the nation, the poverty level has been increasingly concentrated in the less developed regions. It is estimated that more than 60% of the rural poor live in the two least-developed regions (Fan *et al.*, 2001b) even though they account for only 20% of the national population.

The difference in the degree of openness across regions might contribute to the income gap across regions as well (Kanbur and Zhang, 2001). In 1978, with China's adoption of "opening-to-the-outside-world" policy, the degree of the openness of China's economy, measured both by trade and foreign capital flows, increased dramatically. For example, the trade to GDP ratio quadrupled, from 8.5% in 1978 to 36.5% in 1999 (Wei and Wu, 2001). However, due to the difference in geographical and social economic conditions, the degree of openness varies sharply among the provinces and regions. In Table 3, we use the trade to GDP ratio and per capita foreign direct investment figures to measure the gap in openness across provinces and regions in China. As Table 3 shows,

Table 3. Measures of Openness by Province and Region

Province/Region	Trade-GDP Ratio 3-year (97–99) Average (%)	Per Capita Foreign Investment 1999 (US$)
Beijing	68.9	3,129
Tianjin	72.5	3,067
Hebei	8.3	220
Shanxi	12.4	147
Inner Mongolia	7.4	96
Liaoning	31.0	1,033
Jilin	12.8	273
Heilongjiang	10.4	239
Shanghai	74.6	6,156
Jiangsu	30.6	1,011
Zhejiang	29.5	614
Anhui	7.9	145
Fujian	46.8	1,490
Jiangxi	6.3	115
Shandong	23.2	429
Henan	4.4	127
Hubei	7.1	274
Hunan	5.5	110
Guangdong[1]	136.7	2,968
Guangxi	9.5	231
Sichuan[2]	6.9	149
Guizhou	6.6	54
Yunnan	7.7	104
Tibet	12.1	100
Shaanxi	11.7	213
Gansu	5.3	72
Qinghai	6.5	172
Ningxia	11.9	151
Xinjiang	12.3	72
North	22.3	430
Northwest	8.7	92
Northeast	20.5	559
East	40.1	1,452
Central	6.7	163
South	96.6	1,860
Southwest	7.1	121
Nation	33.8	615

[1]Including Hainan
[2]Including Chongqing
Source: Computed from *China Statistical Yearbook*

the three-year (1997–1999) average of the trade to GDP ratio was 97% for the South and 40% for the East. However, it was as low as 7–9% in the Southwest, the Central and the Northwest. Similarly, the per capita foreign investment (in 1999) in the South and the East was US$1,860 and US$1,452, but was only US$90 and US$121 for the Northwest and the Southwest, respectively.

3. The Data and Model

For purposes of our analysis, we developed a China regional CGE model based on various sources of data. The 1997 national level social accounting matrix (SAM) for China is used as the base. However, the original 1997 SAM includes only two aggregate primary agricultural sectors: crops and livestock. Since the focus of our study is agriculture, we need more disaggregated agricultural sectors. For such disaggregation, we follow the GTAP (Global Trade Analysis Project, 2001) version 5 database. Using the production data from China's statistics yearbooks and the input–output relationship provided by the GTAP database, the aggregated crop sector is disaggregated into nine sectors: wheat, rice, corn, vegetables, fruits, soybeans, other oilseeds, cotton, and other crops. (See sectoral details in Appendix.)

An ideal or standard multi-regional CGE model would have production and consumption activities disaggregated at the regional level, including details in inter-regional activities, such as commodity and factor flows across regions. To develop such a multi-region model, it requires data equivalent to a social accounting matrix at the regional level. Unfortunately, such data, especially the regional input–output relationship and inter-regional commodity and factor flows, are not available for China. Given the focus of the study is agriculture, we tried to disaggregate agricultural production data into the seven regions according to *China's Statistical Yearbook* and *China's Agricultural Yearbook*. While almost all crops (i.e. 9 aggregate crop groups included in the national SAM) are produced in each region, the production system, i.e. either the level of productivity, factor endowments, or the combination of land, labor, and capital, are quite different across regions. For example, land is quite abundant in the Northeast, while agricultural production is relatively labor-intensive in the East. It would be inaccurate to use the national level input–output technical coefficients provided by the national SAM for all seven regions. Lacking regional input–output matrices for agriculture, we use the maximum entropy approach, as employed by Zhang and Fan (2001), to estimate region-specific input–output technical coefficients. The entropy approach gives us both production elasticities for inputs by crop and shares of each crop in total input use by region. We then use three-year averages estimated shares for the inputs and output data by region to disaggregate inputs of land, labor, capital, and intermediates included in the national SAM to the regional level.

While the input–output coefficients of crop production (sectors 1–9 in the Appendix) is disaggregated to the regional level, other agricultural production (sectors 11–15 in the Appendix), all non-gricultural production (13 sectors), and other economic activities such as trade and consumption are kept at the national level due to lack of data. This is a shortcoming, as the model simulations cannot capture the resource adjustments between crop and non-crop production within a region or across seven regions. Moreover, the model only includes two aggregate household groups — rural and urban — at the national level and the feedback effect from consumers to the regional production activities is hardly captured. In order to partially amend these deficiencies, we have modified the model's structure as discussed below.

Similar to most CGE models that are neo-classical in their structure, the China-regional CGE model assumes that the representative producer for each production sector (in the case of crop production for each sector within each region) chooses levels of inputs and outputs in order to maximize profits and consumers (aggregated into rural and urban at the national level) maximize their utility by making consumption decisions subject to their income constraint. Labor and capital are categorized as rural and urban, the land is only employed in crop production, and returns to land compensate the rural household.

To take into account the rapid growth in rural non-farm activities, we assume rural labor and capital to be utilized in both agriculture and non-agricultural production, while urban labor and capital are employed in non-agriculture sectors only. The shares of non-agricultural labor and capital in total rural labor and capital supplies are calculated according to the share of the gross value of rural industrial product in the gross value of national industrial product. As rural industries are more labor intensive, we allow the share of rural labor to be high in the labor-intensive sectors, such as the textile, apparel, transportation, sales, and construction sectors, while the share of urban labor is high in the capital-intensive sectors such as the other industry, urban electricity supply and other utility services, financial services, and social services.

In order to amend the deficiencies caused by the lack of data on the non-crop, non-agricultural production, and factor allocation at regional level, the model specification allows factor mobility between crop production within regions and labor migration from regional crop production to non-crop and non-agricultural activities at national level. In the simulations, we allow regions' labor forces to migrate from crop production into a pool of labor force employed by all other production activities at the national level, if the returns to labor in crop production at the regional level declines relatively to the returns to non-crop and non-agricultural production at the national level. The degree of factor mobility is determined in the model by the different employment opportunities for rural labor across sectors and the elasticity of the substitution between rural and urban labor. Even though rural labor and capital can be employed by non-agricultural sectors, rural labor and urban labor are not perfectly substitutable in the model. Moreover, migrant rural labor cannot be employed by urban industries, such as urban electricity supply and other utility services, finance services, and social services, but can be absorbed by textile, construction, transportation, and sales industries, in which production is quite labor-intensive and requires low labor skills.

All agents, producers and consumers, respond to prices. For example, when the relative prices change due to removal or reduction of import tariffs, producers adjust their production level while consumers adjust their demand for commodities. In the international market, the country is assumed to be small in the sense that it takes world prices as given. Following a commonly used assumption in CGE models, there exists imperfect substitution between foreign goods and domestically produced goods, and hence, the domestic price for a commodity, e.g. wheat, is not necessarily equal to (even though highly affected by) the world price.

Detailed discussion of the "standard" structure of the CGE model can be found in Löfgren *et al.* (2001).

With regional disaggregation for crop production, we further allow commodities produced by each region to be differentiated. That is, the same commodity, such as rice, produced in different regions is not perfectly substitutable. As most commodity groups are quite aggregate, many crops and different varieties of the same group constitute a commodity group. Considering the market size of China, the difference in the distance between producers and consumers, and the discrepancies in transportation and other transaction costs, this seems a reasonable and necessary assumption.

We further distinguish the model's seven regions as import-substitutable and export-substitutable according to different crops. The specification of a region as an import-substitutable or an export-substitutable is based on each region's trade-GDP share (Table 3), the income level, and the crop mix. With this distinction, the reduction of trade barriers will cause different effects on the relative prices for commodities across regions. As imported commodities mainly compete with domestic production in the import-substitutable regions, the production effects due to trade liberalization would be relatively large in these regions. On the other hand, trade liberalization may stimulate exports from some sectors, such as vegetables and fruits, in which the trade barriers are relatively low. However, such export opportunities cannot be equally realized among regions. Export opportunities will be mainly captured by regions with advantages in information, transportation, technology, and, hence, relatively easy access to foreign markets. We define such regions as export-substitutable and distinguish them from the other regions.

We report the results of comparative static experiments in which we simulate the reduction of tariff rates and the increase of TRQ levels according to China's commitment for 2002–04. The model is static, and hence we do not explicitly consider other adjustments, such as an increase in total labor supply, capital investment, technology transfer, productivity shifts, etc. all of which might occur due to China's WTO accession. Because TRQ is a quantitative constraint for potential imports, with growth in China's GDP, increase in demand for commodities may cause a TRQ to become binding. In order to capture such a possibility, we allow the country's total factor productivity to exogenously grow such that China's GDP rises by 7% annually in 2002–04 period. This growth rate is quite close to the China's reported growth rate in GDP for the last ten years as well as its predicted growth rate in the next few years.

However, with its static features, the model does not capture many dynamic adjustments, such as the linkage between trade openness and economic growth, which are statistically proven to be strong and important factors in explaining China's economic growth and rural development.

The China regional CGE model is used to evaluate both the national and regional effects of China's WTO accession. Details about the terms of China's commitments for 2002–04 are from the WTO website, and are used as the policy base for the study (Tables 4–5). However, with the exception of TRQs for specific agricultural commodities, the model ignores many other non-tariff barriers to agricultural trade, including import licenses and the use of state trading companies. Given the agricultural focus of the study and the difficulty in obtaining non-tariff barriers data for non-agricultural sectors, the model does not account for any non-tariff barriers in the non-agricultural sectors, such as in the automobile industry and services, which are crucial components of China's commitments and would also generate a large effect on the Chinese economy. Also, the study does not take into account the potential conflicts between China's domestic policies and institutional arrangements and WTO requirements. While the harmonization between China's domestic policies and institutions with China's commitments to WTO is a necessary condition to

Table 4. Tariff Rates Reduction Schedule (%)

	Base Year	2002	2003	2004
Wheat				
In quota	50.0	1.0	1.0	1.0
Over quota	74.0	71.0	68.0	65.0
Rice				
In quota	1.0	1.0	1.0	1.0
Over quota	74.0	71.0	68.0	65.0
Corn				
In quota	60.0	1.0	1.0	1.0
Over quota	70.0	60.0	50.0	40.0
Vegetables	19.4	18.0	16.5	15.1
Fruits	26.1	24.2	22.2	20.3
Soybeans	39.0	19.0	17.0	15.0
Other oilseeds	21.9	19.0	17.0	15.0
Cotton				
In quota	13.0	1.0	1.0	1.0
Over quota	62.0	54.4	47.2	40.0
Other crops	17.8	15.3	12.7	10.6
Livestock	19.4	18.1	16.8	15.6
Other agriculture	22.1	18.7	16.1	15.6
Meat, eggs and dairy products	26.8	21.6	18.5	15.3
Vegetable oils				
In quota	22.0	9.0	9.0	9.0
Over quota	61.0	48.0	35.0	22.0
Grain mill products	18.0	20.4	17.6	14.4
Other processed food	48.4	42.2	35.6	28.0
Cotton textile	13.0	11.0	8.0	4.1
Other textile	20.7	18.1	15.1	11.4
Apparel	21.7	19.4	13.0	10.9
Leather products	18.5	16.3	11.5	8.4
Fertilizers	12.2	11.0	8.0	4.1
Agricultural machinery	10.2	8.4	5.7	2.4
Other industry	20.4	18.3	9.5	6.4

Note: All tariff rates for the commodities without over quota rates are bound rates
Sources: Base year's tariff rates for the agricultural commodities with quotas are calculated by the authors using the gaps between world prices and China's domestic prices in 1999/2000, with the price data from USDA/ERS (http://www.ers.usda.gov/briefing/china/data.htm). Tariff rates for the other commodities are from GTAP version 5 database. Tariff reduction schedule is from WTO website (http://dosonline.wto.org/, WT/ACC/Chn/*)

Table 5. Level of TRQ Quota (1000 Ton)

	Base Year Imports[1]	2002	2003	2004
Wheat	1916	8468	9052	9636
Rice	261	3990	4655	5320
Corn	287	5850	6525	7200
Cotton	787	819	856	894
Vegetable oils[2]	1650	2518	2818	3118

[1]We choose the year in which imports were the highest during 1996–2001 as the base year. 1997 for wheat, rice, corn, and soybean oil and 1996 for cotton
[2]Soybean oil only
Sources: Data for base year from USDA/ERS (http://www.ers.usda.gov/briefing/china/data.htm); TRQ quota level from WTO website (http://dosonline.wto.org/, WT/ACC/Chn/*)

make the following effects happen (Colby *et al.*, 2001), we have to ignore such important linkages in the current study due to the difficulties in quantifying the effects of these domestic policies and institutions.

4. Aggregate Effect of China's WTO Accession

4.1. *Modest Welfare Gains*

At the national level, we focus on evaluating the effect of China's WTO accession on some macroeconomic indicators. We first simulate the "base-run" for 2002–04. In the base-run, we exogenously increase the total factor productivity (TFP) to a level such that the growth rate in GDP is around 6–7%. The trade policy, however, is status quo, i.e. China's WTO commitments are not included in the base-run. In the second group of simulations, China's WTO commitments are implemented according to the time schedule for 2002–04, with the same TFP growth rate included in the base-run. As expected, China's WTO accession, by reducing import tariffs and quota constraints, would benefit its economy at the national (aggregate) level. However, the welfare gains are modest. We use changes in real GDP, total consumption in quantity (weighted by the expenditure share for each sector's commodity), and real income by rural and urban households to evaluate the welfare effect at national level. As exogenous growth in TFP is included in the base-run, gains in welfare originate only from a more efficient allocation of factor endowments. Trade liberalization due to China's WTO commitments would raise GDP by 0.2–0.7% in 2002–04. While total consumption increases, rural consumption would increase less than urban consumption. The domestic price level, measured by the consumer price index, would fall slightly in 2002 due to the inflow of cheap foreign goods, but would stay unchanged thereafter. For the same reason, the real exchange rate depreciates, implying improvement in the terms of trade, which benefits China's exports. While the real income for the rural household group rises, income from agriculture falls in 2002 (Table 6). Moreover, increases in the rural income are much smaller than the increases in urban income in the first year. These results indicate that the income gap between rural and urban areas may be further widened after China's joining the WTO.

While the welfare results are comparable with those from other studies [e.g. China's GDP rises by 1% in USITC (1999) and 1.4–2% in Lejour (2000)], our results are relatively modest. Besides excluding the growth effects associated with trade openness and spillover effects due to trade liberalization, another important reason is that the model's incorporation of seven regions reduces factor mobility across sectors at the national level while facilitating more realistic factor re-allocation.

Other studies have shown, as expected, world prices, especially prices for wheat, corn, soybeans, and some other agricultural products, will be affected (rise) as China increases its grain imports, since China is a large player in the world market for these commodities. In order to capture the effect of China's WTO accession on the world's economy, a global CGE models with

Table 6. Macroeconomic Effects in the Model

	Base-run: Without WTO Commitments			With WTO Commitments					
	2002	2003	2004	2002	2003	2004	2002	2003	2004
	Annual Growth Rate						% Change from the Base-run		
GDP	6.89	6.80	6.71	7.11	7.44	7.50	0.20	0.60	0.73
Total consumption	6.56	6.45	6.35	7.17	7.17	7.22	0.57	0.68	0.81
Rural consumption	6.96	6.82	6.69	7.10	7.54	7.58	0.14	0.68	0.83
Urban consumption	6.99	6.86	6.77	8.06	7.68	7.73	1.00	0.77	0.90
Consumer price index	1.79	1.80	1.80	1.29	1.87	1.94	−0.49	0.06	0.13
Real exchange rate	−0.81	−0.82	−0.82	0.03	2.72	3.93	0.85	3.57	4.79
Rural income, real[1]	6.16	5.98	5.81	6.46	7.92	8.35	0.28	1.83	2.41
from agriculture	7.09	6.82	6.54	6.06	7.85	8.00	−0.97	0.96	1.37
Urban income, real	5.29	5.15	5.05	6.60	7.06	7.48	1.25	1.81	2.32

[1]Normalized by CPI
Source: Model results

endogenously determined world prices is an ideal choice. Indeed, many studies on this issue, such as those we referred above, have been using global CGE model for analyzing China's accession to the WTO. However, as one of the focuses in our study is the regional impacts within China and a sensible allocation of its resources, it is very hard to handle regional disaggregation within China in a global world CGE model framework. A comprehensive trade liberalization after China joining WTO would affect world prices in a wide range of agricultural and non-agricultural products, but many of such price effects would be cancelled out and the relative level of agricultural prices may not rise as much as would be predicted by commodity or sector analysis. In fact, the domestic price level only slightly falls in the first year in our WTO scenarios (Table 6), so the magnitude of possible bias in the model results due to the small country assumption might be minimal.

4.2. *Grain TRQs would not Fill*

Given the emphasis of the study is agriculture and grain imports mainly bear quantitative restrictions under a tariff-rate-quota system, we further look at the possible impact of increasing the level of TRQs, and reducing in-quota and above-quota tariffs on grain imports. Given data availability, we only incorporate TRQs for six agricultural commodities: wheat, rice, corn, cotton, soybean oils and grain mill products, including mainly milled rice and wheat flour.

In general, a TRQ is a quota for a volume of imports at a particular tariff-rate. If a volume of imports is below the level of the quota, an in-quota (lower) tariff is applied. Once the quota is filled, an above-quota (higher) tariff is applied on additional imports (Skully, 2001). Before China's accession to the WTO, its tariff-rate quota system had not actually been implemented. Even though it is well known that grain and some other agricultural imports have been quantitatively controlled for many years in China, China has never officially provided any information about quota levels on its agricultural imports before the year 2001. The TRQ levels for the first year (2001) in China's WTO commitments were set according to the average level of China's imports in the last ten years. Due to the two-year surge in grain imports in 1994/95, imports in the years after 1994/95, especially in the most recent five years, were far below the quota levels for most TRQ commodities. While the applied tariff rates for the in-quota imports are extremely low (e.g. 1% for grain imports), the domestic prices for these commodities are actually higher than the prices for similar commodities on world markets. This implies that there exists, implicitly, a shadow quota rent for imports. For this reason, the model is set up so that the nominal protection rate, i.e. the gap between domestic prices and prices for similar goods in the international markets, is treated as an implicit tariff in the base year. The nominal protection rate is then updated to 1999's level in the model (Table 4, first column).

In the simulations, the nominal protection rates (the initial tariff rates) are first reduced to the level equivalent to the in-quota tariff. Then, quota levels are further increased and the above-quota tariffs are further reduced according to China's commitments. Replacing the base-year's nominal protection rate by the in-quota tariff rate definitely would raise in-quota imports. However, given the fact that the base-year's nominal protection rate for the commodities subjecting to TRQ is often lower than the above-quota tariff rate, increased volume of imports would be below these quota levels, and the quotas will not be filled in the three years. Over time, the quota may be eventually filled. However, if the level of the shadow rent for imports is lower than the above-quota tariff rate by then, it is still hard to observe any imports at the high above- the-quota tariff levels.

In the "base-run" simulations, both imports and exports rise with the growth in GDP. With income growth, demand for food and other primary agricultural products may not rise at the same speed as growth in income. In the model, the crop production (except for vegetables and fruits) either declines or increases less than the increase in livestock, processed food, and non-agricultural sectors (Table 7). Decline in production implies that the demand growth (though slower than the income growth) has to be met by imports. Thus, agricultural imports rise rapidly.

We focus our discussion on the four crops that are subject to quotas, and soybeans. In the base-run, rice, corn, and soybean production falls (the soybean production declines the most) and wheat production rises slightly (Table 7). This results in a rapid growth in imports of these commodities. The annual growth rates are 12% to 15% for rice and wheat imports, 19% to 42% for cotton, soybean, and corn imports.

We calculate the ratio of imports in total consumption for the grain products. Except for soybean imports, imports of each individual grain accounted only for a small share of total consumption in the domestic market. Note that imports of wheat, rice, and corn in the base year are extremely low (Table 8). In total, imported grains accounted for 2% of domestic consumption in the base year. With economic growth, this ratio rises to 2.7% to 4% in 2002–04 period in the base-run scenarios. Even though the annual growth rate of wheat imports is 15%, imports still only accounted for less

Table 7. Growth in Sectoral Production in the Model (Base-run)

	Annual Growth Rate (%)		
	2002	2003	2004
Wheat	1.02	0.99	0.98
Rice	−0.16	−0.06	0.03
Corn	0.08	−0.24	−0.61
Vegetables	2.48	2.39	2.30
Fruits	2.28	2.21	2.10
Soybeans	−8.23	−9.56	−10.82
Other oilseeds	−2.17	−2.14	−2.10
Cotton	−0.54	−0.83	−1.11
Other crops	0.95	0.91	0.87
Livestock	3.52	3.45	3.40
Meats and eggs	3.16	3.26	3.37
Grain mills	1.06	1.06	1.08
Vegetable oils	0.29	0.05	−0.10
Other agriculture	3.15	3.14	3.14
Other food products	5.67	5.51	5.38
Fertilizers	2.08	1.98	1.88
Ag machinery	6.90	6.84	6.77
Cotton textile	3.82	3.83	3.86
Other textile	2.13	2.18	2.26
Apparel	4.82	4.85	4.90
Leather	4.33	4.50	4.69
Other industry	6.35	6.27	6.19
Utility	5.63	5.55	5.48
Construction	9.27	9.03	8.81
Transportation	5.11	5.05	5.00
Sales	5.02	4.99	4.97
Finance	5.56	5.46	5.38
Social services	6.49	6.36	6.25

Source: Model results

than 1% of total wheat consumption in the domestic market in 2002–04 period (Table 9).

Reducing in-quota tariffs and raising the quota levels would further increase grain imports. Corn's imports would triple, and imports of wheat would rise more than 50% annually (Table 10). On the other hand, since China's domestic

Table 8. Imports of Selected Agricultural Commodities 1994–2000 (1000 Ton)

	Wheat	Rice	Corn	Soybeans
1994	10,256	1,998	4,287	
1995	12,531	852	1,476	795
1996	2,705	322	75	2,274
1997	1,916	261	287	2,940
1998	829	178	262	3,850
1999	1,010	278	71	10,100
2000	195	267	88	13,245

Source: ERS database (http://www.ers.usda.gov/briefing/china/data.htm)

Table 9. Ratio of Imports in Total Consumption for Selected Agricultural Commodities

		Base-run: Without WTO Commitments			With WTO Commitments		
	Base Year	2002	2003	2004	2002	2003	2004
Wheat	0.58	0.66	0.75	0.84	1.01	1.15	1.28
Rice	0.15	0.16	0.18	0.21	0.16	0.18	0.20
Corn	2.69	3.87	5.49	7.67	18.45	24.43	30.88
Soybeans	19.77	25.45	31.99	39.15	33.84	42.65	51.11
All grains	2.14	2.67	3.30	4.04	5.45	6.98	8.64
Cotton	10.66	12.45	14.58	17.07	17.46	19.29	21.71
Vegetable oils	14.53	16.88	19.41	22.08	21.69	23.94	26.14

Source: Model results

price of rice is actually lower than the world price, rice imports actually fall slightly.

Even though China would drastically increase wheat, corn and cotton imports in the model due to the rise in the TRQ level and reduction in tariff rates, the gap between the volume of its imports in the base year and the in-quota level is still very high, implying that the quota level would not be filled and the above-quota imports would not be observed. The model simulation results show that for the five TRQ commodities included in the model, quota levels would be filled by 8% to 61% (Table 11). As expected, the lowest fill rate is observed for rice imports, about 8% annually. The highest rate is for vegetable oil imports, about 59% to 61% annually. In reality, however, changes

Table 10. WTO Impact on Value of Imports by Commodity

	Percent Change from the Base-run		
	2002	2003	2004
Wheat	54.37	55.16	53.94
Rice	−2.72	−2.23	−2.81
Corn	406.96	389.33	359.26
Vegetables	2.06	2.41	3.60
Fruits	−6.69	−2.66	−0.58
Soybeans	30.38	33.17	33.22
Cotton	43.81	44.38	41.60
Other crops	1.19	3.61	6.69
Livestock	−2.61	−2.35	−0.72
Meats and eggs	10.51	17.42	26.98
Grain mills	18.41	17.77	16.92
Vegetable oils	30.14	25.51	21.02
Other agriculture	2.43	0.83	3.22
Other food	12.46	25.90	52.91
Fertilizers	0.75	0.29	8.47
Ag machinery	4.17	2.99	11.06
Cotton textile	4.49	7.98	18.90
Other textile	4.39	7.35	16.10
Apparel	2.80	10.08	10.32
Leather	1.60	5.59	9.98
Other industry	2.89	21.69	29.34

Source: Model results

Table 11. Ratio of the Import Volume in the Model to the TRQ Level

	With WTO Commitments (%)		
	2002	2003	2004
Wheat	40.26	43.44	46.21
Rice	8.51	8.22	8.50
Corn	36.33	45.34	54.87
Cotton	18.14	20.69	23.09
Vegetable oils	58.78	59.90	61.22

Source: WTO (http://dosonline.wto.org/, WT/ACC/Chn/*)

in international market conditions, such as a sudden surge in prices because of large-scale natural disasters, timing of TRQ releases from the government, and lower domestic prices caused by extreme bumper harvests or high stocks may also lead China not only fail to fill the TRQs, but also reverse the trade flows.

Our study's outcomes are relatively modest compared to those of other studies. Regional disaggregation enforces reasonable constraints on the mobility of labor and other factors, and hence agricultural production at the national level is more sensible as it is based on feasible allocation of factors. Except for corn and soybeans, in which output declines by 10% to 18% as imported foreign goods replace domestic production, other agricultural commodities experience only slight changes in output (Table 12).

It has to be pointed out that the model results would be different if there were different estimates of the initial gap between domestic and world prices. If the gap were wider than assumed in our base case, the surge in imports would be relatively large. For this reason, we conduct a sensitivity test in which the nominal protection rate for wheat is 87% and that for corn is 94%. Under these assumptions, the TRQs for wheat imports would be filled, but the TRQs for corn imports would not be filled in the 2002–04 period. This result implies that the TRQ filling rate depends critically on the gap price between domestic and global markets. If grain and cotton prices continue to decline in the world market, while China's domestic prices do not fall or rise, China's imports of grains and cotton would rise steadily in the future. However, even though wheat imports would rise significantly in the future, given the high above-quota tariff rate, China's grain and cotton imports would not be likely to rise above the quota level in the near future.

Estimated nominal protection rates for China's agricultural trade vary substantially across studies. For example, using recent survey data on the border prices, Huang *et al.* (2002) found relative low nominal protection rates for many agricultural products: 12% for wheat, 32% for corn, and 15% for soybeans. The information on China's domestic prices used in Huang's study is comparable to that used in our study. However, Huang *et al.* use their own survey data to estimate an average border price for wheat, which is much lower than the hard wheat gulf price used in our study.

5. Differential Effects of China's WTO Accession at the Regional Level

At the regional level, we focus on the possible impact of China's WTO accession on resource allocation and rural income. It is known that non-farm

Table 12. WTO Impact on Production by Sector

	Percent Change from the Base-run		
	2003	2003	2004
Wheat	0.17	0.47	0.67
Rice	1.08	1.79	2.23
Corn	−9.80	−12.01	−14.56
Vegetables	0.18	0.25	0.24
Fruits	1.25	1.29	1.31
Soybeans	−12.99	−15.75	−18.03
Other oilseeds	−2.90	−2.09	−1.12
Cotton	−2.78	3.85	6.12
Other crops	0.78	0.99	0.91
Livestock	1.07	2.01	2.43
Meats and eggs	1.38	3.05	3.69
Grain mills	0.77	1.25	1.55
Vegetable oils	−4.10	−3.27	−2.34
Other agriculture	0.66	1.24	1.43
Other food products	0.80	0.95	0.80
Fertilizers	−0.93	0.36	−0.66
Ag machinery	−0.07	1.07	1.28
Cotton textile	1.76	6.43	7.77
Other textile	3.02	10.14	12.54
Apparel	2.30	7.56	10.86
Leather	3.92	11.31	15.90
Other industry	0.34	−0.15	−0.11
Utility	0.53	1.20	1.57
Construction	0.02	1.07	1.36
Transportation	0.68	2.35	3.04
Sales	0.88	2.49	3.16
Finance	0.62	1.58	2.02
Social services	0.25	1.26	1.59

Source: Model results

income now accounts for about one-third of rural income in China. However, due to a lack of data on rural non-farm sectors, we cannot disaggregate rural non-farm activities from national non-agricultural sectors. Thus, in the model, the effects of China joining the WTO on rural income at the regional level are captured by the net labor migration from agriculture (crop production) within regions to the non-crop and non-agricultural activities at the national level. That is, we only consider the net increase in rural labor income for each region caused by net increase in employment in non-crop or non-agriculture. At the same time, we ignored any change in rural income due to the labor mobility between non-crop and non-agricultural activities. Given the fact that non-farm income accounted for only 10% of rural income in the less-developed regions, far below the one-third of national average level, in the simulations, we assume that agricultural labor in the Northwest and Southwest cannot freely move into non-agricultural activities, chiefly because of lack of employment opportunities. Furthermore, considering natural resource constraints (such as water), difficulty in market access, and lack of export markets, cropping mix is also restricted in these two regions. We assume that agricultural production in these two less-developed regions is only sold on the domestic markets while the other five regions mainly produce exportable commodities. Production of rice, vegetables, and fruits cannot exceed the level observed in the base year's data for the Northwest due to water limitations.

Regional analysis reveals large differential impacts on agricultural production. For example, at the national level, wheat production is expected to rise 0.7%, relative to the base-run for 2004 in the WTO simulations. But at the regional level, wheat production would fall in the regions of Central, East, South, and Southwest by 2.4% to 5%. In the North, a major wheat producing region, which accounts for almost 60% of national wheat output, wheat production would rise at close to the national rate. About 10% of China's wheat production is produced in the Northwest region. Given cropping limitations, wheat production rises by 3.5% in this region. For the Northeast, due to a big drop in soybean and corn production, wheat production would also increase (Table 13).

Given the regional difference in cropping mix, and especially the difference in the share of non-farm income in total rural income, the WTO accession accentuates regional differences in rural income. In the first year in the simulation (2002), there are five regions in which rural income would fall. After the first year's adjustment, rural income recovers and starts to rise in six regions. However, the less-developed Northwest would still suffer, as its total rural income continues to decline. Among the six regions in which total rural income rises in the 2003–04 period, the smallest increase is observed in the Northeast, the major soybean production region in China, and the Southwest, the other less-developed region. For the Northeast, this is mainly due to international competition from soybean and corn imports, while for the Southwest, the limited access to export markets is critical.

Table 13. Change in Regional Crop Production

2004	North	North-west	North-east	Central	East	South	South-west	Nation
	Percent Change from the Base-run							
Wheat	0.72	3.47	12.23	−2.35	−2.98	−4.95	−3.18	0.67
Rice	5.48	17.07	11.57	0.17	−0.70	−0.22	3.63	2.23
Corn	−16.10	−27.61	−7.18	−21.38	−18.00	−21.11	−31.77	−14.56
Vegetables	−0.44	11.79	0.22	−4.56	1.94	−1.57	10.78	0.24
Fruits	2.55	3.48	2.65	−0.93	−0.11	−1.37	−2.20	1.31
Soybeans	−18.48	−27.92	−15.20	−20.73	−21.53	−22.61	−32.83	−18.03
Other oilseeds	1.08	3.71	1.88	−3.22	−1.67	−2.89	−2.04	−1.12
Cotton	6.14	11.19	11.65	2.71	2.97	8.21	8.57	6.12
Other crops	2.39	4.39	3.14	0.32	1.01	0.75	1.54	0.91

Source: Model results

In the more advanced regions, such as the East and South, non-farm income accounted for as much as 70–80% of total rural income (Fan *et al.*, 2001b), while in the less-developed regions, the share was often less than 20%. Table 6 shows that the returns in the non-agricultural activities rise more than those in agriculture, which benefits advanced regions as their non-farm income ratio is high. With more labor moving from agricultural to non-agricultural sectors, the developed regions would further benefit, considering the fact that there are more non-farm employment opportunities in these regions. However, for the less-developed regions, as agriculture still remains the main income source, rural households gain relatively little from engaging in non-farm activities. With the majority of the rural labor force still in agriculture, rural income either declines or stagnates in these regions. Table 15 shows the changes in the rural income by source, which helps to explain model results in Table 14.

6. Conclusions

This study constructs a China regional CGE model to analyze both the national and regional impacts of China's WTO accession on agricultural production, trade, and farmers' income. We divide China into seven regions (for agricultural production) and 28 sectors, including 15 disaggregated agricultural sectors for grain, cash crop, livestock, and processed agricultural activities. We utilize the model to simulate China's WTO accession effects through comparison with a base-run, in which a 6–7% annual GDP growth rate is assumed.

Table 14. Change in Rural Income by Region[1]

	Percent Change from the Base-run		
	2002	2003	2004
North	−0.48	1.05	1.42
Northwest	−2.65	−0.48	−0.24
Northeast	−1.41	0.15	0.38
Central	−0.42	1.30	1.70
East	0.51	1.54	2.02
South	0.49	1.58	2.06
Southwest	−1.94	0.31	0.59
Nation	0.28	1.83	2.41

[1]Income from livestock production is not included in the regional results (non-crop sectors were not disaggregated duo to lack of data), but include in the national results
Source: Model results

Table 15. Change in Rural Income by Source and by Region

	Percent Change from the Base-run		
	2002	2003	2004
Agriculture			
North	−3.07	−0.74	−0.52
Northwest	−2.65	−0.48	−0.24
Northeast	−3.20	−1.21	−1.11
Central	−2.88	−0.57	−0.30
East	−2.73	−0.20	0.12
South	−2.55	−0.14	0.14
Southwest	−1.94	0.31	0.59
Non-agriculture			
North	3.13	3.63	4.33
Northwest			
Northeast	3.35	3.91	4.64
Central	5.63	6.11	7.09
East	1.56	2.12	2.68
South	1.74	2.32	2.90
Southwest			

Source: Model results

In the WTO simulations, we incorporate TRQs as quantitative constraints in agricultural imports. Reductions in both in-quota and above-quota tariffs and increases in TRQ levels are simulated according to China's commitment schedule in the 2002–04 period. Results show that China's WTO accession would generally improve the country's total welfare with modest increases in GDP and household income, but may widen existing gaps among regions and sectors. It is expected that the rural income from agricultural sources may decline. While lifting trade barriers in both agriculture and non-agriculture will benefit farmers at the national level, the increase in rural income would be smaller than the increase in urban income, which implies that the rural–urban income gap may be further widened. Furthermore, among the regions, the less-developed rural areas will benefit little or even be hurt because their major income sources are still from agriculture, especially from traditional agricultural activities such as grain production.

The model results should be read as a general direction to capture the possible impacts of China's WTO accession. Even though the model outcomes of China's WTO accession are relatively modest at the national level, differential regional and sectoral effects remind us of conflicts of interests among different groups within China.

References

Colby H, Diao X, and Tuan F, 2001. "China's WTO accession: conflicts with domestic agricultural policies and institutions." *Estey Center J. Int. Law Trade Policy* 2(1): 190–210.

Development Research Center (DRC), The State Council of People's Republic of China, 1998. "The global and domestic impact of China's joining the World Trade Organization."

Easterly W, and Levine R, 2000. "It's not factor accumulation: stylized facts and growth models." Paper presented at the World Bank Conference entitled "What Have We Learned from a Decade of Empirical Research on Growth?" Washington, DC.

Fan S, Zhang L, and Xiaobo Z, 2001a. "Growth, inequality, and poverty in rural China: the role of public investment," IFPRI research report 125, International Food Policy Research Institute, Washington, DC.

Fan S, Zhang L, Xiaobo Z, and Xiaohe M, 2001b. "Regional priorities of public investment in rural china: a county-level analysis." Report prepared for the project Priorities of Public Investments in Chinese Agriculture, September.

Fan M-T, and Zheng Y-X, 2000. "The impact of China's trade liberalization for WTO accession — a computable general equilibrium analysis." Paper presented for the Third GTAP Annual Conference, Australia, June 2000.

Gilbert J, and Wahl T, 2000. "Applied general equilibrium assessments of trade liberalization in China." *World Economy* 25(5): 697–731.

Huang J, Xie Y, Scott R, Min C, and Dan S, 2002. "The nature of distortions to agricultural incentives in China and implications of WTO accession." Paper presented at the WCC Annual meetings, April 15–16, Washington DC.

Kanbur R, and Zhang X, 1999. "Which regional inequality? The evolution of rural–urban and coastal–inland inequality in China from 1983 to 1995." *J. Comp. Econ.* **27**: 686–701.

Kanbur R, and Zhang X, 2001. "Fifty years of regional inequality in China: a journey through revolution, reform and openness." Center For Economic Policy Research (CEPR), Discussion Paper 2887.

Lejour A, 2000. "China and the WTO: the impact on China and the world economy." Paper presented for the Third GTAP Annual Conference, Australia, June 2000.

Löfgren H, Harris RL, and Robinson S, 2001. "A standard computable general equilibrium (CGE) model in Gams." TMD Discussion Paper No. 75, International Food Policy Research Institute, Washington, D.C.

Martin W, Dimaranan B, and Hertel T, 1999. "Trade policy, structural change and China's trade growth." Memo, The World Bank, Washington, DC.

Ministry of Agriculture, 1988 and 2000. *China's Agricultural Statistical Materials*. China Agricultural Publishing House: Beijing (In Chinese).

National Bureau of Statistics of China, 1988–2000. *China Statistical Yearbook*. China Statistics Press: Beijing (In Chinese).

Rozelle S, 1994. "Rural industrialization and increasing inequality: emerging patterns in China's reforming economy." *J. Comp. Econ.* **19**(3): 363–392.

Skully, DW, 2001. "Economics of tariff-rate quota administration." Technical Bulletin #1893, Economic Research Service, U.S. Department of Agriculture, Washington, DC.

U.S. International Trade Commission (USITC), 1999. *Assessment of the Economic Effects on the United States of China's Accession to the WTO*. USITC publication: Washington, DC.

Walmsley T, Hertel T, and McDougall R, 2000. "China's accession to the WTO: timing is everything." Paper presented at the Third GTAP Annual Conference, Australia.

Wang Z, 1999. "The impact of China's WTO entry on the world labor-intensive export market: a recursive dynamic CGE analysis." *The World Economy* **22**(3): 379–405.

Wazing R, 2001. "Measuring the dynamic gains from trade. The World Bank economic review." **15**(3): 393–429.

Wei S-J, and Wu Y, 2001. "Globalization and inequality: evidence from within China." National Bureau of Economic Research (NBER) Working Paper 8611.

Zhang X, and Fan S, 2001. "Estimating crop-specific production technology in Chinese agriculture: a generalized maximum entropy approach." *Am. J. Agri. Econ.* **83**(2): 378–388.

Appendix

Table A1. Sector Aggregation of the Model

Agricultural and processed food sectors:
1. Wheat
2. Rice
3. Other cereals
4. Vegetables
5. Fruits
6. Soybeans
7. Other oilseeds
8. Cotton
9. Other crops
10. Livestock and products
11. Meat, processing eggs and dairy products
12. Grain mill products
13. Vegetable oil and forage
14. Other agricultural products
15. Other food product
Manufacturing sectors:
16. Fertilizer and pesticides
17. Agricultural machinery
18. Cotton textile
19. Other textile
20. Wearing and apparel
21. Leather product
22. Other industry
Service sectors:
23. Electricity and other utility
24. Construction
25. Transport services
26. Sales services
27. Finance services
28. Social services

Chapter 14

Welfare Effects of Trade and Factor Market Reforms in China

MASAYUKI DOI

Institute of Policy and Planning Sciences, University of Tsukuba, Tsukuba, Ibaraki, Japan

PIYUSH TIWARI

University of Aberdeen Business School, Aberdeen, Scotland, United Kingdom

TETSU KAWAKAMI

Department of Social Sciences, Mie University, Tsu, Mie, Japan

Benefits of the multi-faceted liberalization of the Chinese economy can be found in the high rate of economic growth, increased inflow of foreign investment, improved overall quality of life, and some other forms. While the role of trade reform in the Chinese economy received strong attention in the past studies, labor and capital reforms are equally important issues, but were understudied. Inter-industrial wage and capital differentials and restricted labor mobility from rural to urban sector still persist. In this paper, we analyze the economic effects of labor and capital market liberalization on China using a computable general equilibrium (CGE) model. As a signatory to the WTO agreement, China is required to reform its trade sector by eliminating tariffs. We explicitly model wage differentials in Chinese economy, and experiment the effect of removing factor market differentials in the presence and then absence of tariffs and non-tariff barriers. Our results indicate that factor market reforms are essential to the realization of full gains from accession to the WTO agreement.

1. Introduction

Since the introduction of the Reforms and Open-up Policy in 1978, the multi-faceted liberalization of the economy has generated significant economic growth to China. The average annual real growth rate of GNP is over 10%, and external trade has expanded by more than 15% in the period of 1980–1995. Foreign direct investment in terms of signed agreements and contracts, and the total amount of foreign direct investment that could be utilized and actually used stood at 260,000 cases, US$396 billion and US$135 billion in total, respectively, until 1995. The share of agriculture goods sold at an administered price reduced from 94.3% in 1978 to 10.2% in 1993, and that of consumption goods from 97.4% to 12.2% (Cao *et al.*, 1996).

On December 11, 2001, China formally became a full member of the World Trade Organization (WTO) after negotiations lasting nearly 15 years with the WTO and its predecessor, the General Agreement on Tariffs and Trade (GATT). Since 1990, the Chinese Government has taken a series of important steps to actively promote its trade liberalization in order to respond to the globalization trend of the world economy and participate in international competition on the basis of WTO rules. These steps are composed mainly of tariff reduction and elimination of non-tariff barriers. Accession to the WTO would have a significant impact on the external trade patterns in China. Zhai and Li (2000) have shown that the Chinese economy would gain from accession to the WTO, but the gains are not evenly distributed among either sectors or income groups. In particular, protected sectors such as agriculture would be the losers and rural households would suffer since the dominant role of agriculture is minimized. Fan and Zheng (2000) have shown that tariff cuts induced by trade liberalization have minor, but positive effects on the macro-economy in terms of gains in GDP.

Meanwhile, liberalization of labor and capital sectors has not been adequately addressed in earlier studies. Most of the earlier studies assume equilibrium wage and capital rates in the economy with the assumption that there are perfect divisions of labor and capital. The present factor market distortions are not explicitly reflected in their models. Labor market liberalization in China is an unfinished agenda. Conventionally, Lewis (1954) argued that the economic growth can be enhanced by the migration of surplus labor from the traditional sector with a zero marginal productivity characterized by disguised unemployment to the modern sector to the productivity level similar to that observed in the traditional sector. In economic theory, reallocation of labor and capital from low productivity to high productivity activities emphasizes efficiency.

However, following theoretical analysis by Sachs, Yang and Zhang (2000), Doi, Tiwari and Kawakami (2002) estimated the effects of trade liberalization and factor market reforms caused by the dual economic structure on the Chinese economy using a static computable general equilibrium (CGE) model. They explicitly modeled wage and capital returns in the case of the Chinese economy, assuming *a priori* exogenous wage differentials. Then, taking a view that differential determination is an endogenous process, Tiwari, Kawakami and Doi (2002) extended the model of Doi *et al.* (2002) to incorporate this behavior, in which the government utility function is specified newly into the model.

In this paper, we introduce the CGE models with wage and capital differentials in the Chinese economy by re-presenting the CGE structures developed in Doi *et al.* (2002) and Tiwari *et al.* (2002) and their respective results, and discuss policy implications for factor and trade market reforms. We assume that wage and capital differentials are the outcome of institutional aspects of the Chinese economy that restrict the factor mobility. The objective of this paper then is to estimate welfare gain due to (1) institutional changes that eliminate wage and capital differentials, and (2) trade liberalization after WTO accession of China when there are wage and capital differentials as well as when there are no wage and capital differentials. To illustrate the effects of factor market reforms under each scenario, we introduce two different base models: (1) maintaining exogenous wage differentials, and (2) determining wage differentials in an endogenous process. We indicate that factor market reforms are essential to the realization of full gains from accession to the WTO agreement.

The remainder of the paper is organized as follows. Section 2 discusses the issues of factor distortions and trade barriers in China as well as the past studies on them. Section 3 describes the CGE models for China incorporating wage and capital differentials for trade liberalization evaluation. Section 4 reports the analysis and results of the models, and Section 5 concludes.

2. Trade and Factor Distortions of China and their Studies

2.1. *Factor Immobility*

According to China's National Bureau of Statistics (1996), rural China had 323 million farmers in its labor force in 1995, out of the total of 860 million registered rural residents. However, with only 0.33 ha of cultivated land per farmer, Chinese countryside does not actually support so many fully working farmers. The average labor productivity in agriculture is less than one-fifth of manufacturing industry's productivity and less than one-third of the service sector's productivity. Farmers officially account for over a half of the national labor force, but produce only 20% of GDP (Bhattacharyya *et al.*, 1999). Bhattacharyya *et al.* (1999) have estimated that there is an apparent labor surplus of between 35% and 40% of the total agricultural labor force.

The incentives to out-migrate have always been present in rural China, even though the chances were not available before the reform policy transformed Chinese economies. The migration flows from rural to urban areas in China perhaps are the largest in the world. This has been occurring since the mid-1980s and tens of millions of rural migrants are working and residing in urban areas (Zhao, 1999a). Almost all of those, however, are the so-called "floating population" (*liudong renkou*), which means migrants without official permanent urban registration. Most of these migrants from rural areas find employment in the informal sector of urban areas. This is primarily because these migrants from rural areas do not have legal documents for staying in the urban areas. The formal sector in urban areas is unable to employ this floating labor, and it has to pay higher wages to retain the employees with legal documents. China has an immense wage differential because of this "*hukou*" system of household registration by which the migration from rural to urban areas has been restricted. Under the *hukou* system, rural registered labor is not granted opportunities of employment in urban areas which are given to urban registered labor, and their children do not have equal educational opportunities in urban areas (Yang, 1997; Zhao, 1999b). There are also the psychological costs of being isolated from their families due to illegal migration (Zhao, 1999a).

As a result, the surplus labor in agriculture has distorted the wages between the agricultural sector and other sectors of the economy as shown in Table 1 as of 1995. Agriculture reportedly has a low wage return (5.38 thousand yuan) far lower than the manufacturing (33.7 thousand yuan) and service (15.1 thousand yuan) sectors.

Also found in Table 1 is capital market distortion. The service sector shows a particularly low capital return presumably due to distortions caused by state-owned enterprises (SOEs). The government has subsidized some SOEs, performing poorly, in the energy, transportation and other sectors. A large amount of concessionary loans have impeded the incentives to improve their investment and operating efficiencies, and have become budget burdens for the government. The reform of SOEs and capital allocation improvement among state, collective and individual owned enterprises are indispensable for capital market reform.

Table 1. Wage and Capital Return Differentials Across the Sectors in China

	Wage (1,000 yuan)	Capital (yuan)
Agriculture	5.38	0.51
Manufacture	33.74	1.00
Services	15.07	0.28

Note: As of 1995
Source: National Bureau of Statistics (1997)

It is now empirically accepted that the transfer of underemployed or surplus rural labor to unskilled jobs in urban sectors, and town and village enterprises contributed greatly to China's GDP growth in the post-reform period (see, for example, World Bank, 1997). Even so, labor market reform has lagged behind far from labor reforms in most other countries. Cai, Wang and Du (2002) analyzed the impact of labor market distortions on China's regional economic growth by an econometric approach using a provincial-level panel data set. They incorporated the productivity of agricultural labor into the growth regression model of Solow-type as an indicator of labor market distortion. They found that regional labor immobility has negatively affected regional growth rates over the reform period. Through a growth regression approach similar to theirs, Kawakami (2004) showed that the negative effect on China's regional growth caused by labor market distortion became more critical during the 1990s than earlier.

2.2. *Trade Liberalization*

Until 1992, China's trade barriers were still very high with a simple average nominal tariff rate as high as 43.2% and a variety of non-tariff measures including licensing, quotas, tendering and other controls (Fan and Zheng, 2000). Since then, China has taken steps to sharply reduce tariffs and remove non-tariff measures pursuant to its bilateral commitments and to support its WTO accession bid.

Chinese tariff rates operate as part of an industrial policy to protect its specific industrial sectors and build its international competitiveness. Since 1992, China has speeded up its tariff liberalization. By 1998, China had reduced six times its simple average tariff from 43.2% to 17.0%. In January 1999, the Ministry of Finance announced tariff reductions for 1,014 commodities in the forestry, textile and toy sectors. In January 2000, China adjusted tariff schedule to increase the number of import tax codes from previous 6,940 to 7,062 and partially reduced further tariff rates. A total of 819 textile commodities have undergone tax rate reductions (Fan and Zheng, 2000).

However, the actual tariff collection rate is far lower than the nominal tariff rate both because of legal tariff exemptions and illegal smuggling and corruption. Table 2 illustrates the profile of China's trade pattern and actual tariff collection rates basically in 1995. The simple average actual tariff rate of the three sectors is only 2.3% while the simple average nominal tariff rate is as high as 19.6%. Hence, the official tariff rates should be scaled down to accommodate the tariff exemptions and smuggling so that China's tariff barriers will not be overestimated.

In the Sino–U.S. WTO deal signed on 15 November, 1999 for China's accession to WTO membership, China agreed to reduce its tariff rates on agricultural products to 14.5–15%, a 12% decrease from its 1997 tariff base. China pledged to cut its tariff rates on wood and paper to 5–7.5% by 2005, 55% decrease for wood products and 49% decrease for paper products; and to lower its industrial tariffs to an overall average of 9.4% by 2005, a decrease by about 53.7% from its 1997 tariff base for other industrial products, on average. With China becoming a full member of WTO, the tariffs would have to reduce further in line with the WTO guidelines.

China's non-tariff barriers (hereafter, NTBs) to trade usually include a broad array of licenses, quotas, tendering, state trading and other controls. Combined with high tariffs, Chinese NTBs overlap and serve as a web of protection for particular domestic industries. As a result, the removal of NTBs was also required for its accession to WTO membership. In fact, China has removed over 1,000 quotas and licenses on a wide range of commodities since 1992. So far, the number of products requiring licenses and quotas is said to be only 395 (Fan and Zheng, 2000). Despite the removal of quotas and

Table 2. Trade Pattern and Tariff Rates by Sector in China

	Output	Labor Force	Imports	Exports	Nominal Tariff Rate[1]	Actual Tariff Rate[1]	Tariff Equivalent of NTBs	Net Export (Billion Yuan)
Agriculture	12.40	56.43	3.05	1.37	27.20	1.54	0.00	−16.63
Manufacture	68.76	23.57	89.49	89.91	18.85	2.56	15.09	53.11
Services	18.84	20.00	7.46	8.72	0.00	0.47	0.00	17.80
Total/Average	100.00	100.00	100.00	100.00	19.62	2.34	15.09	54.28

[1]Nominal and actual tariff rates are for 1997. The other values are for 1995

Source: Estimates based on Fan and Zheng (2000)

license requirements during the period 1992–1998, China would be required to remove NTBs. Among the major NTBs, China would be required to eliminate WTO-inconsistent licensing, quotas and tendering requirements, the elimination of China's trade-related investment measures and market openings in specified Chinese serviced sectors, etc.

Sachs *et al.* (2000) have theoretically explored implications for China's WTO membership and trade policy under its dual economy. In their model endogenous and exogenous comparative advantages generate pecuniary positive network effects of division of labor on aggregate productivity. The tradeoff between the network effects and transaction costs implies that if a transaction cost coefficient for a unit of goods traded is large, total transaction cost outweighs economies of division of labor, so that autarky, where aggregate productivity is lower than the PPF (production possibility frontier), is equilibrium. As transaction conditions are improved, the equilibrium network of trade expands (Sachs *et al.*, 2000). Their model shows that if China's transaction efficiency is very low, then China cannot gain from globalization in a dual structure where some Chinese are involved in international trade and others are in autarky since low income in autarchic part forces terms of trade against China, bring all gains from trade to the developed country with a higher transaction efficiency. If China's further reforms can significantly raise transaction efficiency, China can then gain from globalization from a high level of international and domestic division of labor and a fairer division of gains from the division of labor (Sachs *et al.*, 2000).

There are also a number of studies on China using CGE models to evaluate the effect of trade liberalization in association with the free-trade agreements (FTAs) and WTO accession. As mentioned in Section 1, Zhai and Li (2000) and Fan and Zheng (2000) are among them. As pointed out earlier, however, most of the earlier studies assume equilibrium wage and capital rates in the economy in which the present factor market distortions are not reflected. Then, the objective of this paper is, as stated earlier, to discuss welfare gains due to both factor market reform and trade liberalization. For this purpose, we start the discussion by re-presenting the CGE models of Doi *et al.* (2002) and Tiwari *et al.* (2002) which explicitly incorporated factor market distortions.

3. CGE Models with Factor Market Distortions

3.1. *A Stylize CGE Model for Trade Reform Evaluation*

Following Thierfelder and Shiells (1997), Doi *et al.* (2002) and Tiwari *et al.* (2002) used a stylized CGE model to evaluate the economic effects of trade liberalization for China. The model is a modified version of the classic Jones model (Jones, 1971) used in trade theory. Two factors, namely, labor and capital, are used to produce three commodities, agriculture, manufactured goods, and services. Both factors are mobile across the sectors. Output is produced according to a constant elasticity of substitution (CES) production function over labor and capital.

Departing from the standard theoretical trade model, this model assumes that imports and domestic commodities are not perfect substitutes (as in Thierfelder and Shiells, 1997). It applies the Armington assumption, and distinguishes commodities by country of origin. Consumers purchase a composite good that is a CES aggregate of the imported and domestic variety. Likewise, on the output side, the model assumes that output for the domestic market is different from output sold on the export market. There is a constant elasticity of transformation (CET) function describing the relationship between exports and goods for domestic consumption. The Armington specification dampens the price transmission following a trade policy shock. When tariffs are eliminated, for example, domestic prices do not experience the full price change — the changes depend on the degree of substitutability between the imported and the domestic good.

The model develops a single country model in which one country, in this case China, trades with the rest of the world at constant prices (as in Thierfelder and Shiells, 1997). The trade balance is held constant and both the relative price of imports to the domestic competing variety and the relative price of exports to the domestic competing variety adjust. The domestic price index is *numeraire*. Consistent with theoretical trade models, all tariff revenue is redistributed to the consumer in a lump-sum fashion.

The stylized model is summarized in Appendices A and B. Appendix A identifies the variables and the parameters for the model, and the model equations appear in Appendix B. The impact of removing not only tariff but also NTBs in the context of China's WTO accession is simulated by this model with and without factor market distortions which are modeled as described next.

3.2. *Modeling Labor Market Distortions*

Doi *et al.* (2002) and Tiwari *et al.* (2002) modeled the dual structure in the Chinese economy by incorporating the restrictions on factor mobility using the concept of wage differentials. They assume that sectoral wage differences are due to the restrictions on factors to gaining employment in different sectors.

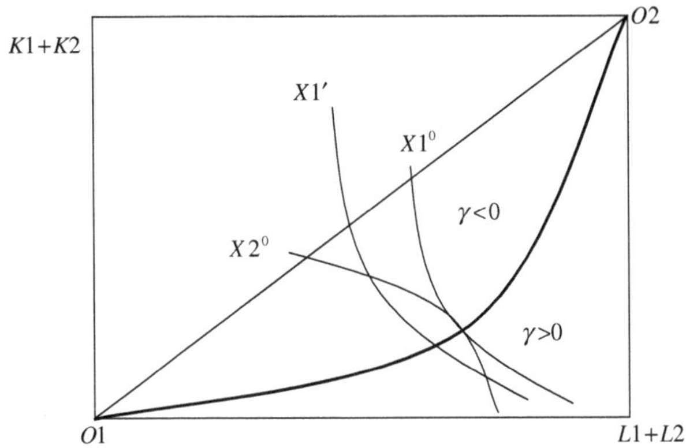

Fig. 1. Wage Differentials in the Hekscher–Ohlin Framework.
Source: Thierfelder and Shiells (1997, p. 440)

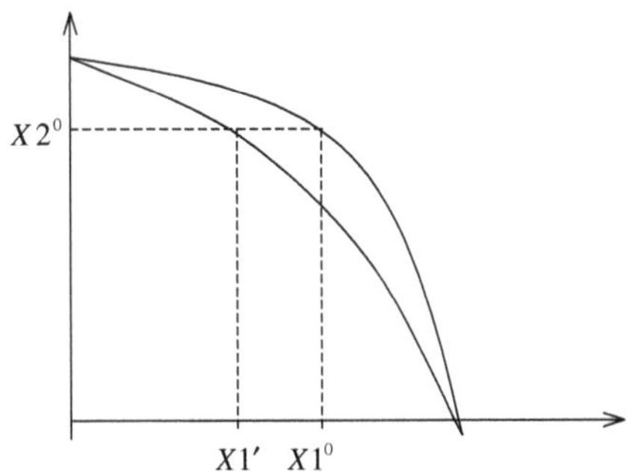

Fig. 2. The Efficiency Effects of Wage Differentials.
Source: Thierfelder and Shiells (1997, p. 440)

The assumption here is that the skill of factor is same[a] and the wage differentials occur due to the restriction on their allocation to different sectors.

To understand the welfare effects of policies such as trade reform in a stylized CGE model, they reproduce the theoretical model with factor market distortions as presented in Thierfelder and Shiells (1997). The effect of wage differentials on resource allocation, and hence the PPF, are illustrated in Figs. 1 and 2. In Fig. 1, a Heckscher–Ohlin model is represented by an Edgeworth–Bowley diagram. The thick line represents allocation of capital and labor in

[a]This is a simplifying assumption. There is a large body of literature that models the wage differentials due to skill (see, for example, Thierfelder and Shiells, 1997).

identical proportions between Sectors 1 and 2. Sector 1 is assumed to be labor-intensive, so that the curved locus between $O1$ and $O2$ represents efficient allocations of resources between the two sectors in the absence of distortions.

A wedge, γ, has been assumed between Sectors 1 and 2 so that

$$W2 = (1 + \gamma) \cdot W1 \qquad (1)$$

Both sectors are distorted when γ differs from zero. In Fig. 1, Sector 1 is assumed to have higher wages ($\gamma < 0$), forcing more capital-intensive production in the labor-intensive sector, and more labor-intensive production in Sector 2. The result is a set of equilibria as represented by the intersection of the $X2^0$ and $X1'$ isoquants.

The implications of moving off the efficiency locus in this way are illustrated in Fig. 2. For a given output $X2^0$, production of $X1$ falls from $X1^0$ to $X1'$ — the PPF contracts. There is also a non-tangency between the private returns (market prices) and the social rate of return (the slope of the PPF). When there is a factor price distortion, there is an inefficient allocation of resources, as evident in the PPF shrinking toward the origin. The equivalent framework can be applied to explain the impact of capital market distortion. The theoretical model above explains why there is welfare loss under factor market distortions. In China, there are wage and capital return differentials across various sectors as shown in Table 1 earlier.

To illustrate the effects of factor market reforms based on the above theoretical model under each scenario of the CGE simulation, we introduce two different base models. In the first model developed by Doi *et al.* (2002), the exogenous wage differentials are maintained evident in the benchmark data. As explained by Thierfelder and Shiells (1997), these factor payment differentials affect the producer's hiring decision. For example, when the factor payment differential exceeds 1, fewer workers will be hired in the concerned sector than when the workers receive the economy-wide average wage. However, since the factor payment differentials are exogenous, once established in the base model, it is the change in the economy-wide average wage that affects resource allocation, as in the case with competitive labor markets (Thierfelder and Shiells, 1997).

3.3. *Government Utility Function for Wage Differentials*

Another model developed by Tiwari *et al.* (2002) considered government behavior in which the wage differentials are determined in endogenous process. The wage differentials in the base data are assumed to be due to government policies restricting labor movements. The government is assumed to maintain high employment in the agricultural sector in order to keep agricultural commodity prices low. The government restricts all exits by labor from the agricultural sector. The government behaves as a monopsonist, by setting wage such that the value of the marginal product of labor in the agricultural sector equals marginal factor cost, determined by the higher labor supply in the agricultural sector caused by restrictions on labor's mobility. In equilibrium, wages in the agricultural sector are lower than all other sectors, which are assumed to be set freely.

Tiwari *et al.* (2002) extended the exogenous wage differentials model and specifically incorporated a government utility function. The government has a maximum acceptable wage rate, presumably the economy-wide average wage, and a minimum acceptable level of employment. The utility function for government is

$$GOVUTIL = (WF_l - WF_l \cdot WD_{\text{agri},l})^{\mu}(L_{\text{agri}} - L_{\min})^{(1-\mu)} \tag{2}$$

where $GOVUTIL$ is the government utility, WF_l is the economy-wide average, $WD_{\text{agri},l}$ is the wage differential in the agricultural sector, L_{agri} is the labor employed in the agricultural sector, and $L_{\min}$ is the reservation level of employment. μ is the weight on the wage markup.

Given a CES production function (see Appendix B), the optimal labor demand in the agricultural sector is

$$L_{\text{agri}} = \left(\frac{PX_{\text{agri}} \cdot X_{\text{agri}}\delta_l}{WF_l \cdot WD_{\text{agri}}}\right)^{1/(1+\rho_{p,\text{agri}})} \left(\frac{X_{\text{agri}}}{A3_{\text{agri}}}\right)^{1/(1+\rho_{p,\text{agri}})} \tag{3}$$

where PX_{agri} is the producer price of agricultural output, X_{agri} is agricultural output, δ_l is the CES production factor share parameter, $\rho_{p,\text{agri}}$ is the CES production function parameter, and $A3_{\text{agri}}$ is the CES production function constant. Substituting this value for labor into the government's utility function and choosing the wage differential to maximize utility, the optimal wage differential is

$$\frac{1 - WD_{\text{agri},l}}{WD_{\text{agri},l}} = \left(\frac{L_{\text{agri}} - L_{\min}}{L_{\text{agri}}}\right)\left(\frac{\mu}{1-\mu}\right)(1 + \rho_{p,\text{agri}}) \quad \text{for } \mu \neq 1 \tag{4}$$

4. Analysis and Results

4.1. *The Base Case*

The CGE model needs to be calibrated first to the benchmark data, which is done so that the balance of trade is held between the economic units such as

Table 3. The Base Case

	Base Case			
	Agriculture	Manufacture	Services	Total
Labor (million person)	342.90	143.26	121.52	607.68
Capital (billion yuan)	435.80	6,611.60	4,668.50	11,715.90
Wage (1000 yuan)	5.38	33.74	15.07	8508.82
Return to Capital (yuan)	0.51	1.00	0.28	8153.29
Output (billion yuan)	2,065.62	11,455.13	3,139.14	16,659.89
Composite good consumption (billion yuan)	2,082.25	11,402.02	3,156.94	16,641.21
Domestic good consumption (billion yuan)	2,050.73	10,476.47	3,061.98	15,589.18
Exports[1] (billion yuan)	14.89	978.66	94.96	1,088.51
Imports[1] (billion yuan)	31.52	925.55	77.16	1,034.23
Exchange Rate	1.00			

[1]Measured by domestic price

households or firms. This model uses Chinese Social Account Matrix for 1995 developed by us and other macro-economic data from the *China Statistical Year Book 1996*. The Base Case data are shown in Table 3. In order to evaluate the impact of removing not only tariff but also NTBs in the context of China's WTO accession with and without factor market distortions which are modeled as described next, the Base Case is calibrated using the actual tariff rates and tariff equivalents of NTBs taken from Fan and Zheng (2000).

4.2. *Exogenous Wage Differential Model*

To evaluate the welfare effects of factor distortion removal and trade liberalization, Doi *et al.* (2002) constructed the following combinations of factor and trade distortions/liberalization as the scenarios.

Scenario 1: There are wage differentials but no capital differentials in all sectors without trade liberalization.

Scenario 2: There are no wage differentials but capital differentials in all sectors without trade liberalization.

Scenario 3: There are no wage differentials and no capital differentials in all sectors without trade liberalization.

Scenario 4: There are wage and capital differentials in all sectors with no tariff and NTBs.

Scenario 5: There are no wage and no capital differentials in all sectors with no tariff and NTBs.

The percentage changes in various macro-economic variables from the Base Case for these scenarios are presented in Tables 4 and 5.

Overall, there are welfare gains — indicated by the equivalent variation — in each of the above scenarios compared with the Base Case as shown in Tables 4 and 5. The factor allocation changes as labor moves into the wage sectors of formally higher wage and capital into the sectors of formally higher capital payment. The results of Scenarios 1, 2 and 3 indicate that the removal of factor payment differentials generates large welfare gain. In Scenario 3, utility increases by 16.4% compared with the Base Case and the welfare gain is estimated to be 2,726 billion yuan. With the removal of wage differentials, labor moves out of agriculture to the manufacturing sector.

Furthermore, counterfactual experiments relating to China's accession to WTO (Scenarios 4 and 5) were conducted assuming that actual tariff rates and the tariff equivalent of NTBs are eliminated upon the complete accession to the WTO agreement. The welfare effects of the two scenarios of trade liberalization are reported in Table 5.

The result of each "no tariff scenario" indicates only a small utility and welfare gain compared with its corresponding "with tariff scenario". It is estimated that the elimination of tariff and NTBs by China's WTO accession with factor differentials leads to increases in the exports and imports by 30.8% and 17.8%, respectively (see the result of Scenario 4). Under Scenario 4, there are only small positive effects with the output increasing only by 0.1%, composite consumption increasing only by 0.02%, utility increasing only by 0.23%, and welfare gains of only 39 billion yuan.

On the other hand, if the elimination of tariff and NTBs is implemented together with the removal of both wage and capital differentials, the macro-economic variables indicate much more positive effects, and the output increases by 27.3%, composite consumption by 26.9%, utility by 16.6%, and welfare by 2,752 billion yuan. (See the result of Scenario 5 in Table 5.)

The results of the above analysis for welfare effect of China's WTO accession shows that even with no tariff rates and NTBs, the growth of GNP and significant welfare gain would not be realized unless factor differentials are removed.

Table 4. The Effects in the Different Scenarios Used in Sensitivity Analysis Under the Wage Differentials Model (Percent Changes Compared with the Base Case)

	Scenario 1: No Capital Differentials				Scenario 2: No Wage Differentials				Scenario 3: No Wage and Capital Differentials			
	Agriculture	Manufacture	Services	Total	Agriculture	Manufacture	Services	Total	Agriculture	Manufacture	Services	Total
Labor	1.04	29.62	−37.85		−41.50	61.60	44.48		−42.25	116.74	−18.41	
Capital	−0.99	27.67	−39.10		−64.08	12.19	−11.28		−64.49	42.09	−53.58	
Wage	6.68	6.68	6.68	16.19	86.60	−70.27	−33.41	−28.35	75.40	−72.05	−37.40	−32.65
Return to Capital	37.20	−30.21	149.21	0.44	40.09	40.09	40.09	48.97	86.07	−5.35	237.98	36.22
Output	0.75	28.67	−38.65	12.52	−42.82	21.20	16.03	12.29	−44.07	59.58	−44.15	27.18
Composite good consumption	1.92	27.18	−35.19	12.18	−40.31	20.78	15.29	12.09	−40.29	56.74	−44.81	25.33
Domestic good consumption	1.12	27.77	−37.55	11.44	−42.50	20.95	15.75	11.58	−43.75	57.85	−43.10	24.65
Exports[1]	−63.28	14.81	−96.38	4.04	−97.13	8.59	−9.66	5.55	−99.21	18.24	−99.14	6.39
Imports[1]	32.50	0.13	85.45	7.48	143.86	4.23	8.22	8.78	212.46	−4.00	130.24	12.62
Producer price	2.20	−18.30	61.10		79.30	−12.80	−9.60		74.40	−35.20	70.60	
Composite good price	1.90	−18.30	58.40		76.50	−12.80	−9.60		70.00	−35.30	65.50	
Domestic price of domestic variety[2]	2.30	−18.50	62.00		79.60	−12.80	−9.60		74.60	−35.40	71.60	
Domestic price of exported good	−16.90	−16.90	−16.90		−12.30	−12.30	−12.30		−33.50	−33.50	−33.50	
Domestic price of imported good	−16.90	−16.90	−16.90		−12.30	−12.30	−12.30		−33.50	−33.50	−33.50	
Exchange rate	−16.90				−12.30				−33.50			
Utility	9.20				9.84				16.42			
Equivalent variation[3]	1,528.37				1,633.20				2,725.91			

[1]Measured by domestic price
[2]Including tax
[3]A positive value for equivalent variation indicates a welfare gain

Table 5. The Effects in the Different Scenarios Used in Sensitivity Analysis Under the Wage Differentials Model (Percent Changes Compared with the Base Case)

	Scenario 4: No Tariffs				Scenario 5: No Factor Differentials and no Tariffs			
	Agriculture	Manufacture	Services	Total	Agriculture	Manufacture	Services	Total
Labor	−0.28	0.29	0.45		−42.49	117.61	−18.76	
Capital	−0.67	0.00	0.06		−64.73	42.34	−53.92	
Wage	0.39	1.11	0.39	1.00	75.48	−72.04	−37.38	−32.62
Return to Capital	0.57	0.57	0.57	0.57	86.86	−4.95	239.41	36.80
Output	−0.32	0.12	0.29	0.10	−44.31	59.95	−44.50	27.34
Composite good consumption	−0.64	0.65	−1.82	0.02	−40.76	57.74	−40.03	26.87
Domestic good consumption	−0.51	−2.13	−1.05	−1.70	−43.99	54.51	−43.47	22.31
Exports[1]	31.40	30.78	31.41	30.84	−98.99	51.00	−98.91	35.87
Imports[1]	−4.95	20.49	−4.69	17.83	198.88	16.56	120.83	29.89
Producer price	0.20	0.50	0.40		74.50	−35.00	71.10	
Composite good price	0.30	−1.00	0.30		70.30	−36.00	66.40	
Domestic price of domestic variety[2]	0.20	−0.10	0.20		74.70	−35.60	72.10	
Domestic price of exported good	5.90	5.90	5.90		−30.00	−30.00	−30.00	
Domestic price of imported good	4.30	−10.00	5.40		−31.00	−40.50	−30.30	
Exchange rate	5.90				−30.00			
Utility	0.23				16.57			
Equivalent variation[3]	38.83				2,751.78			

[1]Measured by domestic price
[2]Including tax
[3]A positive value for equivalent variation indicates a welfare gain

4.3. *Government Behavior Model*

Under the government behavior model where the wage differentials are endogenously determined, Tiwari *et al.* (2002) constructed the following three scenarios.

Scenario 6: The labor market alone is liberalized (i.e. free mobility of labor) without trade liberalization.
Scenario 7: Tariffs and NTBs are removed but the labor market is not liberalized.
Scenario 8: Tariffs and NTBs are removed and the labor market is also liberalized.

The percentage changes in various macro-economic variables from the Base Case for each scenario are reported in Table 6.

There are welfare gains indicated by the positive equivalent variation in each of the above scenarios compared with the Base Case. We calibrate the value of wage markup coefficient μ in the government utility function by replicating the Base Case values. The value of μ is then reduced, indicating labor market liberalization. The minimum value of μ at which the model achieves its optimum value is interpreted to be the maximum extent of possible labor market liberalization. After giving a policy shock, wage rates are determined endogenously in the model. Wage differentials among sectors are also calibrated in the endogenous processes, and are not completely disappearing in this model due to the government behavior of placing a high priority on agriculture.

Firstly, when the labor market alone is liberalized, as the value of μ gets reduced, in Scenario 6, labor moves from agriculture toward the sectors of higher wage and capital into the sectors of higher capital return. As a result, the outputs in manufacturing and services increase substantially. The wage in agriculture increases relative to the Base Case and agricultural output declines. The exports of manufacturing and services goods increase substantially but exports of agricultural goods decline. China becomes even a net importer of agriculture goods. Overall, welfare increases substantially and the GNP increases by 1,600 billion yuan.

Secondly, if tariff and NTBs are completely eliminated with factor distortions retained in Scenario 7, the result is exactly the same as that of Scenario 4 in the exogenous wage differentials model (no tariffs and NTBs with factor market distortions maintained). Recalling the result of Scenario 4, the exports and imports increase in the case of Scenario 7, and only a marginal positive effect is found on GNP increasing by 39 billion yuan.

Table 6. The Effects in the Different Scenarios Used in Sensitivity Analysis Under the Government Behavior Model (Percent Changes Compared with the Base Case)

	Scenario 6: Liberalized Labor Market			Scenario 7: No Tariffs			Scenario 8: Liberalize Labor Market and no Tariffs		
	Agriculture	Manufacture	Services	Agriculture	Manufacture	Services	Agriculture	Manufacture	Services
Labor	−36.61	39.94	56.23	−0.28	0.29	0.45	−59.34	28.92	37.39
Capital	−17.95	0.71	0.67	−0.67	0.00	0.06	−23.18	0.42	1.17
Wage	147.18	−1.84	−1.84	0.39	1.11	0.39	151.18	−1.78	−1.78
Return to capital	15.22	15.22	15.22	0.57	0.57	0.57	15.80	15.80	15.80
Output	−34.92	14.71	29.32	−0.32	0.12	0.29	−55.21	12.78	23.67
Composite good consumption	−33.06	15.24	26.99	−0.64	0.65	−1.82	−51.11	13.84	20.77
Domestic good consumption	−34.56	15.01	27.52	−0.51	−2.13	−1.05	−54.38	10.84	21.32
Exports[1]	−93.09	11.36	84.16	31.40	30.78	31.41	−133.05	33.61	71.42
Imports[1]	101.38	17.83	7.1	−4.95	20.49	−4.69	43.09	48.89	−3.22
Producer price	61.1	−7.4	−15.8	0.20	0.50	0.40	38.92	−7.67	−18.76
Composite good price	59.5	−7.4	−15.9	0.30	−1.00	0.30	38.37	−9.18	−19.14
Domestic price of domestic variety[2]	61.3	−7.3	−16.1	0.20	−0.10	0.20	39.06	−8.19	−19.43
Domestic price of exported good	−8.1	−8.1	−8.1	5.90	5.90	5.90	−3.05	−3.05	−3.05
Domestic price of imported good	−8.1	−8.1	−8.1	4.30	−10.00	5.40	−4.67	−18.93	−3.59
Exchange rate	−8.1			5.90			−3.05		
Equivalent variation[3]	1,600.3			38.83			1,620.5		

[1]Measured by domestic price
[2]Including tax
[3]A positive value for equivalent variation indicates a welfare gain

On the other hand, when trade liberalization is carried out jointly with labor market reforms in Scenario 8, the economic gains are substantially large. The GNP grows by 1,621 billion yuan. Exports of manufacturing and services also largely grow.

Based on the results of the government behavior model, the effects of labor market liberalization, whether tariffs and NTBs remain or are removed, are similar in directions to the equivalent scenarios of the exogenous wage differentials model. However, the government behavior model brings GNP gains slightly lower (1,600 billion yuan in Scenario 6 and 1,621 billion yuan in Scenario 8, respectively) than the case of Scenario 2 (1,633 billion yuan). This is because wage differentials among sectors do not completely disappear under the government behavior model in the case of labor market liberalization.

Despite the smaller effect than the result of exogenous wage differentials model, the government behavior model still suggests that the labor market reform brings a large amount of positive impact on the overall GNP. We can also conclude, therefore, that with China's WTO accession, the growth in GNP and significant welfare gain would not be realized unless labor market is liberalized.

5. Concluding Remarks

China has experienced drastic economic growth due to the multi-faceted liberalization since the Reforms and the Open-up Policy in 1978, and became a full member of the WTO in 2001. In assessing how much China would benefit from joining in the WTO, factor market reforms are the key issue. Historically, policies have restricted migration from rural to urban areas, and have created surplus labor in the rural areas, which constrained growth.

In this paper, we analyzed the welfare effects of trade and factor market liberalization in China using a CGE model. Following Doi *et al.* (2002) and Tiwari *et al.* (2002), we introduced two different models which consider the restrictions on mobility of factors in a CGE framework by specifying wage differentials among sectors in the Chinese economy. One specification is to persist the existing wage differentials exogenously, and the other is to apply a government utility function as an endogenous process. The results of simulating trade liberalization with and without labor distortions are similar in both models, but slightly differ in terms of the extent to which effects arise.

More specifically, the removal of factor constraints leads to substantial growth of GNP. In particular, the positive impact on the overall GNP under the labor market liberalization scenario is slightly smaller in the government behavior model than the exogenous wage differentials model. This is because wage differentials among sectors do not completely disappear under the government behavior model due to the government behavior of placing a high priority on agriculture.

However, labor liberalization brings significant GNP gains in both models. The economic effect of eliminating tariffs and NTBs due to China's accession to the WTO is positive, but not substantial in the presence of wage differentials. It is shown that large economic effects are expected with the trade liberalization only if the factor market reforms are associated. The labor market reform can be achieved particularly if labor mobility restrictions such as the *hukou* system are abolished.

References

Bhattacharyya A, and Parker E, 1999. "Labor productivity and migration in Chinese agriculture — a stochastic frontier approach." *China Econ. Rev.* **10**: 59–74.

Cai F, Wang D, and Du Y, 2002. "Regional disparity and economic growth in China: the impact of labor market distortions." *China Econ. Rev.* **13**: 197–212.

Cao YZ, Fan G, and Woo WT, 1996. "Chinese economic reforms: past successes and future challenges." In: Woo WT, Parker S, and Sachs JD, (eds) *Economies in Transition: Comparing Asia and Eastern Europe*, MIT Press.

Doi M, Tiwari P, and Kawakami T, 2002. "Trade and factor market reforms in China." *Labour* **16**(3): 537–555.

Fan M, and Zheng Y, 2000. "The impact of China's trade liberalization for WTO accession — a computable general equilibrium analysis." Paper presented at the Third Annual Conference on Global Economic Analysis, June 27–30, 2000, Melbourne, Australia.

Jones RW, 1971. "Distortions in factor markets and the general equilibrium model of production." *J. Political Econ.* **73**: 437–459.

Kawakami T, 2004. "Structural changes in China's economic growth during the reform period." *Rev. Urban Reg. Dev. Stud.* **16**(2): 133–153.

Lewis AW, 1954. "Economic development with unlimited supplies of labour." *Manchester School Econ. Social Studies* **22**: 139–191.

National Bureau of Statistics (NBS), 1996. *China Statistical Yearbook 1996*. China Statistical Press: Beijing.

National Bureau of Statistics (NBS), 1997. *Input-Output Table of China*. China Statistical Press: Beijing.

Sachs JD, Yang X, and Zhang D, 2000. "Globalization, dual economy and economic development." *China Econ. Rev.* **11**: 189–209.

Thierfelder KE, and Shiells CR, 1997. "Trade and labor market behavior." In: Francois JF, and Reinert KA, (eds) *Applied Methods for Trade Policy Analysis*, Cambridge University Press: Cambridge.

Tiwari P, Kawakami T, and Doi M, 2002. "Dual labor markets and trade reform in China." *J. Policy Reform* 5(2): 101–113.

World Bank, 1997. *China 2020: Development Challenges in the New Century.* World Bank: Washington, DC.

Yang DT, 1997. "China's land arrangements and rural labor mobility." *China Econ. Rev.* **8**(2): 101–116.

Zhai F, and Li S, 2000. "Implications of accession to WTO on China's economy." Paper presented at the Third Annual Conference on Global Economic Analysis, June 27–30, 2000, Melbourne, Australia.

Zhao Y, 1999a. "Leaving the countryside: rural-to-urban migration decisions in China." *Am. Econ. Rev.* **89**(2): 281–286.

Zhao Y, 1999b. "Labor migration and earnings differences: the case of rural china." *Econ. Dev. Cultural Change* 47(4): 767–782.

Appendix 1. The CGE Model with Factor Market Distortions for China: System Notations

The model used in this paper is an application of the CGE model introduced in Thierfelder and Shiells (1997). The notations and equations that we present here are a modified version of Thierfelder and Shiells (1997). Subscripts i and f represent the sector and factor, respectively.

Price Variables

PX_i: Producer price
PQ_i: Composite good price
PWE_i: World export price
PWM_i: World import price
PED_i: Domestic price of exported good
PMD_i: Domestic price of imported good
PDT_i: Domestic price of domestic variety including tax
PD_i: Domestic price of domestic variety net of tax

Quantity Variables

E_i: Exports
DD_i: Domestic demand
$INTD_i$: Intermediate demand
M_i: Imports
X_i: Production of the composite good
Q_i: Composite consumption good

Sector Tax Variables

td_i: Domestic good tax
te_i: Export subsidy
tm_i: Import tariff

Welfare Variables

$CLIV$: Cost of living index in current prices
$UTIL$: Utility
YN: New income in equivalent variation calculation
EV: Equivalent variation
$Y0$: Income in the Base Case

Macroeconomic Variables

P_{INDEX}: Domestic price index
Y: Gross national product
GR: Government net revenue
WALRAS: Walras law variables
OBJ: Objective function value
ER: Exchange rate
$FSAV$: Foreign savings

Factor Variables

$FDSC_{i,f}$: Factor demand
$FCTRY_{i,f}$: Factor income
WF_f: Economy-wide average wage
$WFDIST_{i,f}$: Factor payment differential

Functional Parameters

σ_i: CES trade substitution elasticity
Ω_i: CET export transformation elasticity
Γ_i: CES production substitution elasticity
$\rho_{c,i}$: CES import aggregation parameter
$\rho_{t,i}$: CET export transformation parameter
$\rho_{p,i}$: CES production function parameter
β_i: CES trade share parameter
α_i: CET export share parameter

$\delta_{i,f}$: CES production factor share parameter
$A1_i$: CES trade constant
$A2_i$: CET export constant
$A3_i$: CES production constant
cs_i: Consumption expenditure share
$pwts_i$: Weight for the domestic goods price index

Appendix 2. The CGE Model with Factor Market Distortions for China: System of Equations

Price Equations

$$PX_i \cdot X_i = PED_i \cdot E_i + PD_i \cdot DD_i$$

$$PMD_i = PWM_i \cdot ER \cdot (1 + tm_i)$$

$$PED_i = PWE_i \cdot ER \cdot (1 + te_i)$$

$$PQ_i \cdot Q_i = PDT_i \cdot DD_i + PMD_i \cdot M_i$$

$$PDT_i = PD_i \cdot \left(1 + td_i\right)$$

$$P_{\text{INDEX}} = \sum_i pwts_i \cdot PD0_i$$

$$pwts_i = \frac{DD0_i}{\sum_i DD0_i}$$

$$PX_i \cdot X_i = \sum_f WF_f \cdot WFDIST_{i,f} \cdot FDSC_{i,f} + PD_i \cdot INTD_i$$

Factor Market in the Base Case

$$FS_f = \sum_i FDSC_{i,f}$$

$$FCTRY_{i,f} = \frac{FCTRY_{i,f}}{\sum_f FCTRY_{i,f}} \cdot (PX_i \cdot X_i - PD_i \cdot INTD_i)$$

$$TFCTRY_f = \sum_i FCTRY_{i,f}$$

$$WF_f = \frac{TFCTRY_f}{FS_f}$$

$$WF_f \cdot WFDIST_{i,f} = \frac{FCTRY_{i,f}}{FDSC_{i,f}}$$

Elasticity Equations

$$\Gamma_i = \frac{1}{(1 + \rho_{p,i})}$$

$$\sigma_i = \frac{1}{(1 + \rho_{c,i})}$$

$$\Omega_i = \frac{1}{(1 + \rho_{t,i})}$$

Production, Factor Demand and Final Demand Equations

$$X_i = A3_i \cdot \left(\sum_f \delta_{i,f} \cdot FDSC_{i,f}^{-\rho_{p,i}} \right)^{-1/\rho_{p,i}} + INTD_i$$

$$INTD_i = \sum_j a_{i,j} \cdot X_j$$

$$WF_f \cdot WFDIST_{i,f} = PX_i \cdot A3_i \cdot \left(\sum_f \delta_{i,f} \cdot FDSC_{i,f}^{-\rho_{p,i}} \right)^{\left[\left(-1/\rho_{p,i}\right)-1\right]} \times FDSC_{i,f}^{(-\rho_{p,i}-1)}$$

$$X_i = A2_i \cdot \left(\alpha_i \cdot E_i^{-\rho_{t,i}} + (1 - \alpha_i) \cdot DD_i^{-\rho_{t,i}} \right)^{-1/\rho_{t,i}}$$

$$Q_i = A1_i \cdot \left(\beta_i \cdot M_i^{-\rho_{c,i}} + (1-\beta_i) \cdot DD_i^{-\rho_{c,i}}\right)^{-1/\rho_{c,i}}$$

$$PQ_i \cdot Q_i = cs_i \cdot \sum_i (PQ_i \cdot Q_i)$$

Trade Equations

$$E_i = DD_i \cdot \left(\frac{PD_i}{PED_i} \cdot \frac{\alpha_i}{1-\alpha_i}\right)^{1/(1+\rho_{t,i})}$$

$$M_i = DD_i \cdot \left(\frac{PDT_i}{PMD_i} \cdot \frac{\beta_i}{1-\beta_i}\right)^{1/(1+\rho_{c,i})}$$

$$FSAV = \sum_i (PWM_i \cdot M_i) - \sum_i (PWE_i \cdot E_i)$$

Welfare Equations

$$CLIV = \prod_i PQ_i^{cs_i}$$

$$UTIL = \prod_i (Q_i - INTD_i)^{cs_i}$$

$$EV = YN - YO$$

Income and Objective Equations

$$GR = \sum_i (tm_i \cdot ER \cdot PWM_i \cdot M_i) + \sum_i (td_i \cdot PD_i \cdot DD_i) - \sum_i (te_i \cdot ER \cdot PWE_i \cdot E_i)$$

$$FCTRY_f = \sum_i (WF_f \cdot WFDIST_{i,f} \cdot FDSC_{i,f})$$

$$\sum_i (PQ_i \cdot Q_i) = \sum_i (PX_i \cdot X_i) + ER \cdot FSAV + GR + \text{WALRAS}$$

$$OBJ = \text{WALRAS} \cdot \text{WALRAS}$$

Market-Clearing Equations

$$\overline{FS}_f = \sum_i FDSC_{i,f}$$

Government Utility Equations

$$GOVUTIL = (WF_l - WF_l \cdot WD_{\text{agri},l})^{\mu}(L_{\text{agri}} - L_{\text{min}})^{(1-\mu)}$$

$$\frac{1 - WD_{\text{agri},l}}{WD_{\text{agri},l}} = \left(\frac{L_{\text{agri}} - L_{\text{min}}}{L_{\text{agri}}}\right)\left(\frac{\mu}{1-\mu}\right)(1 + \rho_{p,\text{agri}})$$

Chapter 15

Sustainable Development and Globalization in a World with Unequal Starting Points*

BRANTLEY LIDDLE

Max Plank Institute for Demographic Research, Rostock, Germany

We develop a simulation model by integrating aspects of economics, demography, and environmental science. The model is used to explore the challenges of development for countries with different initial conditions (i.e. natural resource endowment, physical and human capital, technology, and population) in a world with movement of goods, people, and capital, free substitution in production, flexible economic structures, and the ability to upgrade input factors via investment. We find that the impact of globalization on various countries differs depending on their starting points. In general, capital flows (when accompanied by technology transfer) tend to benefit all countries, migration tends to benefit the destination countries (particularly the aging, rich) and the migrants themselves, and the benefits of trade can be either positive or negative depending on country endowments. A basic revelation of the explicit dynamics is that history matters, a finding that is often highly counter-intuitive from the point of view of conventional models.

1. Introduction and Background

The sustainable development paradigm has lead to a substantial amount of interdisciplinary research. Studies routinely integrate aspects of economics,

*This chapter was originally published in *Review of Urban and Regional Development Studies*, Vol. 14, No. 3, November 2002, and is reprinted here with minor modifications upon the permission from the publisher.

demography, and environment, focus on medium- to long-term direct and indirect impacts, and consider feedbacks within economic, social, and natural systems. Most studies, however, focus on only two of the three important subsystems (economy, population, environment). In addition, studies often consider only one or more developed countries or one or more developing countries, and ignore interactions among levels of development. Lastly, when studies do consider both developed and developing countries, they usually involve cross-sectional analysis, and thus, the studies assume transitions or transformations, rather than directly model or observe them. The simulation modeling technique, in theory, can address the above shortcomings by building complete, multi-country dynamic models and running them over long horizons.

Yet, multi-country, dynamic, computable general equilibrium (CGE) models that include environmental aspects are rare; ones that also treat population change, endogenous growth or endogenous technology change, and developing-developed country interactions are virtually non-existent. Dellink (1999) surveyed the literature on CGE studies with environmental issues. He found only two families of models that are both dynamic and, at times extended to, multi-country, but neither has a sophisticated treatment of population or technical change. However, Loschel (2002) surveyed models that contained technological change and environment and found a number of models that have, to varying degrees, endogenous technical change. Yet, the models were nearly exclusively focused on carbon emissions — as was the technology change (rather than more general, growth enhancing technical change). Furthermore, the models he reviewed did not treat population or other sustainability issues like developing-developed country interactions.

Many dynamic, CGE models use the perfect foresight equilibrium technique. Perfect foresight equilibrium requires model dynamics to be exogenous to some extent since for the model to solve all growth rates must converge to a steady-state rate. But assuming (even eventual) constant growth rates of gross domestic product (GDP) and population is particularly problematic for the type of sustainability analysis intended here. As Pritchett (2000) has noted, GDP growth instability is the norm — especially for developing countries — not steady-state growth. Furthermore, as Williamson and Higgins (2001) argued, it is essential for population-development models to confront transitional dynamics, since it is exactly when some groups of the population are growing faster than others that demography will most impact development. Additionally, even in post-demographic transition, developed countries, the "new" demography of continued declining fertility and mortality rates prevails over constant populations. The answer to this criticism is for dynamic, CGE modelers to run their models over extended time horizons and focus only on a period prior to the achievement of steady-state growth. However, the problem of semi-exogenous dynamics remains: there is no robust way of knowing when the output trajectory generated by the model is dominated by past or current decisions and equilibria rather than by the steady-state convergence requirement. Even Solow (1970), over 30 years ago, said that "the steady state is not a bad place for growth theory to start, but may be a dangerous place for it to end."

Considering models other than the CGE variety, Sanderson has done two literature reviews — about a decade apart — on systems models with economic-demographic interactions (1980) and economic-demographic-environmental interactions (1992). All the models he reviewed (including his own) have some combination (of more than one) of no environment, not multi-country, no endogenous growth, and no developed-developing country interactions. Bloom and Canning (2001) argued that models dealing with the "new" demography — emphasizing age-structure effects rather than total population — should necessarily use a systems framework. Yet, their own model, which does not include environment, is currently at only the schematic level. Other population revisionists that use simulation models (e.g. Williamson and Higgins, 2001 and Lee *et al.*, 2001) develop models that are at most partial equilibrium models and are used to project variables like the savings rate rather than to account for feedbacks or the interrelationships at multiple levels of a complex, integrated system.

Sustainability models should consider aspects of the economy-environment-population nexus. Such models must inherently be dynamic — capable of following important indicators over a long time horizon; however, they must also acknowledge the disparity among actors/countries. The sustainability issue is ultimately about both intragenerational and intergenerational concerns. Lastly, sustainability models should not be programmed either to reject sustainability (e.g. an essential, nonrenewable input) or to affirm it (e.g. costless, endogenous technical change).

We develop a simulation model, borrowing from and integrating aspects of economics, demography, and environmental and political science, to simultaneously consider environment, economic development, and population/politics by focusing specifically on the impact of important flows (i.e. pollution, capital, technology, production goods, natural resources, and people). The model can assess sustainable development on three levels: economic (by determining production, consumption, investment, foreign direct investment, foreign aid, technology transfer, and international trade), social (by calculating population growth/change, migration flows, and political stress levels), and environmental (by calculating natural resource use and the difference between environmental pollution and upgrading expenditures). The model follows "representative" countries that differ in their initial endowments (i.e. natural resource endowment, physical and human capital, technology, and population), and thus in their development levels and prospects.

We model economic growth endogenously — indeed all important parameters and variables change endogenously — by explicitly modeling the choice to invest in technology enhancing (over other investments). Thus, technology improvements are not essentially free as they are in learning-by-doing models. Our treatment of environment includes costs, but not limits. Although our natural resource intermediate good is effectively non-exhaustible, the extraction function allows the good's price to increase with use. Pollution, which cannot be avoided completely via trade, has a welfare impact that increases with income, and environmental quality upgrading has rapidly diminishing returns; however, we do not set a threshold level of pollution. Lastly, our model takes full account of transitionary dynamics (in demography as well as the environment-income relationship). Furthermore, we do not enforce terminal conditions on growth rates; rather, the dynamics unfold period by period in response to specific adaptations by actors (who apply "realistic" foresight). In a world with movement of goods, people, and capital, free substitution in production, flexible economic structures, and the ability to upgrade input factors via investment, we find the initial disparities in circumstances among countries are still vital to their development prospects — i.e. history matters.

The following two sections of the paper describe the simulation model: first, a general overview is presented; next, the basic modules are described. Some results from the base case are discussed in Section 4, focusing particularly on the source of long-run economic growth in the model. Section 5 discusses the impact of our model's three major international flows — traded goods, people, and investment in physical capital — on our stylized versions of rich, middle, and poor countries.[a] Section 6 concludes the paper with a summary of the findings. In addition, an appendix contains some of the important model equations.

2. Overview of Model

The model contains the following major segments: (1) a global economic system, covering seven significantly different "countries"; (2) an

[a]To economize on space, only the impact of migration on rich and middle countries is included.

environmental natural resource system, relating environmental quality and natural resource capacity to welfare and economic production and consumption; and (3) induced changes in population growth and age distribution in each country (including international migration). The economic system comprises sets of relationships in different stages for each country: (1) production of three kinds of commodities (two final goods and one intermediate); (2) patterns of international trade and foreign direct investment; (3) determination of consumption and investment; (4) allocation of investment resources over five investment categories (physical capital, human capital, natural resource capacity, environmental quality upgrading, and development of new technology).

There are four types of decision-makers in the model: (1) all consumers; (2) owners of productive resources, i.e. workers and owners of physical capital and land (or the firms); (3) in each of seven countries, three separate production sectors (thus making 21 individual "firms" overall); and (4) an aggregate national "investor" for each country. The aggregate national investor allocates a country's total investment pool among different types of investment, actually engages all those investment activities, determines the size of the total investment pool via a Keynesian investment function, and determines the market goods-environmental quality tradeoff (by choosing to spend on environmental quality upgrading).

Each type of decision-maker renders decisions via optimization. Consumers choose their consumption mix (between two final goods) to maximize their utility, derived from demand functions. The national optimal consumption mix is based on national utility maximization reflected in consumer goods demand. Since we have no interest in specific consumption preferences, we assume these demand functions all have unitary price and income elasticities; thus, budgetary allocations to these goods are constant and, for simplicity, are equal for the two goods in all countries. Each "industry firm" maximizes its profits. Since there is no leisure or operation-related depreciation, factor owners maximize period returns to their assets by supplying what is demanded. The national investor maximizes present discounted value of all investments performed in each period, based on the marginal productivity of different investment types and on national preference tradeoffs between market goods and environmental quality.

Each type of investment generates, via sectoral production functions and profit-maximizing levels of output, a lifetime marginal value productivity that is transformed into a present discounted value via a single social rate of discount specified for each country as a function of its per capita GDP. Relative rates of return form the basis of allocation. The size of the investment pool is given by a Keynesian consumption-investment function, modified by social provision for rates of population dependency.

The model sequentially, deterministically, and in discrete-time "periods" runs through (i) equilibria (individual country labor markets and internationally traded goods), (ii) optimizations (profit maximization, wage maximization through international migration, final goods consumption mix, and investment mix — including welfare-maximizing goods consumption versus environmental quality choice), and (iii) updates (productive endowments, discount rates, and population — number, age structure, and mortality and fertility rates). Thus, at the end (and as a result) of this sequence of events, each country has a new set of input endowments and prices. In addition, there is a new set of international trade prices. In this manner the whole global system will generate 90–100-period (or year) national trajectories.[b] The model is recursively dynamic: equilibrium in the individual country labor markets and in the international trade markets set the prices (for any specific period) that agents use (along with simple forecasts of the future) to make their decisions (during that period). Again, having the model achieve simultaneous equilibrium in all markets over all time (perfect foresight dynamics) necessitates constant, terminal growth rates for all stocks — a restriction we did not want to impose.

The country initial conditions are based on judgmental stereotypes of Rich, Middle, and Poor countries, as enhanced by empirical data on country factor endowments; however, only the age structure and birth and death rates are taken directly from the empirical data of specific countries (from Keyfitz and Flieger, 1990). Since the different levels of development or per capita GDP (in our model and empirically) are essentially defined in terms of technology, human capital, and physical capital per capita, differences within each level of development refer to population size and resource (land) endowment. Middle countries differ as well in population growth rates.

There are two Rich countries, one with larger total population and higher resource endowment per capita, three Middle countries, varying in population, resource base, and population growth, and two Poor countries, differing in population size. The two Poor countries have the greatest resource endowment,

---

[b]To calibrate and test the limits of the entire model, a series of nested, two-level, full and fractional factorial experimental designs were used. Factorial designs (described in detail in Schmidt and Launsby, 1992) allow study of the effects of changes in levels of independent factors as well as of interaction effects. In general, our model's behavior is not sensitive even to reasonably large changes in parameters — there is numerical sensitivity to changes in some parameters; however, behavior robustness is most important for our findings.

followed by Middle3, then Middle2 and Rich2; Middle1 and Rich1 have the smallest resource endowment. The Rich countries' populations have low birth rates and advanced age structures (based on the European Community circa 1980). The three Middle countries use data from Venezuela in 1975, Chile in 1980, and Taiwan in 1985, and thus, vary in the degree to which they have undergone demographic transition. The Poor countries have high birth rates and young age structures (initial data from Guatemala in 1985).

3. Model Modules

3.1. *Production Module*

In each country, there are three production sectors: resource intensive industry (producing a final good), resource non-intensive ("service") industry (producing a final good), and natural resource extraction industry (producing an intermediate good). Final goods and processed natural resources are tradables, so their prices are the same for all countries; wage and rent rates are determined locally. Because labor (but not capital) is completely mobile (within each country), countries can shift production each period for competitive advantage. Since the producers are treated as profit-maximizing price takers, and since physical capital is not sectorally mobile, the amount of each good produced by each country is a straight-forward optimization calculation. The local wage rate for each country clears the labor market each period (for the purpose of this equilibrium, international migration is not considered; rather differences in the various country wages motivate the subsequent migration decision as will be discussed below). At the end of each period each country's rent rate on physical capital is updated by recalculating the average marginal value product of capital for the three sectors, weighted by the total amount of capital in each sector.

Lastly, world prices for the two final consumption goods and the intermediate, natural resource good are calculated for use in the following period. These prices are calculated iteratively by equating forecasted world supply and demand. This (arguably simplified) solution method results in actual global supplies and demands that equate within ±1% (after an initialization process taking from three to seven periods). The national aggregate adjustments in equilibrium have many lags, constraints, and uncertainties, making for varied speeds of adjustment. These adjustments are too complex to model simultaneously, so we simplify by adjusting prices at the end of each period, and leaving the direction of behavioral adjustments to these new prices to the next period.

Adjustments, therefore, lead to continued temporal changes — a main focus in the model.

The production functions for the two final consumer goods sectors are of "Barro" form (Barro and Sala-i-Martin, 1995). The production function for the resource extraction sector is slightly different in that we include a drag parameter to allow for heavy recent production to increase rapidly the cost of further extraction. This increasing cost to extract can lead to increasing prices for the natural resource, despite its inexhaustibility. All the production functions are assumed to have constant returns to scale. The resource intensive industry is less labor intensive than the resource non-intensive one. The equations as well as the exponents used (Table A1) are shown in the Appendix.

3.2. *Investment Module*

The share of a country's total GDP allocated for investment depends positively on the country's per capita GDP relative to the initial per capita GDP of the richest country (a measure of a minimum consumption necessity), and negatively on the country's young (ages 0–14) and aged (65+) dependency (i.e. the ratio of those cohorts to the total population). This relationship is one of the most important in the model.[c]

$$c = 0.34 - 0.071\ln\left(\mathrm{GDP}/\mathrm{GDP}_0^R\right) + 0.7 \times \mathrm{pop}(0\text{–}14) + 2.1 \times \mathrm{pop}(65+) \quad (1)$$

where c is the fraction of GDP for consumption, GDP is per capita GDP, GDP_0^R is the initial per capita GDP of the Rich country, pop(0–14) is the fraction of population aged 0–14, and pop(65+) is the fraction of population over 65. The GDP ratio term as well as c are constrained (by other equations) to be less than or equal to one. (Because our model does not have a financial sector, countries must invest all income that is not spent on goods consumption in projects commencing in the current period; thus, Eq. 1 does not have a term for the return on investment.)

The coefficients in Eq. 1 were derived econometrically from panel data (observations in 1985 and 1990) from World Bank (1994). All of the coefficients are statistically significant at least at the 5% level (the adjusted R-squared

[c]The one exception to the model's lack of behavioral sensitivity occurs when the coefficients in Eq. 1 are adjusted (by one standard deviation from their econometrically derived values) in the way that constrains investment the most. Under this scenario the rich countries' per capita GDP displays "growth and then collapse," as their share of income for investment eventually reaches zero (driven by their population aging).

for the regression was 0.42). We normalize the per capita GDP term (1) to render its impact indifferent to the magnitude of GDP and, thus, appropriate for the stylized values used in the simulation model, and (2) to lessen some of the regression problems common when the dependent variables are a combination of rates and levels. These results are similar to other econometric models, such as Kelley and Schmidt (1994) and Mason (1987 & 1988); however, we attribute a greater drag on investment to aged dependency (perhaps because those analyses were only concerned with developing countries).[d] Our formulation gives Middle countries (with per capita GDPs about one-fourth of Rich countries') an opportunity to invest, but gives Poor countries (with per capita GDPs 1/20 or less of Rich countries') very little chance to catch up.

Each type of investment has a distinctive production function and cost function. From these functions, rates of return are calculated for each investment type. (To project these production and cost functions over the life of an investment, current prices and factor endowments are assumed to be constant.) These different return rates determine the percentages of the total investment pool that are allocated to each investment type via a logit share equation (thus, investment funds are allocated in proportion to their relative returns).

Each production sector has its own (well-mixed) physical capital allotment, which is increased through investment and decreased by depreciation (set at 5% a year). Physical capital created (by investment) at the end of one period is considered operational (included in the production function) in the following period. The rate of return on physical capital for each sector depends on the marginal value product of capital for that sector.

Technology enters the production functions as a constant multiplier (T in Eqs. 2, 3, and 4 shown in the appendix). There is a ten period lag on technology investment, i.e. the technology multiplier is increased based on technology investment ten periods ago, but the technology multiplier does not depreciate if investment ceases. The increase in the technology multiplier is a logarithmic function of the five-year average of technology investment (ten periods ago). The five-year moving average reflects the fact that innovation is an interactive process that takes time to bear fruit, i.e. labs must "ramp up."

A country's human capital multiple, H (in Eqs. 2, 3, and 4), is based on the average per student spending on education for the work force. The new H for a country is the weighted (by population size) average of the H of the graduating class and the current H of the workforce. The H of the graduating class is based on the average per student spending (i.e. per student human

[d]More detail on Eq. 1 and its estimation can be found in the appendix of Liddle (2000).

capital investment) for the class over their 12 periods in school. Hence, for human capital investment both time lags and age structure are important. A one period increase in per student spending likely will have a marginal effect on the graduating class' H since it will be averaged together with the per student spending for the previous 11 periods. Also, a graduating class's H has a greater impact on the country's H as a whole when the graduating class is large relative to the work force. In addition, the "life" of a human capital investment is limited by the life expectancy of the graduating class.

Investment in the resource base increases land endowment, A (in Eq. 4). This investment is analogous to exploration, but is limited by original land endowment and the sum of past additions to land endowment (via rapidly diminishing returns); thus, countries with small original land endowments but large amount of investment funds could not end up being the major resource producing country. Finally, there is a five period lag between investment in resource replenishment and increases to land endowment.

The three middle countries and two rich countries form a multi-national "investment corporation" that invests in and builds, when profitable, physical capital in the two poor countries. The investment corporation allocates its investment pool (the sum of contributions from the five controlling countries) in six investments (physical capital in the three economic sectors of the two poor countries) according to relative returns. The donor countries decide how much to invest in the pool based on relative returns (compared with their average return on "domestic" investments). The investment corporation has its own wage rate, rent rate, cost to produce physical capital (determined by the same function used by the individual countries), discount rate, human capital, and technology. These factors are a weighted average of the factors for the contributing countries (based on their share of the corporation's investment pool). The corporation receives rent payments (based on the rent rate of capital in the host or poor country) on their capital, which it divides among the members according to their share of the total pool. The individual countries repatriate or reinvest their shares depending on the investment–consumption rate of their home investments (determined by Eq. 1).

The poor countries pay, out of their own GDP, rent on the foreign capital. They also tax the investment corporation's remittances (at 40%, a rate roughly optimal for the poor countries). This tax rate influences the amount of foreign capital, beyond the obvious, by affecting the profitability of foreign direct investment (FDI) since the corporation knows this rate and incorporates it into its return on investment calculation. There is also a technology transfer from the investment corporation to the poor countries. The rate of this transfer depends on the share of a sector's capital that was foreign produced and the technology's "appropriateness" (based on the ratio of human capital of the poor country to that of the investment corporation).

The fact that we only allow FDI flows to go from the wealthier countries to the poorest does run counter to empirical evidence. Most FDI flows occur among countries at similar development levels; indeed, most FDI from developed countries goes into other developed countries. We apply this restriction to FDI in large part to greatly simplify the FDI module; in addition, the sole motivation for adding such a module was to determine how effective it would be in evening growth among the richer, growing countries and the poorer ones.

3.3. *Environmental Quality and Welfare Module*

The environmental module essentially considers air pollution and focuses on local and regional impacts of a flow pollutant. The strategy is to relate emissions to economic activity and, to a lesser extent, economic structure and to allow countries to invest in environmental quality upgrading (or remediation). Pollution results from energy use, which is assumed to be a linear function of production in the resource intensive industry and a log-linear function of per capita final goods consumption. The most important aspect of this relationship is that pollution depends on consumption (which means pollution cannot be avoided completely through economic structural change). The log-linear nature of this relationship could be interpreted as consumption becoming relatively less polluting as countries become richer; however, in the absence of investment in environmental quality upgrading, the relationship between consumption and pollution is unambiguous, i.e. more per capita consumption leads to greater per capita pollution. This model feature captures the (often overlooked) empirical fact that primarily-consumption-driven pollution is significant in developed countries; for example, in the US, personal transport and energy use in the residential building sector account for the majority of total energy consumption and a large percentage of air pollution emissions. In addition, personal transport and personal living space have generally increased, not decreased, with wealth in developed countries.

Environmental quality and per capita final goods consumption are the arguments of a log-linear welfare function. Environmental quality is the difference between the environment in a pure state and "effective pollution," or the amount of pollution produced that is not remediated through investments in environmental quality upgrading. The exponents for goods consumption and environmental quality sum to one, and change so that the welfare weight of environmental quality increases with per capita GDP (equations shown in appendix). Investment in environmental quality upgrading (remediation) is made on a yearly basis. To calculate its return the extra welfare from a cleaner environment must be converted into consumption terms. Unlike the other investments, environmental quality upgrading has a one-time immediate pay-off, so no discounting is required.

3.4. *Population Module*

The mortality rates for infants (0–1), children (1–5), and the aged (approximately 60 and up) are updated every five periods according to changes in per capita GDP (negatively) and time (negatively). Fertility is adjusted at five year intervals according to infant mortality (positively affected) and human capital (negatively affected). Aging is performed based on one year cohorts, i.e. instead of one-fifth of a cohort moving to the next one, the amount of people at each age is known. The school age population consists of 6–17, and the working population consists of 18–64. Although gender differences are not explicitly modeled, we assume half of each cohort is female to calculate births.

Migrants are assumed to come only from the 20–35-age cohort. The motivation for a worker's migrating is to maximize his human capital adjusted wage. The human capital adjusted wage is the country's wage rate divided by its human capital multiple. This operation reflects the fact that lower skilled immigrants expect lower wages than the higher skilled indigenous population. Besides the obvious impacts of a larger and younger population, migrants affect their host countries in more subtle ways. Migrants bring with them their country's human capital multiple and fertility rates, thus affecting the host country's (through a simple weighted average). The direction of migration is from countries with a lower human capital adjusted wage to countries with higher ones (migrants do not return to their source country). The destination country of the migrants is determined from a logit model.

4. Base Case and Sources of Growth

The basic model is one of investment and growth; hence, the two main drags on growth are the two main drags on investment. One drag is population aging, which reduces the percentage of GDP allotted for investment. The other drag is the environment: as countries get richer their assessment of the value of a clean environment (seen through the weight of environmental quality in the welfare function) increases; yet, getting richer means creating more pollution (again through industrial production and, especially, consumption). Countries remedy this conflict by spending on environmental quality upgrading; the consequence of this spending is less money left over for GDP growth producing investments, thus the environmental drag on GDP growth.

Both of these drags can be seen in the following plot of welfare (Fig. 1). In the rich countries, both GDP per capita (not shown) and welfare leveled off in the middle periods, but then rose again. Population aging and the resulting shrinkage of the investment pool, as well as an increased concentration of spending on the environment, caused the leveling off. Migration from the middle and poor countries helped to decrease the dependency ratios, and thus raise investment — this, along with lower pollution levels because of a shift to less industry production, led to the second increase.

The constraint on growth is a drag on investment, specifically spending on environmental quality upgrading and population aging. However, investment in and of itself does not guarantee growth; rather, it is a very specific kind of investment that generates sustained growth, that is, technology investment and, to a lesser degree, human capital investment. Even with the environment and population aging drags removed, and considering we have already disallowed the possibility of resource exhaustion to constrain growth, the key to

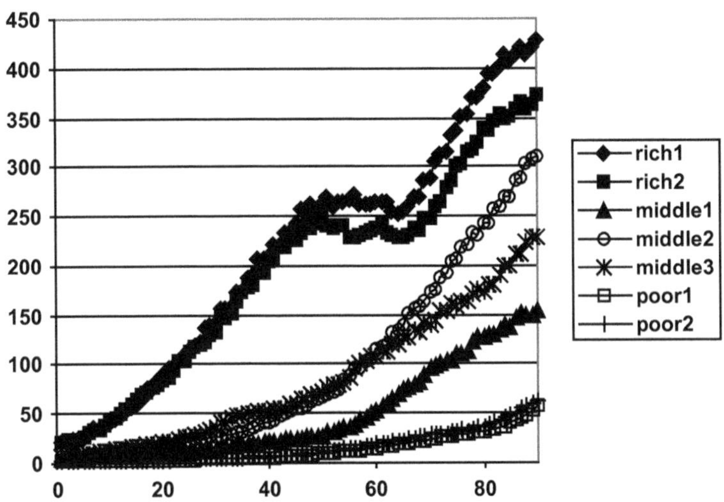

Fig. 1. Welfare Levels for All Countries in the Base Case Run. The Traces of the Two Poor Countries are Nearly the Same

growth is technological advance, not factor accumulation. The following run removes the environment and population dynamics (including migration) — so the share of GDP going toward investment stays essentially constant (and in the rich and middle countries fairly high) — as well as foreign direct investment and technology and human capital improvements. The remaining investments, therefore, are physical capital in the three production sectors and resource base augmentation. In this run GDP initially grew, but then clearly was limited (Fig. 2), despite the fact that the investment pools grew and the labor forces did not decline. Indeed, as economic theory would suggest, in some periods no investment was made because further investment in the physical capital stock would have negative returns.

Thus, some of the basic results of our model agree with two important, emerging stylized facts from the recent economic growth literature. First, Pritchet (1997) as well as Easterly and Levine (2001) found that over the very long run (the last 200 years) the modal behavior of per capita GDP is divergence — and a great deal of it — not convergence among countries. Furthermore, the gap among rich and poor has grown more rapidly since the Second World War. This increase in divergence does not mean the poor are getting

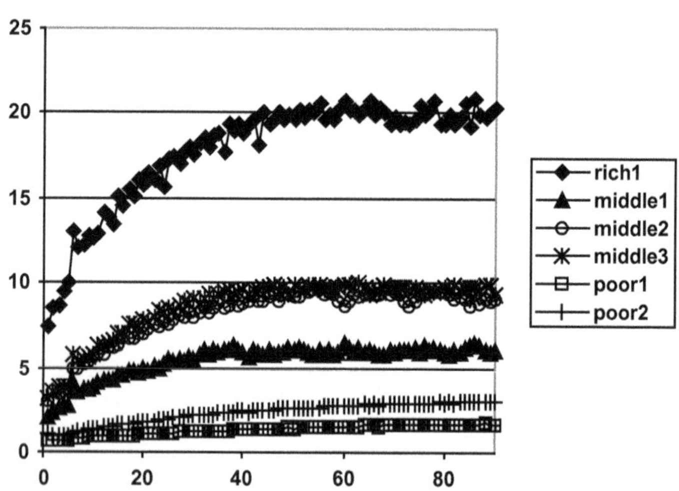

Fig. 2. Per Capita GDP when the Base Case is Run without the Environmental Module (thus, No Environmental Drag), without Population Dynamics (thus, No Population Drag), without FDI, and without the Ability to Increase Technology or Human Capital via Investment (i.e. Constant Technology and Human Capital Levels). The Traces of the Two Rich Countries are Virtually the Same so for Clarity Only One is Shown. The Traces for Middle2 and Middle3 are also Very Similar

poorer, rather the rich are getting richer at a much faster rate than the poor. Second, Easterly and Levine (2001) show that improvements in productivity (both labor productivity and technology improvements), not factor accumulation (i.e. physical capital, population size, natural resource abundance), are responsible for most of the cross-country differences in the level and growth rate of GDP per capita. Both Rodrik (1999) and Easterly and Levine (2001) point out that economic growth is unstable over time, yet investment levels and physical capital are highly persistent, implying that something else must explain variations in economic growth.

5. Impact of Global Flows on Countries with Different Starting Points

5.1. *Trade*

There are two obvious sources of advantage concerning trade in our system: (i) access to cheaper natural resources, and thus, lower production costs of the two final goods; and (ii) the opportunity to buy final goods at lower prices than if a country had to produce all its own consumption by importing and exporting according to that country's relative cost advantages in the various production sectors. Accordingly, we would expect a benefit from trade for countries with low resource endowments and countries with high resource endowments but low technology and human capital (which mean high costs to produce the final goods). Indeed, we find that countries always benefit from trade when they trade with a country (or countries) that has (or have) a greater resource endowment. Thus, the two rich countries and the Middle1 country are major beneficiaries of trade. In general, the poor countries also benefit from trade since they have substantial export potential in the natural resource and often (if not always) produce the final goods at higher costs.

In addition, no country ever does well if it protects one of the final goods sectors. Such protection, predictably, always results in lower purchasing power. If a country protects the good it is relatively worse at producing (i.e. produces at a higher cost), then consumers pay more for that good than they would under trade and the purchasing power of exporting the good that the country is relatively better at producing is muted. (The assumption is that protecting a sector means no imports or exports of that good.) If a country protects the good it is relatively better at producing, it enjoys a lower price for that good, but can no longer use exports of that good to buy (or import) the other good that the country is relatively worse at producing. The one exception to the adverse consequences of a protection strategy involves the middling resource endowed middle countries (Middle2 and Middle3) and protecting the intermediate, resource good — more on this below.

To consider the benefits of trade, as well as various trade regimes, we look at per capita consumption of the two final goods since improving purchasing power is the ultimate motivation for trade. But, we run the model without the environment drag since differences in trade regimes are most obvious in high growth scenarios. Also, to make comparisons between free trade and autarky most robust migration and FDI were not used in any runs.

Poor countries and trade. When the version of the base model, modified as above, is run, the poor countries are investment constrained for a long time until their per capita GDP grows to a level above "subsistence". Under those conditions, free trade is better than autarky since the ability to export the resource (the one production sector the poor countries "begin" at a reasonably proficient level) allows the poor countries to increase their investment pools and then their endowments. However, the superiority of free trade is less clear under conditions where investment is enhanced, for example, where the poor countries introduce an "austerity" program. In runs with an austerity program — the minimum share of GDP for investment is set at 20% — the smaller poor country (Poor2) eventually (after period 80 or so) enjoyed greater consumption (of both goods) under autarky — a gap that showed signs of increasing. This result turns out not to be a condemnation of free trade. Nor does the result support an "infant industry" argument for protection; indeed, the smaller poor country paid higher prices for the two final goods (than under free trade) throughout the run. The country increased productivity to the point where it could afford to buy more even at higher prices.

The counterintuitive result of Poor2 reflects the complexity of an international, endogenous growth system. For the poor countries, trade influences economic structure, which in turn influences investment mixes, which in turn influences future economic growth. The poor countries' endowments lead them to specialize in resource extraction and, in later periods, the more labor-intensive service sector. Naturally, autarky forces the poor countries to develop a more complete economic structure.

The returns to investment in physical capital in the various sectors and resource base augmentation follow predictably from country endowments and economic structure. However, returns to human capital and technology investments — as shown previously, the two most important investments for long-term growth — are more complex. An improvement in technology increases the productive capacity in all sectors equally. An improvement in human capital increases the productive capacity in all sectors too, but weighted by the labor exponent in the production functions — so that the productive capacity of the service sector is increased the most, followed by the industrial sector, and then the extraction sector. The returns on investment calculations are such that the benefits to investment are clear only when there is production in a sector. Thus, when countries specialize (and particularly, when they do so in the extraction sector), the eventual benefits of an increase in technology or human capital are not appreciated in sectors (industry or service) where production is currently zero or very low. The national investor's, arguably, shortsightedness primarily affects countries that are highly specialized or the poor countries under free trade.

Thus, under autarky, Poor2 had production in all three sectors; the benefits of increased production caused by investment in human capital and technology were evident for all three sectors, and the country invested a higher share of its investment pool in human capital and technology. Also, under autarky the final goods had higher prices, further increasing the returns to more production, and thus investments in human capital and technology. Whereas under free trade, Poor2 channeled relatively more investment toward physical capital in extraction and resource base augmentation. The higher investment by Poor2 in human capital and technology under autarky eventually led to greater human capital and technology levels that in-turn led to a larger investment pool, still further increases in human capital and technology, and ultimately enough growth to compensate for the higher final goods prices. By around the 70th period, Poor2 had a larger investment pool under autarky, and near this same time began to have considerably more investment in human capital and technology. Poor2 had an increasingly greater human capital under autarky by the 70th period, and autarky overtook free trade in technology level by the 100th period. In the 84th period, Poor2 begins to have more consumption under autarky, and like the gap in endowments, this difference continued to grow. Figure 3 shows the difference in investment priorities (i.e. shares of the investment pool) for growth enhancing investments that impact all sectors (human capital and technology) and extraction sector specific investments (physical capital in the extraction sector and resource base augmentation) under autarky and free trade.

The larger poor country, Poor1, produced enough in the service sector early on under free trade, that the bias against technology and human capital investment brought on by specialization did not cause its investment mix to differ that much from what it was under autarky. Indeed, it had a similar

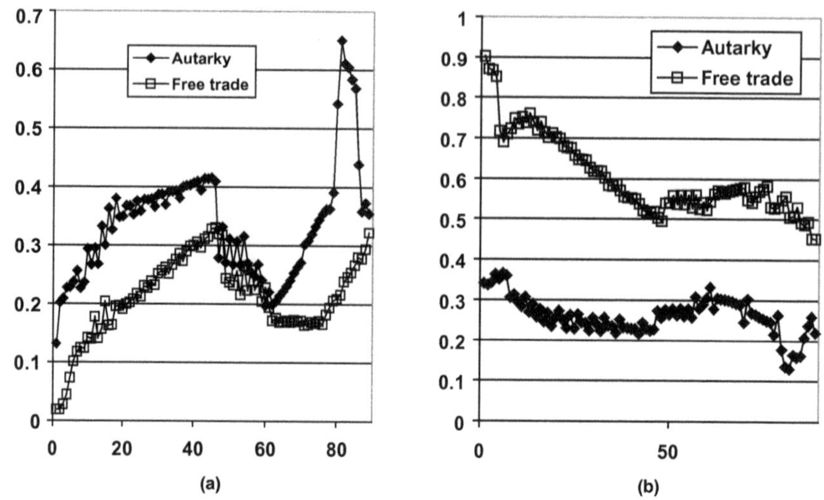

Fig. 3. (a) The Share of the Total Investment Pool for Growth Enhancing Investments in Human Capital and Technology for Poor2 under Autarky and Free Trade. (b) The Share of the Total Investment Pool for Extraction Sector Specific Investments — Investments in Physical Capital in the Extraction Sector and Resource Base Augmentation — for Poor2 under Autarky and Free Trade

investment pool and human capital and technology level under both regimes. In fact, under free trade Poor1 was only a marginal resource base exporter by the end of the run. Poor1 benefited from free trade through lower final goods prices.

Countries can, of course, extract themselves from the free trade induced economic specialization-investment trap. In one such policy, Poor2 reallocated its investment mix to correct for this bias (in this case 25% of investment in physical capital and resource base augmentation were redirected toward human capital and technology). Under this scenario, the country maintained a larger investment pool, higher human capital, and technology, and enjoyed greater final goods consumption under free trade than autarky. This investment policy eventually led to more physical capital investment in the final goods sectors, and thus ultimately less specialization. Hence, the poor countries do indeed benefit from free trade; however, the specialization that free trade induces in the poor countries can cause — in the absence of profound foresight — under-investment in human capital and technology. Under-investments in these areas have significant long run consequences for growth and development.

Middle countries and trade. Middle2 and Middle3, who have natural resource endowments less than the two poor countries but greater than the others, like the poor countries, had higher final goods consumption under autarky than free trade. These two middle countries are usually net exporters of the natural resource, but not major ones. Under autarky their endowments and resulting supply and demand patterns resulted in their local resource price as well as final goods prices being lower than the corresponding world prices under free trade. The greater demand for the natural resource in the rich countries (among other things) drives up the resource price beyond what it would be if these two (middle) countries were solely responsible for the pricing of the resource. Therefore, initially we believed the better performance these middle countries had under autarky resulted from the lower prices they experienced. However, on closer scrutiny, it appears that these countries too suffer from an invest bias imposed by the free trade system. To examine these issues more closely, an experiment like the one used for the poor countries was set up, but using Middle2 only — the two countries have very similar endowments, differing substantially, only in terms of population age structure and dynamics. Thus, the model was run without the environmental drag and FDI and with Middle2's population remaining constant (while the populations of the others changed as in the base case).

Surprisingly, Middle2, with a smaller resource endowment and greater human capital and technology endowment, seemed to fall in the same pattern as Poor2 in terms of performance under autarky versus free trade. Middle2 invested a higher share of its pool in human capital and technology over the first 40–50 periods under autarky compared to free trade. Meanwhile, it invested a considerably higher share of investment in resource base augmentation and physical capital in the extraction sector under free trade throughout the run. This difference in investment priorities meant Middle2 eventually had higher human capital, technology, GDP, investment pool, and consumption of final goods under autarky.

What is meant by a "resource curse" in this context is not that a resource endowment can actually be adverse for growth. On the contrary, all countries do better, under any trade regime, when they begin with more, rather than less, resource endowment. The "curse" refers to a bias that, for countries with relatively high resource endowments, free trade imparts against human capital and technology investment — the two investments most important for long-term growth — and toward investment in resource base augmentation and physical capital in the extraction sector, at least in the early periods. One cure for this investment bias is autarky.

In other words, for countries well endowed in the natural resource, free trade means that they will not do as well as they could do, but these countries still do better with greater resource endowments.

Next we looked at what factors make countries more likely to be susceptible to this investment bias. Two obvious factors are resource base and population sizes, or alternatively, perhaps just per capita resource base. Thus, we examined the investment mix when these two are changed (but other aspects of population remain constant). In general, under autarky, when the resource base was increased (but other things were held constant), per capita measures (like GDP or consumption quantities) increased as well; however, when population increased, per capita measures fell (although total output increased). Under free trade, per capita measures increased both with increases in total population (when there is no population growth) and resource base. As population increased, per capita resource base fell, and the country under autarky began to look more like a country that would benefit from getting the natural resource elsewhere (i.e. from trade). This country had to spend a greater amount of investment on producing the natural resource, and correspondingly, the price of the resource rose. On the other hand, under free trade, as the per capita resource base declined, the country was more likely to import the resource, and appropriately spend less on resource base augmentation or physical capital in extraction. In addition, when a population is young (and unchanging), an increase in total population increases the return to human capital investment. Thus, as the per capita resource base fell, the investment mixes under autarky and free trade converged.

On the other hand, when the resource endowment was increased, resource base per capita increased, and the investment mixes and long-run per capita indicators between autarky and free trade diverged. Under autarky, as the resource base increased, more investment can be channeled away from extraction motivated investments since there is no reason to extract more than is needed by the two final goods sectors. In addition, a higher natural endowment means lower levels of other factors are required to extract the same amount. However, a higher resource base per capita under free trade tends to encourage the exportation of the natural resource, and thus, extraction motivated investments (at the expense, at least in the early periods, of investments like human capital).

In addition to per capita resource base, initial human capital and technology levels were very important in the difference between free trade and autarky. Indeed, when Middle2's initial human capital and technology was set at the starting level for the rich countries (i.e. changed from 2 to 3), free trade out performed autarky at a much lower population, or a much higher resource base per capita than before. Earlier, Middle2's population had to increase to 700 (holding the resource base constant at 10) before free trade led to higher final goods consumption quantities than autarky; but with a higher starting level of human capital and technology, this occurred for free trade with a population of only 300. (Using the original base case population of 200, free trade and autarky were very close.) Under free trade, the higher starting levels of human capital and technology meant a lower share of investment went toward capital in the extraction sector, a higher share to human capital, a lower share to resource base augmentation, and a higher share for technology. Under autarky, increasing initial human capital and technology changed the investment mix much less than under free trade; however, the directions of change were typically the same.

At this point, we briefly summarize why the choice of free trade versus autarky matters. First, countries benefit from access to a lower priced natural resource — and thus, have lower production costs — and factor endowments determine under which trade regime a country will experience these lower costs. Second, countries clearly benefit when they can freely import and export the final goods to achieve consumption baskets in the most efficient manner given their productive endowments. Third, an investment mix skewed toward human capital and technology investment is most likely to support long-run income growth, and for some countries achieving this mix is more likely under autarky, at least in the absence of some other correction to the investment decision. For Middle2 and Middle3, reasons one and three favor autarky while reason two favors free trade. To better understand the relative strengths of these three reasons for Middle2, that country's resulting investment mix under autarky was exogenously applied to a free trade run, and conversely, its free trade investment mix was exogenously applied to an autarky run.

Final goods consumption of the two "hybrid" runs — autarky using free trade's investment mix and free trade using autarky's investment mix — was less than that of the base autarky run but greater than the base free trade run. Typically, there was more industrial consumption under autarky with free trade's investment mix and more service consumption under free trade with autarky's investment mix. These results suggest that it is indeed both the lower prices enjoyed under autarky and the more optimal long-run investment mix that led Middle2 to do better under autarky than free trade. A trade regime that may allow Middle2 to capture the best of all three benefits outlined above would protect its resource industry, but allow it to trade freely in the two final goods. This strategy would allow the country to have access to a lower priced natural resource, but not to be limited in imports or exports of the final, consumption goods, nor to have its investment mix biased in favor of resource extraction investments at the expense of human capital and technology, a bias that free trade of the resource causes.

Final goods consumption under autarky and free trade in final goods plus natural resource protection were very close and, not surprisingly, higher than with free trade in all sectors. Industry consumption was slightly higher under autarky, while service consumption was slightly higher under (free trade with) protection. Although the prices of both final goods were lower under autarky, the difference in price was much greater for the industry good than the service good; thus, the relative industry-to-service good price (the determinant of the consumption good mix) was skewed toward service under protection and toward industry under autarky. The investment mixes for autarky and protection were similar, but resource base augmentation was higher under autarky for the first 25 periods, as was technology investment, and extraction sector physical capital was slightly higher throughout, while human capital investment was slightly higher under protection.

It is somewhat disappointing and hard to say why the protection regime was not clearly superior to autarky for Middle2. One possibility is the benefit of a lower resource price essentially offset the benefit of final goods trade, given Middle2's very particular endowments and the endowments of the other countries in the free trade system. Of course, what could easily tip the scales toward the resource-protection strategy (and away from autarky) are the other global flows, particularly FDI — of which Middle2 becomes a major donor. Indeed, Middle2 definitely does better than autarky when considering FDI and migration (in-migrants are restricted from only the other middle countries and the amount of out-migrants are held to less than the base case). Protection is clearly better than autarky, and free trade catches autarky. When the environment is considered, the benefits both of (1) global flows (i.e. the base case) and (2) protection with migration and FDI over autarky are even stronger.

There are a number of "resource curse" arguments in the theoretical and empirical literature, and some of this literature dates back to at least the 1940s and 1950s. However, the resource curse that we have modeled — quite unintentionally — is completely different from many of these previous arguments and only similar in spirit to others.

Some studies place major emphasis on the failure of resource rich countries to develop final goods industries (particularly manufacturing in these theories), and thus, conclude these countries retard technological progress and long-run growth (e.g. Sachs and Warner, 1995). Manufacturing industries are considered an important source of economic growth because of productivity externalities stemming from, for example, "forward and backward linkages" (Hirschman, 1958) or learning-by-doing (Matsuyama, 1992). This set of arguments is most closely related to the resource curse that occurs in our model, although we do not model learning-by-doing, and final goods production, *per se*, has no great influence on long-run growth. The resource curse in our model comes about because open, resource-rich countries have a tendency early in the run to be biased toward investments specifically focusing on resource extraction, and against sector neutral investments like human capital and technology. This deficiency in investment priorities has long-run consequences, but it can be mitigated when countries also have high initial levels of technology and human capital, and so, the final goods industries are more competitive with the extraction sector, a fact reflected in the investment allocation.

Mikesell (1997) offers a counter example to the resource curse, what he refers to as the resource-curse paradox — namely, that virtually all countries begin their development by exploiting their natural resource base. In our model, poor countries do indeed benefit almost immediately from the ability to trade on their resource endowment. They only do better under autarky in the long-run, and then only because of their higher technology levels achieved because of priority differences in early period investments. If the poor countries correct their initial investment bias, the paradox and resource curse are resolved.

5.2. *Foreign Direct Investment*

There are four ways in which the poor or receiving countries may benefit from foreign direct investment (FDI). First, the poor countries receive physical capital that they may not otherwise be able to afford. This capital, of course, does not come without costs, since it will be foreign owned the poor countries will not capture all the returns to capital from the additional production made possible by the foreign physical capital investment. The poor countries will, however, get all the returns to labor that the additional production affords. Second, the poor countries benefit from technology transfer. We assume that at least part of technology is embodied in new physical capital, and the primary vehicle for international transfer of technology is the FDI "firm" installing its technologically advanced physical capital in the poor countries. The poor countries overtime fully incorporate those technology improvements into their new, indigenously created physical capita. Third, the poor countries could capture additional benefits from FDI by taxing the remittances of the foreign firm. This last method of benefits capture has clear limits since we assume the foreign firm understands fully the poor countries policy in this matter and will adjust the predicted returns to its investment accordingly.

Finally, since we assume all FDI goes toward physical capital, rather than to "crowd out" domestic investment, FDI could "free-up" the domestic investor to concentrate more on the human capital and technology investments key to long-run success.

The poor countries indeed had greater investment in technology and human capital under FDI. It appears the technology transfer aspect of FDI — which helped the poor countries achieve higher technology levels than otherwise possible — was more responsible for this redirection of investment priorities toward long run economic growth than the poor countries spending less on physical capital because of the foreign flows to that area.

To assess the relative strengths of these FDI benefits, and to assess how managing FDI flows will impact the poor countries, the model was run with constant populations and with a "mild" version of the environment drag (i.e. the welfare weight of environmental quality increased more slowly with income and was capped at a lower number than in the base case). If there were no technology transfer or taxing of remittances, then both poor countries did significantly worse — in terms of per capita GDP — with FDI than without it. However, if there were technology transfer, but no way to capture benefits more directly (i.e. no tax), both poor countries did better with FDI. These results suggest that the simple free market goal of equalizing rent rates across countries, i.e. investing in physical capital where its returns are highest, does not provide much benefit to poor countries or meaningfully help them solve their under-investment problem. Moreover, the payments to foreign capital can be greater than the benefits; thus, capturing benefits, or at least controlling foreign ownership, is important for the poor, recipient countries.

In fact, the potential benefit of technology transfer is so great that if technology transfer could be increased, both poor countries would be justified in encouraging FDI by subsidizing the remittances. Furthermore, if the larger poor country could lower the time it takes for the technology of foreign created capital to diffuse throughout the economy enough, a subsidy policy would be substantially better than that country's previous best tax policy. However, it is unlikely the smaller poor country could ever improve the technology transfer mechanism enough for a subsidy policy to perform better than a tax regime with slower technology transfer. The greater value of technology transfer to Poor1 reflects its less specialized economic structure. The investing countries tend to do better as well when the recipient countries have higher technology levels. Therefore, both recipient and investing countries have incentives to find ways — even costly ones — to increase the rate of technology transfer that occurs under FDI.

As an alternative to FDI, the poor countries could reap benefits from general technology diffusion (not tied to capital or trade flows) and foreign aid. A high enough degree of such international technology diffusion can make the poor countries just as well off as under FDI; however, the donor (i.e. rich and middle) countries do not benefit nearly as much. The poor countries, instead, could receive foreign aid directly to their investment pools. If this foreign aid is high enough the poor countries can do as well as under FDI. However, the donor countries have to give much more foreign aid than they did FDI, and those donor countries do not receive nearly as much for their contributions (their per capita GDPs are close to the no FDI/no foreign aid case). One reason for the discrepancy is that the FDI flows into the poor countries are much greater than the sum of the contributions, since some of the returns are reinvested (and not remitted), and thus, enjoy a compounding effect. If the donor countries give exactly the same flows as they invested under FDI, for the poor countries to do as well under FDI, there would have to be a substantial, independent mechanism for technology diffusion (i.e. much greater amounts of diffusion than currently modeled). Yet, again, this program would have little benefits for the donor countries. Thus, FDI is both an effective way to conduct intra-generational transfers and a self-beneficial one for the donor countries.

5.3. *Migration*

(In-)migration and rich countries. As destination countries only, migration provides a clear, substantial benefit to the rich countries whose indigenous populations are aging rapidly. Migration increases the work force directly and lowers aged dependency burdens both directly (the migrants themselves are between 20 and 35) and indirectly, since migrants tend to come from countries with higher fertility rates. Although the migrants also come from countries with lower human capital, the rich countries do not suffer much human capital dilution since the rich countries can continue to increase their indigenous human capital through the increased investment pool the larger, younger population affords them. In addition, the rich countries also receive migrants from the growing, middle countries who too have high human capital. Without migration, aged dependency burdens reach 0.4 by the 80th period, and the share of GDP going toward investment drops to (or very near) zero. With migration, aged dependency burdens fluctuate between 0.3 and 0.25, and the share of GDP for investment fluctuates between 10% and 15%. As a result

of these higher numbers, the total investment pool actually increases in the later periods (after a decline in the middle periods). Migration is a particularly important benefit to the rich countries when the environment is considered. Welfare levels are only slightly lower under migration during the first 50 periods of the run; in the later periods, after a brief plateau, welfare continues to rise under migration, whereas without migration welfare falls in the later periods. This divergence in the last third of the run results in final welfare levels that are two to three times higher with migration than without.

Migration and middle countries. Not surprisingly, migration affects the middle countries differently from either the rich or poor ones. Because the middle countries are both source and destination countries for migrants, migration means for the middle countries, in part, trading their populations for the poor countries' (with those countries' lower human capital and higher fertility rates). In addition, the middle countries have significantly different indigenous population dynamics (different both among themselves and from the other two country "types" or development levels). For each of the three middle countries a series of migration policies, combining both in- and out-migration rules, were run (again, the "mild" version of the environmental drag was used). The three different in- and out-migration rules are: (i) the base case (or normal), (ii) none allowed, and (iii) restricted. For in-migration, the restricted rule means only migrants from the other middle countries are allowed (i.e. no in-migration from the poor countries). For out-migration, restricted simply refers to a lower maximum migration rate for the target population (0.06 instead of 0.15 in the base case). The possible combinations of rules results in nine different overall migration polices. We focus the analysis on Middle1 and Middle3 since they provide the greatest contrast.

Middle1 has the youngest and fastest growing population among the middle countries. In addition, because it is most similar to the poor countries, in terms of human capital and fertility, under the base case conditions it received significant in-migration from those countries. In any run where out-migration is limited (the "none" or "restricted" rule was used), but in-migration was not, Middle1 experienced high population growth and finished with a substantially greater population than under any other policy scenario. Under the policy of "normal" (out-migration)–"normal" (in-migration), Middle1 was very much trading part of the poor countries" populations for part of its own. Thus, it is not surprising that the worst in- and out-migration rules clearly were the "normal" ones. Because Middle1 typically achieved the lowest per capita income of the middle countries, there was little difference in population between the "none" and "restricted" in-migration rules. The "none" out-migration rule produced a slightly higher per capita GDP than the "restricted" rule throughout the run. The "none–none" (and equivalently the "none–restricted") policy led to a larger population and higher percent of GDP for investment than the "restricted–none" (and "restricted–restricted") policy. However, the difference in per capita GDP between the "none" out-migration policy and the "restricted" one was not great. Assuming that eliminating migration is considerably more costly than controlling it, the best policy for Middle1 is probably "restricted–restricted."

Middle3 has population dynamics that allow for a very high percentage of GDP for investment early on, but its population aged rapidly, causing a drop in investment even more extreme than experienced by the rich countries. As a result of its unique population dynamics, Middle3 had the most complex pattern of per capita GDP traces in response to the different migration policies. In general, policies that limited both out- and in-migration ("none–none," "none–restricted," "restricted–none," and "restricted–restricted") were the best policies over the middle periods — periods 30–60. Yet, policies that allowed for significant out- or in-migration ("normal–normal," "normal–none," "normal–restricted," and "restricted–normal") were clearly the worst over this period. Middle3 enjoyed income growth during the middle periods; however, it was still "poorer" than the rich countries, and thus, experienced some out-migration, with this loss of its workers hurting the country. At the same time, an influx from the poor countries and from the slower growing and, by now, lower human capital Middle1 put a drag on per capita growth. Because of the high degree of population aging of the indigenous population, policies that limited in-migration ("normal–none," "normal–restricted," "restricted–none," and "none–none") all led to flat per capita GDP during the last 30 periods.

Policies that allow for in-migration ("none-normal," "restricted–normal," "none–restricted," "restricted–restricted," and "normal–normal") enjoyed sustained per capita GDP growth in the later periods. Among this second group — the "sustained-growth" polices — there was little difference in results over the last 30 periods between the "none" and "restrictive" out-migration rules (i.e. "none–normal" was very similar to "restricted–normal" and "none–restricted" was similar to "restricted–restricted"). This lack of sensitivity to the out-migration rule is not surprising since in situations of income growth people are less likely to want to migrate.

Because the "normal" in-migration rule is clearly the best in the long-run, but the "restricted" rule is much better than "normal" in the short-to-medium-run, choosing an optimal migration policy is difficult for Middle3. Among the

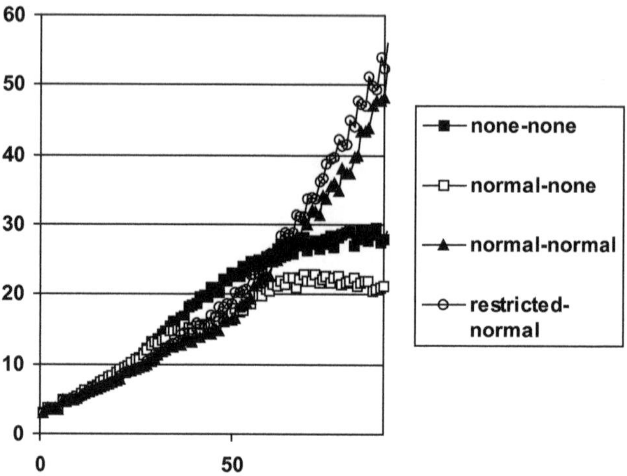

Fig. 4. Per Capita GDP for Middle3 under Four Different Migration Policies. The Out-migration Rule is Designated First Followed by the In-migration Rule. For Example, "Normal–none" Refers to the Policy that Combines the "Normal" Out-migration Rule with the "None" In-migration Rule. See the Text (Section 5.3.2) for Definitions of the Three Rules

policies that allowed for sustained per capita GDP growth, "none–restricted" was the best policy during the first 60 periods, while "none-normal" was the best over the last 30 (although the "restricted" out-migration rule resulted in only slightly lower income when keeping the in-migration rule constant). The choice between these two policies, and equivalently between these two time horizons, could be made using standard discounting, alternatively Middle3 could pursue a dynamic migration policy. Figure 4 shows Middle3's per capita GDP for a selected group of the above policies that produce some of the greatest divergence in the short- and long-runs.

6. Conclusions

We have tried to develop a model that is "more complete" than most, i.e. a fuller treatment of population, an economic module that also considers international capital movements, and some consideration for the environment. But the most important aspects of our work in differentiating it from others, is our modeling of a diversity of "country types," and our explicit modeling of human capital and technology investments/improvements — widely accepted as the drivers of sustained economic growth. We have allowed countries to differ in initial human capital and technology levels, and thus, in initial development or wealth levels, as well as in areas in which there is less likelihood of rapid convergence or change, i.e. natural resource endowment, population age structure, and fertility and death rates. One of the major payoffs of our approach is we find history matters. Our model has both an exogenous history, implied by our initial conditions (human capital, technology, and aspects of population that imply previous changes), as well as an endogenous history — the complex of parameter changes embedded in our simulation runs.

This paper has focused on how individual country histories or starting points impact how those countries will react or prefer to manage three types of global flows: goods (via trade), capital (via foreign direct investment), and people (via international migration). Some findings were not unforeseen; for example, in a trade model with an internationally mobile intermediate good (a natural resource in our model), country factor endowments are important in determining the benefits of free trade. Since trade changes the price that countries can buy the natural resource, it also changes countries' cost structures of production. Another more predictable result was that aging, rich countries would enjoy economic benefits from some in-migration of more fertile populations. As countries go through rapid aging two things happen: (i) the share of GDP for investment and, accordingly, their investment pool fall (because of the link between aged dependency and the investment-consumption trade-off); and (ii) their labor force shrinks (something that can only be partially offset by increases in human capital). Migration mitigates both these problems (an increasing age dependency and shrinking labor force), both immediately and in the longer-run since migrants often have higher fertility rates than the indigenous population.

Other results, however, were much harder to anticipate, e.g. the richness in migration polices for the middle countries, which are both source and destination countries for migrants and have individual past changes in population that imply very different profiles for the future. Perhaps most unexpected to us was that the smaller poor country would do better under autarky because free trade imparted a bias on its investment priorities that had long-run consequences, not because autarky improved the country's terms of trade. Under autarky, that country's higher investment in human capital and technology early on sowed the ground for greater per capita GDP much later in the run — a striking example of the importance of an emergent history, or path dependency in our results.

Acknowledgment

I would like to acknowledge Jerome Rothenberg's substantial contribution in the initial formulation of the model. I appreciate the funding from the Max

Plank Institute that enabled me to present an earlier version of this paper at the Policy Modeling 2002 conference in Brussels. The views expressed in this paper are the author's own views and do not necessarily represent those of the Max Plank Institute for Demographic Research.

References

Barro R, and Sala-i-Martin X, 1995. *Economic Growth*. McGraw-Hill: New York.

Bloom D, and Canning D, 2001. "Cumulative causality, economic growth, and the demographic transition." In: *Population Matters: Demographic Change, Economic Growth, and Poverty in the Developing World*. Birdsall N, Kelley AC, and Sinding SW, (eds) Oxford University Press: Oxford. 165–197.

Dellink RB, 1999. "Environmental-economic modeling: a survey of pollution, abatement and economic growth." Wageningen University, Wageningen, Netherlands.

Easterly W, and Levine R, 2001. "It's not factor accumulation: stylized facts and growth models." *World Bank Econ. Rev.* **15**(2): 177–219.

Hirschman AO, 1958. *The Strategy of Economic Development*. Yale University Press: New Haven, CT.

Kelley AC, and Schmidt RM, 1994. "Population and income change: recent evidence." World Bank Discussion Paper 249, Washington, DC.

Keyfitz N, and Flieger W, 1990. *World Population Growth and Aging: Demographic Trends in the Late Twentieth Century*. University of Chicago Press: Chicago.

Lee RD, Mason A, and Miller T, 2001. "Saving, wealth, and population." In: *Population Matters: Demographic Change, Economic Growth, and Poverty in the Developing World*. Birdsall N, Kelley AC, and Sinding SW, (eds) Oxford University Press: Oxford. 137–164.

Liddle B, 2000. "Population growth, age structure, and environmental impact." *Popul. Envir.* **21**(4): 385–411.

Loschel A, 2002. "Technological change in economic models of environmental policy: a survey." Working paper, University of Mannheim, Germany.

Mason A, 1987. "National saving rates and population growth: a new model and new evidence." In: *Population Growth and Economic Development: Issues and Evidence*. Johnson DG, and Lee RD, (eds) University of Wisconsin Press: Madison. 523–560.

Mason A, 1988. "Saving, economic growth and demographic change." *Popul. Develop. Rev.* **14**: 113–144.

Matsuyama K, 1992. "Agricultural productivity, comparative advantage, and economic growth." *J. Econ. Theory* **58**: 317–334.

Mikesell RF, 1997. "Explaining the resource curse, with special reference to mineral-exporting countries." *Resources Policy* **23**(4): 191–199.

OECD, 1995. *The OECD Input–Output Database*. Organization for Economic Co-operation and Development: Paris.

Pritchett L, 1997. "Divergence, big time." *J. Econ. Persp.* **11**(3): 3–17.

Pritchett L, 2000. "Understanding patterns of economic growth: searching for hills among plateaus, mountains, and plains." *World Bank Econ. Rev.* 14(2): 221–250.
Rodrik D, 1999. "Where did all the growth go? external shocks, social conflict, and growth collapses." *J. Econ. Growth* 4: 385–412.
Sachs JD, and Warner AM, 1995. "Natural resource abundance and economic growth." NBER Working Paper 5398. NBER: Cambridge, MA.
Sanderson WC, 1980. "Economic-demographic simulation models: a review of their usefulness for policy analysis." RR-80-14, IIASA, Laxenburg, Austria.
Sanderson WC, 1992. "Simulation models of economic, demographic, and environmental interactions: are they on a sustainable development path?" Working paper WP-92-87, IIASA, Laxenburg, Austria.
Schmidt SR, and Launsby RG, 1992. *Understanding Industrial Designed Experiments*. 3rd Edn. Air Academy Press: Colorado Springs.
Solow R, 1970. *Growth Theory: An Exposition*. Oxford University Press: Oxford.
Williamson JG, and Higgins M, 2001. "The accumulation and demography connection in East Asia." In: *Population Change and Economic Development in East Asia*. Mason A, (ed) Stanford University Press: Stanford, CA. 123–154.
World Bank, 1994. *World Tables 1994*. The World Bank, Washington, DC.

Appendix. Important Model Equations and Production Function Exponents[e]

The production functions for the two final consumer goods sectors, with all variables and parameters specific to each period t, are:

Resource non-intensive service sector, S:

$$Q_S = T(HL_S)^{\text{bls}} K_S^{\text{bks}} R_S^{\text{brs}} \tag{2}$$

Resource intensive industry sector, I:

$$Q_I = T(HL_I)^{\text{bli}} K_I^{\text{bki}} R_I^{\text{bri}}, \tag{3}$$

where:

Q_S, Q_I: output for two sectors
T: input-neutral technological improvements (same for all sectors)
L_x, K_x, R_x $(x = S, I)$: labor, capital, natural resource input for individual sectors

[e]For complete model documentation and (PASCAL) program code see Liddle B, 2003. "The challenge of sustainability in a global system: documentation of a transdisciplinary, multi-country, dynamic simulation model." MPIDR Working Paper WP-2003-005, Rostock, Germany. Both the paper and code can be accessed through the MPI for Demographic Research's website: http://www.demogr.mpg.de.

H: human capital factor (same for all sectors)
bkx, blx, brx ($x = s, i$): productivity exponents for three inputs and two sectors.

The production function for the resource extraction sector, also specific to each period t, is:

$$R = ATK_R{}^{\alpha kr}(HL_R)^{\alpha nr}\overline{R^{\beta}}, \tag{4}$$

Where:

R: amount of extraction
A: country specific factor representing land endowment
T: input-neutral technological improvements (again, same for all sectors)
L_R, K_R: labor and capital input
H: human capital factor (again, same for all sectors)
$\alpha kr, \alpha nr$: productivity exponents for capital and labor
$\bar{R}$: 8 year moving average of past extraction
β: country specific drag parameter based on the extent of recent extraction (less than -1).

The exponents used in Eqs. 2–4 were estimated from empirical data of factor shares using The OECD Input–Output Database (1995), as applied to the stylized definitions of our aggregate sectors.

Environmental Quality Module Equations, again with all variables and parameters specific to each period t, are:

$$EQ = EQ_0 - P \tag{5}$$

$$P = \bar{P}(1 - \Pi) \tag{6}$$

$$W = EQ^{\theta}C^{\phi} \tag{7}$$

$$1 = \theta + \phi \tag{8}$$

Table A1. Production Function Exponents

	Extraction/Resource Replenishment	Resource Intensive "Industry"	Resource Nonintensive "Service"
Labor share	0.3	0.45	0.6
Capital share	0.7	0.20	0.3
Natural resource share		0.35	0.1

$$\theta = k - dg^{GDP} \tag{9}$$

$$\Pi = 0.99(1 - f^{e}) \tag{10}$$

where EQ is environmental quality, EQ_0 is environmental quality in a pure state (arbitrarily set high enough so EQ is positive), P is effective pollution consumed, $\bar{P}$ is pollution produced, Π is the percentage remediated, W is welfare, C is per capita final goods consumption, GDP is per capita GDP, and k, d, and g are positives constants (all less than 1.0 and $k > dg$) that set bounds for the welfare weight on environmental quality. The percentage remediated is based on the amount of investment in environmental quality upgrading per unit of pollution produced, e, and the ease of remediation, f (currently set to 0.05). Thus, the maximum amount remediated is 99% of pollution produced.

Chapter 16

The Impact of Japanese Economic Cooperation on Asian Economic Development*

KENICHI KAWASAKI

Research Institute of Economy, Trade and Industry, Tokyo, Japan

The main objective of this paper is to overview the developments of Japan's ODA and assess, in a quantitative manner, their economic impacts on Asian countries. The benefits of two alternative measures — one from capital formation by Japan's ODA loans and the other from import liberalization in the Japanese market — are compared. Those economy-wide impacts of aid and trade on six Asian countries — China, Indonesia, Malaysia, the Philippines, Thailand, and Vietnam — are estimated by a CGE model of global trade, incorporating a certain mechanism of dynamic capital formation. Japan's ODA loans are effective for economic growth in the countries. Real GDP gains range from 0.1 to 1.6% annually. Trade liberalization is efficient to improve economic welfare. Utility gains range from 0.2 to 1.9%, which exceed those on account of Japan's ODA. Variations in those economic impacts are much more significantly observed when examined by sector.

1. Introduction

Expansion of international trade and investment has enhanced the mutual interdependencies of the world's economies, both within the developed

*This chapter was originally published in *Review of Urban and Regional Development Studies*, Vol. 16, No. 1, March 2004, and is reprinted here with minor modifications upon the permission from the publisher. The views expressed here are solely those of the author; they do not represent those of any bodies with which the author is or has been associated.

economies and between developed and developing economies. The role that the developed economies will play in the sustainable development of the developing economies has never been as important as it is now. The quality of aid from the developed economies has been reviewed on a number of occasions. Earlier arguments in *Assessing Aid* (World Bank, 1998) have also been re-examined.

Throughout the 1990s, Japan experienced a persistently stagnant economy. In contrast, most of Japan's Asian neighboring economies have succeeded in recovering from the crisis of 1997 and are starting to grow again. Recently, however, Japan's massive amount of ODA to other Asian economies has been questioned by the Japanese people. In addition to the total amount of ODA, its allocation both by region and sector are being reviewed, with the idea that ODA has to be provided with a view toward effectiveness and efficiency in a selective manner.

This paper will provide a quantitative analysis, using CGE model simulations, of the impact of Japanese economic cooperation on Asian economic development. Developments of Japan's ODA, and trade and investment in Asia, will be discussed in Section 2. Following the presentation of the framework of CGE model simulations in Section 3, with results discussed in Section 4. The paper will conclude with Section 5.

2. Developments in Japan's Aid and Trade/Investment

2.1. *Features of Japan's ODA*

Japan's ODA has several salient features[a] that differ from that of other countries. In 1991, the volume of Japan's ODA in terms of net-disbursement[b] exceeded that of the United States and became the largest in the world. Japan had maintained this position of top donor country in the world in the 1990s,[c] during which time Japan's ODA accounted for around a fourth or fifth of the

[a]Those features may be a reflection of a unique Japanese history, having experienced the phenomenon of originally being a large aid recipient to becoming the world's top donor. After World War II, Japan's economic reconstruction was largely undertaken through aid from abroad. The volume of Japanese borrowing from the World Bank was the second largest in the world in the early 1960s. Japan has often been criticized for having no clear or consistent ideas that underlie its Japanese economic cooperation policies. One argument — though it is not necessarily clear — is that Japan is attempting to support the self-help efforts of developing countries.

[b]This is the net amount of deducting the repayments of loans from the total amount of aid.

[c]According to OECD (2004), the volume of Japan's ODA has been the second largest in the world since 2001 following that of the United States.

total world aid. Japan's aid performance, however, is not so excellent when looked at in terms of relative position rather than absolute volume. According to OECD (2004), Japan's ODA over GNI ratio was 0.20% in 2003, which is around the DAC member countries' average of 0.25%. However, it is very far from the international target of 0.7% that the five distinguished countries of Norway, Denmark, the Netherlands, Luxembourg and Sweden have already satisfied.

ODA is comprised of several schemes and can be classified in several ways. One is the determination of ODA as a grant or a loan, depending on whether the initial disbursement is to be repaid. The ratio of loans, in terms of net-disbursement, was around 20% over the total of Japan's ODA in fiscal 2003. Using an international comparison, one distinguishing feature of Japan's ODA has been this higher ratio of loans.

Since ODA loans are to be repaid, distributions by region and sector are different from those of other aid measures such as grant aid, which is not to be repaid. By region, it is shown in Fig. 1 that the ratio of loans to Asia is very high compared with other regions. In contrast, the ratio of grant aid to Africa is strikingly high and that to Asia is relatively low. ODA loans are mainly provided to relatively higher-income developing countries. Grants are primarily intended to aid lesser developing countries with lower living standards.

Moreover, destinations of Japan's ODA loans concentrate to several Asian countries. According to MoFA (2004), the largest four recipients — India, Indonesia, China and Vietnam — shared more than 70% in total in 2003. While, in terms of the cumulated amount of ODA loans at the end of fiscal

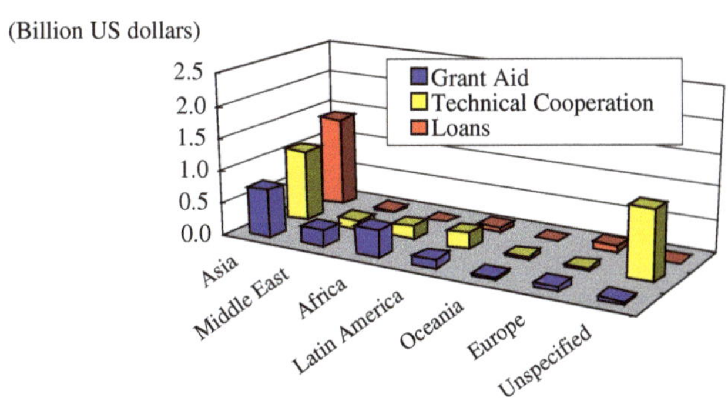

Fig. 1. Geographical Distribution of Japan's ODA (2003). *Source: Japan's Official Development Assistance 2004,* Ministry of Foreign Affairs

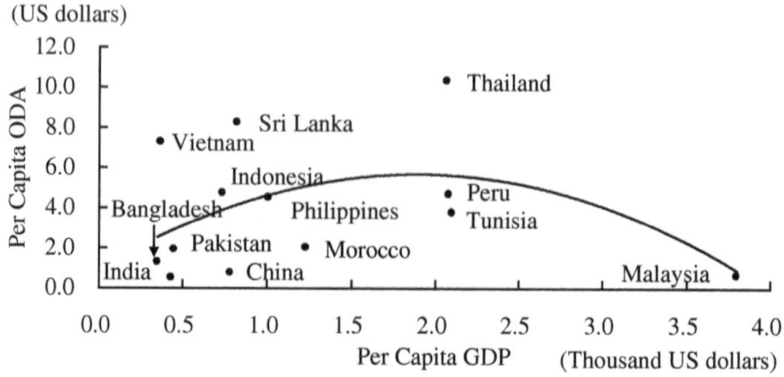

Fig. 2. Relative Level of ODA. *Source: Japan's Official Development Assistance*, Ministry of Foreign Affairs

2003, Indonesia is the top recipient receiving 3.8 trillion yen on the Exchange of Note basis. This is followed by China (3.0 trillion yen), India (2.2 trillion yen), the Philippines (2.0 trillion yen) and Thailand (2.0 trillion yen).

By sector, the ratio of ODA loans is high for economic infrastructure. This includes energy and transportation infrastructures, i.e. the building of roads, railways, bridges, and ports. The ratio of ODA loans for social infrastructure, however, is low. Moreover, grant aid has been allocated mainly to those sectors with low economic profitability. Those are education, health, and sanitation in the social infrastructure sector and agriculture in the production sector.

As shown in Fig. 2, the current level of ODA distributes widely around a theoretical convex curve,[d] it is expected that the relative size of aid will increase to a certain level according to economic development, which is measured by per capita GDP, but will decrease as the economy "graduates" from receiving aid. Several reasons for the variation in per capita ODA levels among countries in light of their stage of economic development can be pointed out. The excess of ODA in Sri Lanka and shortage of it in China and India in this regard may be a reflection of the fact that population is not a significant indicator for the size of ODA. The appropriate amount of ODA to each country may vary when seen in terms of total values or scaled by a certain macro indicator such as population. On the other hand, the lower levels of ODA in Morocco and Tunisia may be attributed to the geographical bias of Japan's ODA going largely to neighboring Asian economies.

[d]The curve is drawn for selected countries of so called "annual consultation countries" for ODA loans. The figures for per capita ODA and GDP are averages of the four years 1997–2000. The convex shape is not always derived; it depends on the choice of country and period.

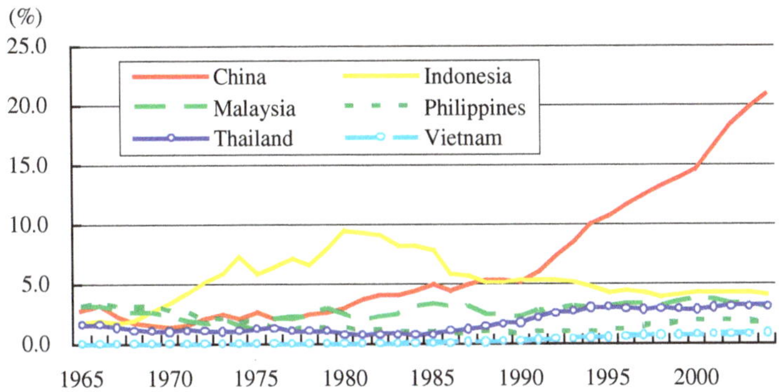

Fig. 3. Sources of Japan's Imports. *Source: Trade Statistics*, Ministry of Finance

Earlier studies that focused on identifying the factors deciding the distribution of Japan's ODA among the countries[e] found a certain correlation between the amount of ODA and economic factors such as population, income level, and trade, but at the same time attributed more or less importance to social and political factors and geographical bias. There may be a good reason why such an argument is made, since Japan's ODA has been said to be a "tool" or even a "weapon" in foreign affairs and diplomatic policy. It is not necessarily decided by economic factors alone. Econometric studies in this field are beyond the scope of this paper.

2.2. *Japanese Trade and Investment in Asia*

The Asian economies, including the Asian NIEs, ASEAN and China, have been the most dynamic part of the world economy during the last decade. One typical feature in the development of Asian economies is that the higher economic growth in the region has been associated with the deepening of economic interdependence within the region. This feature may also be applied to Japan. Long-term trends in the share of selected Asian countries in the sources of Japanese imports are shown in Fig. 3. Asian countries in total are becoming much more significant partners of Japanese trade.

To be more specific, several key structural changes are pointed out. First, what is striking is the rapid growth in both exports to and imports from China. The share of Japanese trade with China exceeded a tenth at the end of 1990s. Second, on the other hand, one distinguishing feature in view of

---

[e]See, for example, Shimomura *et al.* (1999).

the relative position among countries is a larger drop in the share of Japanese imports from Indonesia. This would be a reflection of the structural changes in Japanese imports, in which the share of oils and raw commodities has declined substantially since the oil crises in the 1970s. Indonesia is no longer a special partner of Japanese trade as far as this figure of total share is concerned.

The developments of Japanese capital outflows to selected Asian countries are shown in Fig. 4. Among others, trends in outward FDI and ODA loans[f] are compared.[g] Japanese FDI flows into these Asian countries once peaked at around the time of the 1997 Asian crisis. On the other hand, the amount of ODA loans corresponds to that of FDI in China, the Philippines, and Thailand at the end of the 1990s. Moreover, ODA loans have surpassed FDI in Vietnam. However, the absolute volume of ODA loans in these five countries is in a relatively narrow range, between 50 to 100 billion yen. It should be pointed out that ODA loans have played an important role of offsetting the declining trends in private capital inflows into these Asian countries.[h]

3. Framework of CGE Model Simulations

To analyze the impact of Japanese economic cooperation measures, the Global Trade Analysis Project (GTAP)[i] model is employed for model simulations. In this chapter, an outline of the fundamental structure of the model is presented and simulation designs, including the assumptions of the experiments, are discussed.

3.1. *Past Assessments of Aid and Trade*

The publication *Assessing Aid* (World Bank, 1998) is "intended to bring the results of World Bank research on development policy issues to take stock of what is known and is not known". The two key messages concerning the effectiveness of aid in promoting growth and reducing poverty are "aid works in a

---

[f] The values in the figure are on a gross-disbursement basis.

[g] These two share one common trait: they are spent largely on long-term physical investment, rather than on speculative investment that can be withdrawn quickly.

[h] FDI flows to China from the other countries remained large, amounting to around 40 to 50 billion US dollars in total including those from Japan at the end of the 1990s, according to UNCTAD (2004). Japan's share in FDI flows to China is relatively low compared with that in other countries.

[i] See Hertel (1997) for details of the GTAP model.

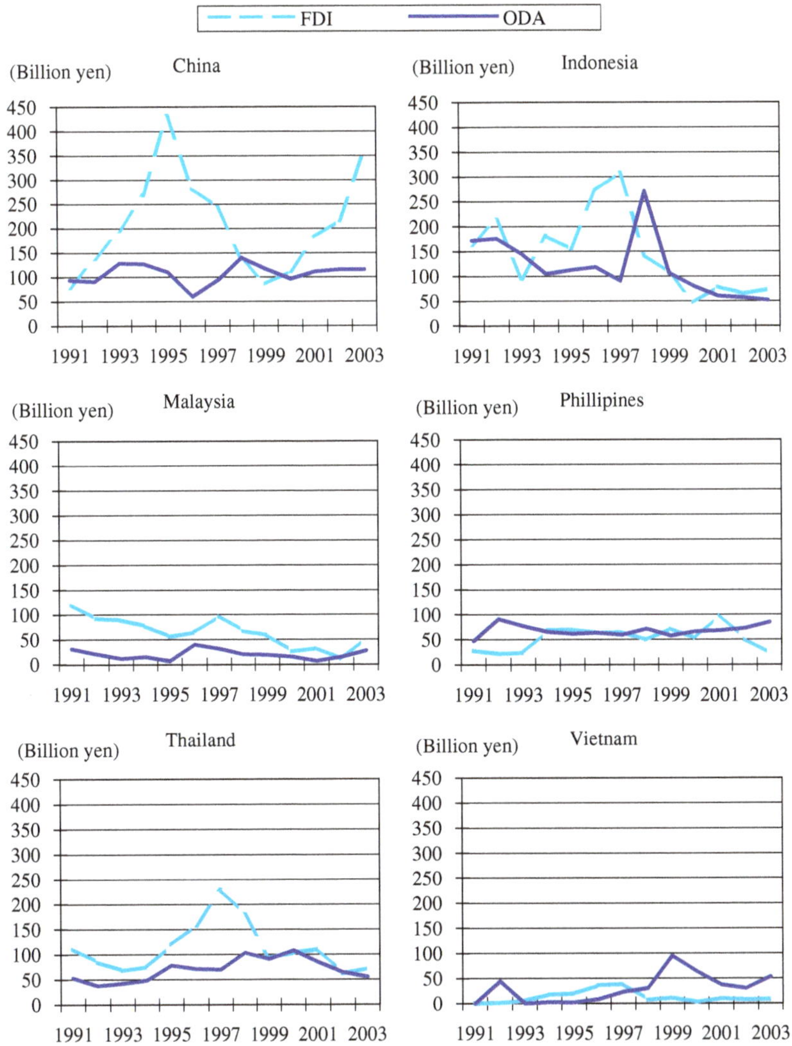

Fig. 4. Trends in Flows of FDI and ODA Loans. *Source: Ministry of Finance Statistics Monthly*, Ministry of Finance; *ODA Loan Report*, Japan Bank for International Cooperation

good policy environment" and "assistance must be targeted more effectively to low-income countries with sound economic management". As far as quantitative assessment is concerned, it states, according to cross-country studies, that under the good-management environments, "1% of GDP in assistance translates to a sustainable increase in growth of 0.5 percentage points of GDP", while it "reduces poverty by 1%".

However, these conclusions have been re-examined. Hansen and Tarp (2000), who address the aid-growth literature, reached rather different conclusions from those presented in *Assessing Aid*. It is pointed out that a coherent and positive picture of the aid-growth linkage emerges, even in countries hampered by an unfavorable policy environment. It is demonstrated that much is still not known about the complex linkage between aid, policy, and growth.

In the areas of global trade policies, the focus has been on relations between developed countries and developing countries. Among others, Shoven and Whalley (1992), who analyze the impact of protectionism of developed countries on developing countries by the general equilibrium model of global trade, argue that the trade costs that developed countries impose on developing countries would be approximately equivalent to the values of annual aid flows. Therefore, it is pointed out that the effects of aid and trade on developing countries would offset one another.

Recently, poverty reduction is an increasingly important issue not just in terms of aid policies but also in conjunction with global trade liberalization. Most past studies that have analyzed the impact of trade liberalization on poverty have looked at average macroeconomic effects. However, it is misleading to judge from average effects, in light of the fact that poverty is not always reduced even under economic growth; therefore, improvements in living standards as measured by per capita income on average are not always a given. Hertel *et al.* (2002) show one departure that focuses on the impact of trade liberalization on households at the edge of poverty. It is expected that ambitious research will continue to push forward, addressing limitations mainly in data availability.

Acknowledging the current states of both policy concerns in aid and trade and developments of tools to empirically analyze those economic impacts, this paper will discuss the impact of Japanese economic cooperation measures by means of CGE model simulations. The recent Japanese policies in aid and trade are compared with an emphasis of relative efficiencies from the perspectives of economic welfare.

3.2. *GTAP Model*

A CGE model numerically simulates the general equilibrium structure of the economy. It is built on the Walrasian general equilibrium system, in which the central idea is that market demand equals supply for all commodities at a set of relative prices. Moreover, a CGE model has solid micro-foundations that are theoretically transparent. Functional forms are specified in an explicit manner, and interdependencies and feedback are incorporated. Therefore, the model provides a framework for assessing the effects of policy and structural changes on resource allocation by clarifying "who gains and who loses".

These characteristics differentiate it from the partial equilibrium model, which is not economy-wide, the macroeconomic model, which is not multi-sectoral, and the input–output model, in which agents do not respond to changes in prices. Moreover, the multi-country model is required to analyze international economic affairs such as trade and investment policies, which affect not just one but a number of economies.

The basic framework of the trade model is guided by the comparative advantage theory by Hecksher–Ohlin. However, the original theory of comparative advantage cannot explain such aspects as the two-way trade seen in actual trading behavior. This is because the theory makes no distinctions between the same goods from different areas of production. Therefore, the general equilibrium model introduces heterogeneity into the same goods according to their production areas, namely, imperfect substitutes of goods between home and abroad, the so-called Armington assumption,[j] and thus describes realistic trade developments as discussed below.

The GTAP model is a standard CGE model that depicts the behavior of households, governments, and global sectors across each economy in the world. It is composed of regional models, which are linked through international trade. Prices and quantities are simultaneously determined in factor markets and commodity markets by accounting relationships, by the equilibrium conditions specified by the behavior of economic agents, and by the structure of international trade. The model includes three main factors of production: labor, capital, and land. Labor and capital are used by all industries, but land is used only in agricultural sectors. Capital and intermediate inputs are traded, while labor and land are not traded between regions.

The GTAP model assumes that firms use a constant-returns-to-scale technology, and minimize the cost of inputs, given a level of output and technology. Firms are assumed to combine a bundle of intermediate inputs in fixed proportion with a bundle of primary factors. The demand for each intermediate input is also assumed to vary in fixed proportion with the level of output. That is, the production function in the GTAP model has the Leontief structure.

---

[j] See Armington (1969) for the description of the Armington assumption.

This production structure yields the demand equations for a bundle of primary factors and intermediate inputs. Within determining the demand for primary factors, the CES functional forms are assumed. The CES production function yields the demand equations for primary factors, and price of value-added in industry evaluated at firms. Firms purchase intermediate inputs, some of which are produced domestically, and some of which are imported. Domestic and imported intermediate inputs are substituted according to a constant elasticity of substitution. Similarly, a constant elasticity of substitution is assumed to capture the degree of substitutability between imports from different sources. The two level CES functional form yields the demand functions.

Regional household behavior is governed by an aggregate utility function specified over composite private consumption, composite government consumption, and savings. The other features of regional household utility function is the use of an index of current government expenditures to proxy the welfare derived from the government's provision of public goods and services to private household in the region. The share of each of private household expenditures, government expenditures and savings are constant in total income. Once the changes in real government spending has been determined, this spending is allocated across composite goods and aggregate demand for the composite is allocated between imports and domestic products under the assumption of constant elasticity of substitution. Private household demand has a non-homothetic nature. The allocation of private household expenditures across commodities is based on the constant difference of elasticity (CDE) expenditure functions.

The GTAP model introduces two global sectors. One is the global transportation sector, which provides the services that account for the difference between fob and cif values for commodities. The other is the global banking sector. The global banking sector intermediates between global savings and investment. It creates a composite investment goods, based on a portfolio of net regional investment, and offers this to regional households in order to satisfy their savings demand. Therefore, all savers face a common price for this saving commodity. A consistency check on the accounting relationships involves separately computing the supply of the composite investment goods and the demand for aggregate savings. If all other markets are in equilibrium, all firms earn zero profit, and all households are on their budget constrain, then global investment must equal global savings by virtue of Walras' Law.

The standard version of the GTAP model includes several key assumptions.[k] Among others, it must be noted that the amount of total labor — one primary factor of production — is fixed. This means that the model assumes full employment and no unemployment. The amount of total capital is also fixed in the standard GTAP model.

A common criticism has often been that a standard CGE model focuses evaluation of static efficiency improvements; therefore the dynamic effects among production, income, and savings and investment are not captured. In this paper, one dynamic aspect of capital formation is studied[l] in the model simulations by modifying the standard version of the GTAP model. The initial increase in income is assumed to increase savings (a fixed share of additional income is saved) and investment. The induced savings and investment (larger capital stock) in turn links to the production capacities and causes a further increase in income. On the other hand, the trade, therefore, current balance is endogenous. However, rates of return on capital are not equalized across the regions through anticipated international capital flows. The model simulations show the outcomes of medium-term adjustments rather than theoretical long-term equilibrium.

The GTAP database currently consists of 57 disaggregated sectors and 66 economies,[m] which are aggregated to the appropriate version for simulations. In this paper, as is shown in Table 1, economies are aggregated into 15 areas, and six areas are allocated to the larger six recipient countries: China, Indonesia, Malaysia, the Philippines, Thailand, and Vietnam, whose benefits from Japanese economic cooperation measures are analyzed in this paper.

---

[k]It must be noted that the outcomes of model simulations may vary according to these macroeconomic assumptions and closures. These variations are suggested not just in terms of magnitude but also in direction. See, for example, Kawasaki (1999) for a diagnostic analysis of such model sensitivities in case of simulations on the impact of trade liberalization.

[l]See Francois, McDonald and Nordstrom (1996) for the methodology to implement this mechanism into the GTAP model. They explore the interaction between trade policy and capital accumulation in the GTAP model. According to the growth theory, a medium-run growth or accumulation effect induces additional savings and investment, which yields more output. In general, a permanent shock to the GDP is translated into a shock to the steady state level of capital. The magnitude of this effect crucially depends on the assumed underlying saving behavior. Under the assumption of a fixed saving ratio, the change in steady states capital stock is proportionate to the change in the steady states level of GDP.

[m]This is the version 5 database, which was released in summer 2002. Although, whose base year is 1997.

Table 1. Regional and Sectoral Aggregation

Countries and Regions		Industries/Commodities	
Japan	Asian NIEs	AGR:	Agriculture, forestry and fisheries
China	Oceania	MFG:	Mining and Manufacturing
Indonesia	USA	EGW:	Electricity, Gas and Water
Malaysia	Canada	CNS:	Construction
Philippines	Latin America	T_T:	Trade and Transport
Thailand	Western Europe	CMN:	Communication
Vietnam	Rest of World	OSP:	Other Private Services
South Asia		PUB:	Public Services

Industries/commodities are aggregated to eight, following a classification in the sectors of ODA loans.

There are four types of behavior parameters in GTAP: elasticities of substitution (in both expenditures and production), transformation elasticities that determine the degree of mobility of primary factors across sectors, the flexibilities of regional investment allocation, and consumer demand elasticities. In this paper, three sets of elasticities of substitution are taken from the GTAP database and aggregated with weights of trade shares. It should be noted that these parameters are commonly applied to all regions in this paper.

The first set of elasticities is a set of parameters for the Armington assumption, which describes the ease of substitution between the domestic goods and the composite import, by commodity. Those Armington elasticities are 2.4 for primary, 2.8 for manufacturing, and 1.9 for services. The second Armington parameter determines the case of substitution among imports from different sources. This is equal to twice the value of the first one. The third set is for primary production factors of labor and capital. Those are 0.23 for primary, 1.16 for manufacturing, and 1.26 to 1.68 for services. The demand of primary sector for primary production factors is less sensitive to the price changes in production factors.

3.3. *Assumptions*

In this paper, two model simulations are carried out. One is on the impact of Japan's ODA capital flows[n] to the six Asian countries listed above. Another is that of unilateral trade liberalization of Japan for imports from those countries. The precise designs of these two experiments are discussed below.

[n]The impact of other schemes of Japan's economic cooperation measures such that grand and technological cooperation is not analyzed in the model simulations.

ODA loans. It is assumed that the entire amounts of Japan's ODA loans[o] are spent for the construction of infrastructures in the recipient countries,[p] which result in expansion of capital stocks.[q] On the other hand, it is assumed that capital formation is reduced in Japan by the corresponding amount of total flows of ODA loans to the six Asian countries compared with instances where this is not the case.

The annual size of such total amount of capital flows is calculated by a simple five- year average (1996 to 2000) of Japan's ODA loans to Asian countries in terms of gross-disbursement,[r] as shown in Fig. 4.[s] Sectoral disaggregation of these total ODA loans[t] is guided by the cumulated ODA loans by sector at the end of fiscal 2000. Exogenous shocks implemented in the model simulation are shown in Table 2.[u]

Trade liberalization. Instead of providing ODA loans, it is assumed that Japan will unilaterally eliminate protection on the import of goods from the six Asian countries. This means that Japanese import protection for the other economies remains unchanged. Moreover, import protection of the other countries, including the six Asian countries and not Japan, also remains unchanged. The magnitudes of such exogenous shocks on Japanese import prices are shown in Table 3, which are compared with the import protection in those six Asian countries that Japan faces.

---

[o]Those are total amounts for project loans. Those for commodity loans are not included.

[p]It is assumed that no part of Japan's ODA loans is tied to contract and procurement of Japanese goods and services. Transactions of goods and services among the regions are solved in the model without any constraints in this regard.

[q]There is no distinction in the model whether such capital inflows are private like FDI, or public like ODA loans. See Hermann (1996) for one methodology to evaluate FDI inflows in the GTAP model. The same methodology is employed in this paper to assess the impact of ODA capital inflows. It is assumed that the firms' usage price of capital is lowered to realize a certain amount of increase in sectoral capital.

[r]This amount corresponds to actual progress in the progress of projects. The net amount of Japan's capital flows is shown in terms of net-disbursement. Moreover, from the viewpoint of measuring the size of expenditures for economic cooperation, it may be noted that concessionaity is not taken in account in either gross or net disbursement.

[s]The annual average total amount of Japan's ODA loans to the six Asian countries accounts for around 0.26% of Japanese capital production.

[t]These figures are not published by the authorities.

[u]Therefore, these figures do not necessarily show the actual amount of Japan's ODA loans to the six Asian countries in 1996 to 2000 by sector. They are more likely the average of much longer trends from the beginning of Japan's ODA loans.

Table 2. ODA Capital Flows to Asian Countries (Average Percentage of Sectoral Capitals in 1996–2000)

	AGR	MFG	EGW	T_T	CMN	PUB	Total
China	0.27	0.02	3.26	1.03	0.43	1.11	0.31
Indonesia	0.39	0.29	28.85	1.46	3.64	1.58	1.11
Malaysia	0.07	0.11	10.11	0.23	0.32	3.22	0.38
Philippines	1.05	0.64	9.09	2.38	3.45	5.65	1.55
Thailand	1.12	0.09	3.99	1.45	4.02	3.51	0.65
Vietnam	0.00	0.19	137.78	22.61	68.29	29.14	4.05

Source: Author's calculations based on GTAP database Version 5 and *ODA Loan Report*, Japan Bank for International Cooperation

Table 3. Import Protection (%)

	Japanese Import			Japanese Export		
	Primary	Secondary	Average	Primary	Secondary	Average
China	33.2	8.0	8.6	11.3	15.6	15.2
Indonesia	14.2	5.6	5.5	11.1	9.9	9.6
Malaysia	2.7	2.0	1.9	40.0	8.5	8.4
Philippines	40.8	3.5	5.6	20.0	6.4	6.2
Thailand	22.8	14.9	13.4	33.3	17.3	16.8
Vietnam	19.7	12.0	11.5	0.0	19.0	17.5
World	42.1	6.8	7.0	12.2	7.0	6.1

Source: GTAP database Version 5

These shocks are derived from the protection data in the current GTAP database.[v] It is shown that Japanese import protection is still significantly high in the primary sectors compared with that in the manufacturing sectors. Moreover, variation in the import protection among the countries within the same sectors is also suggested.[w]

[v] The protection data in the GTAP database are expressed in the form of ad valorem equivalent, tariff, and non-tariff barriers. The best-quality data are those relating to tariffs. Non-tariff information is most complete in the cases of agriculture and textiles/apparel. Data for subsidies are also available distinguishing those for factor-based, intermediates, and ordinary output. However, the data are not comprehensive. Protection of the service sector is especially difficult to quantify and is mostly neglected in the current database.

[w] It may be noted that China's accession to WTO is not reflected in the current GTAP database.

4. Simulation Results

The main purpose of this paper is to compare the economic impacts of Japan's ODA loans to Asian countries with that of other Japanese external policy measures such as trade liberalization, while employing the same version of the economic model for simulation experiments. Before doing such comparison, however, the impacts of these two policy measures will be presented.

It must be noted that the estimated economic impact by the CGE model is not a forecast. As described in Dee *et al.* (1996), economic policy measures will be implemented over time and adjustments to those changes may take time. During the course of such adjustments, other economic changes will also take place. However, those changes, including economic growth and structural changes in trade and industries, are not taken into account in the current analysis. The model simulation shows the differences at a certain point in time between when economic cooperation measures were implemented and when they were not.

4.1. *Impact of Individual Measures*

ODA loans. The macroeconomic impact of capital formation in the six Asian countries by the inflows of Japan's ODA loans is summarized in Table 4. Investment and capital accumulation are key elements for economic growth. Capital inflows from abroad enable the recipient countries to invest more than domestic savings. Expansion of capital stock, and therefore production capacity, would raise the permanent level of real GDP compared instances in which this is not the case. This magnitude ranges from 0.1% in China to 1.6%

Table 4. Impact of Japan's ODA Loans (%)

	Real GDP	Export Volume	Import Volume	GDP Deflator	Trade Balance*	Utility
Japan	−0.10	−0.12	−0.01	0.03	−387	−0.07
China	0.12	0.14	0.05	−0.06	139	0.08
Indonesia	0.50	0.59	0.35	−0.22	67	0.41
Malaysia	0.20	0.19	0.16	−0.13	13	0.14
Philippines	0.71	0.90	0.54	−0.60	6	0.49
Thailand	0.49	0.34	0.20	−0.29	29	0.42
Vietnam	1.65	2.53	1.24	−0.69	28	0.99
World	0.00	0.02	0.02	−0.01	0	0.00

*Deviations in million US dollars

in Vietnam in terms of the rate of change. It is a sizable impact, however, and it must be admitted that the relative contribution of ODA capital flows to economic growth may be limited in light of the recent rapid economic growth (from 5% to 10%) in these countries.

Expansion of production capacity is expected to lower production prices.[x] In fact, the current simulation suggests that the GDP price index would decline by 0.1% to 0.7% in the six Asian recipient countries. Lower production prices would enhance the competitiveness of those countries in the international market. Export volumes would increase due to these price effects. Moreover, import volumes would be stimulated by the income effects according to the expansion of the economy on the one hand, while those could be mitigated by the same price effects on the other hand. The current simulation shows that both export and import volumes would increase but those rates of changes in exports would tend to be larger than those in imports.

One concern in the analysis of the FDI behavior and developments is whether FDI and trade can be substitutes or complements. The theoretical literature indicates that these depend on the assumptions. In the empirical works, earlier general equilibrium modeling studies of FDI[y] have generally concluded that FDI and trade are likely to be complements at the economy-wide level. The current simulation outcomes are in line with these studies that show capital inflows by means of the Japan's ODA loans in the Asian countries would create rather than destroy trade. However, the current framework of a CGE model does not explicitly incorporate the behavior of FDI[z] and other capital movements. Therefore, the relationship between trade and investment is an issue to be further elaborated on in the future.

As far as the efficiency of resource allocation is concerned, capital inflows raise the relative value of labor in the host countries, while a relative value of capital would decline. This would result in increases in wages and therefore a surplus in workers. On the other hand, if capital moves from capital-rich countries to capital-poor countries, the investor country gains a larger return on the capital and enjoys surpluses. It is expected that international capital movements benefit both the investor and host countries by these efficiency effects.

---

[x]In general equilibrium model, only relative prices are important. The price of any factor endowments or goods in the model may be selected as a numéraire. All other prices are shown relative to the numéraire. In the current model simulations, a price index for the average price of capital goods supplied in an each region is chosen as a numéraire.

[y]See, for example, Petri (1997) and Dee and Hanslow (2000).

[z]See Hanslow *et al.* (2000) for the recent developments of a CGE model with FDI.

The overall impact on economic welfare may also vary according to the terms of trade effect. The six Asian recipient countries would generally face deterioration of the terms of trade due to lower prices in the domestic market. In addition to the static impact of efficiency effects and terms of trade effects, the dynamic impact of capital formation may also be a concern.[aa] In fact, welfare gains in the recipient countries are largely explained by capital formation rather than static efficiency and terms of trade effects. The rate of change in utility improvements ranges from 0.1% to 1.0%, which is relatively small compared with those changes in real GDP.

It is not surprising that those welfare gains may vary according to the sectors that ODA loans go into. As concerns welfare changes in recipient countries, which are measured by Equivalent Variation, capital formation in the production and energy sectors tends to show larger gains. Moreover, the impact of capital formation in communication and public services is generally smaller. These outcomes are in line with the expectation that those sectors that gain more from additional investment are economically profitable. From the viewpoint of economic development of the developing countries on average, it may be efficient to concentrate capital formation in those sectors. However, there must be other key concerns, such as poverty reduction, in view of a balanced development in the developing countries.

Moreover, sectoral differences in the efficiency of capital formation are clearly shown when those welfare gains in the world economy as a whole are looked at. Including the spillover effects outside the recipient countries, although those are not the primal concerns of the economic cooperation measures, manufacturing, and trade and transportation are the two distinguishing sectors in which capital formation in those sectors bring about significant economy-wide benefits. The larger impact arising from the capital formation in trade and transportation sector may partly be a reflection of the feature of the model, which is the general equilibrium model of global trade, in which trade linkages among the regions are one of the aspects highlighted.

From the viewpoint of efficient allocation of capital, it may also be pointed out that capital inflows to developing countries in an unspecified manner — as opposed to limiting those directions to certain sectors — would be much

---

[aa]In the current framework model, one important dynamic effect of capital accumulation is already incorporated, as discussed above. However, other dynamic effects, such that through a rise in productivity by, among others, technology transfer, technology diffusion, and promotion of competition are not taken in account.

more beneficial. This is consistent with the expectation that more efficient resource allocation would result in higher economic welfare.

The donor economy of Japan would lose rather than gain both in terms of real GDP and utility. This is primarily due to less capital formation according to the outflows of Japan's ODA capital. However, it must be noted that the income gains arising from investment abroad are not taken into account entirely in the current framework of model simulations. Including such income effects — which may not necessarily be large in the case of ODA loans compared with commercial loans — the negative impact on the Japanese economy could be limited to some extent.

Trade liberalization. According to the conventional simulations by a CGE model of global trade, trade liberalization measures including tariff reductions would stimulate trade by lowering prices on tradable goods. This would result in increases in national output of exporting countries, while increasing access to the markets of trading partners. On the other hand, domestic production resources — land, capital, labor, and intermediate inputs — would be used more efficiently in importing countries in particular, when domestic distortions, including those due to trade barriers, are reduced. These combined effects — one from foreign markets and the other from the domestic market — are expected to result in the expansion of production and an increase in income and welfare.

The macroeconomic impact of import liberalization in Japan from the six Asian countries is summarized in Table 5. Although trade volumes for both exports and imports would generally be stimulated by a sizable amount,[ab] increases in real GDP could be relatively limited. This is not surprising because production in different sectors competes for a limited supply of labor, capital, and land. An expansion of one sector would be accompanied by a contraction of another sector, except when the expansion is the result of significant resource accumulation or technological improvements.[ac]

In comparison with macroeconomic gains in real GDP, those gains measured in utility would be significantly larger in all six Asian countries. This is

[ab]Exports of the Philippines would exceptionally decrease. This is because of higher inflation mainly induced by significant expansion in Japanese demand for imports of agricultural products from the Philippines.

[ac]As it is noted in GATT (1994), a certain amount of increase in exports is not equivalent to the same amount of increase in production. To produce additional exports, resources that could otherwise have been used to produce goods and services for domestic residents must be used. The true net production gain is the difference between the increases in exports and the value of those "foregone" domestic goods and services.

Table 5. Impact of Japan's Import Liberalization (%)

	Real GDP	Export Volume	Import Volume	GDP Deflator	Trade Balance*	Utility
Japan	0.06	2.85	2.87	−0.45	−790	−0.11
China	0.08	1.82	2.73	1.51	1,514	0.78
Indonesia	0.06	0.87	1.51	1.10	168	0.49
Malaysia	0.05	0.10	0.16	0.16	33	0.16
Philippines	0.00	−0.36	0.34	1.10	−72	0.43
Thailand	0.22	2.21	3.52	2.29	617	1.56
Vietnam	0.21	1.80	3.32	4.23	−20	1.86
World	0.04	0.30	0.30	−0.03	0	0.03

*Deviations in million US dollars

mainly due to terms of trade effects. Asian countries would gain larger benefits in terms of changes in Equivalent Variations, and therefore utilities, from unilateral import liberalization in Japan from those countries. It is indicated that terms of trade effects are much more significant compared with the efficiency effects of resource allocation discussed above.

One key issue in north-south trade has been these terms of trade effects on developing countries. There have been several interpretations and empirical studies concerning the reason why the persistent deterioration of terms of trade has been observed in the developing economies. One is to look at differences in the income elasticity of imports between north and south.[ad] Another is to attribute the higher growth in the south compared with the north. Moreover, trade policies of developed economies, which deteriorate the terms of trade in developing economies, have also been discussed on a number of occasions.

The current model simulations support that the trade protection in the developed countries such as Japan has been harmful for the economic welfare of developing countries such as neighboring Asian countries. From the perspective of development of Asian countries, it is also indicated that they could enjoy much more terms of trade gains from unilateral import liberalization in Japan without liberalizing their own markets, compared with those from reciprocal trade liberalization both in Japan and Asian countries. However, it

[ad]This is supported by the argument that export goods of the south are "necessities" whose income elasticity of imports in the north are low, while export goods of the north are "luxuries" whose income elasticity of imports in the south are high.

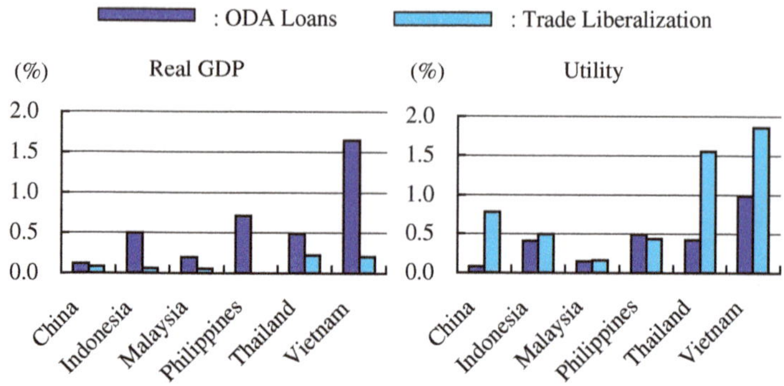

Fig. 5. Comparison of Macroeconomic Gains

must be noted that partial rather than broadly based trade liberalization may have the opposite effects generating significant economic losses.[ae]

The impact of unilateral Japanese import liberalization on the Japanese economy is mixed. Japanese trade, including both imports and exports, would expand. Japanese prices would drop. These would result in increases in real GDP. These are entirely opposite outcomes compared with those according to Japan's ODA capital outflows. However, utility may still be lost because of terms of trade effects, which in turn significantly benefit Asian countries.

4.2. *Benefits and Costs of Aid and Trade*

Macroeconomic benefits of Japan's ODA loans and Japanese import liberalization in the six Asian countries are compared in Fig. 5. It may be argued that entire Japanese import liberalization takes place once and for all, while the disbursement of Japan's ODA loans continue over time. However, it may also be pointed out that both capital expenditures for ODA loans and tariff payment for trade protection are viewed as burdens by the Japanese taxpayers,[af] at a macro level. The impact of annual expenditures for ODA loans is compared with that of tariff payment every year.

As far as ODA loans are used for capital formation, sizable impacts on economic growth are expected. Estimating the impact of the actual amount

---

[ae]See Dee, Hardin and Schule (1998), who examined selected Early Voluntary Sectoral Liberalization (EVSL) by the APEC member economies.

[af]As far as the fiscal balance of Japanese public sector is concerned, capital outflows are viewed as expenditures, while import protection, including custom tariffs, are viewed as revenue. They offset one another, when considering the impact on public balances.

of ODA capital flows to Asian countries, those on real GDP are shown to be significantly larger compared with the potential impact of Japanese import liberalization from those countries. In contrast, as far as improvements in economic welfare are concerned, trade liberalization is shown to be much more beneficial to most Asian countries. This is a reflection of composition of economic gains from two alternative economic cooperation measures. Expansion in production capacities is a primary factor of the benefits from ODA loans. Moreover, terms of trade gains are a crucial source of economic benefits in unilateral — and therefore partial — trade liberalization.

It should be pointed out that capital formation through ODA loans is effective for economic growth, while trade liberalization is efficient in welfare improvements. However, it does not necessarily mean that welfare improvements on average reduce poverty, as discussed above. In any event, two policy measures may more likely be complements rather than substitute for the development of developing countries.

In addition, it should be noted that reallocation of resources to more productive uses usually involves some adjustment costs. Implementation of certain policy measures in general would result in the displacing of employment across industries within the economies. Employment in obsolete industries declines, harming workers in those industries. In a rapidly changing economy, some of these workers may find themselves without the skills required for the new jobs being created.

It is shown from the estimated impacts on the structure of sectoral production that capital formation by Japan's ODA loans would result in increases in sectoral production without any exception in the six Asian countries. Furthermore, the relative magnitudes of increases in production by the sectors may largely be determined by the sectoral distribution of ODA loans.

In contrast, Japanese import liberalization may result in a realignment of regional production. In principle, it would be in accordance with comparative advantage of the regions. According to conventional simulations by a CGE model of global trade, developing and transition economies are expected to expand production and exports of labor-intensive manufactured products as a result of broadly based trade liberalization measures.

However, such an impact may more likely be determined by degree of import liberalization by the sectors in the case of partial trade liberalization. The current simulations do not give such developments by the sufficiently disaggregated sectors. It is suggested that China and the Philippines would gain in primary sectors but lose in manufacturing sectors as a whole. On the other hand, contractions in several tertiary industries are suggested in some countries due to reallocation of production resources within the countries.

On the other hand, Japanese people may be concerned about the total amounts of ODA loans and trade protection in terms of the appropriate size of the government. In addition, sectoral variations in those payments and protections may be a much more serious concern from the viewpoint of distribution effects. ODA outflows are thought to be beneficial to certain exporting industries, while import protection could support non-tradable sheltered industries.

5. Conclusions and Recommendations

The main objective of this paper was to overview the developments of Japan's ODA and assess their economic impacts on Asian countries. It has attempted to provide quantitative evaluation of Japanese economic cooperation measures by means of economic model simulations. The benefits of two alternative measures — one from capital formation by Japan's ODA loans and the other from import liberalization in the Japanese market — are compared in view of the relative efficiencies of the economic policy measures.

The appropriate amount of ODA to each country may vary when seen in terms of total value or scaled by a certain macro indicator such as population. In addition, trends in Japan's ODA over time do not necessarily reflect the structural changes in Japanese trade and investment in Asian economies. In this regard, Japan's ODA to China is not necessarily huge, while that to Indonesia is still over-represented relative to the other countries.

As far as macroeconomic gains of Japanese economic cooperation measures in recipient countries are concerned, capital formation through ODA loans is effective for economic growth, while trade liberalization is efficient in welfare improvements. The two policy measures may more likely be complements rather than substitutes for the development of developing countries. Moreover, it must be noted that sectoral effects would be significantly different between the two policy measures of aid and trade both on the recipient and donor countries. A better policy mix may be sought in view of these distribution effects by sector, in addition to the appropriate size of policy measures in total.

Japan's ODA has been called a "tool" of diplomatic policy. However, the geographical and sectoral distribution of aid need to be reviewed, first, in views of the effectiveness and efficiency of aid and trade for economic development, and second, in light of economic trends such as trade and investment.

References

Armington PS, 1969. "A theory of demand for products distinguished by place of production." International Monetary Fund Staff Paper.

Dee P, Geisler C, and Watts G, 1996. "The impact of APEC's free trade commitment." Staff Information Paper, AGPS, Canberra.

Dee P, and Hanslow K, 2000. "Multilateral liberalization of services trade." Productivity Commission Staff Paper, AusInfo, Canberra.

Dee P, Hardin A, and Schule M, 1998. "APEC early voluntary sectoral liberalization." Productivity Commission Staff Research Paper, AusInfo, Canberra.

Francois JF, McDonals BJ, and Nordstrom H, 1996. "Liberalization and capital accumulation in the GTAP model." GTAP Technical Paper No. 7.

GATT, 1994. *The Results of the Uruguay Round of Multilateral Trade Negotiations.* General Agreement on Tariffs and Trade.

Hansen H, and Tarp F, 2000. "Aid effectiveness disputed." *J. Int. Dev.* **12**(3).

Hanslow K, Phamduc T, and Verikios G, 2000. "The structure of the FTAP model." Research Memorandum MC-58, Productivity Commission, Canberra.

Hermann L, 1996. "Foreign direct investment and technology transfer in transition economies: an application of the GTAP model." Humboldt-Universitat Zu Berlin Working Paper Nr. 28.

Hertel TW, 1997. *Global Trade Analysis: Modeling and Applications.* Cambridge University Press: Cambridge.

Hertel TW, Preckel PV, Cranfield JAL, and Ivanic M, 2002. "Poverty impacts of multilateral trade liberalization." Paper presented at the fifth Conference on Global Economic Analysis, Taipei.

Kawasaki K, 1999. *Applications of the Computable General Equilibrium Model: Simulation Analysis on Trade Liberalization and Regulatory Reform.* Nihonhyoronsya: Tokyo (in Japanese).

MoFA, 2004. *Japan's official development assistance 2004.* Ministry of Foreign Affairs: Tokyo.

OECD, 2004. *2003 DAC Chair's Report.* Organization for Economic Cooperation and Development: Paris.

Petri PA, 1997. "Foreign direct investment in a computable general equilibrium framework." Paper prepared for the conference, Making APEC Work: Economic Challenges and Policy Alternatives, 13–14 March, Keio University: Tokyo.

Shimomura Y, Nakagawa J, and Saito J, 1999. *Political Economy of the ODA Charter.* Yuhikaku: Tokyo (in Japanese).

Shoven JB, and Whalley J, 1992. *Applying General Equilibrium.* Cambridge University Press: Cambridge.

UNCTAD, 2004. *The World Investment Report 2004: TNCs and Export Competitiveness.* United Nations: New York and Geneva.

World Bank, 1998. *Assessing Aid: What Works, What Doesn't and Why.* World Bank: Washington DC.

Chapter 17

Regional Economic Integration and Its Impacts on Growth, Poverty and Income Distribution: The Case of Vietnam*

TIEN DUNG NGUYEN

National Advanced Training Institute, Hanoi, Vietnam

MITSUO EZAKI

Graduate School of International Development, Nagoya University, Nagoya, Japan

Trade liberalization and regional economic integration have recently accelerated in East Asia, where several free trade areas have been established or are under negotiation. After acquiring ASEAN membership in 1995, Vietnam has signed a bilateral trade package with the United States and participated in the China–ASEAN free trade area. This paper attempts to analyze impacts on Vietnam of ongoing regional economic integration, focussing on growth, poverty reductions and income distribution. For this purpose, we have constructed a global linked Computable General Equilibrium (CGE) model and made use of GTAP database version 6.0 and Vietnam's living standards surveys. The simulation analysis shows that regional economic integration generally has positive impacts; and it both enhances welfare and improves income distribution for Vietnam. Household income and consumption increase, and poor and rural household groups benefit more than urban high income groups.

*This chapter was originally published in *Review of Urban and Regional Development Studies*, Vol. 17, No. 3, November 2005, and is reprinted here with minor modifications upon the permission from the publisher.

1. Introduction

Twenty years have passed since Vietnam began profound social and economic reforms, which have transformed Vietnam from a centrally planned economy to a market one. Since the beginning days of the economic reforms, trade reforms and the open-door policies have constituted an integral part of overall economic reforms. The restrictions and limitations on trade activities have been steadily and progressively removed, and Vietnam has successfully developed trade and investment relations with countries in Asia, Europe and North America. Trade reforms have contributed to the rapid growth of exports and the overall economic growth.

Economic integration with the regional and global economy has recently accelerated in Vietnam. Vietnam became a member of ASEAN in 1995, joined APEC in 1998, while negotiating for WTO membership. Vietnam has also concluded a bilateral trade agreement with the United States in 2000, and has participated in the China–ASEAN free trade area. Given the national target of sustained growth and poverty alleviation, Vietnamese policy makers are greatly concerned about the possible consequences of these liberalization movements on growth, poverty and income distribution.

This paper attempts to examine the impacts of ongoing regional economic integration on Vietnam's economy using a global Computable General Equilibrium (CGE) model. The discussion will continue in Section 2 analyzing the trade liberalization and regional economic integration in Vietnam. It is followed by Section 3 examining poverty and income-distribution issues in Vietnam. The structure of the global CGE model is presented in Section 4, and simulation scenarios are performed and discussed in Section 5. Policy implications are drawn and some concluding remarks are given in Section 6.

2. Trade Liberalization in Vietnam

Since the late 1980s, Vietnam's trade reforms have progressed steadily, consisting of the creation and amendment of a system of taxation of imports and exports, the gradual removal of non-tariff barriers and progressive deregulation of trade regimes. The entry to trading activities has been liberalized for both state-owned enterprises and private firms. For the majority of goods, businesses from all economic sectors are currently allowed to conduct export or import activities without the need of acquiring approval or licenses from the authorities. The deregulation of trading rights has increased the competitiveness and efficiency of trading activities.[a]

In regards to the import regime, the tariff system has been simplified and rationalized, and tariff rates have been lowered. The average weighted tariff rate dropped from nearly 20% in the early 1990s to around 15% in the late 1990s (SRV, 1999). Together with tariff reductions, non-tariff barriers have been abolished or relaxed. Quantitative restrictions on imports have been removed for the majority of commodities, with the exception of petroleum products, sugar and some other strategic products. The surrender requirement and other currency control measures introduced in 1997 to cope with the East Asian crisis have been eliminated, and foreign-invested firms are no longer required to balance their foreign exchange account. The number of imports that are subject to the minimum valuation procedure has been reduced considerably.

With respect to exports, export duties and quotas have been removed for the majority of products. Only a small number of exports are being levied with export taxes mainly for the purpose of raising revenue, but the tax rates are low. With the exception of some products regulated due to environmental, health or security concerns, quotas are only imposed on the export of garment and textiles to the EU, the United Sates and Canada. These quotas are imposed by the importing countries, and are determined in the bilateral trade agreements between Vietnam and these countries. The export quotas on garment and textiles are to be removed by WTO members in 2005, as mandated by the Agreement on Textiles and Clothing (ATC). However, Vietnam has to acquire WTO membership before it could open the US and EU market for garment and textile products.

High tariff rates and non-tariff barriers are generally employed to protect consumer goods, while capital goods and production inputs are subject to low tariffs and very few non-tariff barriers. As a result, effective protection provided to many industries is higher than that offered by nominal protection. Several studies have shown that many industries, and consumer goods industries in particular, have enjoyed very high degrees of effective protection.[b] However, imports of some intermediate inputs being domestically produced

---

[a]Vietnam's trade regimes have been the subject in several studies, such as CIE (1998) and CIE (1999a). The non-tariff barriers that were present in Vietnam by 1999 are surveyed in detail in CIE (1999b) and McCarty (1999).

[b]See, for example, CIE (1998) and Fukase and Martin (1998) for the estimates of effective protection rates by industries.

such as cement, fertilizers, or steel, have been subject to very high tariffs. Protection through tariffs and non-tariff barriers is also provided to some so-called infant industries, such as automobile or petroleum products. Unlike the case of consumer goods industries, the protection of upstream industries raises the price of intermediate inputs and negatively affects downstream industries and export activities.[c]

Together with unilateral reform measures, Vietnam has made important commitments to trade liberalization under various bilateral and multilateral agreements. Vietnam became a member of ASEAN in 1995, joined APEC in 1998, while applying for the membership of the WTO. In 2000, Vietnam agreed on a landmark trade package with the United States. Together with other ASEAN members, Vietnam has participated in the recent formation of a free trade area between ASEAN and China. All these bilateral and multilateral agreements are being implemented, and are integral parts of Vietnam's trade reforms.

Under the ASEAN free trade area (AFTA), the member countries are obligated to reduce tariffs on intra-ASEAN trade to less than 5% by 2002. As a later member of ASEAN, Vietnam is allowed to fulfill its commitment to trade liberalization over a longer period. According to the Common Effective Preferential Tariff (CEPT) agreement, products with current tariff rates under 20% have tariffs reduced to 0–5% by the year 2003. For products with tariffs above 20%, rates are to be reduced to 0–5% by the year 2006. In addition to the tariff reductions, Vietnam is also obligated to remove quantitative restrictions and non-tariff barriers as soon as tariff reductions are carried out.[d] The implementation of CEPT began in 1996 but progressed slowly until 1999. Most products that were subject to early tariff cuts were not produced in Vietnam or already had tariff rates of less than 5% and were subject to very few non-tariff barriers. Since 2000, tariff reductions have been carried out for highly protected products and are expected to have a greater impact on the economy. When the tariff reduction under AFTA is completed by 2006, over 97% of Vietnam's tariff lines will have their tariffs reduced to less than 5%.

In November 2001, China and ASEAN agreed to establish a free trade area within ten years, in which tariffs and non-tariff barriers will be removed by 2010 for China and six old ASEAN members, and by 2015 for four new

[c]Fukase and Martin (1998) show that exports-oriented industries suffers negative effective protection as protection given to intermediate inputs raises the cost of production.

[d]See, for example, Forster (1998) and Thang (1999) for the detailed liberalization schedule under AFTA.

ASEAN members, namely Vietnam, Laos, Cambodia and Myanmar. The liberalization measures are planned to take place in 2005 and will be conducted on a reciprocal basis. The formation of this free trade area is expected to serve the interest of both sides with ASEAN members looking for new export opportunities in China's huge market and China seeking for natural-resource based inputs from ASEAN. The China–ASEAN free trade area is, however, one among many efforts made by East Asian countries to liberalize trade and investment regimes in the region. ASEAN is seeking other free trade areas with Japan, Korea, Australia and New Zealand. Meanwhile Japan has concluded two free trade agreements with Singapore and Mexico, and is negotiating with Korea and some ASEAN members. It can be said that all these efforts have been going into promoting a broader free trade area in the East Asian region.

The Asia-Pacific Economic Cooperation (APEC) grouping was established in 1989 with the objective of liberalizing and facilitating trade and investment. The goals of APEC, as defined in the APEC leaders Meeting in Bogor, Indonesia in November 1994, are to achieve free trade and investment for the region by 2010 for developed countries and 2020 for developing countries. As an APEC member, Vietnam has made commitments to unilateral trade liberalization, including free trade, liberalization of investment regimes and the opening of service sectors to foreign providers (SRV, 1999).

It is worth-while to make some notes about the geographical composition of Vietnam's trade, which has greatly changed over the last two decades, reflecting the dramatic changes in the international situation and the implementation of the country's open-door policies. Until the late 1980s, Vietnam traded mainly with the Soviet Union and the Eastern European countries. The collapse of the former Soviet Union interrupted the trading relations with these countries, and forced Vietnam to redirect trade toward Asian countries, which dominated Vietnam's trade in early 1990s. Since the mid 1990s, particularly after the Asian crisis led to a sharp contraction of export markets in the region, Vietnam has managed to expand trade toward Europe and North America.

Vietnam's trade with its ASEAN neighbors has been relatively small, and surprisingly, the share in total trade has been on decline despite the implementation of AFTA. In 2003, only 23.6% of imports were sourced from ASEAN, and 14.7% of total exports were shipped to ASEAN. Among ASEAN countries, Singapore is the largest trading partner, accounting for more than 50% of imports from ASEAN and around 30% of exports to ASEAN countries. As can be seen in Table 1, the decline in trade with ASEAN countries is largely caused by the fall in the bilateral trade between Vietnam and

Table 1. Trade Direction of Vietnam 1995–2003

	1995	2000	2001	2002	2003
A. Exports					
Total value (million dollars)	5448.9	14483.0	15029.0	16706.1	20176.0
Composition of exports (% of total)					
ASEAN	18.3	18.1	17.0	14.6	14.7
Of which Singapore	12.7	6.1	6.9	5.8	5.1
Other ASEAN countries	5.6	12.0	10.0	8.8	9.6
NIEs	17.1	9.8	10.2	9.7	8.0
Japan	26.8	17.8	16.7	14.6	14.4
China	6.6	10.6	9.4	9.1	8.7
EU	12.2	19.6	20.0	18.9	19.1
US	3.1	5.1	7.1	14.7	19.5
Others	15.9	19.0	19.6	18.4	15.7
B. Imports					
Total value (million dollars)	8155.4	15636.5	16218.0	19745.6	25226.9
Composition of imports (% of total)					
ASEAN	27.8	28.5	25.7	24.2	23.6
Of which Singapore	17.5	17.2	15.3	12.8	11.4
Other ASEAN countries	10.4	11.2	10.4	11.3	12.2
NIEs	31.6	27.1	27.3	28.4	25.9
Japan	11.2	14.7	13.5	12.7	11.9
China	4.0	9.0	9.9	10.9	12.4
EU	8.7	8.4	9.3	9.3	9.8
US	1.6	2.3	2.5	2.3	4.5
Others	15.0	10.1	11.8	12.2	11.9

Source: Vietnam's Statistical Yearbook, 2003 (GSO, 2004)

Singapore.[e] As for other ASEAN members, imports from these countries nearly doubled between 2000 and 2003 following the reduction in tariffs imposed on ASEAN exports. However, Vietnam seems to have not

[e]It should be noted that Singapore, like Hong Kong, has been acting as a sub-contractor for Vietnam's exports and imports. A significant proportion of trade with these two countries may have been re-exported to or re-imported from other countries. The fall in trade with Singapore, therefore may largely reflect the fact that Vietnam has become increasingly familiar with the international market and it can export or import goods without going through trading companies in Singapore or Hong Kong.

exploited the advantage of the tariff reductions in ASEAN trading partners, and exports of Vietnam to these markets increased only modestly during the same period.

North East Asian countries have been the major trading partners of Vietnam, which account for nearly one third of Vietnam's exports and a half of its imports. While trade with Japan and the East Asian new industrialized economies (NIEs) has been declining in importance, two-way trade with China has been on a steady and rapid increase since the mid 1990s. Both exports to and imports from China increased more than ten times during the last 10 years, and China has recently passed Japan to become Vietnam's largest import markets. Given the fact that the two economies are growing fast, bilateral trade between Vietnam and China is expected to continue on rapid rise in the foreseeable future. With the exception of Japan, Vietnam has usually suffered from large trade deficits with ASEAN and other East Asian countries. In the case of East Asian NIEs, large imports from these countries are mainly caused by the inflows of foreign direct investment. For China and some ASEAN countries, the large trade deficits reflect the lack of competitiveness of Vietnam's exports in these markets.[f]

Another interesting fact about Vietnam's trade direction is that the European Union and the United States of America have become increasingly important for Vietnam's exports. Trade with European countries increased rapidly during the latter half of the 1990s, when Vietnam managed to expand the market for its exports in response to the slowdown in trade with East Asia caused by the East Asian economic crisis. Until the signing of the bilateral trade agreement between Vietnam and the US in 2000, trade between two countries had been relatively small. The granting of the US's most favored nation status to Vietnam has opened the US market for Vietnam's exports, and the US now becomes Vietnam's largest export market. Combined together, exports to the US and the EU amounted to nearly $8 billion in 2003, or equivalent to 40% of Vietnam's total exports. These are also the major markets for exports of labor-intensive products such as agricultural products, wearing apparel, textiles and footwear. However, Vietnam's exports of textiles and wearing apparel to the US and the EU are expected to face more competition from China after the phase-out of the Multi-Fibre Agreement (MFA) in 2005.

[f]As an example, the textile and clothing industries are the major exporting industries in Vietnam, but they exports mainly low-quality products to the low end of markets. These industries even cannot compete with China's exports in the domestic markets without tariff protection.

3. Poverty and Income Distribution

When Vietnam started economic reforms 20 years ago, it was a very poor country with a per capita income of less than 200 $US. Most Vietnamese people then lived below the poverty line with the estimated poverty incidence of over 70%. The rapid economic growth over the last decade has not only increased the national income, but also sharply reduced the incidence of poverty. The percentage of poor people fell sharply to 50% in 1993, 37% in 1998 and 15% in 2002 (GSO, 2000, 2003). The absolute poverty incidence based on the food poverty line also fell from 25% to less than 10% between 1993 and 2002.

Despite the impressive achievement in poverty alleviation, the poverty incidence is unevenly distributed among regions. Most of poor people, around 90%, are living in rural areas, while the remaining 10% are urban dwellers (World Bank, 1999). This implies that the poverty in rural areas is more serious than the average national-wide level. The poverty incidence is also found very high in mountainous and remote regions, particularly in Northern Uplands and Central Highland, which are the poorest regions of Vietnam with relatively slow economic growth. This indicates that focussing on rural development and allocating more resources toward poor regions are essential for further poverty reductions in Vietnam.

There are several reasons that can explain the rapid reduction in poverty. Firstly, agriculture grew quite fast and contributed to the income increase in rural areas where the majority of the poor live. The growth of agriculture and agricultural exports also helped Vietnam to stabilize the economy during the late 1980s. Secondly, the agricultural terms of trade changed in favour of agriculture and rural areas. Over the last decade the food prices increased faster than non-food prices largely thanks to the liberalization of the agricultural product market and the increase in export prices. As a result, rural income rose quite fast and brought benefits to the rural poor. Finally, as pointed out by World Bank (1999), a large proportion of population initially lived just below the poverty line. The increase in income, even a small increase, could lift them up above the line. This also means, however, that those people are vulnerable to the change in economic environment, and they could easily fall back below the poverty line.

Vietnam has remained a relatively equitable country by international standards, and this is attributable to the relatively equal income distribution in rural areas. However, inequality has increased slightly during the years of rapid economic growth. Gini coefficient increased from 0.33 to 0.35 between 1993 and 1998, and the income ratio between the poorest and the richest quintiles rose from 4.9 to 5.5 during this period (Kinh *et al.*, 2001). The increased inequality is largely due to the widening income gap between rural and urban areas that, as indicated by World Bank (1999), accounted for 96% of total rise in equality. The urban economy based largely on manufactures and services grew as twice as much the rural economy, and the ratio of urban to rural income rose from 1.8 in 1993 to 2.2 in 1998.

Table 2 provides a profile of income distribution with respect to income, expenditure and employment. The table is processed using the latest household survey conducted by Vietnam's General Statistical Office in 2002 (VLSS 2002). The survey data covering 30000 households is aggregated into 20 household groups. These households are classified based on the level of expenditure and consist of 10 urban groups and 10 rural groups. As can be seen in Table 2, there are larger income gaps among household groups. Income per capita of the richest urban group is almost 8 times higher than that of the urban poorest, while the figure for rural areas is 6.4, suggesting that inequality is higher in urban areas than in rural areas. The share of the poorest decile group in total income is only 3.4%, while the richest decile accounts for nearly 27% of total income.

Poor households tend to rely more on agriculture and informal services, partly reflecting their lack of physical capital and the low level of educational attainment. The urban lowest income group spends nearly 70% of their working time on agriculture, whereas the figure for the rural lowest income group is 88%. Low-income groups are also involved more in trade and other low-productivity services in the informal sector, and by contrast, higher income groups tend to work more in industries and formal services.[g] From the survey data, we also find that poor households are involved more in small-scale, labor-intensive manufactures, while the rich usually have jobs in capital-intensive and highly protected manufactures. Due to the differences in skills and the characteristics of jobs, the average wage rates of poor groups are considerably low compared to high income groups. For example, the average wage rate of the rural lowest income group is around 40% of the national average wage, and the figure for the urban lowest income group is only 30%. The difference in the composition of jobs also results in the different compositions of income between the rich and the poor. Income of poor households largely originates from agriculture, labor-intensive industries and informal services, while the rich have income sources mainly from capital-intensive industries and formal

[g] The formal sector consists of the state sectors and foreign-invested sector, while the rest of the economy can be considered as informal.

Table 2. Income Distribution in Vietnam

	Unit	Total	Urban			Rural		
			Total	Lowest Decile Group	Highest Decile Group	Total	Lowest Decile Group	Highest Decile Group
Average household income	1000 VND	20972	33444.3	9009.418	53328.7	17050.06	8336.474	36319.45
Share of household income	%	100.0	38.1	0.2	20.9	61.9	3.2	5.9
Composition of income by sources	%	100.0	100.0	100.0	100.0	100.0	100.0	100.0
Self-employed agriculture	%	31.4	6.9	44.4	2.7	46.5	66.6	25.5
Self-employed non-agricultural	%	21.7	30.6	25.5	30.3	16.2	5.2	26.4
Wage income	%	30.5	42.3	20.0	42.8	23.2	19.8	21.0
Transfers	%	16.4	20.2	10.1	24.2	14.1	8.4	27.2
Annual income per capita	1000 VND	4510.3	7468.9	1650.6	12905.7	3624.6	1520.1	9790.8
Income ratio	Unit	1.0	1.7	0.4	2.9	0.8	0.3	2.2
Annual expenditure per capita	1000 VND	3414.1	5829.6	1120.2	10579.9	2691.1	1100.3	9265.3
Expenditure ratio	Unit	1.0	1.7	0.3	3.1	0.8	0.3	2.7

Table 2. (*Continued*)

	Unit	Total	Urban			Rural		
			Total	Lowest Decile Group	Highest Decile Group	Total	Lowest Decile Group	Highest Decile Group
Annual working hours (per workers)	Hours	1583.2	2034.7	1340.9	2276.8	1474.6	1404.6	1746.8
Average wage rate (per hours)	VND	3840.9	5537.0	1156.6	7809.9	2854.5	1613.2	5182.4
Wage ratio	Unit	1.0	1.4	0.3	2.0	0.7	0.4	1.3
Composition of employment by economic sectors	%	100.0	100.0	100.0	100.0	100.0	100.0	100.0
Formal	%	14.8	29.5	6.1	38.8	10.0	2.7	24.8
Informal	%	85.2	70.5	93.9	61.2	90.0	97.3	75.2
Composition of employment by industry	%	100.0	100.0	100.0	100.0	100.0	100.0	100.0
Agriculture	%	51.3	13.7	69.7	3.6	63.9	87.7	30.2
Industry and construction	%	19.5	27.3	10.3	27.4	16.8	7.1	21.7
Services	%	29.2	59.0	19.9	68.9	19.3	5.1	48.1

Sources: Authors' calculation based on Vietnam's Living Standard Survey, 2002 (GSO 2003)

services. This income pattern is what can be expected from a developing country like Vietnam, and it also brings about an important implication for development policies; that is promoting agriculture and labor-intensive industries is essential for reducing poverty and improving income distribution in Vietnam.

According to the official statistics, the unemployment rate is around 7% of labor force, which is a moderate figure when compared to both developed and developing countries. However, despite the low unemployment rate, underemployment is a serious problem in Vietnam. Based on the assumption of the full-time annual work of 2000 hours, around 50% of urban workers and 70% of rural workers can be classified as underemployed.[h] On average, a Vietnamese worker works slightly less than 1600 hours a year, suggesting an underemployment rate of more than 20%. The incidence of underemployment varies across regions and household groups. Reflecting the limited availability of arable land and off-farm jobs, underemployment is particularly high in rural areas where an average worker uses only three-fourths of his working time. In urban areas, underemployment is generally less serious, with the average year-round number of working hours amounting to over 2000. However urban low-income groups have less working time than high-income groups. A similar trend is also observed in rural areas, where underemployment mainly affects low-income groups.

4. Model Specification

This section discusses the major characteristics of the global CGE model used in this paper. Our model generally follows the standard neoclassical CGE model (Dervis *et al.*, 1982), but extends the standard model by allowing for several countries and regions and international link mechanisms.[i] Our model specifies ten industries and eleven countries or regions. The ten industries consist of crops, other agricultural activities, mining, food processing, light manufactures, heavy manufactures, machinery and equipment, public utilities, construction and services. The countries and regions in the model are specified with the focus on the East Asian region. Eleven countries and regions are China, Indonesia, Malaysia, Thailand, Philippines, Vietnam, East Asian newly

[h]This is calculated based on the assumption of full-time work of 40 hours per week and 50 working weeks a year.

[i]Our model of Vietnam and global link system originate from, Nguyen (2002), Ezaki and Nguyen (2001), Ezaki (2001).

industrializing economies (NIEs), Japan, the North American free trade area (NAFTA), the European Union (EU) and the rest of the world.

4.1. *Each Economy's Models*

In each economy's model, domestic output in each sector is a Constant Elasticity of Substitution (CES) function of capital and labor. Domestic producers, who seek to maximize profits, decide how much they sell in domestic and foreign markets, depending on the domestic and export prices. Domestic output is supplied to domestic or foreign markets according to the Constant Elasticity of Transformation (CET) function, in which domestic products and exports are treated as imperfect substitutes. The supply of domestic products and exports is derived from the revenue maximization condition.

The factor demand is derived from the profit maximization condition, and factor remuneration is equal to the value added price times the partial derivative of the production function with respect to each factor. Since our model focuses on the long-term impact of regional integration, the factor market is modeled with the assumption of full employment. Capital is intersectorally immobile, and the capital stock in each sector is fixed, letting the first-order condition to determine capital rents. The treatment of the labor market allows for labor mobility, but takes into consideration distortions in the labor market. The model generally specifies two kinds of labor, that is, skilled labor and unskilled labor. Sectoral labor demand is a CES function of skilled and unskilled labor, and the demand for each type of labor is derived from the first-order condition. Sectoral wages are equal to the average wage level times the exogenous coefficients, which represent wage differentials between economic sectors and types of labor. With the adoption of exogenous wage differentials, we implicitly assume that the different wage rates reflect the productivity differentials pertaining to each industry and labor type.

In regards to the model for Vietnam, each type of labor is further divided into formal and informal labor in order to capture the characteristic of the segmented labor market. Labor can move between these two sectors, but the wage rates of formal and informal labor are subject to different adjustment mechanisms. For workers in the formal sector consisting of workers in the state sector and foreign invested firms, the real wage rates are fixed by institutional factors. Since the informal sector, inclusive of agriculture and non-agricultural small businesses, is largely unregulated in Vietnam, the informal wage rate is treated as flexible. The supply of labor to the informal sector is determined as the difference between total supply of labor and the demand for formal labor.

Household income consists of labor and capital income, which is allocated to each household by using fixed coefficients. To allow for a detailed inspection of the impact of trade liberalization on income distribution in Vietnam, the household sector in Vietnam's model is disaggregated into 20 household groups, consisting of 10 urban groups and 10 rural groups. Government revenue consists of indirect taxes, import tariffs and export duties. Savings by each institution are the difference between income and expenditure. On the demand side, household consumption demand is based on a Cobb–Douglas utility function, with fixed expenditure shares. The government demand for final goods is defined using fixed expenditure shares of government real spending. The demand for inventory investment is determined by using the fixed proportions of sectoral output, and the sectoral demand for capital goods is computed through exogenous share coefficients.

Total domestic demand is satisfied through domestic production and imports. The demand for imports is modeled using the Armington structure, in which domestic and foreign goods are imperfect substitutes. The sectoral composite good, or total domestic demand, is a CES function of imported and domestically produced goods, and the demand for imports is derived from the cost minimization condition. In this treatment, the demand for imports and domestic products varies with the changes in the relative prices of domestic products and imports.

4.2. *International Linkages*

Each economy's models are linked through bilateral trade flows. Since our model allows for different tariffs on imports depending on the countries of origin, the domestic prices of imports varies with the import sources. Specifically, the import price at the domestic market is equal to the export price of the country of origin times the corresponding tariff rates. Domestic consumers and producers differentiate imports by sources, that is, imports coming from different countries are considered as imperfect substitutes. This characteristic is also modeled using the Armington structure. At the aggregate level, total imports are a CES function of imports from different sources, and the demand for imports from each sources is then derived from the cost minimization condition.

On the export side, exporters do not differentiate exports by countries of destination, that is, commodities supplied to foreign countries are seen as perfectly homogenous and are sold at the same price. The trade consistency is held so that total exports supplied by home countries must be equal to the sum of imports by foreign countries. To put it more specifically, imports from a country or region must be added up to total exports by that country or region. The model does not allow for any movement of labor and capital between countries or regions, that is, labor and capital are internationally immobile. Thus trade flows provide the only channel, through which any change in the economic policy or economic environment in one country transmit its effect to other countries.

4.3. *Equilibrium Conditions*

Equilibrium conditions consist of the conditions in factor, commodity and foreign exchange markets. In the capital market, capital stocks are fixed and capital rents serve as equilibrating variables. In the labor market, total supply of skilled and unskilled labor is held fixed at the base-run level, and the labor market equilibrium determines wage rates. In the model for Vietnam, there are two different equilibrating mechanisms for formal and informal labor markets. In the formal sector, wage rates held fixed by institutional factors and the equilibrium condition determines the demand for formal labor. In the informal labor market, wage rates adjust flexibly to attain the equilibrium between supply and demand.

Equilibrium in product markets equates the supply of the domestic good in each sector to the demand with domestic prices serving as equilibrating variables. The fiscal balance is implied in the treatment of the government sector, in which government consumption and savings are determined as fixed shares of government revenue. As for the savings-investment identity, we adopt a so-called savings-driven closure, in which total nominal investment is determined by available savings. In the foreign exchange market, foreign savings held fixed and equilibrium is achieved through price adjustments. We also fix the exchange rates of all countries and regions at the base run level. In this setting, the domestic price level changes and causes the exchange rate to adjust in real terms to attain the equilibrium condition between the market supply of and the demand for foreign exchange.

5. Simulation Analysis

5.1. *Data and the Model Calibration*

To run the model, we make use of GTAP database version 6.0, which is constructed for 2001. GTAP database is a highly disaggregated global input-output table, differentiating 57 industries and 87 countries or regions. These data are then aggregated into 10 industries and 11 countries or regions in accordance with the model. We take 2001 as the benchmark year and use GTAP data to calculate most of the parameters used in the model, such as consumption shares, saving rates, tax rates and wage rates. In regards to labor and capital, GTAP database provides only information on total labor and capital stock for each country or region. Total labor and capital stock is then allocated to each industry by assuming uniform wage rates and uniform capital rents.

To calculate the share and scale parameters in trade and production functions, we follow the calibration procedure commonly employed in CGE modelling. The elasticities of substitution in trade and production functions are taken from GTAP database, consisting of the elasticity of substitution between labor and capital, the elasticity of substitution between domestically produced goods and imports, and the elasticity of substitution between imports from different sources. GTAP database gives high values to the elasticities in trade functions, while assigning relatively low values to the elasticity of substitution in production functions. We assign a value of 1.2 to the elasticity of transformation in the export supply function for all industries. Given the type of functions and the value of the elasticities, the scale and share parameters can be calculated directly from the benchmark data.

In regards to the model for Vietnam, the household sector is constructed using Vietnam's living standard survey (VLSS) conducted by Vietnam's General Statistical Office in 2002. From the VLSS 2002, we process data on household income, which is disaggregated for around 70 industries and each type of primary factors. Income shares are then computed and are used to allocate the data on factor income taken from GTAP database to each household groups and industries. Based on VLSS 2002, household expenditure disaggregated for 67 commodities are calculated for each household group. From this information, the expenditure shares are computed, and are used to allocate GTAP data on private consumption to household groups. Data on household employment is also derived from the VLSS 2002, and is based on the number of working hours instead of the number of workers.[j] This data is computed for each type of workers, i.e. formal and skilled workers, informal and skilled workers, formal and unskilled workers and informal and unskilled workers, and is used to allocate employment data derived from GTAP database to each household group.

---

[j] Because each worker can have more than one job and underemployment is widespread, using the number of working hours could reflect better the household's employment composition.

Quantitative restrictions and other non-tariff barriers have actually been the important instruments of protection in many countries, but unfortunately, they are not quantified in this version of GTAP database. The database provides only data on tariffs and the export-tax equivalent rates of the Multi-fibre Agreement (MFA). To a certain extent, this data also shows the degree and structure of protection of the countries and regions in investigation. High average tariff rates are observed in the case of Vietnam, China and Thailand, suggesting a high degree of protection of domestic industries in these countries. The average rates for the remaining countries and regions are relatively low. For China and ASEAN countries, highly protected products are crop products, processed food and light manufactures, in which high tariffs are observed. The high degree of protection is also provided to crop products and the food processing industry in Japan and East Asian NIEs. For other industrial countries and regions like the EU and NAFTA, tariff imposed on agricultural products and light manufactures are moderate, since these sectors are mainly protected through non-tariff instruments, such as domestic subsidies or export restrictions.

5.2. *Simulation Results*

The model described in Section 4 is employed to analyze the effect on Vietnam of different economic integration scenarios. Five simulations are performed and described briefly in Table 3, and simulation results are reported in Tables 4 to 7.[k] These five simulation scenarios have been formulated to cover the

Table 3. Simulation Scenarios

S0	Base Run
S1	Removing tariffs on the bilateral trade between Vietnam and ASEAN-4
S2	Removing tariffs on the bilateral trade between Vietnam, China and ASEAN-4
S3	Removing tariffs on the bilateral trade between Vietnam, China, ASEAN-4, East Asian NIEs and Japan (East Asian Economic Community)
S4	Removing tariffs on the bilateral trade between Vietnam, China, ASEAN-4, East Asian NIEs, Japan and North America
S5	Multilateral Trade liberalization

[k]There is a concern that, in a global CGE model, the computational errors can be allocated to the small countries like Vietnam. However, our model has replicated well the benchmark data set in the base run, for Vietnam as well as other countries and regions.

Table 4. Effect of Economic Integration on Countries and Regions

	China	Indonesia	Malaysia	Philippines	Thailand	Vietnam	NIEs	Japan	NAFTA	EU	ROW
Simulation Scenario S1											
Real GDP	0.02	0.01	0.04	0.00	−0.01	−0.06	0.00	0.00	0.00	0.00	0.00
Private consumption	−0.05	0.37	4.03	0.95	1.64	2.21	−0.07	−0.02	0.02	0.00	−0.02
Imports	−1.66	−0.73	−0.89	1.65	1.02	3.15	−0.27	−0.60	0.86	−0.02	−0.11
Exports	0.74	1.25	1.26	0.52	1.82	1.73	0.04	0.23	−0.37	0.01	0.03
Simulation Scenario S2											
Real GDP	0.00	−0.01	0.06	0.02	−0.02	−0.18	0.00	0.00	0.00	0.00	0.00
Private consumption	0.47	0.95	5.95	1.18	3.46	4.66	−0.22	−0.04	−0.01	−0.01	−0.02
Imports	1.63	3.61	4.21	1.90	5.04	4.62	−0.46	−0.49	−0.07	−0.05	−0.07
Exports	1.14	0.73	1.09	1.11	2.10	5.31	−0.12	−0.14	−0.02	−0.01	−0.03
Simulation Scenario S3											
Real GDP	−0.20	0.00	0.11	0.05	−0.11	−0.68	0.06	0.00	0.00	0.00	0.00
Private consumption	2.27	1.14	6.71	0.89	6.34	9.05	1.93	0.36	−0.04	−0.06	−0.06
Imports	8.63	3.15	4.15	1.18	8.64	10.87	2.95	3.54	−0.43	−0.19	−0.28
Exports	4.98	1.18	2.11	1.52	3.97	12.31	2.36	1.97	−0.11	−0.02	−0.12

Table 4. (*Continued*)

	China	Indonesia	Malaysia	Philippines	Thailand	Vietnam	NIEs	Japan	NAFTA	EU	ROW
Simulation Scenario S4											
Real GDP	−0.21	−0.02	0.13	0.08	−0.12	−0.56	0.00	0.00	−0.01	0.01	−0.01
Private consumption	3.41	1.41	7.74	1.16	6.56	9.43	2.80	0.70	0.20	−0.14	−0.13
Imports	11.69	4.68	5.02	1.61	8.81	11.78	4.28	5.29	1.48	−0.34	−0.51
Exports	6.66	1.09	2.27	1.95	4.36	13.91	3.05	3.43	1.94	−0.03	−0.33
Simulation Scenario S5											
Real GDP	−0.51	−0.10	0.08	0.09	−0.34	−0.55	−0.01	−0.02	−0.01	0.04	−0.01
Private consumption	5.22	2.56	9.21	0.81	8.61	11.23	3.28	0.83	0.30	0.07	2.47
Imports	18.49	9.27	7.45	1.00	11.77	15.39	5.36	6.57	2.12	0.51	6.37
Exports	8.87	1.13	2.56	2.30	5.61	18.24	4.18	4.45	3.46	0.95	4.84

Sources: Authors' calculation

Table 5. Effect of Trade Liberalization on Vietnam

	Unit	Base Run S0	Percentage Change (%)				
			S1	S2	S3	S4	S5
Consumer price index	Unit	1.00	−5.83	−1.02	−3.70	−3.22	−1.80
Exchange rate	Unit	1.00	0.00	0.00	0.00	0.00	0.00
Average wage rates	Thousand USD	0.28	−3.61	3.33	4.80	5.91	9.54
Skilled labor	Thousand USD	0.55	−4.03	2.55	3.83	5.06	8.23
Unskilled labor	Thousand USD	0.21	−3.27	4.11	5.71	6.67	10.67
Capital rent	Unit	0.18	−3.91	3.38	3.97	4.65	7.59
Real GDP	Million USD	30340.73	−0.06	−0.18	−0.68	−0.56	−0.55
Output	Million USD	66170.38	0.45	0.84	1.63	2.07	2.96
Private consumption	Million USD	27213.19	2.21	4.66	9.05	9.43	11.23
Government consumption	Million USD	2607.05	−12.89	−26.42	−43.36	−43.03	−43.17
Real investment	Million USD	12938.58	2.48	−1.25	−3.13	−3.63	−4.76
Imports	Million USD	27434.05	3.15	4.62	10.87	11.78	15.39
Exports	Million USD	15015.96	1.73	5.31	12.31	13.91	18.24
Household income	Million USD	28121.22	−3.78	3.42	4.37	5.21	8.45
Labor income (skilled labor)	Million USD	4740.35	−4.03	2.55	3.83	5.06	8.23
Labor income (unskilled labor)	Million USD	6852.58	−3.27	4.11	5.71	6.67	10.67
Capital income	Million USD	16528.29	−3.91	3.38	3.97	4.65	7.59
Government revenue	Million USD	5180.36	−17.24	−25.92	−43.02	−42.32	−41.61

Sources: Authors' calculation

Table 6. Effect on Income Distribution of Vietnam

	Household Income					Household Consumption				
	S1	S2	S3	S4	S5	S1	S2	S3	S4	S5
	Percentage Changes Compared to the Base-run (%)									
Urban group 1	2.43	4.86	9.13	9.38	11.77	2.58	4.42	10.35	10.74	13.06
Urban group 2	2.52	5.19	9.73	10.21	13.02	2.70	4.79	11.00	11.59	14.33
Urban group 3	2.44	4.47	7.57	7.53	8.88	2.58	4.08	8.53	8.58	9.85
Urban group 4	2.24	4.22	8.09	8.45	10.49	2.31	3.72	8.68	9.11	11.05
Urban group 5	2.41	4.60	8.51	9.07	11.43	2.57	4.27	9.49	10.14	12.42
Urban group 6	2.36	4.47	7.90	8.35	10.17	2.40	4.04	8.27	8.75	10.49
Urban group 7	2.10	4.04	7.69	8.17	9.89	2.13	3.72	8.06	8.57	10.23
Urban group 8	2.10	4.39	8.40	9.05	11.17	2.06	4.00	8.34	9.00	11.02
Urban group 9	1.87	3.73	7.51	8.15	9.94	1.84	3.53	7.58	8.21	9.96
Urban group 10	1.64	3.55	7.12	7.68	9.16	1.72	3.85	7.70	8.23	9.73
Rural group 1	2.80	5.99	9.34	8.97	10.73	3.06	5.71	11.14	10.92	12.62
Rural group 2	2.77	5.78	9.30	9.14	11.09	3.02	5.49	10.89	10.83	12.72
Rural group 3	2.61	5.55	9.17	9.15	11.17	2.84	5.26	10.64	10.72	12.67
Rural group 4	2.61	5.60	9.49	9.68	12.15	2.79	5.29	10.68	10.95	13.34
Rural group 5	2.49	5.38	8.91	9.02	11.00	2.65	5.12	9.96	10.12	12.03
Rural group 6	2.37	5.37	9.14	9.34	11.44	2.54	5.24	10.20	10.44	12.48
Rural group 7	2.17	4.82	8.37	8.61	10.52	2.35	4.91	9.47	9.74	11.63
Rural group 8	2.20	4.87	8.58	8.88	10.78	2.41	5.25	9.81	10.12	12.01
Rural group 9	1.93	4.51	8.12	8.54	10.36	2.18	5.32	9.49	9.88	11.74
Rural group 10	1.66	3.88	7.09	7.53	9.14	2.19	6.07	9.86	10.24	12.04

Sources: Authors' calculation

Table 7. Effect on the Trade Direction of Vietnam

	Imports					Exports				
	S1	S2	S3	S4	S5	S1	S2	S3	S4	S5
China	−11.55	167.60	95.22	91.75	83.56	−6.51	156.86	132.17	103.02	71.79
Indonesia	134.86	75.88	20.88	17.34	3.34	21.35	16.30	13.19	23.54	30.80
Malaysia	94.03	45.13	3.42	2.94	−5.89	4.81	−9.47	−13.22	−14.74	−18.97
Philippines	112.14	79.52	13.85	9.70	8.30	112.06	102.58	88.74	93.39	87.54
Thailand	143.97	41.75	6.32	6.99	4.00	167.44	152.52	118.08	114.84	87.64
NIES	−12.04	−29.78	29.43	29.30	26.68	−6.58	−11.67	20.05	17.48	3.05
Japan	−13.34	−37.12	−13.82	−12.57	−12.73	−8.56	−10.82	12.75	6.28	−4.98
NAFTA	−2.45	−5.89	−8.72	−1.90	1.99	−7.29	−11.27	−12.26	29.92	17.90
EU	−4.25	−11.62	−16.29	−15.38	−2.95	−2.26	−4.59	0.15	−2.07	24.61
Rest of the World	−5.55	−11.02	−20.67	−20.37	−4.87	−5.82	−10.44	−9.57	−7.58	7.61
ASEAN-4	124.95	50.34	8.23	7.60	0.87	95.24	83.25	66.21	67.36	56.25
ASEAN-4 plus China	55.20	110.25	52.68	50.59	43.12	55.66	111.89	91.87	81.24	62.29
East Asia	11.43	18.27	29.91	29.34	25.44	10.37	24.06	37.43	30.85	16.51
Total	3.15	4.62	10.87	11.78	15.39	1.73	5.31	12.31	13.91	18.24

Sources: Authors' calculation

different economic integration options for Vietnam, including the ASEAN free trade area, the China–ASEAN free trade area, the possible formation of an East Asian economic community, APEC trade liberalization and the world-wide multilateral trade liberalization. In all these simulation, we focus on the impact of tariff reductions and simply assume a complete removal of tariffs.

Simulation S1 is designed to evaluate the impacts of the ASEAN free trade area on Vietnam. We remove all tariffs on the bilateral trade between Vietnam and four ASEAN members, i.e. Indonesia, Thailand, Malaysia and Philippines.[1] The tariff removal stimulates the bilateral trade between ASEAN countries, and both exports and imports increase in all countries. The extent to which exports or imports increase, however, depends on the structure of protection and the composition of trade in each countries. Since foreign savings are fixed in the model, the exchange rate will adjust to attain the current account balance. The exchange rate depreciates if imports increase more than exports and it appreciates otherwise. At the aggregate level, the real exchange rate depreciates in all ASEAN countries with the exception of Indonesia. GDP falls slightly in Vietnam and Thailand in real terms, but increases in Malaysia and Philippines. The increase in imports put a downward pressure on domestic demand and force domestic prices to fall. Combined with the increase in income, this leads to an increase in consumption. The gain in consumption can be seen in all countries, with the biggest gain is observed in Malaysia.

In regards to Vietnam, real household income and consumption rise by around 2.0% on average. The welfare gain for Vietnam comes from both the tariff removal in Vietnam and the removal of tariffs imposed on Vietnam's exports in ASEAN trading partners. While the tariff removal in Vietnam reduces the cost of imported goods and improves resource allocation, the removal of tariffs in other ASEAN countries expands the market for Vietnam's exports. The ASEAN free trade area mostly brings benefits to agriculture and labor-intensive industries, and generally has positive effects on poverty reduction and income distribution in Vietnam. Income to unskilled labor, which constitutes a large share in poor households' income, increases more than income to skilled labor and capital. All household groups have income gains, with the poor groups having slightly higher gains than the rich. However, the AFTA tariff removal also causes trade diversions, although not to a large extent. Both exports to and imports from ASEAN countries rise sharply, while trade with non-ASEAN countries or regions falls.

[1]Hereafter we will refer to these countries as ASEAN-4.

The impact of the recently established China–ASEAN free trade area is considered in simulation S2, in which tariffs on the bilateral trade between China, Vietnam and ASEAN-4 are completely eliminated. Similar to S1, exports and imports rise in all countries, and all countries experiences gains in consumption, with the biggest gains observed in Malaysia. The real exchange rate depreciation occurs in all countries, except for Indonesia and Malaysia. The inclusion of China seems to have a negative impact on Japan and East Asian NIEs, since the volume of trade declines slightly in these countries.

For Vietnam, the gain in consumption increases to more than 4%. This is the combined result of a greater tariff reduction in Vietnam and the removal of Chinese tariffs imposed on Vietnam's exports. Similar to S1, the China–ASEAN free trade area appears to have a positive impact on income distribution and poverty reduction. All household groups have gains in income and consumption, and the poor has bigger gains than the rich. Rural household groups also benefit more than urban groups. The establishment of the free trade area between China and ASEAN, however, causes a considerable trade diversion to Vietnam. Imports from China and exports to China rise sharply at the expense of trade with other regions. The biggest falls are seen in imports from Japan and East Asian NIEs, which decline by 37% and 30% respectively from the base-run values.

In simulation S3, we examine the effect of the possible formation of the East Asian economic community. In this simulation, we remove all tariffs on the bilateral trade between East Asian countries, including Japan and East Asian NIEs. The bilateral trade between East Asian countries increases, and both exports and imports rise in all countries. The establishment of the East Asian free trade area, however, causes a trade diversion to the EU and North America, where there is a slight decline in exports and imports. All East Asian countries experience a gain in income and consumption, and real GDP increases with the exception of Thailand, China and Vietnam.

The welfare gain for Vietnam increases significantly as regional integration is expanded to include Vietnam's large trading partners such as Japan and East Asian NIEs. The inclusion of Japan and East Asian NIEs benefits mostly to agriculture and labor-intensive industries in Vietnam, since the corresponding tariffs employed by Japan and East Asian NIEs are relatively high. Household consumption and income rise by 9.1% and 8.1% respectively. Income to unskilled labor rises more than income to capital and skilled labor, and benefits mostly poor and rural household groups. In terms of the trade direction, Vietnam's trade is diverted from the US and the EU, and exports from these countries to Vietnam to fall by 8.7% and 16.3% respectively. Both exports to and imports from East Asian NIEs rise, while imports from Japan fall to a lesser extent as compared with S2.

In simulation S4, we remove the tariffs on the bilateral trade between North America and East Asian countries. This simulation is designed to evaluate the effect of trade liberalization under the APEC forum, which has set the objective of liberalizing trade and investment regimes by the year 2020.[m] All APEC countries experience gains in income and consumption. Imports and exports increase in all APEC members but at the expense of the EU and the rest of the world. The removal of the NAFTA tariff also brings additional welfare gains to Vietnam, where household income and consumption rise by 8.4% and 9.4% respectively. As may be expected, Vietnam's trade is redirected toward APEC region, and trade with the EU and the rest of the world falls.

Finally, the effect of a multilateral liberalization is considered in simulation S5, in which tariffs are completely eliminated for all countries and regions. Exports and imports rise, with the total world exports increase by 3.4%. The welfare gain is also significant. Total world consumption rise by 0.9%, or equivalent to $180 billion. The tariff removal on a multilateral basis significantly increases the welfare gain for Vietnam, where household consumption increases by 11.2% and exports increase by 18.2%. Multilateral trade liberalization also reduces the extent of trade diversions caused by regional integration as it is seen in the previous simulations. The increase in Vietnam's imports from ASEAN members falls to less than 1.0%, while imports from the EU and North America still decline, but to a lesser extent compared with the previous simulations.

It should be stressed that the impacts on Vietnam, particularly on the pattern of trade and production, vary with the integration scenarios, depending on whether the countries and regions included are developing or developed. For example, the participation of Japan in S3 has a big impact on the light manufacturing sector, which is a major exporting industry in Vietnam. The output and export of this sector increase by 18.4% and 24.5% respectively.[n] A substantial expansion in the light manufacturing sector is also observed with the inclusion of NAFTA and the EU in S4 and S5. However, with the participation of a developing country with an economic structure similar to Vietnam

[m] In this simulation, we assume tariffs are removed for only member countries. Indeed, as it is commonly believed, the APEC forum adopts the open regionalism, in which trade liberalization measures are applied to both member and non-member countries.

[n] The simulation results on the sectoral output and exports are not reported, but they can be obtained from the authors on request.

like China in S2, the simulation results show only a limited effect on the light manufacturing sector.

One of the main reasons for Vietnam to pursue regional integration and trade liberalization is the expectation that regional integration would stimulate the inflow of foreign investment through the improved economic environment and a greater market access for Vietnam's exports. The increasing competition among the developing countries for foreign investment also provides Vietnam with another incentive to quickly improve its investment environment. Even we do not explicitly model capital inflows or outflows, the simulation results give some indication of the impact of regional integration on foreign investment. As can be seen in Table 5, capital rents of Vietnam increase in all simulations. Moreover, although it is not shown in details, the increase in the capital rents of Vietnam is the highest as compared to other regions or countries. The rising capital rents obviously imply an increase in foreign investment. To put it differently, regional economic integration and trade liberalization may make investments in Vietnam more profitable, and makes Vietnam more attractive to foreign investors.

Despite the positive impacts on income distribution, export expansion and foreign investment, regional integration raises some macroeconomic issues for Vietnam. Real GDP falls in all simulations, although the GDP loss is not large. The decline in real GDP is largely due to the decline in government revenue and consumption following tariff reductions, and this fiscal loss is not fully offset by the increase in factor income. Since tariffs constitute a major source of fiscal revenue in Vietnam, tariff reductions can cause a sharp decline in fiscal revenue and should be accompanied by complementary tax policies to accommodate the loss in tariff revenue.[o]

In addition to fiscal issues, regional integration appears to have adverse impacts on the trade balance of Vietnam. In all simulations, the exchange rate depreciates in real terms, indicating a worsening of the trade deficit. Moreover, the real exchange rate depreciates most in the simulation of the ASEAN free trade areas, while it depreciates to a lesser extent in other simulations. The implication here is that the adverse impact on the trade balance would be smaller when regional integration is expanded to include Vietnam's large export markets such as Japan, the United States or the European Union. The possible

[o]In an effort to compensate for the loss in tariff revenue, the government of Vietnam has planned to raise the special sales tax imposed on cars and some other luxury goods. However, further tax reforms are needed to fully compensate for the revenue loss.

adverse impact on the trade balance also indicates the need of adopting a flexible exchange rate during the process of regional integration.

6. Summary and Conclusions

In this paper, we have constructed a global CGE model, which specifies 10 industries and 11 countries and regions. We have employed the model to examine the impact of regional economic integration on Vietnam's economy, focussing on growth, poverty reductions and income distribution. As discussed in the previous section, the impact of trade liberalization and regional economic integration on Vietnam's economy is basically positive. Regional integration both enhances welfare and improves income distribution for Vietnam. Household consumption and income rise significantly, and the poor and rural groups gain more than the rich. The removal of tariffs in trading partners provides a greater market access for Vietnam's exports, thereby contributing to the expansion of labor-intensive and exporting industries in Vietnam. Regional integration also increases the profitability of investing in Vietnam and helps in attracting foreign investment.

However, regional integration and trade liberalization also produces some undesirable outcomes. In terms of growth, regional integration may cause real GDP to fall, largely due to the sharp decrease in tariff revenue. The fiscal and trade balance could be negatively affected by tariff reductions, raising the need of adopting complementary macroeconomic policies to mitigate the adverse impact of regional integration on the macroeconomy. Beside that, certain regional integration scenarios could significantly divert Vietnam's trade from its major trading partners. The possibility of trade diversion and the different impacts resulting from different integration partners should be paid adequate attention in establishing integration policies for Vietnam.

From the above discussion, it is obviously desirable for Vietnam to pursue ongoing regional integration, including the ASEAN free trade area and the recently established China–ASEAN free trade area. However, Vietnam should not confine itself to these trading areas. As the simulation results shows, the gain from these trade areas is limited, and the welfare gain for Vietnam could increase significantly when trade liberalization is carried out on a broader basis that involves Vietnam's major export markets. Broader regional integration also reduces the extent of possible trade diversions and further increases the market access for Vietnam's exports.

The global linked CGE model employed in this paper has proved to be useful in evaluating the impact of regional economic integration on Vietnam's economy. However, there remain some limitations in the model, and it needs to be further elaborated to capture better the characteristics of Vietnam's economy and regional economic integration. Among possible extensions, we consider incorporating foreign capital inflows in our model. Allowing for the international capital mobility would make it possible to quantify the changes in foreign direct investment resulting from regional economic integration, and this would probably further increase the welfare gain for Vietnam. In order to analyze the process of resource reallocation over time, we also consider performing some dynamic simulations, in which labor and capital are allowed to move between industries and countries.

Acknowledgment

We are grateful to Prof. Masayuki Doi, Tsukuba University, for the useful comments and insights. This research was financially supported by the Grants-in-Aid of Japan Society for the Promotion of Sciences (JSPS) in the fiscal year 2004.

References

Centre for International Economics (CIE), 1998. "Trade policies in Vietnam 1998." Canberra and Sydney.

Centre for International Economics (CIE), 1999a. "Trade and industry policies for economic integration." Report prepared for CIEM and UNIDO, Canberra and Sydney.

Centre for International Economics (CIE), 1999b. "Non-tariff barriers in Vietnam: a framework for developing a phase out strategy." Canberra and Sydney.

Dervis K, de Melo J, and Robinson S, 1982. *General Equilibrium Models for Development Policies*. A World Bank Research Publication, Cambridge University Press.

Ezaki M, 2001. "Asian economy in future: an econometric analysis of growth perspectives." In: *Economic Achievement in Asia*. Watanabe T, (ed) Toyo-Keizai: Tokyo, pp. 171–196 (in Japanese).

Ezaki M, and Nguyen Tien Dung, 2001. "Medium-run prospects of Viet Nam's economy: CGE simulation analysis of the 7th five-year plan." Ministry of Planning and Investment (The Socialist Republic of Vietnam) and Japan International Cooperation Agency, Study on the Economic Development Policy in the Transition toward a Market-Oriented Economy in the Socialist Republic of Vietnam (Phase 3), Final Report, Vol. 1, General Commentary, Ch. 4, pp. 113–141.

Forster N, 1998. "Vietnam's integration with ASEAN: a policy reader." United Nations Development Program, Project VIE 95/015, Hanoi.

Fukase E, and Martin W, 1998. "A quantitative evaluation of Vietnam's accession to the ASEAN free trade area (AFTA)." Development Research Group, World Bank: Washington DC.

General Statistical Office (GSO), 2000. *Vietnam Living Standards Survey 1997–1998*. Statistical Publishing House: Hanoi.

General Statistical Office (GSO), 2003. *Vietnam Living Standards Survey 2001–2002*. Statistical Publishing House: Hanoi.

General Statistical Offices (GSO), 2004. *Statistical Yearbook 2003*. Statistical Publishing House: Hanoi.

Kinh DT, Le DM, Lo TD, Nguyen NM, Tran Q, and Bui XD, 2001. "Inequality." In: *Living Standards during an Economic Boom*. Haughton D, Haughton J, and Phong N, (ed) Statistical Publishing House: Hanoi, Ch. 2, pp. 33–46.

McCarty A, 1999. "Vietnam's integration with ASEAN: survey of non-tariff measures affecting trade." A report prepared for the Office of the Government of Vietnam, United Nations Development Program, Project VIE 95/015, Hanoi.

Nguyen TD, 2002. "Trade reform in Vietnam: a CGE analysis," *Forum of Int. Dev. Stud.* **21**: 189–209.

Socialist Republic of Vietnam (SRV), 1999. "Individual action plan, 1999." Document submitted to the APEC Secretariats. www.apecsec.org.

Thang NX, 1999. *Khu vuc mau dich tu do ASEAN va tien trinh hoi nhap cua Vietnam*, (ASEAN free trade area and Vietnam's integration). Statistical Publishing House: Hanoi (in Vietnamese).

World Bank, 1999. "Vietnam development report 2000: attacking poverty." Report No. 19914-VN, World Bank: Washington DC.

Index

www.ingramcontent.com/pod-product-compliance
Lightning Source LLC
La Vergne TN
LVHW051057210926
848486LV00002B/137
* 9 7 8 9 8 1 2 5 6 4 7 1 9 *